THE
FUTURE IS
ASIAN

Commerce, Conflict, and Culture in the 21st Century

PARAG KHANNA

Simon & Schuster

New York London Toronto Sydney New Delhi

Simon & Schuster
1230 Avenue of the Americas
New York, NY 10020

Copyright © 2019 by Parag Khanna

First Simon & Schuster hardcover edition February 2019

SIMON & SCHUSTER and colophon are registered
trademarks of Simon & Schuster, Inc.

For information about special discounts for bulk purchases,
please contact Simon & Schuster Special Sales at 1-866-506-1949
or business@simonandschuster.com.

The Simon & Schuster Speakers Bureau can bring authors to your
live event. For more information or to book an event, contact the
Simon & Schuster Speakers Bureau at 1-866-248-3049
or visit our website at www.simonspeakers.com.

Interior design by Silverglass Design

Manufactured in the United States of America

10 9 8 7 6 5 4 3 2 1

Library of Congress Cataloging-in-Publication Data is available.

ISBN 978-1-5011-9626-3
ISBN 978-1-5011-9627-0 (ebook)

FOR MY FIVE BILLION NEIGHBORS

Contents

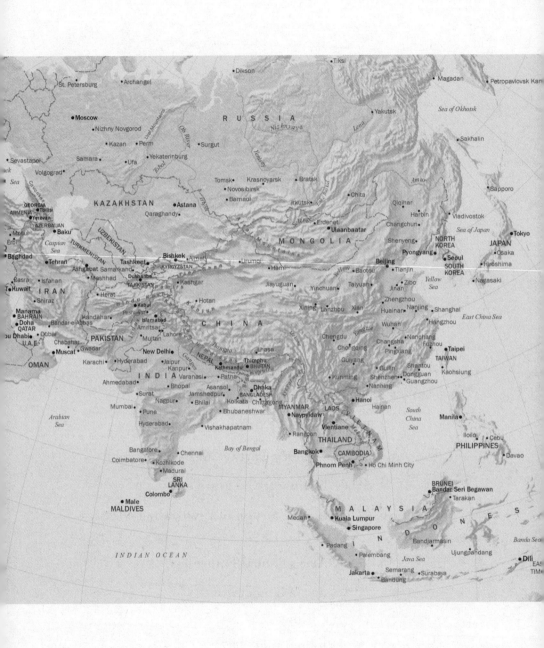

Introduction: Asia First

When did the Asian century begin?

Forecasts of Asia's rise to global preeminence go back two centuries to Napoleon's alleged quip about China: "Let her sleep, for when she wakes she will shake the world."

Nearly a century ago, in 1924, the German general Karl Haushofer predicted a coming "Pacific Age." But Asia is much more than the countries of the Pacific Rim. Geographically, Asia stretches from the Mediterranean and Red Seas across two-thirds of the Eurasian continent to the Pacific Ocean, encompassing fifty-three countries[1] and nearly 5 billion people—only 1.5 billion of whom are Chinese. The Asian century will thus begin when Asia crystallizes into a whole greater than the sum of its many parts. That process is now underway.

When we look back from 2100 at the date on which the cornerstone of an Asian-led world order began, it will be 2017. In May of that year, sixty-eight countries representing two-thirds of the world's population and half its GDP gathered in Beijing for the first Belt and Road Initiative (BRI) summit. This gathering of Asian, European, and African leaders symbolized the launch of the largest coordinated infrastructure investment plan in human history. Collectively, the assembled governments pledged to spend trillions of dollars in the coming decade to connect the world's largest population centers in a constellation of commerce and cultural exchange—a new Silk Road era.

The Belt and Road Initiative is the most significant diplomatic project of the twenty-first century, the equivalent of the mid-twentieth-century founding of the United Nations and World Bank plus the Marshall Plan all rolled into one. The crucial difference: BRI was conceived in Asia and launched in Asia and will be led by Asians.

This is the story of one entire side of the planet—the Asian side—and its impact on the twenty-first-century world.

For most of recorded history, Asia has been the most important region of the globe. As the late British economist Angus Maddison demonstrated, for the past two thousand years, until the mid-1800s, China, India, and Japan together generated a greater total gross domestic product (GDP) (in purchasing power parity, or PPP, terms) than the United States, United Kingdom, France, Germany, and Italy combined. But with the Industrial Revolution, Western societies modernized their economies, expanded their empires, and subjugated most of Asia. After two centuries of Europe ruling the world, the United States rose to become a global power through its victory in the Spanish-American War (which gave it control of Cuba and the Philippines) and its decisive role in ending World War I.

But only after World War II—when Western powers stopped trying to conquer one another—did a stable Western order emerge. It was embodied in US military and economic power, the transatlantic North Atlantic Treaty Organization (NATO) alliance, and international institutions such as the United Nations, World Bank, and International Monetary Fund (IMF). Seventy years ago, nobody knew how enduring those agreements and bodies would be—especially as the Cold War divided much of the world. Only at the end of the Cold War could the West be confident in the triumph of its liberal, democratic, capitalist system. And only in the 1990s did the world order become truly global as numerous former Soviet republics joined the European Union and NATO, while dozens of developing countries joined bodies such as the World Trade Organization (WTO) that promoted what was known as the "Washington Consensus" of free trade and economic deregulation. Western laws, interventions, money, and culture set the global agenda.

But the nearly two decades spanning the September 11, 2001, terrorist attacks and the 2003 Iraq War through the 2007–08 financial crisis to the November 2016 election of Donald Trump as US president will be remembered as a period of profound rupture with the previous decades of Western dominance. The failures of the Afghanistan and Iraq wars, the disconnect between the financial (Wall Street) and real (Main Street) economies, the inability to integrate Russia and Turkey into the West, and democracy hijacked by populists—these are among the salient episodes that have brought many Western elites to question the future of their political, economic, and social values. Today Western societies are consumed with domestic ills: mounting debt, rising inequality, political polarization, and culture wars. American millennials have grown up with a war on terror, declining median income, mounting racial tension, arbitrary gun violence, and political demagoguery. European youths struggle with economic austerity, high unemployment, and out-of-touch politicians. The West has pioneered wondrous technological advances from communications to medicine, but its populations have not enjoyed the benefits evenly.

As the West was fighting and winning the Cold War, Asia began to catch up. Over the past four decades, Asians have gained the greatest share of total global economic growth and Westerners, especially middle-class industrial workers, the least—a trend driven by the rise of manufacturing in Asia.[2] Billions of Asians growing up in the past two decades have experienced geopolitical stability, rapidly expanding prosperity, and surging national pride. The world they know is one not of Western dominance but of Asian ascendance. In 1998, my Singaporean colleague Kishore Mahbubani published a provocative collection of essays titled *Can Asians Think?* warning Westerners that the global tide was turning and that Asia has as much to teach the West as the reverse.[3] As Asians come to adopt some semblance of a common worldview, it is time to explore not *if* Asians can think but *what* they think.

Asians once again see themselves as the center of the world—and its future. The Asian economic zone—from the Arabian Peninsula and Turkey in the west to Japan and New Zealand in the east, and from Russia in the north to Australia in the south—now represents 50 percent of global GDP and two-thirds of global economic growth.[4] Of the estimated $30 trillion in middle-class consumption growth estimated between 2015 and 2030, only $1 trillion is expected to come from today's Western economies. Most of the rest will come from Asia.[5] Asia produces and exports, as well as imports and consumes, more goods than any other region, and Asians trade and invest more with one another than they do with Europe or North America. Asia has several of the world's largest economies, most of the world's foreign exchange reserves, many of the largest banks and industrial and technology companies, and most of the world's biggest armies. Asia also accounts for 60 percent of the world's population. It has *ten* times as many people as Europe and *twelve* times as many people as North America. As the world population climbs toward a plateau of around 10 billion people, Asia will forever be home to more people than the rest of the world combined. They are now speaking. Prepare to see the world from the Asian point of view.

What Is Asia?

Halfway through his decadelong mission to circumnavigate the planet *on foot* following the paths of the earliest humans, I reached the *National Geographic* explorer Paul Salopek as he was crossing the Pamir Mountains in Kyrgyzstan. A modern Marco Polo (and then some), Paul has been showered with literary accolades (including two Pulitzer Prizes) for his reportage. But his current Out of Eden Walk is his most ambitious undertaking, something few if any have attempted before and none has completed. With so much of Asia behind him—and so much still ahead—I sought his assessment of the region. He told me, "Asia is so huge and complex that I feel like I'm moving through a vast mosaic of microworlds, loosely knitted together by forces beyond my ken." This tangible yet spiritual description elegantly captures Asia's combination of enormous size and mystical unity.

Most people literally don't understand *what* Asia is—even in Asia. Asia's vastness and range of self-contained civilizations, combined with a recent history dominated by Western or internal concerns, has meant that most Asians today have contrasting views of the parameters of Asia and the extent to which their nations belong to it.[6] Yet even though Asia is the most heterogeneous region of the world, there is a growing coherence in its dizzying diversity: some psychological underpinning, some aesthetic familiarity, some cultural thread that permeates Asia and differentiates it from other regions.

From kindergartens to military academies, Asia is still mistakenly referred to as a continent even though it is strictly speaking a megaregion stretching from the Sea of Japan to the Red Sea.[7] Asia contains half of the world's largest countries by land area, including Russia, China, Australia, India, and Kazakhstan.[8] Asia also has most of the world's twenty most populous countries, including China, India, Indonesia, Pakistan, Bangladesh, Japan, the Philippines, and Vietnam. Asia is home to some of the wealthiest countries in the world on a per capita basis, such as Qatar and Singapore, but also some of the smallest (Maldives, Nauru), least populous (Tuvalu, Palau), and poorest (Afghanistan, Myanmar).

"Asia" is first and foremost a geographic descriptor. We often impose convenient but false geographic labels that suit our biases. In recent decades, Russia, Turkey, Israel, and the Caucasus countries have all sought to brand themselves as culturally and diplomatically Western states (and group themselves with Europe at the United Nations). But just because Russians and Australians hail (mostly) from European races does not mean they cannot be Asian. Even through an ethnic lens, Russians and Aussies should be seen—and see themselves—as white Asians. Many experts hold "Asia" to be synonymous with "Far East." But Asia cannot be narrowly defined as just China and East Asia. China borders other major Asian subregions, but it does not define them. Hence we should use the term "East Asia" when referring to the Pacific Rim. After all, it is particularly odd for Americans to use the term "Far East" since the region lies to their *west* across the Pacific Ocean. "East" should therefore be used as a relative directional orientation and "Asia" as a geographic region. Similarly, it remains all too common to use "Middle East" to connote everything from Morocco to Afghanistan, spanning a melange of subregions stretching from North Africa to Central Asia. (Even Al Jazeera International's anchors use the term "Middle East"—because they are speaking English.) But North African countries from Egypt westward have little relevance to Asia, even though they are mostly Arab populated. It makes far more sense to refer to West Asia and Southwest Asia to capture Turkey, Iran, the Gulf states, and the nations lying between them. Neutral geographic labels are ultimately much more revealing than colonial artifacts.

Asia for Asians

More than two millennia ago, Asia's disparate civilizations had already established commercial ties and engaged in conflict from the Mediterranean and Caspian seas to the Indus valley. By the fifteenth century, Asia was a diplomatically, economically, and culturally connected realm stretching from Anatolia to China. European colonialism, however, fractured Asia, reducing it to a collection of adjacent territories too poor and subservient to Western powers to congeal meaningfully. The Cold War further splintered Asia into competitive spheres of influence. Over time, Arabs and Turks came to see themselves as the "Middle East" and Chinese and Japanese identified as the "Far East." Asia ceased to be a coherent whole.[9]

After two centuries of division, today's post–Cold War period marks the advent of a new phase of Asia knitting itself back together into a coherent *system*. A system is a collection of countries that are bound together not only by geography but also by the forces of diplomacy, war, and trade. The members of a system are all sovereign and independent but also strongly interdependent with one another in matters of economics and security. A system is formed through alliances, institutions, infrastructure, trade, investment, culture, and other patterns. When nations graduate from common geography into meaningful interactions, a system is born.

As the British scholar Barry Buzan elucidates in *International Systems in World History*, human history is to a large degree the stories of disparate regional systems.[10] The ancient city-states of Mesopotamia, the Delian League led by Athens, and the Warring States of China are all examples of small-scale systems. By contrast, empires such as the Mongol and British governed large regional and international systems. Only in recent centuries has a global system emerged, but to a large degree this consists of the relations among numerous regional systems—with Europe, North America, and Asia being the most important.

Europe today is the most integrated regional system. From the ashes of World War II, European countries not only rebuilt physically but fused important industries through the European Coal and Steel Community. Back then, nobody knew that the original half-dozen members—including rivals France and Germany—would expand to nearly thirty members with supranational institutions and a common currency and even build joint military capabilities. Europe today is far more powerful as a system than merely as a region.

North America is the next most integrated system. The United States, Canada, and Mexico are strategic partners and among one another's top trading partners as well.[11] They also have by far the two busiest border crossings in the world. Even as the more-than-two-decades-old North American Free Trade Agreement (NAFTA) is renegotiated, the broader economic, demographic, cultural, and other ties effectively make the region a North American union even if it never adopts that name.

ASIA BUILDS ITS OWN DIPLOMATIC SYSTEM.

Asian nations are rapidly building their own diplomatic bodies to coordinate, regulate, and govern issues such as trade, infrastructure, and capital flows. The Asian Infrastructure Investment Bank (AIIB) has nearly ninety members, and the Regional Comprehensive Economic Partnership (RCEP) is emerging as the world's largest free-trade area by both GDP and trade volume.

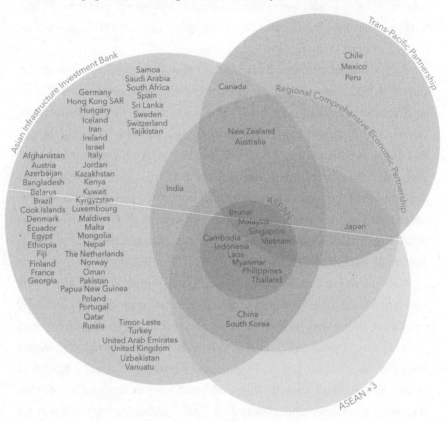

Despite its vast geography and cultural diversity, Asia is evolving from faint historical and cultural linkages to robust economic interdependence to strategic coordination. In 1993, the Japanese scholar and journalist Yoichi Funabashi wrote a prescient essay in *Foreign Affairs* about the "Asianization of Asia."[12] He spoke of a new regional consciousness, one not focused on backward-looking anticolonialism but rather proactively responding to American Cold War triumphalism and Europe's single market. Globalized competition, he rightly argued, would require Asia to Asianize, beginning with the "chopsticks" civilizational area encompassing China, Japan, South Korea, and Vietnam and eventually reaching beyond to reforming countries such as India. Funabashi believed that the combination of economic growth, geopolitical stability, and technocratic pragmatism would give rise to distinctly Asian ideas about world order.

That time has come. The same ingredients of industrial capitalism, internal stability, and search for global markets that propelled Europe's imperial ascendancy and the United States' rise to superpower status are converging in Asia. In just the past few years, China has surpassed the United States as the world's largest economy (in PPP terms) and trading power. India has become the fastest-growing large economy in the world. Southeast Asia receives more foreign investment than both India and China. Asia's major powers have maintained stability with one another despite their historical tensions. They have formed common institutions such as the Asian Development Bank (ADB), ASEAN Regional Forum, East Asian Community (EAC), Regional Comprehensive Economic Partnership (RCEP), and Asian Infrastructure Investment Bank (AIIB)—all of which facilitate flows of goods, services, capital, and people around the region and will steer trillions of dollars of financing into cross-border commercial corridors. A quarter century after the United States won the Cold War and led the Asian order, it is now excluded from nearly all of these bodies.

East and South Asia's rise has compelled West Asia to rediscover its Asian geography. My grandfather, a veteran Indian civil servant and diplomat, always referred to the Gulf states as "West Asia"—never the "Middle East." This seems ever more appropriate as the Gulf petromonarchies trade far more with other Asians than with the West.[13] In fact, in the late 1990s, Arab oil producers began to lock in long-term contracts with energy-thirsty Asian powers the way they used to with Europe and America. With East and South Asians driving global economic growth and West Asians reorienting toward them, the Asian failed states in between such as Iraq and Afghanistan are also closing their chapters of US occupation and plotting their futures within the Asian system.

THINK PPP FOR GDP: ASIANS PAY ASIAN PRICES FOR ASIAN GOODS.

Measured in PPP terms, China has already surpassed the United States as the world's largest economy, while Asia as a whole represents about half of global GDP. The more Asian economies trade with one another, the better able they are to maintain low prices for goods.

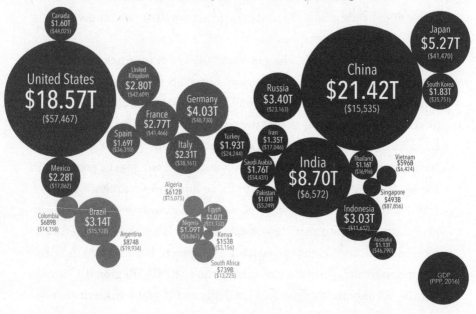

These disparate Asian awakenings are congealing. In 2014, Chinese president Xi Jinping declared to a gathering of Asian leaders in Shanghai, "It is for the people of Asia to run the affairs of Asia, solve the problems of Asia, and uphold the security of Asia."[14] As much as China's neighbors fear its meteoric rise and ambitions, they also share Xi's sentiment. Asians don't want to play by outsiders' rules. No Asian nation—not even US allies Japan, South Korea, and Saudi Arabia—will do anything for the United States that isn't first and foremost in its own interest. It is as if Asians are saying "Asia first." US president Donald Trump's popular slogan "America first" has been a rallying cry that captures the sense of US economic victimization—primarily by Asian economies with large trade surpluses vis-à-vis the United States. Asians, too, want to ensure that global rules suit their preferences rather than allowing them to be exploited.

Yet there are deep differences in worldview between the West and Asia today. Western commentators tend to describe the present geopolitical landscape as a "global disorder" and point to their own errant policies as the cause of declining Western influence—implying that once the United States and Europe get their act together again, the West will be back on top. Asians, by contrast, see their return to the cockpit of history as a natural destiny irrespective of anything the United States or Europe does. Rather than disorder, they are presiding over the construction of a new Asian-led order encompassing the vast majority of the world's population.

This is not to say that Asia will be devoid of conflict. Most of the world's major geopolitical flashpoints lie in Asia, from the Sunni-Shi'a rivalry between Saudi Arabia and Iran to the Korean Peninsula. China has territorial and maritime disputes with India, Vietnam, and Japan. The Arab states and Israel are squaring off against Russia and Iran in Syria, with fragile Iraq caught in the middle. Paradoxically, it is part of the process of becoming a system that neighbors square off violently against each other rather than an outside yoke restraining them. War is as much a part of a system as trade or diplomacy. Friction is evidence of just how important a system's members are to each other, whether as allies or as adversaries. Recall that European states congealed into the European Union only *after* the horrors of World War II, not before. Asia's wars—past, present, and future—and their settlement are thus intrinsic to the process of building an Asian system.

While scenarios for Asian conflicts abound, however, Asia has in recent decades maintained an overarching stability. Asia's big three powers—China, India, and Japan—all have strong leaders with long-term mandates. They are nationalistic, spend massively on their militaries, and have skirmished directly on land or sea. But they have also prevented their altercations from escalating past the point of no return. The United States still helps its allies deter China, while Asian powers such as Japan, India, Australia, and Vietnam are strengthening their bonds to counter Chinese aggression. Meanwhile, new institutions embed China into patterns of restraint with its neighbors and rivals. The more Asian nations are drawn into this maneuvering, the more dynamic and complex the Asian system will become.

This constant multidirectional hedging among ever more pairs of Asian countries is how the Asian diplomatic system is forming from the bottom up. The Asian system does not, and will not, have rules as formalized as those of Europe. There is no supranational Asian parliament, central bank, or military—no "Asian Union," as former Australian prime minister Kevin Rudd once boldly proposed.[15] Instead, the Asian approach to integration involves building complementarities and deferring dangerous issues. Fundamentally, Asians seek not conquest but respect. A sufficient degree of respect for one another's interests is enough.

Europe's postwar decades do, however, show the way in one of the most fundamental aspects of forming a stable system: socialization among political elites, businesses, academics, think tanks, journalists, sports clubs, youth groups, and other communities. For a long time, many Asian citizens have been fed historical narratives of animosity about their neighbors. Yet, though suspicions and negative stereotypes remain strong—especially between Indians and Pakistanis, Chinese and Japanese, Saudi Arabians and Iranians—Asians are getting to know one another better than ever through diplomacy, business, tourism, student exchanges, and regional media. From Al Jazeera to CCTV, Asian youths are becoming more knowledgeable about their fellow Asians and comfortable with their Asian-ness. Over time, perceptions will shift, interests will align, policies will change, and coordination will deepen. The more Asians socialize with one another, the more confidence they will have in solving their problems together.

Asia in the Global Order

In the fall of 2017, German president Frank-Walter Steinmeier invited me to participate in a televised discussion on the future of Western civilization. He began the conversation by asking me, "What's the view from Asia?" My response: The view from Asia is that history has not ended but returned. Asia commands most of the world's population and economy, has catapulted into modernity, maintains stability among its key powers, and has leaders who know what they have to do—and are doing it—to prepare their societies for a complex world. Complacent Western intellectuals conflate material circumstances and ideas, as if the latter remain triumphant despite no longer delivering the former. But ideas compete not in a vacuum but rather on the basis of their impact in the real world.

GROWING TOGETHER: EUROPE AND ASIA FORM THE MOST SIGNIFICANT AXIS OF GLOBAL TRADE.

Europe and Asia are the two most significant regions in global trade, and their trade with each other comprises a greater trade volume than any other pair of regions. As infrastructural linkages and trade agreements expand, Eurasian trade is accelerating and far outstripping either region's trade with North America.

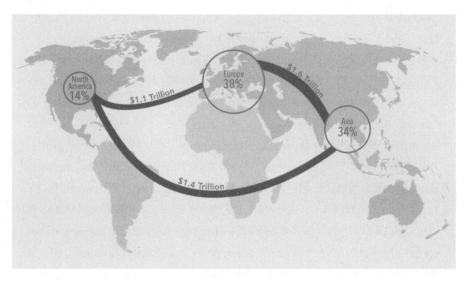

The biggest geopolitical phenomena of the past three decades have come in rapid succession: the dissolution of the Soviet Union, the consolidation of the European Union, the rise of China, the US shale energy revolution, and now the emergence of an Asian system. Global order is about the distribution of power and how that power is governed. The anchor of global order isn't necessarily a single country or set of values, as was the case with the currently waning Western liberal international order. Instead, the foundations of the emerging global order are the US, European, and Asian systems—all at the same time. Each provides vital services around the world, such as military protection, financial investment, and infrastructure development. Rather than one superpower simply fading away to be replaced by a successor, we are living—for the first time ever—in a truly multipolar and multicivilizational order in which North America, Europe, and Asia each represents a major share of power. Asia is not replacing the United States or the West—but it is now shaping them as much as they have shaped it.

To appreciate just how rapidly global order can realign, consider the arc of the post–World War II era. The United States inherited the mantle of preeminence from its wartime ally Great Britain, then provided the security umbrella for Europe to rebuild itself during the Cold War. Today the European Union is a larger economy, plays a greater role in world trade, and exports more capital than does the United States. The United States also provided a Cold War security umbrella for Japan and South Korea, enabling their economies to lift off after decades of conflict. As economic globalization accelerated from the 1970s onward, China leveraged the US-designed global trading system to displace Japan as Asia's largest economy, surpass the United States as the world's largest economy, and become the top trade partner of twice as many countries as the United States. Though the collapse of the Soviet Union meant that the United States stood alone as the world's sole superpower, its "unipolar moment" of the 1990s and 2000s proved to be just a moment as failed wars and a financial crisis turned the rhetoric of invincibility into a fear of imperial overstretch. Meanwhile, both of the regions that America had protected in the postwar years—Europe and Asia—now call their own shots. Trade between Europe and Asia now far exceeds either of their trade with the United States. Both view the Belt and Road Initiative (BRI) as a lucrative opportunity to boost commerce across the Eurasian megacontinent. Neither cares for the United States' suspicion of BRI, for it comes from outside the tent. Once the bedrock of global order, the transatlantic relationship is now an uncomfortable nostalgia, like driving forward while looking in the rearview mirror. That is how quickly the geopolitical world spins.

Asia is the most powerful force reshaping world order today. It is establishing an Asia-centric commercial and diplomatic system across the Indian Ocean to Africa, reorienting the economies and strategies of the United States and Europe, and elevating the appeal of Asian political and social norms in societies worldwide. Geopolitical forecasters like to identify a neat global pecking order, always asking "Who is number one?" But power can't be measured simply by comparing static metrics. The United States is still the leading global military power with the deepest financial markets and largest energy production. Europe still leads the world in market size, the quality of its democratic institutions, and overall living standards. Asia in general, and China in particular, boasts the biggest populations and armies, highest savings rates, and largest currency reserves. Each has different types of power, quantities of power, and geographies of power. There is no definitive answer to who's number one.

Interestingly, China's rise is not as significant a development as it would have been when the United States was the world's sole superpower. For decades, the United States had the most powerful military and largest economy. It protected the global commons, was the consumer of last resort, and had the world's only major currency. By contrast, today the United States, Eurozone, and China each represents more than $10 trillion in GDP. A dozen other countries have economies larger than $1 trillion. Many countries have powerful militaries capable of protecting their own domains, alone or in partnership with others. China is a superpower, but its rise affirms the world's multipolarity; it does not replace it.

Equally important, just as the global landscape is multipolar, so, too, is Asia's. Japan was once Asia's most powerful nation. Today the most powerful nation is China. India has a younger population and will soon be more populous than China. Russia and Iran are flexing their muscles. In Samuel Huntington's *Clash of Civilizations* schematic, most of the world's cultural zones are Asian—Hindu, Buddhist, Sinic, Islamic, and Japanese—and much of the Orthodox realm is as well.

None has ever dominated over more than one of the others for very long. The Asian system has never been an Asian bloc. To the contrary, for most of history, there has been stability across the many Asian sub-regions and fluidity rather than hierarchy. There will be therefore be no Chinese unipolarity—neither globally nor even in Asia. Asians are much more comfortable with the idea of global multipolarity than are Americans, for whom recent history (and most scholarship) has focused on unipolar orders—especially their own. But the more multipolar the world becomes, the more the global future resembles Asia's past.

Getting Asia Right

The time has come to approach Asian dynamics from the inside out. The histories and realities of Asians shouldn't have to be qualified or apologized for. Westerners must be placed, even briefly, in the uncomfortable position of imagining what it's like when about 5 billion Asians don't care what they think and they have to prove their relevance to Asians rather than the reverse.

Americans are just beginning to pay attention to the long and complex cycle of feedback loops tying the United States to Asia. The outsourcing of US jobs to Asia and the erosion of the country's industrial base were among the most salient causes of working-class frustration that propelled Donald Trump into the White House. Thousands of US troops still have their lives on the line in Iraq, Syria, and Afghanistan; East Asia is home to even more US soldiers based in Japan and South Korea. Asia is now a prime destination for US energy, with oil exports across the Pacific increasing by 500 percent between 2011 and 2016—especially to China. (In fact, the United States' trade deficit with Asia would be much worse were it not for rising oil exports.) These realities clearly betray Americans' prevailing mood of wanting to shift their focus inward.

Though the United States' biggest strategic questions revolve around Asia, Asians aspire to what North Americans already enjoy: a high degree of autarky. US arms sales to Saudi Arabia, India, and

Japan have picked up, but Asian defense spending is motivated by the desire either to push the United States out of the region (as China is doing) or to diminish dependence on the United States (as South Korea and others are doing). Asians are working hard to expand access to energy supplies from the Arctic, Russia, Central Asia, and Africa, as well as to invest in their own alternative and renewable energy sources such as natural gas, nuclear power, solar power, wind power, and biomass. The US dollar is still the world's main reserve currency, but Asians have started denominating ever more trade in their own currencies, as well as shedding some of their dollar reserves. And from Amazon to Apple, US corporate profits depend considerably on sales in Asia, but Asian regulators and companies will stop at nothing to capture greater market share for themselves, both in Asia and worldwide.

These examples reflect how Asians view the United States: not as a hegemon but as a service provider. US weapons, capital, oil, and technology are utilities in a global marketplace. The United States is a vendor, and Asia has become its largest customer and competitor at the same time. There was a time when the United States was the default option for the provision of security, capital, and technology, but Asian countries are increasingly providing these services for one another. The United States is more dispensable than it thinks.

To see the world from the Asian point of view requires overcoming decades of accumulated—and willfully cultivated—ignorance about Asia. To this day, Asian perspectives are often inflected through Western prisms; they can only color to an unshakable conventional Western narrative, but nothing more. Yet the presumption that today's Western trends are global quickly falls on its face. The "global financial crisis" was not global: Asian growth rates continued to surge, and almost all the world's fastest-growing economies are in Asia. In 2018, the world's highest growth rates were reported in India, China, Indonesia, Malaysia, and Uzbekistan. Though economic stimulus arrangements and ultralow interest rates have been discontinued in the United States and Europe, they continue in Asia. Similarly, Western populist politics from Brexit to Trump haven't infected Asia, where pragmatic governments are focused on inclusive growth and social cohesion. Americans and Europeans see walls going up, but across Asia they are coming down. Rather than being backward-looking, navel-gazing, and pessimistic, billions of Asians are forward-looking, outward-oriented, and optimistic.

These blind spots are a symptom of a related oversight often found in foreign analyses of Asia, namely that they are actually about the United States. There is a presumption that Asia (and frankly every other region as well) is strategically inert and incapable of making decisions for itself; all it is waiting for is the US leadership to tell them what to do. But from the Asian view, the past two decades have been characterized by President George W. Bush's incompetence, President Barack Obama's half-heartedness, and President Donald Trump's unpredictability. The United States' laundry list of perceived threats—from ISIS and Iran to North Korea and China—have their locus in Asia, but the United States has developed no comprehensive strategy for addressing them. In Washington it is fashionable to promote an "Indo-Pacific" maritime strategy as an antidote to China's Belt and Road Initiative, failing to see how in reality Asia's terrestrial and maritime zones cannot be so neatly separated from each other. For all their differences, Asians have realized that their shared geography is a far more permanent reality than the United States' unreliable promises. The lesson: the United States is a Pacific power with a potent presence in maritime Asia, but it is *not* an *Asian* power.

The most consequential misunderstanding permeating Western thought about Asia is being overly China-centric. Much as geopolitical forecasters have been looking for "number one," many have fallen into the trap of positing a simplistic "G2" of the United States and China competing to lead the world. But neither the world as a whole nor Asia as a region is headed toward a Chinese *tianxia*, or harmonious global system guided by Chinese Confucian principles. Though China presently wields more power than its neighbors, its population is plateauing and is expected to peak by 2030. Of Asia's nearly 5 billion people, 3.5 billion are *not* Chinese. China's staggering debt, worrying demographics, and crowding of foreign competition out of its domestic market are nudging global attention toward the younger and collectively more populous Asian subregions, whose markets are far more open than China's to Western goods. The full picture is this: China has only one-third of Asia's population, less than half of Asia's GDP, about half of its outward investment, and less than half of its inbound investment. Asia is therefore much more than just "China plus."

Asia's future is thus much more than whatever China wants. China is historically not a colonial power. Unlike the United States, it is deeply cautious about foreign entanglements. China wants foreign resources and markets, not foreign colonies. Its military forays from the South China Sea to Afghanistan to East Africa are premised on protecting its sprawling global supply lines—but its grand strategy of building global infrastructure is aimed at *reducing* its dependence on any one foreign supplier (as are its robust alternative energy investments). China's launching the Belt and Road Initiative doesn't prove that it will rule Asia, but it does remind us that China's future, much like its past, is deeply embedded in Asia.

BRI is widely portrayed in the West as a Chinese hegemonic design, but its paradox is that it is accelerating the modernization and growth of countries much as the United States did with its European and Asian partners during the Cold War. BRI will be instructive in showing everyone, including China, just how quickly colonial logic has expired. By joining BRI, other Asian countries have tacitly recognized China as a global power—but the bar for hegemony is very high. As with US interventions, we should not be too quick to assume that China's ambitions will succeed unimpeded and that other powers won't prove sufficiently bold in assrting themselves as well. Nuclear powers India and Russia are on high alert over any Chinese trespassing on their sovereignty and interests, as are regional powers Japan and Australia. Despite spending $50 billion between 2000 and 2016 on infrastructure and humanitarian projects across the region, China has purchased almost no meaningful loyalty. The phrase "China-led Asia" is thus no more acceptable to most Asians than the notion of a "US-led West" is to Europeans.

China has a first-mover advantage in such places where other Asian and Western investors have hesitated to go. But no states are more keenly aware of the potential disadvantages of Chinese neomercantilism than postcolonial nations such as Pakistan and post-Soviet republics such as Uzbekistan and Kazakhstan. They don't need shrill warnings in Western media to remind them of their immediate history. One by one, many countries are pushing back and renegotiating Chinese projects and debts. Here, then, is a more likely scenario: China's forays actually modernize and elevate these countries, helping them gain the confidence to *resist* future encroachment. Furthermore, China's moves have inspired an infrastructural "arms race," with India, Japan, Turkey, South Korea, and others also making major investments that will enable weaker Asian nations to better connect to one another and counter Chinese maneuvers. Ultimately, China's position will be not of an Asian or global hegemon but rather of the eastern anchor of the Asian—and Eurasian—megasystem.

The farther one looks into the future, therefore, the more clearly Asia appears to be—as has been the norm for most of its history—a multipolar region with numerous confident civilizations evolving largely independent of Western policies but constructively coexisting with one another. A reawakening of Western confidence and vitality would be very welcome, but it would not blunt Asia's resurrection. Asia's rise is structural, not cyclical. There remain pockets of haughty ignorance centered around London and Washington that persist in the belief that Asia will come undone as China's economy slows or will implode under the strain of nationalist rivalries. These opinions about Asia are irrelevant and inaccurate in equal measure. As Asian countries emulate one another's successes, they leverage their growing wealth and confidence to extend their influence to all corners of the planet. The Asianization of Asia is just the first step in the Asianization of the world.

The Asianization of the World

The legacy of the nineteenth-century Europeanization and twentieth-century Americanization of the world is that most nations have been shaped by the West in some significant way: European colonial borders and administration, US invasions or military assistance, a currency pegged to the US dollar, American software and social media, and so forth. Billions of people have acquired personal and psychological connections to the West. They have English or French as a first or second language, have relatives in America, Canada, or Great Britain, cheer for an English Premier League football team, never miss films starring their favorite Hollywood actor or actress, and follow the ins and outs of US presidential politics.

In the twenty-first century, Asianization is emerging as the newest sedimentary layer in the geology of global civilization. As with its predecessors, Asianization takes many forms but is universally palpable: selling commodities to China, recruiting software engineers from India, buying oil from Saudi Arabia, taking vacations in Japan or Indonesia, recruiting nurses from the Philippines, hosting construction crews from Korea, doing apprenticeships in the UAE, and other relationships. Asian businesspeople strut around the world as their passports gain more visa-free privileges. Singapore and Japan have overtaken Germany in Henley & Partners' "most powerful passports" index, South Korea also ranks ahead of most European nations, and Malaysia has nudged ahead of many European passports as well. A new layer of Asian-ness is creeping into people's identity and daily life as well. Around the world, students are learning Chinese and Japanese, entrepreneurs are launching businesses in Asian metropolises, travelers are flocking to beaches from Oman to the Philippines, intermarriage is rising among Indians and Thais, youths are converting to Islam, movie theaters are showing Bollywood movies, and more.

The Asian way of doing things is spreading. Governments are taking a stronger hand in steering economic priorities. Democratic impulses are being balanced with technocratic guidance. Social discourse in the

West not only boasts of rights but speaks of responsibilities. Western officials, businesspeople, journalists, scholars, and students are touring Asia to observe how to build large-scale, world-class infrastructure and futuristic cities, study how governments use scenarios and data to align industries and universities, and examine social policies that promote national solidarity. In many ways, rather than "them" aspiring to be like "us," we now aspire to be like them. The name of the flagship publication of Singapore's Lee Kuan Yew School of Public Policy aptly captures the transition to this new paradigm: *Global-is-Asian*.

At the same time, becoming more Asian does not necessarily mean becoming less American or European. Asianization is like an additional layer of paint on an already colorful canvas; it adds texture and hues. As the great British historian Arnold Toynbee documented, civilizations do not merely displace each other, discarding rivals' ideas and substituting their own fully formed ideologies. In this spirit, Asianization borrows much from the past even as it inserts its principles into the world as it already is. Nineteenth-century Europeanization brought with it colonial inclusion in a world economy, modern forms of government administration, and exposure to liberal Enlightenment philosophies. These in turn gave rise to nationalism as colonies sought to become independent nations—an idea strongly supported by the United States as it became the world's leading power. Twentieth-century Americanization ratified democratic self-determination through formal multilateral organizations such as the United Nations, promoted the spread of capitalism and industrialization through global trade and investment treaties, and inspired an appreciation for the great potential of unencumbered freedom. Asianization absorbs but also challenges aspects of these earlier eras. Asians practice neomercantile industrial policy rather than free-market capitalism, with government and business colluding to gain the biggest share of commercial arrangements. Asia is also highly bureaucratized and multilateral, but via new Asian-driven institutions that both complement and compete with incumbent Western ones. Many Asian countries have inherited Western parliamentary systems, but have grafted on more technocratic mechanisms in pursuit of societal welfare. Asianization, then, is not about replacing the past wholesale but about modifying it.

Historical eras are accumulating in ways that do not allow for one model to fully impose itself on the others. Instead, as Asian institutions and norms take their place alongside those of the West, they synthesize into a fusion that itself becomes the global norm. Some aspects of global Westernization will remain central to global life, especially the English language, capitalism, and the pursuit of scientific excellence and technological disruption. But over time, others will fade, such as the appeal of American-style democracy and unsustainable consumerism. The question is not which order will prevail, but rather in which ways is Asia shaping a new global order that encompasses all of us?

We are only in the early phases of Asia penetrating all other civilizations as the West did over the course of centuries. Much as one could not have foreseen the impact of European commercial exploration in Asia or across the Atlantic nor the United States' entry into World War I, the outcome of this process is uncertain. As with previous centuries of Europeanization and Americanization, Asianization is a double-edged sword. You may or may not like some (or many) aspects of global Asianization—the same has certainly been true for the billions of people worldwide on the receiving end of Americanization. Nonetheless, it is widely observed that the United States managed to remake the world in its image. Asia is now doing the same. Everyone can articulate how "American" or "European" he or she is. Now we are learning to grasp how "Asian" we are as well. How Asian are you?

For the past four decades, I've had a front-row seat to the beginnings of global Asianization. I was born in India. My family migrated to the UAE in the 1970s, as did countless other Indians and Pakistanis supporting the Arab oil boom. Then over the course of a decade in New York, my family went from being one of the only to one of dozens of Indian American families in just one small town. Each year of college I saw ever more Asian students major in Asian studies or express their cultural pride in student festivals. Then, in the narrow world of Washington think tanks and foreign policy, I saw growing numbers of Asians take mainstream roles. During my stints in Berlin, Geneva, and London, the rising presence of Asians in academic and daily life was palpable. Now I reside in Singapore, the unofficial capital of Asia, a melting pot that embodies Asia's potential to make the most of the Europeanization and Americanization of the past and, most important, the Asianization of today and tomorrow.

I have also witnessed just how urgently the world needs a better understanding of Asia. From Syria and Iran to China and North Korea, Asia occupies Western headlines while policy makers and the public lack a contextual knowledge of Asia's history. Asian economic policies have been reshaping US industry for decades, yet even as they take center stage in US politics, leaders fail to fully grasp the dynamic feedback loops between the US and Asian economic systems. US and European companies have prioritized China but have little appreciation for its citizens' tastes—and know even less about those of the other 3.5 billion Asians whose markets are their newest growth frontier. Asians, too, have major gaps in knowledge to fill. Chinese are spending hundreds of billions of dollars in new investments across Asia, buying influence in some places and stoking backlash in others, unsure which will happen and where. Indians, Arabs, Turks, and Persians are crisscrossing Asia as well, confronting unfamiliar political and social systems. How much we have forgotten! For many centuries, Asians understood one another through their constant interactions along the Silk Roads, while the West discovered and absorbed Asia through colonialism. Before exploring our Asian future, then, let us refresh our memories about Asia's past.

1

A History of the World:
An Asian View

A typical history textbook in the Western world begins with the civilizations of ancient Mesopotamia and Egypt, followed by chapters on the Greeks and Romans, the Middle Ages and Renaissance, Columbus and Copernicus, Napoleon and Enlightenment, British colonialism and American independence, concluding with the two world wars. As students advance through the years, the curriculum revisits the ancient, medieval, and modern eras in more detail and with more dramatis personae: Caesar and Cleopatra, the Holy Roman Empire and Black Death, Martin Luther and Louis XIV, the slave trade and Industrial Revolution, the Congress of Vienna and Crimean War, Franklin D. Roosevelt and Josef Stalin . . . and then the baton is passed to social studies.

Generally speaking, non-Western societies are brought into the picture to the extent that they had contact with the West. After all, the Mongols did reach the gates of Vienna in 1241. But the life and times of the Buddha and Confucius, the legacies of the Mughal Empire, the oceanic ventures of China's Ming Dynasty, and many other foundations of Asia's heritage might draw blank stares even after a university-level history course. Europeans, because they colonized the world between the fifteenth and twentieth centuries, tend to know quite a bit more than Americans about foreign regions. But as much as colonialism enriched the West, it still doesn't feature much in the Western teaching of the past. Asian textbooks, of course, also focus on their own national and civilizational histories, generally at the expense of the Egyptians and Greeks. Furthermore, Chinese, Japanese, and Koreans are just as willing as Europeans are to whitewash—or omit—their subjugation of, or crimes against, one another. Because of colonialism, however, Asian history cannot wash out the West the way Western teaching does to Asia.

The deep linkages between West and East underscore the need for a more balanced account of global history. However, as Sebastian Conrad persuasively argued in his *What Is Global History?*, the discipline still suffers from Eurocentrism and a nation-state centered lens, diminishing the role of non-European civilizations as well as global processes such as capitalism that sustained linkages across regions.[1] The essence of global history, by contrast, is to recount the coevolution of diverse cultures and appreciate their mutual influence. Remember that both the history of today and the rules for tomorrow are written by the winners—and Asia is gaining ground. As Asia's ascendancy continues, the biggest gap in Western historical knowledge will be filled by Asians in their own words. What does history look like from an Asian point of view?

Ancient Asia: The Dawn of Civilization

The birth of human civilization as we know it today began in West Asia. In Mesopotamia and Asia Minor (Anatolia), the advent of basic farming tools during the Neolithic Revolution enabled humans to evolve from hunter-gatherer tribes into more settled agricultural communities that domesticated animals such as horses and dogs. The Natufian people of the eastern Levantine region were hunter-gatherers who began to grind and bake wheat into bread nearly 15,000 years ago. Fortifications found in Byblos, Aleppo, and Jericho indicate settlements dating to 7000 BC, making these the world's oldest continuously inhabited cities. Archaeological excavations at Göbekli Tepe and Çatalhöyük in modern-day Turkey have uncovered patterned pottery, uniform brick housing, and even religious icons. By 3800 BC, the great Sumerian city-states of Ur, Kish, and Babylon thrived near the confluence of the Tigris and Euphrates rivers.

Prehistoric civilizations also flourished in East Asia. Agriculture became widespread in peninsular Southeast Asia by 6000 BC, in Japan during its Jōmon period around 5000 BC, and in China around 4000 BC. By 3500 BC, during the early Bronze Age, the largest centers of the ancient world were Harappa and Mohenjo-Daro in the Indus Valley (today's Pakistan), which featured wide streets, bathing platforms, drainage, and reservoirs. The Indus peoples worshipped a range of deities, including terra-cotta statues of the female goddess Shakti. With the migration of Aryan ("noble") peoples from Central Asia around 1800 BC, Indo-Aryan civilization expanded southward into the Ganges plain, where its pastoral traditions and social structures were captured in the Sanskrit-language hymns of the world's oldest religious texts, the Vedas, which formed the basis of Hinduism.

During the middle Bronze Age, around 2300 BC, Sumerian city-states gave way to the powerful Akkadian Empire and its successor, the Assyrians, who ruled over ever larger expanses as they subdued their Anatolian neighbors the Hittites, who had developed iron smelting for tools and weapons. Assyrians and Babylonians (especially under King Hammurabi) developed complex legal codes governing social life and a sophisticated division of labor among the working classes. They also engaged in diplomacy and trade with Egypt, selling it olive oil, wine, cedar wood, and the resin used for mummification. By 667 BC, Assyria had vanquished Egypt, putting an end to its age of pyramids.

Asia's civilizations spread their advances in all directions. By 1500 BC, the seafaring Phoenicians of the Levant devised an alphabet system that was documented on Egyptian papyrus and adopted by the Greeks, a major Mediterranean trading partner. Inland, in the Caspian region, the nomadic Scythians mastered mounted warfare, occupied the Central Asian steppe region, and raided settled civilizations such as the Median people (in present-day Iran) while presiding over a vast trading network linking Greeks, Persians, and Indians that flourished from the eighth century BC onward.

These overland routes of commerce and culture reached as far as China, which by the first millennium BC had consolidated its administrative power in the Yangtze River valley. The procession of the Xia, Shang, and Zhou dynasties expanded the area of Chinese civilization through alliances and conquest, assimilating the Rong barbarians on their western frontier. At the same time, the Zhou engaged in sporadic trade with the various nomadic peoples of southern Siberia and the more sedentary peoples of Bactria, who made wide use of single-axle chariots. This Western Zhou Dynasty first articulated the notion of a *Zhongguo* ("Middle Kingdom") to differentiate their imperial state from those of their vassals and the powerful fiefdoms of the northern plains. The Zhou also produced the cosmological *I Ching*, a text that sought to align human behavior with the cyclical patterns of nature.[2]

Three thousand years ago, the forces of commerce, conflict, and culture ebbed and flowed across the vast expanse from the Mediterranean to China in increasingly intense patterns of exchange. Around 550 BC, the nomadic Achaemenid people pushed aside the Scythians as they settled in the Persian region and built an empire that stretched from the Balkans to the Indus valley, the largest empire of the ancient world. Cyrus the Great's Royal Road stretched 1,700 miles from Susa to Saris in western Anatolia, with horse-mounted couriers covering the distance in only seven days, making them the fastest postal service of antiquity. Cyrus and Darius I established opulent cities such as Persepolis, their administrative authority becoming the envy of Mediterranean peoples. (For the Greek historian Herodotus, Persia represented most of what was known of Asia.) The Achaemenids shared a linguistic kinship with the Sanskrit speakers of South Asia as well as a social stratification of priests, rulers, warriors, and farmers. Their faith, known as Zoroastrianism, was a philosophical monotheism that influenced local religions such as that of the Judaic peoples located on the eastern Mediterranean shores between Mesopotamia and the Nile River.

During the mid–6th century BC, India was the epicenter of new religious awakenings. In the eastern Ganges region (today's Bihar province, as well as southern Nepal and western Bangladesh), ancient kingdoms flourished that differed from the Indo-Aryan strongholds to the north. In the Magadha Kingdom, Prince Siddhartha Gautama broke away from the prevailing Vedic Hindu *dharma* (eternal order or law), becoming an ascetic sage who attained enlightenment at Bodh Gaya and gave his first sermon at Sarnath. The first Buddhist council, convened soon after the Buddha's death, was held in Magadha's capital, Rajgir.[3]

To the north, in China, the Zhou Dynasty's transition from bronze to iron made it a pioneer of farming plows, while hydrological technologies such as dams, dikes, and canals enabled it to harness the upper Yangtze River for irrigation. Other Zhou inventions included the decimal system in mathematics and the efficient weaving of silk. Even as the Zhou Dynasty's stability gave way to the Warring States period (481–206 BC), "a hundred schools of thought" flourished. The military theorist Sun Tzu compiled his treatise *The Art of War*, which revealed strategies in espionage and battlefield tactics. Great sages such as Mozi, Mengzi (Mencius), and Confucius produced deep philosophical reflections on social values. Naturalistic philosophies such as Daoism also emerged, proposing the duality of *yin* and *yang* as seemingly opposing forces that actually belong to the same Oneness.

By 221 BC, the Qin Dynasty had risen and restored stability. Its first emperor, Qin Shi Huang, unified China's language, units of measurement, currency, tax system, and census. To ward off the nomadic Xiongnu in the west, the Qin began the construction of the Great Wall. Meanwhile, as the Qin crushed their rivals to the east and south, many Chinese migrated across the Yalu River, overrunning the Gojoseon Kingdom on the Korean Peninsula. Both Chinese and Koreans also migrated across the Tsushima Strait onto the Kyushu Islands of Japan, which during its Yayoi period had developed distinctive pottery, bronze bells, and Shinto and animist belief systems. The mainland migrants brought with them Chinese script and characters, which became foundational to Japanese and other East Asian languages. Han people from central China also shifted in large numbers to northern Vietnam, where the Chinese commander Zhao Tuo established the Nanyue Kingdom, which spanned the Chinese provinces of Yunnan, Guangxi, and Guangdong.

The Qin quickly collapsed with the death of Qin Shi Huang's son in 207 BC and, after another period of unrest, were supplanted by the even more powerful Han Dynasty, which promoted Confucianism both as a national religion and as a curriculum for the imperial bureaucracy. Particularly under the half-century-long reign of Emperor Wu-di (140–87 BC), the Han united disparate kingdoms into a vast empire, including subduing the Nanyue to the south. Their strength also allowed them to incorporate the territory of the nettlesome Xiongnu into a tributary region and to push through the fertile Gansu corridor into the Tarim basin toward the Pamir Mountains of Central Asia. The Han also forged connections over land and sea with India, Ceylon, Egypt, and Rome, together forming the first trans-Asian trading networks.

The Han westward push forced Yuezhi nomads from Xinjiang to the other side of the Karakoram and Pamir mountains, where they established the Kushan Empire with its center at Peshawar. The Yuezhi assimilated Buddhist culture from the Ganges valley lying to their south and disseminated it northward into Central Asia, where the Sogdian people, who occupied lands between the Amu Darya and Syr Darya rivers, were laying the foundations of the great Silk Road cities Samarkand and Bukhara (in today's Uzbekistan). Meanwhile, from the other direction, the Achaemenid continued their push eastward into this strategic terrain, absorbing Sogdiana as a surrogate province.

The Achaemenid, however, faced a greater challenge from their western frontier as the armies of Alexander III of Macedon ("Alexander the Great") penetrated eastward as far as the Indus River. Alexander defeated Emperor Darius III but maintained the efficient Achaemenid administrative and tax structures. The eastern Achaemenid stronghold of Gandhara remained a rich mélange of Persian Zoroastrian, Indian Hindu, and Ganges Buddhist cultures with capitals shifting between great cities such as Charsadda and Taxila. The

Mauryan Empire, which emerged from the eastern Ganges Magadha region, conquered northward toward Taxila, with King Chandragupta advised by the great strategist Chanakya (also known as Kautilya). As the Mauryans secured their base at Taxila, Chandragupta's grandson Ashoka adorned Gandhara with Buddhist stupas. The Mauryan Empire weakened with Ashoka's death in 232 BC, opening the door for King Demetrius of Bactria, a successor to Alexander of Macedon, to capture Gandhara by around 200 BC. Subsequently, King Menander, born at Bagram (north of Kabul), propagated the Grand Trunk Road, which stretched from Central Asia through the fertile Punjab all the way to the mouth of the Ganges.

By that time, the Parthians, heirs to the Achaemenid civilization, had arisen from their stronghold just east of the Caspian Sea to dominate as far west as Anatolia and across the Euphrates River valley and Persia to the fringes of China in the east. Even as they skirmished with the Romans (who had succeeded the Greeks in regional power) in the Mediterranean basin and Caucasus region, the Parthians and their Sogdian middlemen fostered the Silk Road of trade in Indian spices and Chinese tea and porcelain bought by Romans and Roman glass, silver, ivory, and gold bought by the Chinese, who sent diplomatic envoys such as Zhang Qian on extensive westward tours to build ties with the Parthians.

Despite the region's vast geographic and cultural diversity, Buddhism was the glue that held numerous Asian civilizations together. Bamiyan became a major center of Buddhist learning where monks nurtured a distinctive artistic style developed fusing Iranian, Indian, and Gandharan forms. Dunhuang in the Tarim basin, the site of stunning Buddhist grottoes chiseled into mountainsides, was the crossroads of several trade routes linking Mongolia and Tibet to Parthia and the Levant. As Han monks and merchants traveled the Silk Road in search of inspiration, they brought back Buddhist texts translated by Sogdians. Buddhism thus extended its reach through the Han Empire in a pincerlike movement from the west and south from India and Southeast Asia. By AD 155, the Han emperor Huan introduced Buddhist ceremonies into the imperial curriculum to complement Confucian teachings. In East Asia, then, Confucianism came to provide the rules of social organization premised on righteousness and benevolence, while Buddhism, Chinese Daoism, and Japanese Shintoism enabled people's spiritul aspirations.

The maritime routes linking components of the ancient Asian system were even more significant than those over land. By the first century BC, up to 120 Greek ships per year sailed through the Red Sea and captured the monsoon winds to arrive at Indian ports, returning with jade, beads, and spices brought from Southeast Asian island kingdoms such as Sumatra and Java. Robust trade with the Indian subcontinent accelerated Southeast Asia's Indianization, especially in the Kingdom of Funan in the lower Mekong Delta and the Khmer people, with whom Indian merchants intermarried, bringing Hinduism and Indian scripts to the Burmese, Javanese, and Thai languages. Indian knowledge of medicine also flowed along this route, finding its way into Chinese pharmacological texts. Funan's successor, the Srivijayan Kingdom, was a famous Buddhist crossroads. King Songtsen Gampo of the mighty Tibetan Kingdom also adopted Buddhism due to the influence of his Nepali and Chinese wives.

This Indian-Chinese, Buddhist-Confucian exchange spanning India and China via Central and Southeast Asia made ancient Asia a rich cultural zone, lasting well beyond the disintegration of the Han Empire in the second century. The decline of the Han and subsequent Six Dynasties period of chaos empowered the Goguryeo Kingdom of Korea to liberate itself from the Han yoke, creating the largest independent state of the Korean Peninsula; it spanned the Yalu River and the Liaodong Peninsula. Another Korean kingdom, the Baekje, also held its own in territory and trade with China. The Baekje welcomed monks from Gandhara who brought Buddhism to the kingdom in the fourth century, and subsequently many more Indian monks who initiated the construction of monasteries and temples. The princess of Ayodhya in India even married into Korean royalty.

As in Korea, disparate Japanese kingdoms awakened, with the Yamato coalescing into a formidable regime that governed from AD 250 to

710. Under the reign of Prince Shōtoku (AD 593–622) in the Asuka period, Buddhism flourished in Japanese society while Confucianism took hold in the bureaucracy. The Yamato adopted the Chinese calendar and sent Japanese students to China to study both Buddhism and Confucianism. At the same time, Japan sought equality with the Chinese emperor and refused to accept a subordinate status. Even as China, Korea, and Japan contested territory, constant migration brought them together into a common East Asian system of commerce and cross-cultural learning.

South Asia, too, continued with its intellectual and cultural advances. The Kushan Empire, led by Emperor Kanishka, strengthened in the wake of the Mauryans' demise but continued Ashoka and Menander's nurturing of Buddhism. By the year AD 150, Kanishka came to rule over a vast realm spanning the Bactrian regions of the Tarim basin (today's Xinjiang) all the way to the Ganges. The Gupta Empire, which subsequently dominated the Ganges region after 320, marked a golden age of cultural and scientific accomplishment with the completion of the epic tale Mahabharata and the invention of the mathematical zero and the game of chess. The great university of Nalanda attracted students from as far as Central Asia and Korea and hosted the reputable late-seventh-century Chinese monks Xuanzang and Yijing, who translated dozens of Buddhist texts from Sanskrit into Chinese. The Guptas also expanded eastward through Bengal and built strong trade ties with the Srivijaya Kingdom, which over a period of nearly a century constructed the world's largest Buddhist temple at Borobudur on the island of Java. The Guptas exported textiles and perfumes to Rome—until both the Guptas and the Romans succumbed in the fifth century to Hun invaders from the Altai region east of the Caspian Sea (today's Kazakhstan).

Still, Asia's continental connectivity continued to thrive. Paper, silk, gunpowder, and luxury goods traversed the Silk Roads in all directions, as did philosophical ideas and religious doctrines. New faiths also emerged from West Asia. In Roman Palestine, followers of the preacher Jesus Christ began to spread his message across the Levant and Caucasus; early missionaries such as St. Thomas the Apostle baptized Christians as far away as Kerala in southern India. Meanwhile, the Nestorian Church of Byzantium, splitting from that of Rome, anchored itself at Constantinople in Anatolia and grew its following in the Sassanian Empire, through which it spread eastward across Central Asia and as far as China. Ancient Asia was a richly diverse milieu of civilizations engaging through the forces of commerce, conflict, and culture.

Asia's Imperial Expansions

Byzantium was not the only religious empire that surged eastward in the centuries following the sacking of Rome. In Arabia, long home to a polytheistic mix of Zoroastrianism, Judaism, Nestorianism, and numerous indigenous faiths, the revelations of the prophet Muhammad in Mecca in AD 610 CE inspired Arabs across the land. After his death in 632, Muslim tribes unified under the Rashidun Caliphate, which launched conquests across Egypt and North Africa and overran the Sassanians and Persians to the east. This early Islamic unity, however, gave way to disputes over succession, causing a rift within the ruling Umayyad Caliphate between rival Sunni and Shi'a sects. Already by the early eighth century, Islam had advanced to reach both the Iberian Peninsula of Europe and the fringes of India.

The Umayyad's successors, the Abbasids, converted the powerful Turkic tribes of the Ferghana valley (in today's Uzbekistan) and allied with them—as well as the powerful Tibetan Empire, which ruled a vast expanse covering the Tarim basin, the Himalayas, Bengal, and Yunnan—together defeating the Tang Dynasty's armies (led in part by the Goguryeo Korean commander Gao Xianzhi) at the momentous Battle of Talas near the Tian Shan Mountains in present-day Kyrgyzstan, in 751. Despite its victory over the Tang, the Abbasid Dynasty came in 755 to aid the Tang to put down a rebellion launched by its own half-Sogdian, half-Turk general An Lushan.

While the Arab-Turkic-Tibetan alliance expelled China's garrisons from Central Asia, its armies and merchants (including those of the nomadic Uighur people) took westward China's sophisticated knowledge of papermaking. The Abbasids' second caliph, Al-Mansur, established a new capital city, Baghdad, on the banks of the Tigris River (just north of the former Sassanid capital city of Ctesiphon). Subsequently, Caliph Harun al-Rashid (r. 786–809) built a House of Wisdom that gathered scholars such as the Persian mathematician and astronomer Muhammad al-Khwarizmi, who pioneered algebra (*al-jabr*) and the study of Indian numerals, and Hunayn ibn Ishaq, a Nestorian Christian polymath who translated more than one hundred works of the Greek philosophers Plato and Aristotle into Syriac and Arabic. Leveraging this collection of translated knowledge, the esteemed mathematician and astronomer Al-Biruni stood at the Nandna Fort in the hills of Punjab and calculated the circumference of the earth in the year 997. The caliphate's contributions to the region were thus religious, intellectual, and economic.

Despite its defeat at the Battle of Talas, China under the Tang experienced a great awakening of cosmopolitan culture. Just before the Tang, the short-lived Sui Dynasty managed to unite the northern and southern Han and construct the Grand Canal, which linked the capital Chang'an (Xi'an) with eastern cities such as Beijing and Hangzhou, accelerating the movement of troops and grain. The Sui also sinicized major ethnic minorities and elevated Buddhism into the national religion. The Tang then continued to welcome Malay, Arab, and Persian merchants, even inviting them to live in permanent communities in Chinese cities. Such immigrants made up two-thirds of the 200,000 inhabitants of Guangzhou (Canton), where the Huaisheng Mosque became the first of its kind in China. Tang Dynasty merchant ships reflected this diversity, with crews made up of Christians, Parsis, Muslims, and Jews. Tang vessels crossed the Java Sea and Malacca Strait carrying tens of thousands of fine porcelain bowls and other items to be exchanged for Indian fabrics and Abbasid glassware.

At the time, the Tang Empire's estimated 60 million people accounted for a quarter of the world's population, and its cities were larger than any in Europe or India. The Tang leveraged this strength to expand aggressively into Manchuria in the north, Tibet in the west, and Annam (Vietnam) in the south. By the eighth century, nearly one hundred Asiatic peoples were sending tributes to the Tang emperor. Tang influence also reached a peak in Korea and Japan, where Buddhist sects came to rival the Asuka for power in the late eighth century. Japan's two main Buddhist centers, Nara and Kyoto, were modeled on Chang'an (Xi'an). The internal strife that plagued the later Tang had dramatic consequences, including the independence of Vietnam and Korea. It also left a power vacuum in Central Asia filled by the nomadic Turks. Turkic peoples such as the Seljuks came to dominate from the fringes of China across Persia, subduing the Abbasid Dynasty in 1051 and defeating the Byzantines at Manzikert in 1071, advancing their Persian-Turkic synthesis across Anatolia. Born to a Turkic father and Persian mother, the Abbasid sultan Mahmud of Ghazni embodied this fusion of Sunni Islam with the warrior spirit of the Seljuks, waging relentless campaigns of *jihad* into Hindustan. The rise of the Delhi Sultanate all but wiped out Buddhism in favor of a syncretic Indo-Islamic culture in literature, music, and architecture.

As Seljuk raiders sacked north India's disparate Hindu kingdoms, southern India flourished under one of its longest-ruling dynasties, the Chola, who by the ninth century had reached the zenith of power as a seafaring empire. The Chola Dynasty invaded Sri Lanka, the Maldives, Bengal, and Southeast Asia, spreading both Hindu and Buddhist culture across Khmer territory (Cambodia) and Java. The Chola achieved a decisive conquest over the Srivijaya in 1025, making them the masters of the Indian Ocean maritime network, with merchant guilds and temple banks financing ambitious commercial voyages to Yemen and East Africa.

As the Song Dynasty of China reconstituted centralized control in the late tenth century, it rejoined the thriving Indo-Pacific trade and shared its invention of the navigational compass and its mastery of shipbuilding. The expansion of the Delhi Sultanate eastward and its conquest of Bengal in 1200 spread Islam through Malacca, Sumatra, and Java. Such were the Muslims' seafaring capabilities that by the later Song Dynasty, many had become dominant traders in China's import-export industry.

Though the Song never achieved the splendor of the Tang, their prosperity grew as they embraced a capitalist culture and the use of paper money. Indeed, the Song were the first Chinese dynasty to commercialize the "tribute system" that focused on gains from trade with secondary powers rather than heavy taxation of the populace. Meanwhile, the Kingdom of Pagan unified central and coastal Burma as well as the Malay Peninsula, strengthening overland trade routes that linked the Bay of Bengal via Yunnan to China. The Chola, Song, and Srivijaya all competed to control strategic maritime passageways such as the Strait of Malacca but also amplified the linkages between their external trade and internal economies.

Meanwhile, on the other side of Eurasia, Europe had been stagnant for centuries after the fall of the Roman Empire. In the eleventh century, the pope sought to reconcile with Byzantium to repulse the advancing Turks and reclaim the holy land of Palestine. But by 1204, western Christian crusaders had instead plundered Constantinople, further dividing the Christian world and enabling greater gains by the Seljuk Sultanate of Rum. The mystic scholar and poet Rumi came of age in this Turkic-Persian milieu, composing literary volumes that both preached a personal love of God and venerated music and dance as pathways to spiritual union. In Central Asia, the Seljuks faced tough resistance from the Karakhanid confederation of nomadic Turkic tribes, which held firm from Kashgar to Samarkand before splintering into several khanates that became Seljuk vassals. Turkic language and Islamic culture thrived in the *madrassa*s of Bukhara.

The Seljuk khanates and smaller Turkic protostates, however, could not withstand the rapacious armies of the Mongols. After uniting disparate northeast Asian tribes in 1206, the young warrior Temujin took on the name of Genghis Khan, or "universal ruler," and led savage campaigns across Eurasia. By the time of his death in 1227, Genghis

Khan ruled the largest contiguous empire in history, stretching from the East Sea (also known as the Sea of Japan) to the Caspian Sea. The conquests continued under his sons and grandsons, who swept across Russia and sacked Kiev in 1240, laid siege to Hungary in 1241, and reached the gates of Vienna. In 1258, the Mongols sacked Baghdad. In 1276, the Song Dynasty succumbed to Genghis Khan's grandson Kublai Khan. A decade later, all of China—as well as the Gobi Desert and Siberia to the north—had fallen under the reign of the Mongol Yuan Dynasty, which Kublai Khan ruled from Shangdu (Xanadu) and eventually from Khanbaliq (Beijing).

For all its brutality, the Mongol Empire was strikingly tolerant: three of the four major khanates were heavily Muslim populated, while the Yuan adopted Buddhism. The Mongols were also shrewd in coopting diverse cultures and intermarrying with leading families. They rounded up hundreds of thousands of Arabs, Persians, and Turks and brought them back to China as administrators, diluting the influence of Chinese Confucian bureaucrats. The Persian physician Rashid al-Din, who served in the court of Genghis Khan's grandson Hulagu Khan, authored a three-volume compendium (*Jami al-Tawarikh*) chronicling this blending of Mongol, Persian, and other cultures.

The Mongols' provision of reliable security across a vast swath of Eurasia also enabled flourishing trade between numerous civilizations along the Silk Road. Merchant caravans from as far as Europe—including that of the late-thirteenth-century Venetian traveler Marco Polo—brought goods and visitors to the court of Kublai Khan. The rapid connectivity the Mongols enabled, however, also facilitated the rapid spread of a great plague that emanated from Central Asia. By the mid–fourteenth century, about one-third of Persia's population had died; farther west, half of Europe's population perished. That pestilence curtailed Silk Road trade and accelerated the decline of Mongol influence.

The Turkic Ottomans were thus able to reclaim Mesopotamia in the 1300s, while also conquering the Balkans, Arabia, and most of North Africa. After defeating the Byzantine army, Sultan Osman I transformed the land from a Greek-speaking Christian region to a Turkish-speaking Muslim one, while preserving autonomy for Christian and Jewish communities. But a major rival quickly emerged. Claiming descent from Genghis Khan, Amir Timur (Tamerlane) led his armies to restore a vast Persianized Mongol Muslim dynasty covering Central Asia and northwest India. Upon Tamerlane's death in 1405, the Ottomans wrested control of eastern Anatolia back from the Timurids. The spread of field artillery such as cannon and muskets spurred an arms race among Asian empires.

Timur's legacy migrated southward into India. Beginning in the early fifteenth century, Babur, a descendant of Genghis Khan and Tamerlane, laid the foundations of a multigenerational succession of Mughal (the Persian translation of Mongol) rulers whose domain stretched from the Fergana valley across most of the Indian subcontinent. Given their partial Turkic heritage, the Mughals soon began exchanging diplomatic missions with the Ottoman sultans. Initially, the Mughals were less tolerant than their Ottoman brethren, destroying India's Hindu shrines and persecuting non-Muslims. Yet as Babur's son Humayan and grandson Akbar expanded the empire both north and south, they increased trade with Europeans, modernized the court's bureaucracy, and instituted a radical degree of religious tolerance. Akbar's son Jahangir put down numerous revolts to consolidate the empire in the early seventeenth century, and his grandson Emperor Shah Jahan elevated Mughal opulence with Islamic monuments such as the Taj Mahal.

During India's Mughal era, the Shi'a Muslim Safavids of Isfahan, whose ancestry included Turkic, Kurdish, and Azeri heritage, rose above numerous competing dynasties to become the first indigenous power to unify the Persian realm since the Sassanids, taking control of eastern Anatolia, the Caucasus, and western Turkestan. The Safavids enabled the north–south trade routes connecting Europe to India. An estimated 20,000 Indian traders lived and worked across the Safavid Empire, with Mughal merchants establishing dozens of caravanserai in major trading hubs such as Shemakha and Baku, where they collected

Russian furs, copper, and caviar and brought them back to India via Afghanistan or by ship from Bandar-e-Abbas to Surat.

During the Timurid and Mughal periods in Central and South Asia, internal rebellions in China loosened Mongol control, and by 1368, the Ming Dynasty controlled the Yangtze River valley and claimed its place as the successor to the great Tang. In contrast to Song Dynasty capitalism and Mongol openness, however, the Ming emperor Hongwu curtailed private foreign trade and instituted a highly statist trade regime to project power over neighbors such as Tibet and Korea, which became a Ming vassal state and underwent a cultural sinicization. By contrast, Japan kept its distance from China, with neither the imperial military Kamakura Shogunate, which had fended off numerous Mongol naval incursions, nor its successor, the Ashikaga, submitting to the emperor Hongwu. Only in the fifteenth century did they reestablish ties through a series of diplomatic and trade missions.

Hungwu's fourth son, Yongle (Zhu Di), continued to expand the Ming Empire by protecting the Uighurs from the Timurids, annexing Annam (as the Tang had done) and cultivating relations with the Karmapa of Tibet. Upon Timur's death, Yongle reestablished peaceful ties with Persia. Ming China was an export juggernaut, trading from its Yellow River port of Guangdong and the Yangtze River ports of Shanghai and Nanjing, perhaps the largest city in the world at the time with half a million residents. To demonstrate China's incredible wealth, Yongle ordered the Chinese Muslim admiral Zheng He to undertake grand expeditions that established relations with Luzon and Sulu (today's Philippines), Brunei, and Sumatra, and across the Indian Ocean to East Africa. At home, Yongle reconstructed the Grand Canal, built the Forbidden City (modern-day Bejing), instituted a rigorous Confucian examination system, and commissioned a comprehensive encyclopedia of Chinese culture and history. Even though the Ming under Yongle set the global standard for weaponry and shipbuilding, by the 1420s the emperor became preoccupied with defending the northern frontier against the Mongols and Turkic Tatars, turning China inward to focus on agriculture and limiting foreigners' access to southern ports.

One major consequence of the Ming shift inward was that large numbers of Chinese migrated to Southeast Asian kingdoms, intermarrying with local women and assimilating into the societies of the Banten Sultanate (Java), Manila, Ayutthaya in Siam, Hoi An (in Vietnam), and Phnom Penh (Khmer). In Siam, Chinese migrants often changed their last names to be considered more local, while King Rama I of Siam was of partial Chinese descent. As a result, from the Malay Peninsula through the Mekong valley and across the waters to Luzon, Southeast Asia in the fifteenth century became a tapestry of blended ethnicities. It was also a complex religious patchwork, with Islam continuing to spread from Sumatra east to Java and north to Malacca, where King Paramesvara converted to Islam in 1414 and changed his name to Iskander Shah. Although Christianity had already established a strong presence in the southern Indian kingdom of Kerala, the arrival of missionaries and explorers from Portugal and Spain greatly accelerated its advance.

Asia and the Western Empires

The Ottomans completed their triumph over Christian Byzantium with the sacking of Constantinople in 1453, at which time most European nations descended into civil war. Seeking more secure routes to the wealthy markets of Asia, Europe's maritime centers plied multiple long-distance routes in the hope of reaching the Moluku Islands to buy nutmeg and cloves. Toward the end of the fifteenth century, the Italian explorer Christopher Columbus ventured across the Atlantic Ocean, reaching not the Asia he expected but the Caribbean islands. Several years later, the Portuguese explorer Vasco da Gama rounded the cape of Africa to establish trade ties and entrepôts in Calicut and Gujarat. And in 1521, the Portuguese explorer Ferdinand Magellan, aided by the skills of his Malaccan interpreter, Enrique, rounded the tip of South America and leveraged the Pacific Ocean trade winds to make landfall at uninhabited islands near the Kingdom of Cebu. Collectively, these maritime passageways weakened the Turkic-Arab-Persian Silk Roads across Eurasia. By the 1580s, the Portuguese confronted and defeated the Ottoman fleet in the Indian Ocean, entrenching Europe's positions from Mombasa to Gwadar, with Portuguese bridgeheads in Goa and as far away as Macao.

With the Ming having withdrawn their Indian Ocean fleets, Europeans took advantage of the latest technologies in shipbuilding and weaponry to advance trade among Europe, Africa, the Americas, and Asia. As they collaborated with the robust trading network of the southern Japanese Ryukyu Kingdom, they also established durable beachheads of political and religious control. As the Iberians spread across the region (soon followed by the Dutch and British), their merchants drove Indo-Muslim traders from their stronghold of Malacca, began widespread conversions to Christianity, and leased Macau from China in 1557. In 1571, the Spanish colonized Manila, making it the hub of the transpacific trade in silver brought on galleon ships from Acapulco and used to purchase Ming goods sent onward to Europe.[4] The enormous Ming appetite for silver became a major vulnerability as both Spain and Japan reduced silver exports to China, causing huge monetary and trade imbalances. With China weakened, the Japanese general Toyotomi Hideyoshi, who reunified the country in 1590, invaded Korea and China, but Korean resistance and Ming resilience thwarted his efforts. Upon Toyotomi's death, the Tokugawa Shogunate rose to power but, paranoid about the proselytizing Europeans, chose an isolationist foreign policy from 1640 onward.

By 1644, the Ming had declined and were replaced by the Manchu Qing Dynasty, who put an end to the nomad-warrior Seljuks and Mongols (to whom they were related culturally) and reorganized the disparate Buddhist nomads and steppe Muslims of Dzungaria into the province of Xinjiang. Under Emperor Hong Taiji, the Qing invaded Korea twice, with Chinese princes marrying Korean princesses. The Qing Dynasty's successive Kangxi, Yongzheng, and Qianlong emperors ruled over continuous prosperity and security, making China the wealthiest empire of the eighteenth-century world.

Casting off the Mongol yoke also enabled the Grand Duchy of Muscovy to pursue a more expansionist course. Through the sixteenth century, the Russian tsardom grew by approximately 14,000 square miles per year as it swept eastward across the tundra and plains, brushing aside the Khanate of Sibir to cement its claims west of the Irtysh River, after which it crossed the Lena River and reached the Pacific Ocean. Pushing south, Russian merchants and armies reached the Amur River, where they first clashed with the Qing but then signed the Treaty of Nerchinsk, exchanging their claims to the Amur valley for all territory east of Lake Baikal and trade routes to Beijing. Stability on Russia's eastern and southern flanks set the stage for the four-decade rule from 1682 to 1721 of Tsar Peter I, who expanded into Scandinavia and fought a series of wars with the Ottomans for control of the Black Sea. Over the following century, Russia also wrested control of the entire Caucasus region from Persia's Qajar Dynasty.

The Qing, meanwhile, could not sustain their grandeur, with rapid population growth, fiscal pressures, and corruption bringing the dynasty to the brink of disintegration. As Asia's large imperial and bureaucratic powers resisted change, smaller European nations outmaneuvered them to achieve global dominion. Through the late 1600s and 1700s, the Dutch displaced the Portuguese from Hormuz to Malacca, and in 1800 they nationalized their corporate colonies across Batavia, Java, Sumatra, and Moluku, including seizing the Qing Dynasty's Lanfang tributary in Kalimantan. European expansion in Southeast Asian economies relied on long-standing Chinese and Indian diaspora networks of credit that connected European businesses to local Asian markets. As the 1800s progressed, the French colonized Vietnam, Laos, and Cambodia, fusing them into a French Indochina union. Only by shrewdly balancing the interests of Western powers did King Rama of Siam and his successors manage to maintain the kingdom's independence. Still, over the nineteenth century European powers transitioned from colonial intruders to global empires.

The durability of European conquest was enabled by a new set of industrial technologies pioneered in Great Britain, including steam power for ships, locomotives, and factories. As England accumulated large stockpiles of finished goods such as cotton-based textiles, it looked to Africa and Asia as markets to exploit. After its initial forays and skirmishes with Mughal princes on India's western coast, the British East India Company established a stronghold at the mouth of the Ganges River in Calcutta in Bengal, from which it built out its revenue collection and governance functions across ever greater swaths of India. In 1784, the British Crown took over control of the company, beginning a period of direct rule of the subcontinent from Punjab through Southeast Asia, including Burma, Malaya, and the port of Singapore. During this nineteenth-century "Raj" period of rule, India was the hub for governing all territories east of the Suez Canal, meaning all of British olonial Asia. In India itself, the British built a national railway network and established institutions such as universities and a modern administrative bureaucracy. At the same time, they enslaved millions of Indians, with tens of millions more dying in famines, undercut domestic industries, and fomented divides between Hindus and Muslims.

Colonialism also stirred Asia's ethnic pot. The British took Indians to Burma to work as schoolteachers and civil engineers, and Tamils populated Malaya to work on rubber plantations. Tens of thousands of Indians were moved to East Africa as well to build the Uganda railway. Meanwhile, an estimated 20 million Chinese living in or around British coastal concessions such as Canton, Fujian, and Hong Kong shifted to Southeast Asia, where many married locals and deepened Southeast Asia's multiethnic patchwork.

The British Empire also had grand designs for Central Asia. With India and the kingdoms of Nepal and Bhutan firmly under control, England sought a direct trade route to the Emirate of Bukhara. It also hoped to use the Ottomans (with whom England had allied to push back tsarist Russia in the 1850s Crimean War) and the Persians as buffers to prevent Russia from accessing the Indian Ocean. As it pushed northward from Punjab into Afghanistan, it skirmished with the Sikhs and pushed the Qajars out of Herat. A "Great Game" of maneuvers pitting Anglo and Russian proxies unfolded from Turkestan to Tibet, resulting in an 1893 agreement between the two powers to keep Afghanistan as a buffer state. But to the north, Russia rapidly expanded its railway lines eastward, easily taking the khanates of Khiva, Khokand, and Bukhara and the city of Tashkent. After clashes with the Qing Dynasty over the Illi River region at the border of Xinjiang, it also cemented its control over Turkestan.

British expansionism compounded the Qing Dynasty's difficulties. Seeking to grow its trade surpluses, the British forced the Qing to absorb ever greater volumes of opium from India, leading to widespread addiction. In 1838, the British responded to the destruction of 20,000 cases of opium with military force, sailing up the Pearl River delta with gunboats and bombarding Chinese defenses, repeating the intrusions in the 1850s. These humiliations were exacerbated by European imperialists seizing Chinese ports as their own dominions in Shanghai, Tianjin, Ningbo, Fuzhou, Xiamen, and Hong Kong. China was also plagued by civil wars such as the Taiping Rebellion. In the late nineteenth century, the reformist Guangxu emperor attempted to establish a constitutional monarchy, but a coup d'état led by the conservative dowager empress Cixi thwarted him. The Yihetuan militia also launched a violent uprising (the "Boxer Rebellion") to expel foreign intruders, but an alliance of Western powers, including England, France, Germany, and the United States, along with their Qing sympathizers, put it down. The failed rebellion further burdened the Qing with indemnity payments and reparations.

The arrival of Western powers brought very different results in Japan. Americans sailed into Edo Bay in 1868, opening the Tokugawa Shogunate to modernizing reforms that restored the Meiji emperor to the throne. The Meiji renamed Edo to Tokyo, centralized governance, built a national railway, and undertook major economic initiatives around industries such as shipping. As Japan became the leading East Asian power, it sought to emulate the West while also competing with it to dominate regional trade. It asserted itself militarily, defeating China in 1895 to take control of Manchuria, Korea, Taiwan, and the Ryukyu Islands. The United States' efforts to dislodge Europe from the Western Hemisphere also had reverberations in Asia: In the aftermath of the Spanish-American War over the liberation of Cuba, the United States took possession of the Philippines as well as Spanish islands in the Pacific including Palau, Guam, and the Marianas.

Russia also continued to assert itself in the Far East, forcing Japan to return Manchuria to China so that Russia's Trans-Siberian Railway could be extended to reach the naval base at Port Arthur (Dalian). By 1905, Japan secured a major victory over Russia at the Battle of Tsushima, winning back Manchuria, gaining the southern half of Sakhalin Island, and forcing Russia to recognize Korea as part of the Japanese sphere of influence. The Japanese further annexed Korea in 1910, sending Korea's government into exile in Shanghai and then Chongqing. In 1911, Chinese revolutionary nationalists overthrew the Qing, ending China's last great imperial dynasty. Sun Yat-sen was elected the first president of the new republic, whose seat was in Guangzhou, but warlordism continued to increase across the country.

Japan's victory over Russia galvanized Asians to shed their fears of foreign aggressors and colonialists. The Ottomans, for example, were inspired by Japan's defeat of their northern nemesis Russia as well as its ability to modernize without Westernizing. With his mantra "Asia is One," the Japanese philosopher Okakura Tenshin became a leading voice of Pan-Asianism through his writings on the historical linkages not only among East Asians but also between Chinese and Muslims. Okukura's Indian counterpart, the Nobel laureate Rabindranath Tagore, traveled from Japan and Korea to Persia, advocating a return to Asian ideals and traditions. Tagore's host in China was the renowned intellectual Liang Qichao, who lamented how European colonialism had severed Asia's historical interconnectivity and turned Asians against one another. The civil rights lawyer Mohandas K. Gandhi stepped up his campaigns of nonviolent disobedience against British rule in India throughout the 1920s, as did Aung San in Burma.

By 1914, escalating tensions between European empires and their proxies exploded into war. With the promise of having Shandong returned to its possession, China sided with the Allies (Britain, France, Russia, Italy, and the United States). But after Germany's defeat in 1917, the Allies handed China's territories to Japan at the 1919 Paris Peace Conference. Bewildered at this betrayal—and inspired by the 1917 Bolshevik Revolution in Russia in which Vladimir Lenin dismantled the czarist regime in favor of the interests of workers and peasants—Chinese nationalism surged. Chinese blamed themselves for allowing their own victimization at foreign hands. Seeking to avoid a repetition of the prior century of humiliation, Chinese. officials studied Japan's rapid late-nineteenth-century industrialization and invited many Western scholars to tour China in the early twentieth century. In 1921, intellectuals including Chen Duxiu and Li Dazhao founded the Chinese Communist Party. Still, it was the Nationalists under Sun Yat-sen's ally General Chiang Kai-shek who united China in 1926, establishing a government at Nanjing in 1928. Meanwhile, with Russia's postrevolutionary civil war finally ended, the newly created Soviet Union's socialist empire undertook agricultural collectivization and industrial modernization. Agreements with China secured Russia's vast eastern Siberian flank.

The end of the great European war of 1914–1917 also brought about the dismemberment of the Ottoman Empire, with the last Ottoman sultan, Mehmed VI, forced to abdicate in 1922. Within a year, the Ottoman military commander and secular modernizer Mustafa Kemal Atatürk established a new Turkish Republic with its capital at Ankara. The partitioning of the Eastern Ottoman Empire through the Sykes-Picot Agreement created a French mandate over Syria and Lebanon and a British mandate in Palestine and Iraq, which became independent in 1932 with the nationalist Rashid Ali al-Gaylani as prime minister. Saudi Arabia annexed Ottoman possessions in the Arabian Peninsula, with the exception of small British protectorates such as Kuwait, Bahrain, and Qatar.

Lethargic and strife-ridden Persia also reinvigorated itself in the wake of the Ottoman collapse. In 1925, Reza Khan was formally appointed Iran's new monarch, crowning himself Reza Shah of the Pahlavi Dynasty. He oversaw a major modernization program of infrastructure and schools. He also declared Iran (the country's name in Persian) neutral among Europe's hardening alliances, though he elevated trade ties with Germany, which had no colonial history in the region, and canceled the Anglo-Iranian Oil Company's exclusive concessions, for which Iran received only a minimal profit share. Germany's dictator, Adolf Hitler, sought to expand the country's territories for settlement by German populations (*Lebensraum*) and reneged on his secret pact with the Soviet Union to carve up Eastern Europe, instead invading the Soviet Union in 1941. British fears that Germany might conquer the Soviet Union and proceed to take control of Iran's oil refineries prompted a joint Anglo-Soviet invasion that created a corridor for US supplies to the Soviets. The British conscripted hundreds of thousands of troops from India, while the Soviets utilized Central Asian cotton and tank production to overwhelm Iranian forces and hold off the Nazis.

In the early 1930s, Japan, which had an anti-Communist alliance with Germany, seized on the ongoing conflict between China's Communists and Nationalists to invade Manchuria again. Appropriating the same language of regional unity it had used to rally pan-Asianism, Japan conjured up an imperialist vision of a "Greater East Asia Co-Prosperity Sphere." While the Allies (Great Britain, France, and the United States) focused on confronting the Nazis in Europe and Iran, Japan unleashed devastating attacks on the Allies' interests in Pacific Asia, beginning with air strikes against Pearl Harbor in Hawaii and Guam in 1941. Japan's army then marched across French Indochina, Burma, Malaya, and Singapore, taking more than 80,000 British, Australian, and Indian soldiers as prisoners in Singapore alone. British prime minister Winston Churchill mourned the fall of Singapore in early 1942 as the "greatest capitulation" in British history. Japan's conquest of Asia spelled the end of European empires in Asia.

Warfare in Europe and Asia was equally devastating. Japan's pillaging of China caused more than 14 million deaths, displaced more than 100 million people, and enslaved hundreds of thousands of Chinese and Koreans. The United States' economic embargo and naval onslaught between 1942 and 1945 then battered Japan across the Pacific islands. While liberating Burma, the Allies also supported the Chinese resistance and the Korean Liberation Army, which retook southern China and the Korean Peninsula. The Soviet Union entered the Pacific war as well, crushing the Japanese army in Manchuria. In August 1945, US forces dropped two atomic bombs on the Japanese cities of Hiroshima and Nagasaki, after which Japan surrendered.

Asia in the Cold War

The defeat of Japan, combined with the crippling of the European empires, created a power vacuum in East Asia that was rapidly filled by the United States. Under the guise of Allied occupation, the United States, under the leadership of General Douglas MacArthur, imposed a new democratic constitution and barred Japan from any offensive rearmament. The occupation ended only in 1950. Determined to counteract US influence in East Asia, Soviet forces poured into Manchuria and onto the Korean Peninsula, whose southern half the United States had occupied after liberating it from Japan. While the United States and USSR negotiated at the newly founded United Nations to manage Korea as a trusteeship for a period of five years, both the Soviet-influenced Democratic People's Republic of Korea (DPRK) in the north and the Republic of Korea (ROK) in the south agitated for full independence. As Communist forces moved south across the 38th Parallel, MacArthur's army pushed back, sparking a full-scale war involving China.

China's civil war, which erupted after Japan's surrender, had just ended in 1949 with victory for the disciplined Communist forces led by

Mao Zedong over the Nationalist army of Chiang Kai-shek, whose Kuomintang retreated from the mainland onto Taiwan, which had been returned to China after the Japanese occupation. There the Kuomintang established the Republic of China. In 1950, Mao's forces pressed across the Yalu River to aid their brethren in North Korea. In 1951, Chinese Communist forces absorbed Tibet. And in 1955, Mao's forces attacked and seized the Yijangshan and Tachen islands from Taiwan, halting only due to the presence of the US Seventh Fleet and the threat of nuclear reprisal against further Chinese advances.

Mao's victory in China prompted many US lawmakers to urge President Harry Truman to adopt an "Asia First" strategy aimed at containing the advance of communism in East Asia. The United States committed to stationing more troops in Japan and South Korea, continued to deploy its navy to deter mainland aggression against Taiwan, and established the ANZUS Treaty with Australia and New Zealand in 1951. The United States' "hub-and-spoke" alliance system became the scaffolding of Asian order.

The US military also surged into Southeast Asia. In Vietnam, the United States had provided covert support for the nationalist Ho Chi Minh's forces to oust the Japanese from the country's north. Upon declaring independence from France in 1945, Ho Chi Minh had hoped for continued US support, but the United States instead assisted the colonial French army in the south, which sought to preserve the Indochinese Federation. By 1954, France had to evacuate South Vietnam and grant independence to the kingdoms of Laos and Cambodia. US forces deployed into the country to prop up the South Vietnamese government of Ngo Dinh Diem against the North Vietnamese Communists, whose Vietcong guerrillas the Soviet Union and China backed.

In other major Asian states, independence also came at a high price. The immediate postwar years brought full independence for India, which in 1947 was partitioned along religious (Hindu and Muslim) lines into India and Pakistan, led by Jawaharlal Nehru and Muhammad Ali Jinnah, respectively. Nearly 15 million people crossed in each direction between the newly created states, with an estimated 1 million perishing along the way. Independence for Burma and Ceylon followed in 1948. But borders remained unsettled: India and Pakistan entered into a conflict over the Muslim-majority state of Kashmir, which had been ceded to India. In Indonesia, the anticolonial leader Sukarno declared independence from the Dutch almost immediately upon Japan's surrender, but nationalists had to fight several more years until Indonesia won full independence in 1949. The Malay Peninsula, North Borneo, and Singapore were granted independence as Malaysia in 1963, but racial and economic tensions flared between ethnic Malays and the majority-Chinese-populated port of Singapore, which the Malaysian parliament expelled from the federation in 1965. On the whole, whether by liberation or partition, independence brought triumphant moments for Asians even though it meant adopting a new form of rigidly bordered, and contested, statehood.

During the numerous Cold War proxy struggles across the region, US, Soviet, and Chinese factions competed for influence. The United States supported anti-Communist authoritarian regimes such as that of Indonesia's Sukarno and helped suppress the Communist Hukbalahap insurgency in the Philippines. It also led the formation in 1954 of the region's primary security pact, known as the Southeast Asia Treaty Organization (SEATO)—meant to be an Asian version of the NATO alliance—that included disparate regional states such as Australia, Pakistan, the Philippines, and Thailand. Great-power meddling also encouraged authoritarian dictatorships across Southeast Asia. In Burma, the failure of Prime Minister U Nu's democratic government to quell Communist insurgencies led to a military caretaker government in 1958; by 1962, a coup led by General Ne Win had established a formal military government. Likewise in Thailand, a brief experiment with democracy was followed by a succession of military dictatorships that coexisted with the respected monarchy of King Bhumibol. In the Philippines, President Ferdinand Marcos took office in 1965 and soon declared martial law in the country, citing unrest caused by a Communist insurgency.

The United States supported these anti-Communist, military-backed regimes in Indonesia, Thailand, and the Philippines, which together with Malaysia and Singapore in 1967 formed the anti-Communist Association of Southeast Asian Nations (ASEAN).

In Southwest Asia, British and French dominions—Jordan, Syria, and Lebanon—gained (or regained) independence by the late 1940s. The Arab League was founded in 1945 to give voice to pan-Arab nationalism. Arab interests clashed with the Zionist movement, led by the Jewish diaspora, that claimed Jerusalem and Palestine as its homeland. Despite the recommendation of a UN commission to create separate Jewish and Arab states in Palestine, the expiration of the British Mandate in 1948 brought both civil war and a regional Arab war against the newly declared state of Israel. Israel repulsed Arab armies and took much of the territory that had been intended for Arabs under the defunct partition plan. An influx of Jews from Europe and neighboring Arab states fortified Israel's strength, while more than 1 million Palestinian Arabs became refugees.

The United States became a more intrusive power across Southwest Asia as well, especially as the region's hydrocarbon wealth expanded. After the Anglo-Soviet invasion of Iran, Great Britain and the Soviet Union divided and occupied the country, deposing Reza Shah in favor of his son Mohammad Reza Pahlavi and not withdrawing until 1946. The Soviets then backed a separatist Azeri state in northern Iran with its capital at Tabriz and an independent Kurdish republic (both of which were short lived) and created Iran's Communist Tudeh Party. The United States got involved as well. In 1953, US and British intelligence services sponsored a coup against Prime Minister Mohammad Mossadegh, who had nationalized Iran's petroleum industry, and restored to power Shah Mohammad Reza Pahlavi. Competition for influence spread across the region. While the United States protected Israel and secured its energy interests in Iran and Saudi Arabia, the Soviet Union appealed to the Arab world, aligning itself with anti-Israel nations such as Egypt, Syria, and Iraq (whose monarchy was overthrown in 1958).

Many strong Asian states refused to be Cold War pawns. Rather than accept subordinate status to the Soviet Union in a Communist bloc, China under Mao insisted on an independent agrarian socialism. More than 40 million people perished during his late-1950s "Great Leap Forward." Mao also claimed the mantle of leadership against imperialism and capitalism, competing with the Soviets for influence. Syngman Rhee in South Korea and Kim Il Sung in North Korea also played great-power politics to their advantage, enlisting the United States and China, respectively, to strengthen their national modernization goals. Under Nehru, India actively worked with Indonesia, Yugoslavia, Egypt, and other nations to forge a Non-Aligned Movement that sought to achieve collective security without choosing sides between the United States and the Soviet Union.

India's nonaligned status helped keep the United States and the Soviet Union mostly out of South Asia, while India forged a close partnership with Iraq, its largest oil supplier. But tensions with China flared as Tibet's spiritual leader, the Dalai Lama, fled to India, where he was granted asylum in 1959. Subsequent border disputes culminated in the two-front war of 1962 in which China cemented its de facto control over the strategic Aksai Chin territory linking Tibet with Xinjiang. India and Pakistan's dispute over Kashmir continued with a 1965 war that resulted in a United Nations–supervised stalemate, after which India drifted closer to the Soviets while Pakistan received greater aid from China. In 1971, India's aid to Bengali nationalist forces helped East Pakistan secure independence as independent Bangladesh.

With Northeast Asia stabilized, economic modernization became the pathway to geopolitical clout, especially for Japan. The country's nexus of government regulators, especially the Ministry of International Trade and Industry (MITI), and business groups (*keiretsu*) together engineered a liftoff of the country's electronics and automative sectors, propelling the country's growth by an average rate of 10 percent per year between 1958 and 1965. By the mid-1970s, just three decades after its surrender, Japan had become the world's second largest economy. The "Four Asian Tigers" of South Korea under Park Chung-hee, Taiwan under Chiang Kai-shek, Hong Kong under British administration, and Singapore under Lee Kuan Yew also experienced rapid economic growth as they followed Japan's model of state-guided capitalism focused on export-led growth while also welcoming foreign investment.

But Asia's two most populous societies either remained stuck or went backward. India was in a quasi-socialist stasis due to the government's 1950s nationalization campaign, heavy regulation of private enterprise, and imposition of tariffs to discourage trade. China also continued to subject itself to radical Communist experiments, particularly Mao's decade-long "Cultural Revolution" between the late 1960s and mid-1970s. Mao sought to rid China of old ideas, customs, habits, and culture by destroying historical artifacts and eradicating the intellectual class.

The 1970s witnessed significant regional geopolitical realignments. The rift between Mao's China (which became a nuclear power in 1964) and the Soviet Union under Nikita Khrushchev escalated into clashes in 1969 at the border region of Xinjiang and the Soviet Tajik republic, but negotiations between Soviet prime minister Alexei Kosygin and Chinese premier Zhou Enlai prevented escalation. China began to reconsider its hostility toward the United States and through secret negotiations with President Richard Nixon's administration cleared the way for the US president to visit China in 1972. Though the United States hoped to use its new direct relationship with China to restrain North Vietnam, instead it had to withdraw from Vietnam in defeat in 1973, followed by the unification of the country in 1975 after the fall of Saigon, which was renamed Ho Chi Minh City. That same year, Pol Pot's revolutionary forces captured Phnom Penh and took over Cambodia, establishing the Communist Khmer Rouge regime in the newly declared Democratic Kampuchea. Pol Pot's commitment to autarky and social uniformity led to widespread famine and genocide until Vietnamese forces toppled the Khmer regime in 1979. Vietnam and China fought a brief border war as well in 1979, but China withdrew its forces once satisfied that the Soviets would not assist Vietnam.

Starting in 1978, Mao's successor, Deng Xiaoping, sought to blend socialism with the opportunities of the global economy. He decollectivized agriculture, allowed private enterprise, and opened the country to foreign trade and investment as the "tiger" economies had done in the preceding decade. In May 1980, Shenzhen in the Pearl River delta became the first Chinese Special Economic Zone, luring foreign capital with tax exemptions and light regulation. It rapidly achieved a 30 percent annual growth rate and mushroomed from a village with a population of 30,000 to a bustling city of 10 million. While making China the leading developing-country destination for foreign investment, Deng also signed a landmark Treaty of Peace and Friendship with Japan and improved ties with both the US and USSR.

While the Cold War froze relations between the West and the Soviet Union, Turkey joined the Council of Europe (1949) and NATO (1952). It later applied for associate and then full membership in the European Economic Community, a diplomatic process that kicked off in 1959. Elsewhere in West Asia, instability mounted. Several wars erupted in the late 1960s and early 1970s between Egypt and Israel over the Sinai Peninsula and between Syria-led Arab forces and Israel over the Golan Heights. In the midst of the 1973 Arab-Israeli War, the Saudi Arabian–led oil cartel known as the Organization of Arab Petroleum Exporting Countries (OAPEC, later OPEC) imposed an embargo against major Western states, shocking the global economy. The Gulf countries used this oil windfall to kick off massive infrastructural modernization powered by millions of South Asian laborers and white-collar workers. From the mid-1970s to the mid-1980s, 1 million Koreans also went to the Gulf states to complete megaengineering projects.

Other upheavals shook the Arab and Islamic domains. In early 1979, more than two thousand years of Persian monarchic tradition collapsed as the Ayatollah Khomeini ousted Iran's Pahlavi monarchy and declared an Islamic Republic. Later that year, Sunni extremists held 100,000 worshippers hostage at the Grand Mosque in Mecca. Both Saudi Arabia and Iran began to push their respective strains of

Islam outward, especially in Pakistan. In December 1979, amid political chaos in Afghanistan, the Soviet Union invaded the country
to install a loyalist government, inspiring fierce resistance from Muslim nations backed by the United States. In 1980, motivated by fears
that the Iranian Revolution would inspire Iraq's own Shi'a majority,
Saddam Hussein invaded Iran, igniting a decade-long war in which
Sunni Arab nations rallied behind Iraq while Iran sought to empower
Shi'a movements elsewhere in the region such as the Hezbollah political party in Lebanon. As Iraq expended its energy on warfare and
Iran consolidated its revolution in theocratic isolation, Saudi Arabia
raised its profile as the world's largest oil producer and a pillar of regional security, bringing together Arab Gulf monarchies in 1981 to
form the Gulf Cooperation Council (GCC), which aimed at achieving
a single market, unified military force, and common currency with its
petromonarchy neighbors. In 1985, Iran, Turkey, and Pakistan formed
the Economic Cooperation Organization (ECO) to promote greater
cross-border trade and investment.

By 1985, the drain of the Afghanistan war and economic hardship at
home forced the Soviet leadership under Mikhail Gorbachev to undertake a concerted reform program toward greater political, economic,
and social openness (*perestroika* and *glasnost*), establishing détente with
the United States and abandoning its policy of overt interference in
Communist Eastern European nations. Grassroots revolutions spread
in Poland, Czechoslovakia, and other Soviet client states, each prevailing eventually. In 1991, the Soviet Union itself splintered into fifteen
independent republics. The Cold War came to an end, sparking geopolitical and ideological realignments favorable to Asia's return to center
stage in the global order.

Asia Reawakens

As the Cold War ended, West Asia grabbed the spotlight away from
Europe. In the aftermath of the 1988 cease-fire between Iran and Iraq,
Iran was weakened by war, economic isolation, and the death of its

supreme leader, Ayatollah Khomini, in 1989. Iraq sought to rebuild its strength by turning on its oil-rich southern ally Kuwait. Within months, the United States sent 200,000 troops to defend Saudi Arabia, which became the staging ground for the liberation of Kuwait and massive retaliation against Saddam Hussein's forces. With US military preponderance established in the region, the United States pursued a policy of "dual containment" against both Iraq and Iran. Despite long-standing US efforts to find a diplomatic solution to the Palestinian question, Israel's relations with its Arab minority continued to deteriorate. In 1987, a Palestinian *intifada* (uprising) against Israeli occupation began, led by the Palestine Liberation Organization (PLO), the pan-Arab Muslim Brotherhood, and a new Islamist faction called Hamas. The *intifada* calmed only five years later with the Oslo Accords, which set down principles for establishing Palestinian autonomy in the occupied West Bank (and the Gaza Strip).

Between 1990 and 1991, the Soviet Union's collapse thrust new states into independence. Georgia, Armenia, and Azerbaijan in the Caucasus and Kazakhstan, Uzbekistan, Kyrgyzstan, Tajikistan, and Turkmenistan in Central Asia all came to be ruled by their Soviet-era party chiefs. But bereft of Soviet economic support, the reformulated Commonwealth of Independent States (CIS) soon succumbed to conflicts between Armenia and Azerbaijan along with a civil war in Tajikistan. The victory of the Islamist mujahadeen in Afghanistan over Soviet forces just three years earlier had made the nearby Muslim societies of former Soviet Central Asia fertile ground for the rise of new militant groups such as the Islamic Movement of Uzbekistan (IMU) and Hizb ut-Tahrir. The Soviet collapse also meant that China bordered more former Soviet republics in Central Asia than did Russia. China settled its outstanding boundary disputes with these Turkic neighbors and used its largest province, Xinjiang, as a portal to access the raw materials of Kazakhstan, investing in new pipelines stretching from the Caspian Sea to the Tarim basin. As a way of establishing regional coordination with the newly independent republics, it also founded the Shanghai Cooperation Organisation (SCO) in 1996. Turkey also pressed for stronger ties with its Turkic brethren in Central Asia, but a succession of pragmatic Turkish prime ministers continued to focus on Europe, bringing Turkey into the European customs union in 1995 (though tensions with Greece flared over numerous island disputes such as Cyprus).

East Asian economic fortunes continued to shift with the 1990s expansion of globalization. As the Cold War backdrop faded, South Korea reopened diplomatic ties with its former foes China and Vietnam. China continued its rapid economic liberalization but maintained its centralized political regime, as evidenced by the brutal suppression of protesters in Beijing's Tiananmen Square in June 1989. Western leaders such as US president Bill Clinton, elected in 1992, sought to sanction China for its suppression of political freedom, but Western commercial interests focused on accessing China's massive customer base. Japan's economy, meanwhile, suffered a "lost decade" due to the bursting of a speculative-asset bubble, creating space for South Korea's family-run industrial conglomerates (*chaebol*) to leverage their government's tax incentives and cheap credit to challenge Japan's dominance in heavy industries and electronics.

East Asia's geopolitical tensions heightened as China's confidence grew. In 1995, fearing Taiwanese president Lee Teng-hui's independence aspirations, China mobilized forces in Fujian province and conducted missile tests and amphibious exercises in the Taiwan Strait, with the United States responding by sending two aircraft carrier battle groups to compel it to back down. China did, however, regain sovereignty over Hong Kong from Great Britain in 1997 and Macao from Portugal in 1999, marking the formal disappearance of colonialism in Asia. During the mid-1990s, China also became more assertive in the South China Sea, prompting ASEAN to establish the ASEAN Regional Forum to bring China, the United States, Russia, Australia, and other powers under one diplomatic umbrella. ASEAN also expanded to include Vietnam in 1995 and Laos and Myanmar in 1997.

Despite the tense regional atmosphere, China and South Korea began a dialogue with isolated North Korea, which had lost its Soviet patron. However, despite pledges to maintain nuclear-free status on the Korean Peninsula, North Korea announced its withdrawal from the Treaty on the Non-Proliferation of Nuclear Weapons (NPT).

Outside China, democratization was a major phenomenon in East Asia. In South Korea, former army general Roh Tae-woo won the country's first direct presidential election in nearly two decades in 1988, remaining in office until 1993. In Taiwan as well, the incremental Kuomintang political reforms of the 1980s gave way to full-fledged electoral democracy in the 1990s. Political change came unevenly to Southeast Asia. The kleptocratic Marcos regime in the Philippines was toppled, replaced through democratic elections in 1986 by Corazon Aquino, who was hailed as the "mother of Asian democracy," followed by Fidel Ramos in 1992. Southeast Asia's export-led growth surge suffered a significant setback with the financial contagion of 1997, in which insufficient foreign currency reserves forced major devaluations and skyrocketing debt in Thailand, Malaysia, the Philippines, and even mature economies such as South Korea. The collapse of local currencies laid bare the crony capitalism governing countries such as Indonesia. After three decades of rule, Suharto lost the backing of the army and resigned in 1998 amid waves of demonstrations.

The Soviet collapse was also a major precipitating factor in India's 1990s shift toward an open economy. As the once significant trade volumes with the Soviet Union plummented and the Persian Gulf War caused a doubling of oil prices, India's prime minister, P V. Narasimha Rao, and his finance minister, Manmohan Singh, set about reversing Nehru-era central planning, dismantling the notorious "license Raj" of regulations, and welcoming foreign investment, all of which contributed to lifting India above what had come to be known as the "Hindu rate of growth." At the same time, an insurgency in Kashmir and intermittent conflict with Pakistan soured relations, with both countries covertly accelerating their nuclear weapons programs and conducting nuclear tests in 1998. Pakistan also faced instability on its western border as the chaos of Afghanistan's civil war resulted in the radical Taliban movement's rise from the refugee camps of Peshawar to the takeover of Afghanistan in 1994, after which it began to set its sights on spreading Islamist revolution by harboring terrorist groups such as Al Qaeda.

In the aftermath of the Asian financial crisis, the region's economic conditions recovered in the late 1990s and 2000s thanks to increased outsourcing of manufacturing by Western companies and accelerated trade integration. By 2004, Asia's intraregional trade surpassed its trade with developed countries, insulating the region's economies from the demand shock of the 2007 Western financial crisis. India, too, continued to grow despite lackluster economic reforms and began a "Look East" policy to capitalize on the rising opportunities for trade and strategic collaboration with East Asia. Meanwhile, Indians, Pakistanis, and other South Asians streamed in ever larger numbers to work in construction or government bureaucracies in the thriving petromonarchies of the Gulf region, whose economies surged on the back of a rapid growth in oil and gas exports to the fast-growing markets of East Asia. In the reverse direction, China expanded its infrastructure projects across Central Asia toward Iran, Pakistan, and the Gulf states.

This growth wave linking West and East Asia deepened despite the sudden turbulence emanating from the US invasions of Afghanistan in 2001 and Iraq in 2003 in response to the 2001 Al Qaeda terrorist attacks on New York and Washington, DC. The United States toppled both the Taliban in Afghanistan and Saddam Hussein's Baathist regime in Iraq, but insurgencies led by local militias and Al Qaeda against the US-led occupation forces in Iraq and NATO forces in Afghanistan took a heavy toll, with Iraqi refugees crowding into neighboring Jordan and Syria. Meanwhile, a second Palestinian intifada against Israel broke out in 2000 and carried on through the death of PLO leader Yassir Arafat in 2004. In Iran, the strident Mahmoud Ahmadinejad was elected president and pursued a confrontational path with the United States, including ramping up the country's covert nuclear program. As tensions with Iran mounted, violence flared around the Arab region. In early 2011, food insecurity and public agitation against corruption fueled antigovernment riots across many Arab states. Civil war shattered Syria, with radical groups such as Islamic State in Iraq and Syria (ISIS) spreading westward from Iraq and millions of refugees fleeing the country for Jordan, Lebanon, Turkey, and Europe.

Most South and East Asian societies spent the 2010s focused on political stability and economic growth. China became the world's largest economy (in PPP terms) in 2014, Japan's prime minister, Shinzo Abe, launched a major stimulus and reform program, and South Korea became the first country to transition to national high-speed Internet. In 2014, India elected Narendra Modi prime minister for his agenda of infrastructure investment, streamlining of regulation, and national pride. In Southeast Asia, Myanmar's military junta relaxed its grip on power and allowed Aung San Suu Kyi, the daughter of the nation's independence-era hero, to come out of house arrest and become a national political figure; a coup in Thailand against the kleptocratic Shinawatra family led again to military government, albeit focused on infrastructure and economic reform; and Vietnam took off as an industrial production center. The ASEAN nations of Southeast Asia overtook India in GDP and China as a recipient of foreign investment.

East Asia's economic stability and integration helped mitigate significant geopolitical tensions over historically disputed territories such as the Senkaku/Diaoyu Islands between China and Japan and the Spratly and Paracel islands between China and littoral Southeast Asian nations. Tensions escalated on the Korean Peninsula, however, as North Korea sank a South Korean warship in 2010 and conducted successive nuclear and ICBM missile tests in 2017. Pan-Asian integration nonetheless moved forward in large strides: almost all Asian countries joined the Asian Infrastructure Investment Bank (AIIB), founded by China in 2014, and the Belt and Road Initiative (BRI) summit in 2017, committing trillions of dollars of capital to greater commercial and cultural exchange across the full breadth of Asia—and beyond.

2
Lessons of Asian History—for Asia and the World

T he preceding account of Asian history will not be familiar to most readers, both because of the Eurocentric nature of Western historical narratives but also because Asia itself has been fragmented for so long that many societies have lost touch with the bonds that once tied them together. The purpose of such an abridged history, therefore, is both to establish a common understanding of Asia's past and to reestablish Asia's central role in global history: European empires became wealthy global powers because they subjugated Asia, and the United States' global influence today hinges on its relevance in Asia. Perhaps most important, Asians can be reminded of what their collective historical achievements have been and consider what is possible in the future.

Seeing the world from the Asian point of view involves a range of both smaller and larger modifications. Nomenclature is one area that is easy to redress. The Turkic tribes and Sogdian peoples east of the Amu Darya River had richer identities than the Western term "Transoxiana" ("Land beyond the Oxus") suggests. Western history also refers to Southeast Asia as "Indochina," the French colonial term for the region, but Burmese and Khmer people would never refer to themselves merely as the intersection of two larger states. The term "Middle East," too, is a useless colonial holdover referring to where British ships stopped for refueling. And Asians don't have a collective "Dark Ages" as if there had been no meaningful activity across the lands stretching from the Mediterranean to Japan from AD 435 to 1000. For numerous Asian civilizations, this era was one of several Golden Ages.

There are also matters of substantive emphasis. Western history tends to be absorbed with the lore of Alexander the Great's conquests in Central Asia, but the diplomatic strategies of the Mauryan emperor Chandragupta and his adviser Chanakya are far more important for the region's history. For most of history prior to the Industrial Revolution, Asia far outstripped Europe on indicators of development, while Europe was a peripheral upstart. Trade across vast distances between the Mediterranean and China along the Silk Roads long predated Europe's fifteenth-century voyages. Far from being an undiscovered continent prior to European colonialism, Africa was for centuries an integral part of the Afroeurasian trading system. And well before Europe held any colonies at all, the Mongols presided over the largest territorial empire ever known.

At a minimum, this brief historical sweep gives basic context to understand certain current events. When you see the Taliban destroying the Buddha statues of Bamiyan, you know how Buddhism got to a country thought of today as home to Muslim fundamentalists. When you witness the Canton Fair with 200,000 visitors from two hundred countries signing $30 billion in trade deals, you know that Guangzhou has been a cosmopolitan trading hub for more than a millennium.[1] Or if you are at a garden party in New Delhi's diplomatic quarter of Chanakyapuri, you now know how the neighborhood got its name. But beyond the facts, there are lessons from Asian history for Asia's future—and the world's.

Culture Matters

A panoramic arc of West, Central, South, East, and Southeast Asian history going back thousands of years shows that Asia's linkages have been continuously propelled through commerce, conflict, and culture. Turkic, Arab, and Persian civilizations, as well as those of China, Japan, and Korea, have been uninterruptedly accumulating and sharing knowledge for nearly three thousand years. The most basic example is language.

Ancient Indian Sanskrit served as a model for written Thai, Tibetan, and other regional languages, while in East Asia, the Chinese writing system came to Japan via Korea. The Arabic script became the basis of numerous oral traditions such as Farsi, Kurdish, Pashto, and Urdu as they crystallized into written languages. The linkages across the Turkic, Persian, and Indic worlds have resulted in thousands of modern cognates between Turkish, Farsi, and Hindi. Linguistic influence also flowed from west to east: Persian, not Chinese, was the lingua franca of the Silk Roads. The Tang Dynasty set up Persian schools to train its traders and agents to communicate with their counterparts in the western regions. East Asian societies were also willing recipients of cultural ideas that arrived with commerce along the Silk Roads, especially Buddhism.

Commerce and conflict also enabled the intermingling of ethnicities and bloodlines through migratory settlement and marriage. China, Japan, and Korea have all had ethnically mixed dynasties. Chineseness is often perceived of as hewing to the Han ethnicity, but there is no one pure "Chinese" genetic stock, given the historical importance of the Mongol-Turkic Sui rulers, Mongol overlords, and Manchu dynasties. The Chinese imperial administration, especially under the cosmopolitan Tang, employed countless bureaucrats and generals from other Asian cultures, with communities of Arabs, Turks, Persians, and Mongols settled throughout the empire. During the Ming Dynasty, the admiral Zheng He, a distant descendant of a Song-era Muslim Persian migrant, led the Ming's famous maritime voyages as far as Africa. The later Qing military was dominated not by Han but by Mongols and Manchus. Similarly, Arab, Persian, and Turkic fusion made the Abbasid Caliphate an impressive intellectual, cultural, and military power, one capable of penetrating India and establishing the Delhi Sultanate. Mongol DNA is significant in the lineage of numerous Asian peoples. Asian identity has long been more syncretic than ethnic.

Religious diversity has also been a pillar of Asian civilization stability. Vedic Brahmanism, Zoroastrianism, Shintoism, and Buddhism were established faiths centuries before the advent of Christianity, which along with Islam emerged from West Asia. These religions often coexisted in harmony as they adapted to local circumstances. Buddhism is inseparable from the religious and cultural psyche of East Asia, where Confucianism was also a common bond that provided a means through which elites could understand one another even when their relations were adversarial. In Tang China, it was declared that "Buddhism is the sun, Taoism is the moon, and Confucianism the five planets." Upon the arrival of Nestorian Christians and their idea of "one God," the Tang emperor issued an edict stating "The Way has more than one name. There is more than one Sage. Doctrines vary in different lands; their benefits reach all mankind." The early caliphates, Mongols, Mughals, and Ottomans are all examples of Asian empires whose inclusive religious tolerance aided their expansion by reducing fear among their new subjects. Though discriminatory taxes were levied on minorities in many societies, in most cases they did not amount to persecution. The third Mughal emperor, Akbar, decreed that any Hindus converted to Islam could return to Hinduism without penalty. Fascinated by all regional faiths, he even attempted to craft a syncretic doctrine of his own fusing Zoroastrianism, Islam, and Hinduism.

It is almost impossible to explain the historical role of one faith without the others. In South and Southeast Asia, syncretism between Hinduism and Buddhism was most common, with an Indianized Mahayana Buddhist culture emerging in many of the early Southeast Asian kingdoms. The Khmer Empire that dominated much of peninsular Southeast Asia from the ninth to the thirteenth centuries was a Mahayana Buddhist Hindu dominion. The resplendent Angkor Wat in Cambodia began as a Hindu temple in honor of the Lord Vishnu but by the twelfth century had become a Buddhist temple. Even the nihilistic Pol Pot dared not desecrate it. Today it is the only building on a national flag. The Srivijaya Empire of Sumatra was also a Hindu-Buddhist civilization.

On top of this layering, South and Southeast Asian culture cannot be explained without Islam, brought by Arab traders along maritime networks and its coexistence for more than one thousand years with Hinduism, Buddhism, and Christianity. Though Islam has Arab origins, Muslim populations are larger the farther east one travels through Pakistan and India toward Indonesia, the largest Muslim-populated country in the world. Today the vast majority of the world's 1.6 billion Muslims live in Asia (and 300 million in Africa).[2] For Asians, Islam cannot be viewed as foreign and adversarial. One might suggest that the fundamental differences among Asia's dominant religions are the reason they have been able to coexist in stability: they are so dissimilar yet each is so numerically robust that the conquest of one by the other is both spiritually unthinkable and logistically impossible. Asians have no choice but to live and let live.

Generally speaking, Islam's relations with the prevailing political orders also become more accommodating farther east of the Arab world. Despite the gruesome 2017 ISIS siege of the southern Philippine citiy of Marawi on the island of Mindanao, which ended with martial law and the killing of key Indonesian militant leaders, Muslims represent at most 5 percent of the Philippines population and appear to be motivated as much by drug money as by ideology. With its overwhelmingly Muslim population, Indonesia remains the center of debates about whether Islam can coexist with secular governance. In recent years, some Indonesian (and Malaysian) citizens have returned from fighting in Syria and pledged loyalty to ISIS. Religion has also become a political football in recent elections in Indonesia. But Indonesia, Malaysia, and the Philippines have established a task force to track and confront ISIS and other militants operating across the archipelago, while Muslim clerics from organizations such as Muhammadiyah and Nahdlatul Ulema (which combined have nearly 100 million members) speak out against radicalism and avoid politics in order to focus on social development. In keeping with their country's history, they urge Muslims to respect both democracy and religious pluralism.

Asia's other most significant Muslim countries are also prioritizing a subordination of Islam to pragmatic governance. In Saudi

Arabia, Crown Prince Mohammed bin Salman has initiated a broad liberalization program, especially around the rights of women, while also curbing the radical Wahhabi clergy's grip on the nation's Islamic identity. In Pakistan, the government has banned radical Islamist groups from political campaigning while the growing urban class is taking a stand against Islamist intimidation. Central Asian states have also succeeded in controlling the Islamist groups that gained converts during the fragile 1990s. In Uzbekistan, the most at-risk country in the former Soviet Union, the government of President Shavkat Mirziyoyev has launched a program to train imams in government-sponsored centers. Unlike in the fourteenth century, West Asia today looks up to East Asia's success—and is learning lessons from it on how to manage political Islam flow from east to west.

Asia and the West

In addition to Asia's history of diversity, there are also lessons to be learned from its rich history of precolonial connectivity. Asia's commercial and cosmopolitan cities formed a network of hubs spanning numerous multiethnic and multilingual empires. In the tenth century, the Tang Dynasty's imperial library had 80,000 volumes, while the largest library in northern Europe at the time, in the monastery of St. Gall in Switzerland, had only 800. European explorers themselves remarked at how India's and China's cities were larger than London and Paris. Over many centuries, cities from Baghdad to Delhi to Chang'an served to exchange and revitalize knowledge from near and far. In key areas of science and technology—irrigation and bridge building, clock making and gunsmithing, papermaking and navigation—Asia was the inventor and Europe acquired the knowledge secondhand. Paper entered the Islamic domain after the Arab victory over the Tang in AD 751, after which imprisoned Chinese papermakers transmitted their skills to Muslim craftsmen in Baghdad and Damascus, then Egypt and Morocco, and eventually Spain and Italy.

In each phase of Asian history, geopolitical competition for territory and trade routes expanded the reach and intensity of the whole system. Encounters between Arabs and Mongols pushed both each to explore new pathways (and allies), to subdue or evade each other, and to reach key markets. Already in the thirteenth century, the Mongols managed to link much of the world known at the time. For numerous Song Chinese and Southeast Asian maritime entrepôts, external trade was crucial to the survival of local economies. The Chola, Srivijaya, and Ming all jockeyed for control over Indian Ocean trade routes long before the arrival of European merchants.

For most of history, then, Asians have been far more aroused by one another's imperial ambitions, especially the expansionist Arabs, Mongols, Timurids, Qing and other powers. Until the sixteenth century, the West remained on the sidelines of the thriving Asian system, and before 1800, trade flows among Chinese, Indians, Japanese, Siamese, Javanese, and Arabs were still much greater than those within Europe. Only in recent centuries have Western societies actually been a geopolitical concern in Asia. Yet even as European empires persisted into the twentieth century, it was Japan that besieged the Pacific Rim from Vladivostok to Darwin. Today, despite the US military presence in East Asia, China's ambitions consume the region's geopolitical forecasting far more than do those of the United States.

Asians view Europeans' arrival and ascent in their terrain far more as the product of luck than ingenuity. Had it not been for the Ottomans' sacking of Constantinople and threatening of Europe from the east, Europeans would have been less motivated to explore westward in search of East Asia (landing in America instead). And had the Ming Dynasty not chosen to retreat inward in the late fifteeenth century, it is unlikely that Europe's East India companies would ever have established advantageous positions against the Ming fleets. Europe thus gained the most from Asia's premodern globalization, acquiring knowledge of weaponry and navigation from Asia that it used on trade routes opened by India and China. When Asians look at the colonial period, therefore, they see an era of complacency, not inferiority. Their collective lesson is that when they are in conflict with one another, outside powers will exploit them.

For European nations—small and geographically insignificant as they were—to become global empires, they had to become Asian powers first. The Spanish first brought Asia into a global transoceanic trading system, but commerce did not connote dominance. Rather, the global trading system would merely have been a transatlantic one without Asia's participation as a customer and supplier. Only by militarizing trade could Europe assert hegemony. Still, even at the peak of European imperialism, Western powers were not able to displace the cultural, religious, and linguistic systems of Asia. English today is widespread as a global language of convenience but has not displaced indigenous languages anywhere. French has all but disappeared, even from its former colonies. When it comes to religion, West Asians had much more success on the rest of Asia than did European proselytizers. Christianity is dominant only in the Philippines but numerically overshadowed elsewhere in Asia. By contrast, from the eastern Mediterranean through Iran, Pakistan, India, and Indonesia, Islam's hold on much of Asia's Indian Ocean littoral has been unbroken.

Colonialism's mix of capitalism, technology, and manpower did, however, give areas of Asia a head start into the modern world. Hong Kong and Singapore became leading financial centers, drawing Asian talent from near and far, Gulf monarchies harnessed oil deposits through joint ventures with Western companies, and railways helped forge a more united Indian subcontinent. When it comes to migration, colonialism's lasting legacy has been to make Asia even more Asian. European empires from the Portuguese to the British moved Malay and Indian merchants and slaves by the millions across the greater Indian Ocean realm. Steamship ferry services across the Bay of Bengal and South China Sea galvanized regional migration. At the same time, the pan-Asian anticolonial movements of the nineteenth and twentieth centuries inspired Asians to rediscover a common spatial and political understanding of Asia. Though colonialism was a humiliating experience, it nonetheless provided a common layer on which Asians are now building a post-Western future. Asians are realizing that they have much more to learn from one another than from the West. Ultimately, perhaps the greatest Western legacy will have been to accelerate the self-actualization of Asia.

Asia After the West: Uses and Abuses of Western Experience

Given Asia's rich historical record of intercivilizational interactions, it is odd when Western scholars make analogies to European history to explain Asian states' behavior. Is Germany's nineteenth century rise a better way to interpret China's ambitions today than a combination of Tang and Ming history? Should the United States really hold up India as a continental counterbalance to China when India's golden era was under the seafaring Chola Dynasty, which ruled the waves? Can Iran be confined to its present national boundaries when for much of history Persian empires reached the Mediterranean Sea? Since we are talking about China, India, and Iran, surely it makes more sense to assume that Chinese, Indians, and Iranians think and act more through analogies with their own histories than with the West's.

Unlike in the West, where religious conflict has been a defining attribute of the system's formation, Asians have long tolerated one another's belief systems, demonstrating over many centuries a capacity for interethnic and religious coexistence at the international level. They have managed, in the words of the German strategic scholar Andreas Herberg-Rothe, "harmony with difference." Today, despite religious differences, India's ties with the Gulf Arabs, Iran, and Indonesia are getting stronger with each passing year of military and commercial cooperation. Confucian and Muslim societies at opposite ends of Asia have little to fear from each other. They form not a geopolitical axis but a restoration of the Silk Road commercial axis.

A similar logic applies in the geographic domain. Whereas European history features consistent fear of a singular regional hegemon, Asia's geography makes it inherently multipolar. Natural barriers absorb friction. Vast distances, high mountains, and other natural boundaries such as rivers protect Asians from excessive encroachment on one another. Taken together, the combination of geography, ethnicity, and culture has significantly contributed to Asia's recent wars among neighboring powers—China and India, China and Vietnam, India and Pakistan, Iran and Iraq—ending in stalemate. And whereas European history teaches that wars occur when there is a *convergence* in power among rivals, in Asia, wars occur when there is a perception of significant *advantage* over rivals. Thus the more powerful China's neighbors such as India, Japan, and Russia grow, the less likely conflict among them becomes.

Additionally, though European and Asian history both feature major sedentary empires, Asia's many nomadic tribes played a crucial role in advancing Asia's dizzying linguistic, ethnic, and religious diversity. Bridging societies and cultures such as the Sogdian supplied the missionaries, scholars, and translators of the ancient Silk Road. Nomadic cultures also wielded significant geopolitical power. The Huns plundered through India and Europe, the Scythians and Parthians controlled trade networks spanning from Rome to China, the Seljuks roamed patches of eastern Anatolia and Mesopotamia, the Arabs marched across Central Asia and sailed to India and Southeast Asia, and the Mongols showed how nomadic peoples could build the largest empire of the premodern world.

To the extent that Western scholarship uses Asian analogies to divine the future, it often chooses the wrong ones. The most common is to suggest that Asia's future will resemble China's tributary system, which operated primarily from the late sixteenth to mid-nineteenth centuries, during the Ming and Qing dynasties. But the geographic scope of the tributary model never reached meaningfully beyond East Asia. Furthermore, the tributary system revolved around trade; China exercised minimal political or military hegemony. China has never been an indestructible superpower presiding over all of Asia like a colossus. Indeed, China's defeat at the Battle of Talas in the eighteenth century, submission to the Mongols in the thirteenth century, partial colonization by Europeans in the nineteenth century, and invasion by Japan in the twentieth century all remind us that China itself has not been immune to conquest. Western theoretical abstractions paint a false choice for Asia between hegemony and anarchy, whereas the reality is much more rooted in Asia's multicivilizational, multipolar past.

There are, however, Western colonial influences that have been baked into the fabric of the region, perhaps only slowly (if at all) to be undone: state sovereignty over fluid borders, religious and ethnic national divisions over multiethnic identities, consumerism and materialism over clan and kinship. There are exceptions to these shifts, but each has shaped Asia to a considerable degree. Asians must now decide to what extent Western legacies will be Asianized and what elements of Asian history will be recovered.

The most pertinent questions facing Asia are about neither ideology or hegemony but rather about how to demarcate and share territory. Asia's main tensions are not between civilizations but between nations. Asian civilizations have maintained deep patterns of mutual respect and learning for millennia, while post–World War II sovereignty and nationalism have left a legacy of boundary disputes that still need to be resolved for Asia to fully return to its precolonial fluidity. The zero-sum nature of sovereignty requires clarity as to who owns what territory or water. Modern international law has imposed a sense of finality and permanence. The desire to ratify territorial claims has sharpened dormant tensions. Had India never been partitioned, would Kashmir have become the site of an international war, civil conflict, and insurgency claiming more than 100,000 lives since 1947? As a multiethnic princely state, Kashmir was made up of Buddhist Tibetans, Hindu pandits, Sunni and Shi'a Muslims, and Punjabi Sikhs. After centuries of misrule by Mughals, Afghans, and Sikhs, it was far from a well-run and cohesive society. But it is hard to imagine a worse outcome than what has happened since the cementing of ethnoreligious divide-and-rule after Britain's hasty departure. Kashmir and Palestine are just two examples of how Asia today remains littered with conflicts that combine the legacies of European colonialism, exigencies of state sovereignty, and local ethnolinguistic factions. Even Asia's foreign-manufactured security challenges have become regional ones. Many Asians, especially Arabs and Indians, continue to blame the West for their unresolved boundaries and sectarian politics, but this is of little value in conflict resolution. Asians, not Westerners, will suffer the most from fighting over terrain they have long shared.

The principal lesson from Asia's geopolitical history is that no one power's dominance has lasted for very long before meeting sufficient resistance—internally, from neighbors, or both—to dash its hopes of eternal hegemony. Whether the Mongols, Ming China, or imperial Japan, Asia's disparate societies have proved too diffuse and impenetrable to be fully absorbed by others. Over the millennia, Turkic, Persian, Arab, Indian, and Russian empires have also sought to establish hierarchies in Asia with themselves as the core power. Asia will always be a region of distinct and autonomous civilizations, a number of which, including China, India, and Iran, have an ingrained sense of historical centrality and exceptionalism. As a result, the most any power has achieved is to be a thriving subregional anchor in a multipolar Asia—very much the scenario unfolding today.

3

The Return of
Greater Asia

After centuries of colonialism and Cold War division, coherence is returning to Asia. All of Asia's subregions are bending toward a common gravity. In the two countries that bridge western and eastern Eurasia—Russia and Turkey—Asian geography has been considered secondary to European political orientation. But today, both powers are embracing their roles in the Asian system. The same is true for key geographies of the so-called Middle East—the Mashriq (Levant) and Khaleej (Gulf)—whose nations and kingdoms are loosening their dependencies on the West and turning to Asia to build future strategic ties. Even core geographies such as Iran, Pakistan, Central Asia, and Southeast Asia, which were once too underdeveloped or isolated to participate fully in the greater Asian story, are now pillars of it. And regional anchors Australia and Japan, whose Western leanings have defined their global orientation, are discovering their inevitable Asianization as well.

The Asianization of Russia

In July 2017, I was jogging through Moscow's Red Square on the eve of the launch of the Silk Way Rally. On the cobblestone path descending from Lenin's mausoleum, dozens of shiny, colorful trucks with giant treaded tires and covered with corporate decals were prepped to race from Moscow across the Ural Mountains and Siberia through Kazakhstan to Xi'an in central China. On that day, Moscow felt not only like Russia's present capital but also like the capital of the Northern Silk Road.

More than 80 percent of Russia's 140 million people live in its European zone west of the Ural Mountains, while less than 20 percent of its population is spread across the 80 percent of its territory in Asia, mostly bordering Kazakhstan, Mongolia, and China. Its federal capital, Moscow, and strategic port (and second largest city), Saint Petersburg, are both in Europe, but most of the country's enormous oil and gas reserves are located in Siberia and serve Asian markets. Is Russia simply a wayward Western empire or a great Asiatic conduit between Europe and East Asia?

From repelling the Mongols to maneuvering against the British in the nineteenth century "Great Game" to challenging the Qing to defeating Japan in World War II and tilting the balance in the Korean and Vietnam wars, Russia has long had Asian interests. A decade ago, speculating about Russia's seemingly inevitable geopolitical drift to Asia was taboo. At the time, the Kremlin was launching incremental measures to stimulate its vast and dilapidated Far East region. A decade on, Russia's fears over losing its eastern flank have eased. Unlike a century ago, today neither Japan nor China will provoke Russia by invading it to take the oil and gas that they can easily buy—and Russia is eager to sell. Russia's Asianization has graduated from a censored topic to an explicit strategy.

Western strategists have been telling themselves since the collapse of the Soviet Union that Russia would come to accept NATO expansion and a junior partnership with the United States and Europe. After all, the story went, Moscow's ultimate goal would have to be acceptance by Washington and European capitals. In the 1990s, the Clinton administration had declared Russia a "strategic partner and friend." Now, two decades later, Western analysts lament Russia's rejection of the Western rules-based order—as if it were not vesting itself in any order at all.

But Russia is positioning itself as a pillar of the Asian system. By the time President Obama and his secretary of state declared America's "pivot to Asia," Russia had already launched its "pivot to the East" strategy, accepting massive Chinese investments into its oil, gas, and mining sectors to make them serve China's voracious demand more efficiently. Then came the sanctions imposed on Russia after its invasion of Ukraine and seizure of Crimea in 2014, which, combined with collapsing oil prices, forced Russia into a series of desperate deals to accept large-scale Chinese stakes in upstream gas fields. After Russia's cyberhacking of the US Democratic Party and interference in its 2016 presidential election, a Cold War–like atmosphere ensued. Dmitri Trenin, a respected Russian geopolitical scholar, told me over tea in Moscow that he believes Russia's relations with the West are fundamentally conflictual: even if Hillary Clinton had won the 2016 election, the stalemate over Ukraine, Syria, and other hot spots would have persisted.

True to its geography, Russia still has significant European ties. Half its trade is with European countries, and its largest investors are France and Germany. Despite tough talk against Russia after its seizure of Crimea, former German chancellor Gerhard Schröder has both chaired Gazprom and become a director of Rosneft, which is 20 percent owned by Great Britain's BP. European companies despise the Western sanctions on Russia, which undercut their business interests, and resent US efforts to block their planned Nord Stream 2 pipeline to Russia so America can instead boost its own liquefied natural gas (LNG) exports to Europe. Given how divided the West is about Russia, it is common— and naive—for Western commentators to stand by their belief that Russia's interactions with Asia are superficial as Moscow waits for the West to reopen the door. Yet it is Western relations that have become both shallow and outright hostile due to Russia's transgressions from Ukraine to Syria, its usage of toxic nerve agents to assassinate its opponents on British soil, and aggressive cyberscams and propaganda aimed at influencing Western elections. There is clearly a lot to be sorted out before Russia can be considered a member of the West.

Once sanctions ease, Russia will welcome the return of large-scale European investment into its energy, real estate, finance, and other sectors. But Europeans have also learned their lesson from the unpredictable natural gas supply cutoffs that Russia has inflicted in the past and have made significant efforts to secure oil and natural gas from the United States, Algeria, the Arctic, and the Caucasus and to increase alternative energy inputs from their own wind, solar, and nuclear sources. Europe may be just a decade away from relying on Russia for just 10 or 15 percent of its oil imports. Meanwhile, Asia is ever more a destination for Russia's energy exports.

Russia and China are today strategically closer than at any point since the heyday of their 1950s Communist alliance. Since 2014, they have moved toward an entente they call an "all-embracing strategic partnership." Two-thirds of Chinese military hardware imports come from Russia, which has sold it Su-35 fighter jets and S-400 missile defense systems that enhance China's control over the South China Sea. Their navies have conducted drills together both in the Pacific Ocean and even at NATO's doorstep in the Mediterranean and Baltic seas, and they are increasingly coordinating their militarization of space. For his first overseas visit since becoming China's defense chief in 2018, General Wei Fenghe traveled to Moscow and stridently stated that the purpose of his visit was to "let the Americans know about the close ties between the armed forces of China and Russia."[1] At the 2018 G7 summit in Canada, Donald Trump called for Russia to be readmitted to the group—but Russian president Vladimir Putin was busy receiving China's highest award while attending the Shanghai Cooperation Organisation (SCO) summit.

Sino-Russian energy ties are also deepening. While Japan and Korea have traditionally been larger destinations for Russian energy than China, the parallel Gazprom Power of Siberia gas pipeline and Transneft's Eastern Siberia–Pacific Ocean (ESPO) oil pipelines pump energy from Yakutia to the Sea of Japan and, as of 2019, directly to China. Russia's Arctic geography is also strategically critical to East Asia. Whereas Norway and Canada are the primary diplomatic brokers for the North American and European portions of the Arctic, Russia is the gatekeeper for Asia's Arctic access. That is why the Export-Import Bank of China and China Development Bank have provided half the capital for Russia's Yamal Peninsula gas extraction, the world's largest LNG megaproject. In preparing to drink up Russia's Arctic gas output, Japan, China, and South Korea have sped their production of LNG tankers to haul gas from the Barents Sea through the Bering Strait to East Asia. Along this northern sea route, China is also investing in port and rail facilities from Murmansk to Arkhangelsk to facilitate the flow of Russia's inland commodities to world markets.

Russia and China are harmonizing their respective efforts—China's Belt and Road Initiative (BRI) and Russia's Eurasian Economic Union (EEU)—to ensure fluid commerce across the former Soviet Union. Former Soviet republics such as Belarus and Kazakhstan were far less enthusiastic about Russian proposals for a customs union until the endeavor became less about Russian hegemony and more about collecting fees for allowing seamless transit from China to Europe. To strengthen its role as a logistics hub for BRI, China is investing $7 billion in upgrading Ukrainian infrastructure from farms to roads to ports. (Ukraine has declared 2019 the "Year of China.") China is upgrading many Russian railway links such as that from Moscow to Kazan and the fabled Trans-Siberian Railway. Millions of Chinese tourists are lining up at border towns such as Manzhouli (near the intersection with Mongolia), a gateway to Russia's majestic natural treasures such as Lake Baikal, and Bianjiangzhen (whose name literally means "border town"), where a third of the population is Russian or Chinese Russian and Russian men take Chinese names. In Peking University's index of BRI member countries ranked according to their trade, financial, and policy coordination ties to China, Russia ranks first.

While Russia's total trade with Europe is still higher than that with Asia, the latter is growing far more rapidly. China recently replaced Germany as Russia's largest trade partner, and Sino-Russian trade has reached as high as $88 billion in 2015. China has gained a surplus as the price of Russian oil exports has fallen while the value of Chinese electronics exports rises. Jack Ma, the founder of the Chinese technology conglomerate Alibaba, who meets regularly with Vladimir Putin, has witnessed the revenues of AliExpress.com jump by double digits annually since 2010 despite the ruble's slump. Shortly before Putin's flag-ship Valdai Discussion Club forum in 2017, Ma announced that Moscow would be the site of one of Alibaba's seven new research labs due to the strength of Russia's engineering research community. Unlike Europe-ans, Asian investors are willing to comply with Russia's very Asian-style "localization" laws, which require companies to bring technology into the country and create local jobs. No Western defense contractor would ever open a joint industrial park for next-generation weapons outside Moscow, as China is doing. Russian state-owned companies have been replacing Western computers with Chinese-made ones.

Russians are aware of their vast economic and demographic mis-match vis-à-vis China. For Russia, this asymmetry is why it must main-tain good relations with China in the first place—much as Canada does with the United States. For its part, China needs Russian resources and prefers that Russia's nuclear strategy remain focused on the West rather than on the East. Russia's growing ties to Asia are thus less about cultural affinity than economic complementarity and strategic neces-sity. Though two-thirds of Russians view their relations with China as friendly, Russian officials say they need Asian partners more than they trust them. Indeed, Russia wants China to be included in any future arms-control agreements for precisely this reason.

Russia's relations with Asian states are often portrayed as an authori-tarian axis, but the reality is much more complex. Russia is equally keen on elevating ties with democracies such as Japan and India. Like China, Japan seeks to tame rather than awaken Russia. Japanese businesses are as annoyed as their European counterparts with Western sanctions that penalize their interests in Russia, especially as bilateral trade between Russia and Japan had risen to $35 billion in 2014. Indeed, from the Jap-anese viewpoint, the sanctions have only pushed Russia further into Chi-na's arms. Russia has also been rekindling the ties with India that lapsed after the Cold War. Today a full 40 percent of Russia's arms exports go to India. Despite China's frosty strategic relations with India, Russia lobbied successfully for India to be included as a member of the Shanghai Cooperation Organisation (SCO) in 2017. Between 2014 and 2017, Russia and India signed more than forty agreements covering frigates, jet fighters, nuclear reactors, and fertilizers, increasing their bilateral trade volume to nearly $20 billion. Russia's trade with Southeast Asia's ASEAN countries had already reached that amount in 2014 and continues to grow at 20 percent per year, with Russia seeking to export nuclear power technology to Vietnam and boosting arms sales to the Philippines to aid that country's counterinsurgency campaign. Several ASEAN countries are now buying Russian cyberdefense products to fend off Chinese hackers.

Russia's Asia strategy is also visible in its forays into Southwest Asia. Russia and Iran have propped up the Bashar al-Assad regime in Syria (which has allowed Russia to enlarge its Mediterranean fleet at the port of Tartous), angled to commercialize Syria's modest oil and gas industry, and signed $30 billion in new energy cooperation agreements that protect Iran from the uncertainty of Western sanctions policy. Their cooperation was visible in the first-ever international gathering of Russia's elite Valdai Discussion Club held in Tehran in April 2018, with senior officials and academics from both sides building channels of communication to coordinate strategies. One month later, Iran was admitted to the Eurasian Economic Union in spite of US efforts to tighten sanctions on Iran. More such gatherings will be necessary in the years ahead to navigate regional contradictions such as Russia's selling weapons to the Kurds, who are opposed by Russia's nominal friends Syria, Iran, and Turkey. Despite the spike in tensions with Turkey after it shot down a Russian jet over Turkey in 2015, Putin and Turkish president Recep Erdoğan quickly reconciled. Their trade has grown to $20 billion annually, with Russia sending Turkey metals and wheat in exchange for machinery and vegetables. Russian nuclear reactors are being sold to Turkey as well to gradually reduce the latter's enormous energy costs.

Despite Russia's historical rivalry with Saudi Arabia in global oil markets (and tensions over Russia's warm ties with Iran), the two have collaborated to suppress oil production to prop up prices, something both countries need to fund economic diversification, as well as launched a partnership to increase joint gas exploration and production activities. Saudi Arabia also wants to move away from its dependence on US goods, indicating a willingness to buy Russian products from weapons to nuclear reactors. Russia's sale of the S-400 missile defense system to Turkey and potentially Saudi Arabia and Qatar (as well as India) demonstrates how Asians are keen to do military business with each other despite US sanctions against Russian entities.

Separately, even as Russia has blocked Qatar's efforts to build a trans-Syrian gas pipeline, it has gladly taken $3 billion in Qatari investment into the state-run energy giant Rosneft. One of the UAE's leading sovereign funds, Mubadala Investment Company, is the anchor investor in the $6 billion Russian Direct Investment Fund (RDIF), which targets infrastructure and growth businesses across both Russia and Central Asia. It helps that for nearly a decade the Emirati ambassador to Moscow has been the charismatic Omar Saif Ghobash, who happens to be half Russian. And even though Russia and Israel are on opposite sides of the Syria conflict, Russia has turned to Israel for high-tech weaponry, and the two countries maintain robust cultural ties spanning historical migrations and religious pilgrimages by Jews and Orthodox Christians. "Moving forward, it looks like all the new deals are with Asians," a European expat confidently observed over lunch with me at the base of the glittering towers of the new Moscow City district, most of whose commercial occupants are Arab or East Asian companies.

With all of the positive momentum in Russia's twenty-first-century diplomacy coming from Asian partners, Russia is reorienting. For centuries Russians have debated whether their cultural soul belongs to Europe or Asia or represents values unique to their motherland. As Westernizers sought greater ties to Europe, Slavophiles wanted Russia to maintain its independent identity, and anti-Westernizers emphasized Russia's organic historical linkages to Turkic, Mongolian, and Chinese peoples. With an authoritarian government and commodities-dependent economy, Russia fits more into the broader Asian scheme than into the

Western liberal democratic paradigm. Putin and his coterie prefer unitary rule to confronting the uncertainty, risk, and opportunities they see surrounding them.

No doubt many Russians—especially the largely Slavic population concentrated closer to the heart of Europe—still retain the West as their psychological pole. Russian elites keep their money in Europe, send their children to schools in the West, buy EU passports through the citizenship schemes of countries such as Cyprus and Malta, and take vacations on the Riviera and in the Alps. Even though Europe may never grant them visa-free travel, they nonetheless feel they belong to Europe. But this doesn't make Russians European. It makes them ethnically European people in an increasingly Asian state. Thousands of Russians have become fed up with Western visa holdups and discovered Thailand to be a sunny, visa-free hideaway for their children and their money—or Goa, where the Russian mafia is increasingly active.

Nor are all Russians Slavic people claiming European heritage. Vladimir Lenin himself descended in part from the Mongol Zhungarian Kalmyk people who migrated to the western Caspian region in the seventeenth century. Russia today is far from a monochrome society. Travel to Moscow or other major cities such as Kazan or Novosibirsk, and you'll notice that the societal complexion is not the same as that of the country's ice hockey team. Russia is home to nearly 6 million Tatars, almost 4 percent of the population. It is also a magnet for migrants, especially from the poorer Central Asian republics whose economies have barely modernized in the past quarter century. Its food markets, construction sites, and taxi lines are full of Azeris, Uzbeks, and Tajiks.[2] The same country whose polyglot empire dominated these minorities a generation ago now racially profiles and harasses them, but these Muslim Asians and their higher birth rates are a reminder that there is not a single Russian ethnic reality. And as the size of Russia's workforce declines with Russians' lower fertility rate, Russia will need ever more minority migrants, not just for its urban bazaars but for the vast eastern expanses that form its economic foundation.

Climate change will further accelerate Russia's Asianization. Global temperatures are rising fastest at the polar latitudes, meaning that the world's two largest countries—Canada and Russia—could have climates resembling that of the United States by 2040. In the past decade, Russia's wheat harvests have doubled and its grain exports have tripled. For the first time, Russian grain exports in 2017 beat out those of both the United States and the European Union, with exports to South and East Asia growing by 60 percent in a single year. As arid southwest Asian countries suffer crippling droughts, Iraq, Syria, Saudi Arabia, and Iran will become ever larger importers of Russian wheat, alongside the hungry East Asian importers China and Korea. Russia's largest private equity funds, such as Sistema, are not only expanding their agriculture and infrastructure portfolios but also opening more Asian offices to attract investment to Russia's eastern frontier. Russia is Asia's twenty-first-century breadbasket.

To connect Russia's expanding food output to Asia's demand, Japan, China, and South Korea have each found a role, turning Russia's Far Eastern capital of Vladivostok ("Lord of the East") into a special economic zone for food processing and export. Vladivostok lies on a sliver of eastern Russia that blocks northeast China from having its own port on the Sea of Japan; hence China must use Russia's port. The other growth business in Vladivostok is casinos, owned and operated by Chinese hospitality magnates for high rollers coming from nearby Harbin, from which China is upgrading the railway line. In the early 1700s, Tsar Peter the Great founded Saint Petersburg as Russia's capital in an attempt to bring Russia closer to the European center of the world. "If he were alive today," jokes Dmitri Trenin, "he would move the capital to Vladivostok."

Russian strategists are keen on taking advantage of the power shift to Asia, making sure the next generation of diplomats will have enough Farsi, Turkish, Mandarin, and Japanese speakers in its ranks. The centuries-old tension in Russian strategic identity between European Westernizers and nationalist Slavophiles thus no longer captures Russia's intentions, which call for a "Grand Eurasia" in which Russia will straddle the European commonwealth and the Asian megaregion.

Turkey Marches East

From the Huns to the Seljuks to the Ottomans, Turkic peoples have been knocking on Europe's door for well over a millennium. In the fifteenth century, the Ottomans sacked Constantinople and prevailed over Christian Byzantium. But in the early twentieth century, Europeans dismembered the Ottoman Empire. After that, Mustafa Kemal Atatürk's vision of Turkey marching culturally (not militarily) westward to join the civilized nations of Europe animated much of Turkey's twentieth-century foreign policy, particularly its application for EU membership. But whereas the late 1990s and early 2000s were a time of earnest optimism about Turkey's prospects, the lack of agreement over how to resolve its dispute with Greece over Cyprus, tensions with the United States over using NATO air bases in Turkey during the 2003 invasion of Iraq, and the Erdoğan government's escalating crackdowns on opposition froze meaningful negotiations. Since that time, the Arab refugee crisis and Erdoğan's heavy-handed response to a botched coup attempt against him in 2016 have poisoned relations further.

When the Arab uprisings broke out in 2011, many claimed that a secular, moderate, democratic Turkey could be a role model for its Arab neighbors. Instead, the violent spillover of the Arab vortex fueled Erdoğan's metamorphosis into a modern oriental despot who imprisons military officers and opposition figures, intimidates intellectuals and journalists, and sends former allies into exile. He further wants to Islamicize Turkey's educational system through a new curriculum in Arabic and Koran studies intended to produce a "pious generation." With no predictable timeline for his stepping down, the neo-Ottoman Erdoğan has surrounded himself with a praetorian guard of so-called Eurasianers who believe that the West is out to isolate Turkey. As bitter as its relations with Europe have become, Turkey will remain a member of the Council of Europe and European Customs Union, while also drawing more than half of its inward investment from Europe, whose banks need to support Turkey's recovery from its economic crisis precisely because they are so exposed to its market. But Turkey has lurched toward Asia in response to both its political rejection by Europe and the mix of turbulence and opportunities lying to the east.

As with Russia, most of Turkey's territory lies squarely in Asia, but unlike in Russia, most of Turkey's population does as well. Also, Turkey is nearly 100 percent Muslim (with 80 percent of the population Sunni and 20 percent varieties of Shi'a), making it less schizophrenic about its Asian spirit. Turkish ethnic, linguistic, and cultural affinities stretch across the Caucasus and Central Asia (the former "Turkestan") all the way to Mongolia, to which Turkish Airlines began nonstop flights in 2013 and where Turkey has undertaken large-scale preservation of cultural monuments. Turkey's overtures to its Turkic brethren in Central Asia have laid the foundations for the landlocked region to achieve greater westward connectivity. In the past five years, coordinated investments have made serious headway to link Central Asia and Anatolia in a twenty-first-century Silk Road of freight railways, upgraded ports on the Caspian Sea (Baku in Azerbaijan, Aqtau in Kazakhstan, and Turkmenbashi in Turkmenistan), and energy corridors across Kazakhstan to China. Already Turkey is the passageway for Caspian energy to Europe via the Baku-Tbilisi-Ceyhan (BTC) pipeline to the Mediterranean Sea, helping Europe reduce its dependence on Russia. Soon it will be the conduit for natural gas from Turkmenistan and Iran as well.

Turkey has been the eastern pillar of the NATO alliance since 1952, yet it is poised to join the Shanghai Cooperation Organisation (SCO), which many refer to as the "NATO of the East." No doubt joining an Asian security group is the kind of revenge against the West that Erdoğan seeks and why Russia is backing Turkey's bid. Turkey also purchased $2.4 billion worth of surface-to-air missiles in 2017 despite the hostile state of NATO-Russian affairs. In Washington and Brussels, strategists have yet to consider how such a move would force them to recalibrate their policies toward Turkey—but they should as Turkey forms an entente with its two former rivals from the Ottoman era—Russia and Iran—to protect their (admittedly divergent) interests in the Arab theater from US and NATO encroachment.

Though it is hard to imagine a Chinese military base in Turkey, the economic dimensions of Turkey's accelerating Asianization are evident. Turkey's annual trade with China doubled to $27 billion from 2007 to 2016, with China accounting for 13 percent of Turkey's imports (with another 8 percent coming from other Asian countries). To correct the massive imbalance in China's favor, China is sending business delegations to buy from Turkey and inviting Turkish businesses to sell in China, even loosening visa regulations for Turks. In 2015, the Industrial and Commercial Bank of China (ICBC) bought Teksilbank, providing more capital for it to finance trade for Turkish companies. Turkey's commerce with Iran, South Korea, India, and the UAE is also growing quickly and on par with its trade volumes with major European countries. In its broad ties across Asia, Turkey's exports of marble, copper, and other commodities has grown, as have its imports of textiles, computers, and other machinery. Though there is no free trade agreement between Turkey and India, Japan, or China, improvements in infrastructural connectivity have gone a long way toward boosting the efficiency of their trade. Japanese investors were crucial to stabilizing the Turkish lira during the country's 2018 currency slide.

Investment will prove more important than trade in facilitating Turkey's eastern outreach. The Chinese phone handset maker ZTE has bought nearly 49 percent of Türk Telekom, setting the stage for the two to jointly execute infrastructure contracts in the dozen countries lying between them. Turkish State Railways has plans to lay 9,300 miles of new high-speed and conventional rail lines domestically and into its neighbors Georgia and Iran, most of which will be built by Chinese companies. One freight line already connects Turkey via Iran to Pakistan, and new freight railways will soon launch regular service between Istanbul and Urumqi by 2020. Not surprisingly, Turkey enthusiastically joined the Asian Infrastructure Investment Bank (AIIB) as one of the dozen largest shareholders and was immediately rewarded in 2016 with a $600 million loan to complete the Trans-Anatolian Natural Gas Pipeline from Azerbaijan all the way across Turkey to southern Europe. Europeans may resent Turkey's Asian tilt but will benefit from it nonetheless.

Iran's opening also positions Turkey to leverage its geography as an Asian gateway. Not only do European luxury trains now traverse Turkey carrying European tourists to Iran for holidays, but new European investments (despite US sanctions) in Iranian gas production will mean that more Iranian pipelines via Turkey to Europe will be built. Even though Turkey and Iran differ on policy toward Syria and Iraq, Turkish banks, businesses, and money changers have long colluded in sanctions evasion, bartering energy, gold, and other commodities. As sanctions ease, Turkish entrepreneurs are likely to be the largest cohort of foreigners in Iran, supplying ever more gold jewelry, tobacco, and foodstuffs.

Turkey and Iran have also renewed their defense cooperation to protect their borders from Arab instability and suppress Kurdish aspirations. As host to more than 3 million Syrian refugees, Turkey does not have the luxury of pretending it can focus on Europe when it shares a six-hundred-mile-long border with Syria and is constantly battling Kurdish militias. But as Syrian reconstruction gets under way, Turkey will feel commercial pressure to restore trade ties with Syria as Iran moves ahead with lucrative contracts to rebuild the country's electricity grid, water and sewage facilities, and telecommunications infrastructure. Iraq's future also remains uncertain as Iran's influence penetrates its military, politics, and economy; Mosul and other cities demolished by the war against ISIS rebuild; and Kurdistan continues to chafe for independence. With numerous scenarios still possible and the outcome beyond any single power's control, Turkey will have little patience for Europe, the United States, or others attempting to dictate its interests. It will seek instead both to buffer against the instability of its Arab neighbors and to profit from their rehabilitation.

Eastern Sunrise: The "Middle East" Looks East

While parts of East Asia have surpassed the West in living standards, pockets of West Asia have become a smoldering ruin. The further west one goes in Asia, the more violently societies are burning in a cauldron of sectarian fragmentation, civil war, and state failure. An estimated 200,000 Iraqis have been killed since the US invasion in 2003 and an estimated 500,000 Syrians since 2011. Syria's civil war has resulted in many of its cities being bombed into ruins, their remaining residents scavenging in barbaric conditions. West Asia's refugee crises are also the worst in the world. Europe's challenges in hosting 1 million refugees arriving in recent years is numerically trivial compared to the burden carried by Asians themselves. Turkey is dealing with 3 million refugees within its borders, Pakistan is home to 1.5 million more, and Lebanon and Iran each has 1 million.

Turkey, Saudi Arabia, and Iran are the three most significant powers reorganizing the West Asian zone they anchor. This Mashriq ("place of sunrise") region corresponds largely with the eastern Mediterranean region Europeans have called the "Near East" and refers specifically to Iraq, Syria, Lebanon, Jordan, Israel, and Palestine. This subregion of West Asia is experiencing today what Southeast Asia did in the 1970s: postcolonial disintegration and proxy geopolitical cockfighting among foreign powers as Sunni Arab states and Shi'a Iran back irreconcilable sectarian militias. The weapons employed in Syria by the government and rebels come from as far as the United States, Russia, Croatia, and Qatar, but Syria has become today's most terrifying example of Asian blood on Asian hands.

The Saudi-Iranian rivalry is equally prominent in smaller and more vulnerable states. Saudi Arabia has long treated Lebanon as a wholly owned subsidiary, and in 2017, when it suspected Lebanon's prime minister, Saad Hariri, of cooperating too closely with the Iranian-backed Hezbollah, he was summoned to Riyadh to tender his resignation and held under house arrest. Meanwhile, for Iran, both Syria and Lebanon are not only passageways to the Mediterranean but also staging grounds for strategic leverage against Israel. And in Yemen, where Saudi Arabia seeks to quash the Iran-backed Houthi rebels, the world's worst humanitarian disaster continues to unfold, with widespread famine and starvation. The UAE runs Aden's airport and seaport, its military guides the security services, and Emirates Red Crescent tries to rebuild hospitals.

For the past quarter century, the Arab world has been the West's problem, with Asians free riding on Western military involvement and financial contributions. But now that most of the significant long-term energy contracts, infrastructure projects, and diplomatic initiatives are tied to Asian powers, the Asian-Arab nexus will determine West Asia's future more than any diktats from Washington or London. As legacies of the Western colonial past such as arbitrary borders are reorganized, the only clear trend in the present chaos is that the United States' role will be far less decisive. Whereas the United States sees the region mainly through the prism of ISIS and Hezbollah, regional anchors are searching for a power balance that will reorder the entire region. The recently established Saudi-Iraqi Coordination Council advances Saudi interests, while Iranian-backed parties and paramilitaries kowtow to Iran. At the February 2018 Iraq Reconstruction Conference, the United States provided a mere $3 billion in credit lines versus the $30 billion pledged by Asian and multilateral donors.[3] Syrians used to proudly call themselves "eastern Mediterranean." Now they know their future is Arab-Asian. The next ring of Asian powers is also busy developing the economic infrastructure that will ensure that those countries—however they stabilize—will be far more tied to the East than to the West in their next incarnation. China and India are already the largest purchasers of Iraqi oil. The Iraqi army used Chinese-made killer drones in its successful 2017 assault on ISIS, and China's Huawei Technologies outbid European bidders to win the contract to build Iraq's telecom infrastructure, which it rolled out in just twelve months. Ben Simpfendorfer, a veteran observer of Asian commerce who advises business delegations from East Asia exploring Iraq's economy, feels that political risk and cultural distance are manageable obstacles. "Businesspeople are businesspeople. Where there's an opportunity to make money, they'll find a way to do it," he says.

Other Arab countries that have failed to build meaningful post-colonial identities are also seizing the chance to deepen strategic ties with the world's largest and fastest-growing economies. Jordan is trying to graduate from its reputation as an Arab and Western aid orphan by inviting in Asian investors to help build its economic base. Saudi Arabia has begun the construction of a $500 billion city called Neom located at its border with Jordan to assert its commercial reach into the Mashriq region. Jordan also became a founding member of the AIIB, rewarded with immediate approval of financing to construct new shale-oil and renewable-energy power plants, a special economic zone for manufacturing and logistics near the strategic port of Aqaba, and a $3 billion deal for China to build a national railway network. Within a decade, the old Ottoman-era Hejaz Railway will become part of the new Asian Silk Road network.

Israel is also working to draw more support from across Asia. Israel's unique historical circumstances make it the most Western society in West Asia. In this multireligious, multiparty democracy, most of the Jewish population (75 percent) are second- and third-generation native-born citizens, with the largest share claiming European descent. Despite the turbulence in the region, Jewish migration to Israel from France, Germany, Italy, the United Kingdom, and Belgium has risen over the past decade. With terrorism and anti-Semitism on the rise in Europe, the government of Prime Minister Benjamin Netanyahu has called upon all Jews to return to Israel and fortify its demographic base. Yet, like Turkey and Russia, Israel feels increasingly shunned by the European Union, which has pushed for an independent state for Palestinian Arabs, while European groups have launched divestment and boycott campaigns against it. Israel's response has been to double down on democratic illiberalism: in 2018, its parliament passed a resolution declaring the state's raison d'être as being a home for Jews and

Jewish values, with no mention of minority rights. Even though the United States provides robust military assistance to Israel—and Donald Trump recognized Jerusalem as Israel's capital—Israeli leaders know that many American Jews challenge the need for a special alliance they feel provides the Israeli government excessive impunity.

Israel has therefore begun to court China and India heavily. For more than a decade, Israel's growing ties with India have been described as a potential "axis of democracy" amid an arc of hostile Muslim authoritarian states. In 2017, Narendra Modi became the first Indian prime minister to visit Israel, a public recognition of Israel being India's third largest arms supplier, with cooperation deepening across critical areas such as cybersecurity and missile defense, as well as crucial economic priorities such as agrotechnology and water recycling, both areas in which Israel excels.[4] Israel is home to nearly 90,000 Jews of Indian origin, and the country's new talent visa, meant to fast-track foreign engineers into the tech sector, is targeting a new generation of Indians. In 2017, Netanyahu traveled to India for six days, bringing a delegation of 130 officials and business leaders.

Israel has also set its sights on increasing its exports to China, even at the risk of providing sensitive dual-use technologies codeveloped with the United States. Not only has this arrangement caused friction with the US Department of Defense, but China may be passing such technologies onward to Iran, which may use them against Israel. Such a feedback loop is a telltale sign that countries coexist in a common regional security complex—even if they don't appreciate it. The Chinese footprint in Israel is also growing. To alleviate the housing shortage in Tel Aviv, Israel has brought in nearly ten thousand Chinese construction workers, while Israel's renowned universities such as the University of Haifa and the Technion in Tel Aviv are welcoming hundreds of new Chinese students each year. The Technion also has a joint campus in Guangdong focused on artificial intelligence research. The less the United States allows Chinese investments in sensitive US tech companies, the more China may divert its interest to Israel, where it already has $16 billion in investments and has launched a Sino Israel Technology Innovations fund to invest in dozens of Israeli start-ups each year.

The more embedded China becomes in the thorny eastern Mediterranean, the more it must learn to navigate both the legacies of colonialism and the labyrinth of overlapping and conflicting interests in play today. China has called for an independent Palestinian state (with its capital in East Jerusalem) in exchange for support for its diplomatic priorities, placing it in opposition to US policy while also raising suspicions in Israel. Yet China's involvement in Israel's logistics sector could establish new pathways for cooperation between Israel and its Arab neighbors. In 2014, China Harbour Engineering Company began construction of a new port at Ashdod that is larger than Israel's current main port at Haifa. Witnessing the project's rapid progress in 2016, the Israeli transportation minister declared to the Chinese executives, "You've stepped into Moses's shoes, turning water into land."[5] Meanwhile, Israel is planning a new freight railway from Ashdod to Eilat on the Red Sea (the so-called Red-Med link), which would allow goods to bypass the Suez Canal. This will also require Israel to massively expand Eilat's capacity, even extending the rail line to Jordan's much larger neighboring port of Aqaba. At the same time, China has become the largest investor in the Suez Canal Economic Zone, leading a herd of Asian industrial exporters including Malaysia and Indonesia, who want to use it as a bridgehead to boost sales across the Mediterranean.

There is no doubt that Israel is entrenched in the security complex within its Arab and Asian neighborhood. In the past decade, it has fought across its border with Lebanon, supported an independent Kurdistan, launched hundreds of air strikes on Syrian military facilities, destroyed Iranian military installations in Syria, and carried out a much harder line—including cyberattacks, sabotage, and military operations—to thwart Iran's nuclear program. Interestingly, this activity has brought Israel into closer contact with the Gulf Arab states to its south. Israel has had economic ties with Qatar since the 1990s, and Qatar has also been an important back channel for Israeli communication with the militant group Hamas. In 2015, Israel opened a diplomatic mission in the UAE to represent its interests at the International Renewable Energy Agency (IRENA) in Abu Dhabi. In 2017, the Israeli and Emirati air forces (as well as those of Greece, Italy, and the United States) participated in joint military exercises. Both Saudi Arabia and the UAE have made explicit overtures to Israel, promising a lifting of trade restrictions and allowing flyover rights in exchange for progress toward a Palestinian settlement. Both Gulf states are also growing customers for top-tier Israeli surveillance technologies needed for their counterterrorism operations. And all three nations share an overt hostility toward Iran that has translated into high-level strategic coordination that is not even masked. As Benjamin Netanyahu said at the Munich Security Conference in February 2018, Iran's aggression has had the positive consequence of bringing "Arabs and Israelis closer together as never before" and "may pave the way for a broader peace."[6] Thus far, these instances of normalization have not been followed by formal recognition of Israel, but they do represent substantive interactions on common interests among countries that until very recently were sworn enemies. Whereas Israel once sought to wall itself off from the Arab world and brand itself an outpost of Europe, it is becoming ever more a part of the Asian system.

The Persian Gulf: Asia's Western Anchor

After the massive growth liftoff in Asia in the 1980s and 1990s, Arab oil flows began to shift in ever greater proportion toward Asia. The two-decade-long "supercycle" linked Arab energy with Asian demand in a symbiosis of high commodities prices and surging consumption, with East Asia today being the Gulf oil and gas exporters' largest market. West Asia thus began an economic and even strategic detachment from the West that is visible in its economic and even military affairs.

One of the primary purposes of the United States' military encroachment into the Arab world over the past half century has been to protect the flows of oil to Europe and the United States. Four decades ago, Gulf countries used oil as a weapon against the West, embargoing their exports to the United States after President Nixon pulled the United States off the gold standard. When the United States backed Israel in the Yom Kippur War, the Gulf exporters pushed oil prices up five-fold. But the increasingly self-sufficient United States and the renewables-focused Europe require less and less Gulf energy. Once the energy-focused "Carter Doctrine" to unilaterally protect Saudi oil flows expired, US priorities shifted toward boosting arms sales to Gulf nations, stabilizing Iraq, and containing Iran. Yet nearly thirty years after rallying the Gulf countries to expel Saddam Hussein's armies from Kuwait and establishing a massive network of bases to promote Arab military cooperation, the United States found that its efforts to turn the Gulf Cooperation Council into a "NATO of the Middle East" had failed.

In 2017, Saudi Arabia and the UAE, in their power struggle with fellow GCC member Qatar, demanded that the United States close its Al Udeid Air Base in Qatar. Even the Trump administration's enormous arms sales to GCC countries have not made it any easier for the United States to navigate among its Gulf "allies." The episode also revealed the Asianization of regional loyalties. While Saudi Arabia sought to convince Asian powers to curb their ties with Qatar because of its alleged support for regional terrorist groups, Turkey and Iran swooped into Qatar with food and other goods usually supplied via Saudi Arabia. When the UAE pulled its companies out of Qatar, India sent in its steel and construction contractors. Qatar initiated a minimum wage for South Asian guest workers to burnish its image with India and Pakistan. The United States' military presence guaranteed Qatar's sovereignty, but Asian powers provided an equally important lifeline. Even though the United States continues to lead arms sales to the Gulf and maintain robust bases in Saudi Arabia, Qatar, Bahrain, and the UAE, Saudi Arabia has become an eager buyer of Chinese missile systems and drones. The kingdom hopes to achieve as strong a relationship with China as China has with Iran. If Iran crosses the nuclear threshold, Saudi Arabia's likely response will be to acquire the necessary components for its own nuclear weapon from its longtime Asian ally Pakistan.

Economic shifts mirror the Gulf region's changing strategic outlook. Every single GCC country has declining trade with the United States, while their trade with Asia is surging. Two-thirds of East Asia's goods exports and four-fifths of its oil imports pass through the Strait of Malacca and then either the Suez Canal or the Strait of Hormuz. Almost 100 percent of India's goods trade transits through either the Suez Canal or the Strait of Malacca. ASEAN energy consumption is expected to double between 2015 and 2030, with much of the additional supply coming from the Gulf. Hence Saudi Arabia's Saudi Aramco and the UAE's Abu Dhabi National Oil Company (ADNOC) are competing ferociously with Iran, Iraq, Nigeria, and others to be Asia's top oil and gas supplier. As a result, the OPEC unity of the 1970s and '80s has given way to a collapse of coordination, with oil producers jockeying to secure long-term Asian customers. South and East Asia are thus able to import stable oil supplies from West Asia without importing the area's political instability.

The Arab Gulf nations have long had intense trade ties with Asia. The GCC exports petroleum and gold to India and imports jewelry and textiles amounting to nearly $200 billion per year. China also has nearly $170 billion in trade with the GCC countries, and their growing use of the renminbi is rekindling plans for a free-trade agreement. In the past decade, Japan and South Korea have also increased their trade with the Gulf states, and Japan is pursuing a free-trade agreement with the GCC. Both Japan and South Korea have been crucial in providing the high-end industrial machinery and electronics necessary for the Gulf states' ambitions for economic transformation. Meanwhile, ASEAN exports of meat, fruit, tea, and other agricultural goods to the Gulf states have doubled in less than a decade, contributing to their $130 billion in annual trade.

Fresh investments spanning the breadth of this new maritime Silk Road from the Strait of Hormuz to the Strait of Malacca—the world's most significant energy passageways—are further evidence of the Asianization pulling all corners of the region together. In early 2017, Saudi Arabia's King Salman spent one month traveling to Malaysia, Indonesia, Japan, and China, inaugurating new petrochemical refineries for their oil imports from the kingdom. Many of his generation studied in India, and now thousands of young Saudis are returning to Indian universities as King Abdullah Scholarship recipients. All Gulf states have launched eastward-facing campaigns. Kuwait and Qatar have invested in large new refineries in Indonesia, while the UAE's Mubadala Investment Company is underwriting gas exploration in Thailand and Vietnam. Of course, more local gas production in Southeast Asia will displace some imports, but by owning portions of those facilities, Gulf Arabs profit anyway.

In the reverse direction, China has bought into the UAE's oil fields by acquiring a stake in ADNOC's onshore drilling operations, while both the Jiangsu Province Overseas Cooperation and Investment Company and Cosco have signed thirty-five-year and fifty-year leases, respectively, on facilities at Abu Dhabi's Khalifa Port. Across the Arab world, China invested $26 billion in 2016 alone, versus only $7 billion in investment by the Unitd States. Arabic is the fastest-growing language at Beijing's Foreign Studies University. Cross-Asian investment growth is inspiring plans for a great decoupling between oil and the dollar. In return for a strong investment in Saudi Aramco, Saudi Arabia may begin to sell China oil priced in renminbi. Welcome to the petroyuan.[7]

Gulf economies cannot achieve their goal of economic diversification without support from East Asia. GCC countries' sovereign wealth funds (SWFs) manage a total of $3 trillion, and parking that money in London or low-yield US Treasury bonds is less and less a sensible option. Instead, they are rapidly repatriating hundreds of billions of dollars from the United States and United Kingdom to spend with the Asian and

European contractors that are building their future transportation networks and industrial parks. In 2015, Saudi Arabia's Public Investment Fund (PIF) purchased a 38 percent stake in South Korea's POSCO Engineering & Construction, after which Saudi Aramco turned to Korea's Hyundai to construct the Gulf's largest shipyard. In 2018, South Korea signed agreements securing its role in providing nuclear power plants and special forces training for the UAE. Bahrain and Oman are turning ever more to East Asian banks for trade financing and joint investments. GCC countries need to invest an estimated $131 billion just on electricity generation and transmission, and European utilities and Asian nuclear power plant operators are lining up to bid on projects.[8] The Gulf region is looking more and more to Asia for its future, with or without oil.

Asia's SWFs and financial conglomerates are also working with high-growth Asian countries on crucial infrastructure projects. The UAE's Mubadala Investment Company has a $10 billion joint venture with China Development Bank, while Dubai Ports World has a $3 billion fund that is targeting investments across India's rapidly growing logistics sector. Asian tech companies are also leading the drive to capture the Arab world's 400 million customers, half of whom are regular Internet users. Alibaba has begun a $600 million investment into a "tech town" near the UAE port of Jebel Ali that will house robotics and mobile app companies. Tencent is launching WeChat services across the region, facilitating payments and remittances for the millions of migrant laborers from South Asia, while Xiaomi has begun selling an $88 smartphone targeting low-wage workers.

In Muscat, Oman, all conversations are about the country's growing Asian ties. China's investment in industrial parks at Oman's new megaport of Duqm on the Arabian Sea will help Oman expand nonoil industries such as shipbuilding and auto assembly. And as the country diversifies its economy, it is the wealthy Indian merchants and businesspeople (Indians constitute more than one-third of the country's population) who will benefit most by providing consulting, financial, legal, and technology services to the country's broader commercial base.

The more South and East Asians engage with the Gulf region, the more they will want to protect their investments. China, India, Japan, and numerous other Asian powers have all stepped up their freedom of navigation, counterpiracy, and other naval drills in the western Indian Ocean. India, seeking to recover the Chola Dynasty's maritime might, has increased its naval acquisition to more than a quarter of its defense spending with the aim of becoming the gatekeeper of the eponymous Indian Ocean. In the name of maintaining a "free and open Indo-Pacific," India and Japan cooperate in the annual Malabar Exercise with the United States, which has renamed its Pacific forces to Indo-Pacific Command. China is also seeking to recover its Ming Dynasty glory, sending flotillas to the Indian Ocean led by modern-day Zheng Hes. China alone has four times as many destroyers, frigates, and other surface warships as India (though still fewer than the United States and Japan). In the coming years, it may anchor more of them in Sri Lanka's Hambantota port—which the government leased to China in 2017 for ninety-nine years after being unable to repay the loans for the port's construction—or even the Maldives, which has agreed to become a maritime hub of the Belt and Road Initiative. China's more active presence in India's maritime theater has the country on high alert. Sri Lanka first reached out to India to develop the Hambantota port, but India was indecisive. Now India is offering instead to upgrade and manage Hambantota's airport, from which it can monitor Chinese activity.

The growing complexity of ties among Southwest Asian states is a reminder of how much less US dependent the regional system is becoming as countries establish a more diverse array of partners: the Arabs detest Israel but increasingly partner with it for their own security and to deter Iran; Saudi Arabia lavishes aid on Pakistan but courts India as an energy market and relies on the nearly 3 million Indians in its labor force. Yet even Iran's leadership declared in 2018 that it was open to direct talks with Gulf Arabs about finding a regional accommodation—even proposing a "regional dialogue forum"—provided that no Western powers were present. Whether or not Saudi Arabia and Iran have a direct military confrontation, it is inevitable that trade between Arabs and Persians will return to the centuries-old pattern of dhow-boat diplomacy, exchanging food for goods across the narrow strait between them—even if they never agree on the name of the gulf.

Iran Rejoins the Silk Roads

Iran's nearly four decades of isolation are an anomaly for a country that for thousands of years has sat at the geographic center of the Eurasian Silk Roads. Modern Iran, whether led by the shah or the ayatollahs, has chafed under British, Soviet, and US pressure, always seeking to ward off foreign interference and return to Persian hegemony. Iran's western forays have gotten the most attention in the West. Its manipulation of Shi'a politics in Iraq, its propping up of Bashar al-Assad in Syria, backing of Hezbollah in Lebanon, and its arms shipments to Houthis in Yemen all show that it already is more important than the United States in much of the region. US officials decry Iranian attempts to create a "land bridge" to Lebanon, but from Iran's point of view, its westward campaign across Iraq, Syria, and Lebanon to the Mediterranean Sea is less trespassing and more the restoration of the Safavid Empire's dominion over the Tigris and Euphrates river valleys. In more recent terms, Iran is revisiting the 1980s Iran-Iraq War with the latter now in a far weaker condition than it was then.

At the same time, Iran's strategic outlook is equally oriented around its eastern opportunities. Like Saudi Arabia, Iran wants to ensure safe passage for its oil and gas exports to East Asia. Iran and China have conducted regular joint naval exercises in Gulf waters since 2014, with the Chinese flotilla docking at Bandar-e-Abbas near the Strait of Hormuz. The new Shanghai-Tehran freight railway, which arrives via Turkmenistan, takes twelve days rather than the thirty required by sea. Like Turkey, Iran is on the cusp of membership in the Shanghai Cooperation Organisation (SCO), through which it hopes to stabilize Afghanistan and more easily trade with China. Together, Iran and China want to tackle the "Golden Crescent" zone, which leads the world in the production of heroin and other opiates; drug addiction in Iran has doubled in just the past six years. Iran is also plotting to get more water from Afghanistan's Helmand River, on which Iran's second largest city of Mashhad depends. In the large western Afghanistan border province of Farah—also known as "Little Iran"—Iran runs its own commercial and espionage networks.[9] Afghanistan's largest trading partners are already China, Iran, and Pakistan, a reminder of how temporary, if painful, the United States' foray into the country has been. The less the United States does to stabilize Afghanistan, the more Asians will do.

The overlapping maneuvers of allies and rivals across Southwest Asia has created a plot as difficult to navigate as the geopolitical thriller *Syriana*. Saudi Arabia has recruited significant numbers of Pakistani military personnel to fight on its behalf in Yemen against Houthi rebels backed by Iran, which has caused tension between Iran and Pakistan—which China would like to reconcile to stabilize the Baluchistan region, which straddles their border, to avoid any interruptions to its gas, electricity, road, and port projects. Despite the complexity, Asians remain undeterred in their simultaneous pursuit of Arab and Iranian commercial opportunities. They have not been shy about making deals with Iran despite US sanctions and are far more comfortable interacting with Iran's Islamic Revolutionary Guard Corps (IRGC) and its many commercial interests. China has financed the Tehran-Mashhad railway, along which Chinese factories are springing up to supply goods to Iranian and Chinese trading businesses. The Korean and Iranian banking federations signed an agreement in 2017 to offer trade financing in their own currencies rather than the US dollar or euro. With many European companies lacking credit lines from European banks, which fear US reprisals for dealing with Iran, Asians are racing ahead to lock in investments to their advantage. When European energy companies such as Total bend to US pressure and exit their stakes in the Iranian gas fields, the China National Petroleum Corporation takes over. A planned Iran-to-India undersea natural gas pipeline would make importing natural gas from Iran even cheaper for India than producing it domestically. As they maneuver for influence across the region, Arabs, Persians, and other Asians are also resurrecting their ancient ties.

Central Asia: The Crossroads of the New Silk Roads

The Central Asian republics' transformation from former Soviet castaways to Chinese-financed Silk Road passageways has been a generation in the making, starting in the 1990s with the first pipelines across Kazakhstan from the Caspian Sea to China and the founding of the Shanghai Cooperation Organisation (SCO). By 2005, China and Kazakhstan had declared a "strategic partnership." A decade later, the Belt and Road Initiative was under way across numerous Central Asian states. Although China is the key instigator of Central Asia's new arteries, the outcome of the BRI process will be not Chinese hegemony but a new crossroads for Eurasia. Contrary to the US view that China's infrastructure projects constitute a neocolonial intrusion, Central Asian nations are eager to host these new east–west corridors. Khorgas, a logistics hub on the Sino-Kazakh border, has become a much-visited visa-free transit zone for migrant laborers and businesspeople participating in the region's modernization. As in the ancient past, large numbers of Iranians, Turkic peoples, South Asians, and Chinese are visible in the marketplaces of Central Asian states. Almaty, Kazakhstan's commercial hub located near the borders of Uzbekistan, Kyrgyzstan, and China, has become a melting pot for regional merchants and traders. This is a reminder that many Asians welcome China's infrastructural forays in Asia because they provide cover to pursue their own commercial agendas—not China's.

Were China not taking the risk to kick-start a new modernization phase for the former Soviet republics, commentators would lament that those countries are risky backwaters no sane investor should dare enter. But now China is the biggest investor in Kazakhstan's railways and pipelines, Uzbekistan's energy and transport infrastructure, Turkmenistan's gas fields, Kyrgyzstan's mineral sector, and Tajikistan's hydropower plants. Chinese capital has done more than just perpetuate local corruption; it has provided a kick of bootstrapping discipline in states known more for the brutality of their regimes. Now that most of the region's Soviet-era leaders have passed away, how will these fragile nations build a meaningful future? If it were not for Chinese investment in landlocked Uzbekistan's cross-border infrastructure, its new government would not have declared the goal of doubling its GDP through regional integration—nor would it be one of the world's two fastest-growing economies year over year.

China's annual steel output of more than 1 billion tons per year matches that of the rest of the world put together, with 200 million tons to spare annually for export to its BRI partners. With fifty-six special economic zones functioning in BRI countries, there will be plenty of demand. Chinese policy banks and the Asian Infrastructure Investment Bank (AIIB) will together finance many of the $150 billion in annual projects, providing a jump start and incentives for private investors to come in.

Some have criticized the AIIB as a rival of the World Bank, but the AIIB became necessary because the World Bank turned away from financing major infrastructure projects more than five decades ago. The AIIB has thus corrected for the massive market failure in providing regional infrastructure. The template of the AIIB is not the World Bank but the mainly Japanese-funded Asian Development Bank (ADB), headquartered in Manila. Founded in 1966, in the early 2000s the ADB began to implement transport and energy projects as far away as the Caucasus. Today its more than 170 projects, valued at more than $30 billion, financed by Asians and European funders such as the European Bank for Reconstruction and Development (EBRD) as well as multilateral bodies such as the World Bank's International Finance Corporation (IFC). Importantly, ADB projects adhere to COP21 environmental objectives such as investing in renewable energy. No doubt these established development funders were skeptical about the AIIB, but its potential to catapult the volume of capital deployed for the region has inspired dozens of their senior officials to decamp to the AIIB, bringing with them the knowledge of project management standards that many feared the AIIB would lack. Recently, both the World Bank and ADB have committed to finance projects jointly with the AIIB. After all, the ADB itself estimates that Asia needs $26 trillion in infrastructure investment by 2030. Now more than eighty countries and most of the world's development institutions have formed a network to ensure that that target is met. While suspicion will persist about many dealings related to BRI, the process embodies mostly what one Pakistani minister calls a spirit of "cohesive sincerity."

Though BRI is a multilateral initiative, it is one that is market-based, not driven by ideology. Though it may make loss-leading investments, it is a commercial initiative, not a charitable one. China's state-owned enterprises and banks are learning to share the risks of project finance with new financial institutions that are more focused on quality governance and decent returns on investment. Though the main shareholders in the $40 billion Silk Road Fund are the People's Bank of China, China Investment Corporation, China Development Bank, and Export-Import Bank of China, it operates much like the World Bank's IFC with capital raised from a wide range of partners. It seeks efficient operations and meaningful profits. Renminbi-denominated funds that manage Belt and Road assets are launching IPOs and listing on exchanges, attracting investors from around the world.

At its launch, Chinese president Xi Jinping claimed that the BRI "is not a soloist but a chorus." He rightly gambled that even states that rival China would invest in the BRI vision, realizing that criticizing from the sidelines looks like little more than jealousy. India, for example, is not only the second largest shareholder in the AIIB but also its largest loan recipient. BRI has also teamed up with Japan to launch a parallel set of infrastructure projects. The United States, too, has recognized the inevitability of BRI, with wise voices counseling Washington officials, in the words of one former State Department official, to join the game of "ramp[ing] up trade, investment, and infrastructure building across Asia."[10] GE decided to partner with the Silk Road Fund to make joint investments in power grids across BRI member countries. In 2018, President Trump signed the Build Act, which established a new United States International Finance and Development Corporation (USIFDC) with a budget of $60 billion to support American commercial operations in Asia. While such US investments—should they materialize—may restore some US credibility, more fundamentally they will help Asians achieve their own goals. Taken together, all these funds will pay for the services of thousands of companies from all over the world—but especially Asia—that provide construction, manufacturing, technology, consulting, legal, and all manner of project-related needs. What is built in Asia stays in Asia and is first and foremost for Asians.

Xi Jinping, in his speech to the 2017 Communist Party congress, stated that China's approach to foreign policy "offers a new option for other countries and nations who want to speed up their development while preserving their independence."[11] Where so much new investment is made, however, a great deal of debt piles up as well. The only way for Central Asia to manage its rising debt is through radical economic restructuring—a challenging task in an era of low commodities prices. Kazakhstan is the first to try. The national welfare fund (Samruk-Kazyna) aims to reduce the government's share in the economy from nearly 90 percent to under 20 percent, allowing investors to transform state bureaucracies in banking, real estate, and energy into modern enterprises. With no major financial hub between Moscow and Beijing, Kazakhstan's fast-growing new capital city of Astana, the host of Astana Expo 2017, has launched a Dubai-style Astana International Financial Centre (AIFC), with the Shanghai Stock Exchange as an anchor investor, to serve as a regional headquarters for both foreign and local companies. Chinese banks and firms have agreed to list shares there so that Kazakhs can own a stake in the companies financing their future.

Kazakhstan has taken the lead as the hinge nation between Europe and Asia. Sixty percent of the current volumes of China-to-Europe rail cargo cross its territory versus the 30 percent that begins in Russia and the 10 percent that begins in Mongolia. Kazakhstan and Mongolia, the world's two largest landlocked countries, are vast natural transit spaces. They are also giant power stations for the unfurling Silk Road corridors. Kazakhstan not only is an oil and natural gas power but is investing heavily in solar power, wind power, nuclear power, and biomass, all of which can feed into the planned ultra-high-voltage DC (UHVDC) electricity transmission system linking population centers in Central Asia. In Mongolia, Japan's SoftBank is helping develop the country's massive solar- and wind-power potential, which, together with the country's hydropower resources, can reduce its costly imports of fuel from Russia and China, to which it exports almost all its coal and copper.

With Asia's two geographic giants as its neighbors, the eternal question for Mongolia is how to be more than a buffer between Russia and China or a venue for their maneuvering over mining concessions and railways. Russian soldiers built Mongolia's railways a century ago, and their descendants still live there. Mongolia's current president, Battulga Khaltmaa, with his soft spot for Russia, has kicked the country's "third neighbor" campaign into high gear. The goal of attracting non-Chinese investors goes by the acronym ABC: "Anyone but China." During the recent mining boom, however, only China came. Now that Mongolia has to find ways to modernize with less mineral revenue, it is reaching out much farther for development strategies. Like Australia and Bhutan, it is reemphasizing some of its premining industries, such as leather making and organic farming. Mongolia does, after all, have only 3 million people against 50 million horses, cows, camels, goats, and especially sheep, whose wool generates everything from fine cashmere sweaters to cozy, eco-friendly insulation for nomadic *gers* (tents). Asians aren't moving to Mongolia, but Mongolia should be part of sustainable Asian homes.

China has first-mover advantage in many of its neighboring countries, having invested in them when no one else would. But this does not pave a linear path to dominance. Instead, China's robust entry into these markets elevates their profile in attracting other investors who can help them grow and pay down their debts to China, even substituting for Chinese loans and capital on less onerous terms. Small economies such as those of Kyrgyzstan, Laos, Mongolia, and Tajikistan owed the majority of their debt to China before BRI but now are gaining a sturdier platform for growth and recognition. Governments such as that of Kazakhstan have gained the confidence to declare strategic commodities and industries off limits to foreign investors, thus rejecting some of China's debt-for-leverage plays. China's neighbors will accept Chinese investment and trade for mutual benefit, but they won't be coerced into strategic traps. They want to prosper in an Asian system, not a Chinese one.

From Mountain to Sea: Asia's Vertical Axes

Pakistan is a young state in search of new meaning. Conceived as a home for South Asian Muslims, Pakistan nonetheless has only the same number of Muslims as its great rival, Hindu-majority India. In the seventy years since independence, only once has a democratically elected government completed a five-year term. Though it has become an established nuclear power, its internal sectarian violence is its greatest threat. After the September 11, 2001, terrorist attacks, Pakistan became the major conduit for NATO supplies into Afghanistan, making the country an indispensable front line in the US-led "war on terror," but as the weapons, funds, and political support dry up,[12] Pakistan needs a new strategic raison d'être.

The answer—becoming Central Asia's reliable conduit to the Arabian Sea—has been in the works for decades but has now taken pole position among the numerous competing visions for Pakistan's future. After India and China's early-1960s border disputes in the western Himalayas, China began to extend the high-altitude Karakoram Highway through Pakistan along the Indus River to Karachi. Though this north–south traversal has been useful for transportation within Pakistan, it has done little to heal the country's east–west divide between the fertile Punjab and Sindh east of the Indus River and the barren, rugged Pashtun and Baluch regions on its west. The United States' $20 billion in military assistance to Pakistan since 2001 has focused on counterterrorism, but has done little for long-term economic growth: only in 2014 did Pakistan's textile exports to Europe surpass a mere $6 billion, less than a third of the country's total exports. And as ever more Pakistanis have returned from construction labor in the Gulf region, bringing back conservative Wahhabi Islamic values, Pakistan's government has faced a growing backlash against any deals with the United States.

It was once a truism that to comprehend Pakistan you needed to grasp the roles of Allah, the army, and America. The first two still hold sway, but America has been decisively replaced as the third "A"— by Asia. Pakistan, like other Asian countries, has become fed up with being a supplicant to the United States. The former cricket star turned national political leader, Prime Minister Imran Khan, says what almost everyone in the country seems to feel, that Pakistan should stop being a "hired gun"[13] for the United States and a "scapegoat for US failures in Afghanistan."[14] Furthermore, the more the United States threatens to withhold IMF funding to stave off Pakistan's debt crisis, the more the country is pushed into the arms of China and its historical patron Saudi Arabia, which quickly provided a $6 billion bailout in 2018.

Indeed, Pakistan is fully embracing its Asianization. In 2015, Pakistan signed an "all-weather strategic partnership" with China, and as soon as Trump reduced US military assistance in 2017, Pakistan and China declared that all their trade would be denominated in their own currencies rather than the dollar. Pakistan's consulates in Shanghai and Chengdu have been working overtime to dole out visas to Chinese merchants heading over the Karakoram Mountains—or flying directly on new routes between Chengdu and Pakistani cities. The total value of the China-Pakistan Economic Corridor (CPEC) is set to exceed $60 billion in capital allocated to electricity generation, roads, railways, fiber-optic Internet, manufacturing, and agriculture projects. An estimated 3 million jobs in power plants, leather tanneries, and industrial parks making everything from medical devices to solar panels are attributable to CPEC. Eighty-two percent of Pakistanis have a favorable view of China, and TV commercials show recently arrived Chinese families welcomed into local homes to share fragrant meals. With more than 30,000 Chinese taking residency in Pakistan from 2014 to 2016 (and 71,000 short-term visas issued in 2016 alone), the *Huashang Weekly* has begun a Pakistan edition to inform Chinese of local affairs.

China is not Pakistan's main patron for charitable reasons; it wants unfettered access to the Arabian Sea and demands that Pakistan's army and infighting ministries coordinate better and rein in corruption. When they don't, China doesn't hesitate to suspend funding for projects. These are not the environmental and social standards Western agencies demand, but it is conditionality nonetheless. The massive incentives China has put on the table are instilling Pakistan with a discipline it has lacked for decades. Never amid the largesse of the US-financed "war on terror" was national development so front and center in Pakistan's national conversation. As a frequent visitor to Pakistan, I am amazed by the candid and focused number crunching being aired in public fora and media. Which new debts can Pakistan afford to take on? What growth rates need to be achieved to pay them off? How can labor productivity increase and the tax base be expanded? These are the questions Pakistan must ask—and correctly answer—to avoid CPEC becoming what its critics claim it stands for: Colonizing Pakistan for the Enrichment of China.

Pakistan is yearning to graduate from a spasmic Islamist democracy to a reliable moderate partner within the Asian system. This bootstrapping attitude is why Asian investors have gotten excited about Pakistan. For decades, Saudi Arabia's main export to Pakistan besides oil has been radical Islamist ideology. Now it has declared that Pakistan will become one of its top destinations for investment in mining, chemicals, and livestock. In 2018, China launched a pricey marketing campaign promoting the port of Gwadar as the "gateway to emerging Pakistan" with giant posters on the sides of London buses. At the same time, Pakistan is playing hardball and has canceled several significant Chinese projects, including a hydroelectric dam in Gilgit. It resists exporting cotton and marble to Chinese factories, preferring to focus on boosting its own textile and masonry industries and exports. Pakistan has no interest in reliving the British East India Company with China playing the role of England.

China's determined presence in Pakistan is a major driver of Asia's eastern, western, northern, and southern subsystems coming together, benefiting both countries and a number of their neighbors. Iran is keen to join CPEC as a secure corridor for accessing China, while a rumored Chinese naval base on Pakistan's Jiwani peninsula near the Iranian border would strengthen Iranian-Chinese cooperation in challenging the US Navy's Persian Gulf–based Fifth Fleet. At the same time, Iran and India have launched the International North-South Transport Corridor (INSTC), which allows India to circumvent Pakistan and send goods via container ship to Iran's Bandar-e-Abbas port and then via rail through Baku in Azerbaijan and Astrakhan in Russia and onward to Europe. Though some observers portray the CPEC and INSTC initiatives as rivals, in truth they represent Iran cleverly playing to China's and India's simultaneous interest in its energy supplies and geography, while increasing the burden on Pakistan to protect both Chinese and Iranian interests—especially as it pertains to keeping Afghanistan stable. Pakistan's logic has long been to weaken Afghanistan to enhance its own "strategic depth." But with CPEC projects under way, Pakistan has redeployed a full division of 15,000 soldiers away from its Afghan border toward its new functional spine to ensure security for Pakistani and Chinese workers. Since China has become Afghanistan's largest investor and needs it as a gateway to Iran, Pakistan's military adventurism and support for Taliban factions have been curtailed. In fact, Pakistan's government now prioritizes completion of the Iran-Pakistan gas pipeline.

Pakistan's newfound deference to China and Iran may well portend a positive turn for the rugged, war-torn country. After fifteen years of NATO efforts in Afghanistan, the country remains fragile and vulnerable—yet at NATO's 2017 summit, Afghanistan was neglected as the agenda focused on Russia instead. Meanwhile, Pakistan has

substituted the United States with Russia in counterterrorism cooperation, running large exercises together. In 2018, spy chiefs from Russia,
China, and Iran gathered in Pakistan to coordinate their own counter-
ISIS strategies. Additionally, all of Afghanistan's neighbors—as well as
Russia and the Gulf countries—have moved ahead with regional negotiations with the Taliban. China has begun training Afghan batal-
lions in the country's narrow, rugged eastern border region known as
the Wakhan Corridor. At the 2018 Central Asian summit, Kazakhstan
and Uzbekistan agreed to finance $2 billion worth of new railway and
power projects for Afghanistan.

China, too, is starting to back up its investments in Afghanistan
with protective action. In 2017, Chinese troops began deploying mobile patrols with Afghan National Army units in key border provinces,
harkening back to a millennium ago, when the Tang Dynasty had garrisons in Turkestan. Radical Islamist groups such as Al Qaeda and
ISIS have warned that China's encroachment into the region and the
ethnic dilution of Muslim Turkic Uighurs in Xinjiang represent a casus
belli against China. But China's grip on its western provinces is quite
unshakable, with thousands of Uighurs forced into detention and re-
education camps.[15] Furthermore, allusions to the Battle of Talas—in
which Arabs pushed back the Tang Dynasty—betray the reality that
Arab Muslim countries are far too distracted by their own civil wars
to launch a coordinated assault to reclaim Turkestan. Afghan and Pakistani societies find Chinese infrastructural rehabilitation superior to
both Soviet suppression and US manipulation.

As China, Iran, and even Russia enhance their activities in Afghanistan and Pakistan, India sees itself as being on the back foot. India has
long sought cultural fraternity with China, only to witness China race
ahead economically and militarily. As a consolation, China has welcomed
India into the Shanghai Cooperation Organisation (SCO) alongside
Pakistan, but China's CPEC projects traverse Pakistan-occupied Kashmir (PoK), ratifying Pakistan's control over territory that India still also
claims. India's Narendra Modi boycotted the 2017 Belt and Road summit

in Beijing for that reason, though it did not stop the Chinese from feting then Pakistani prime minister Nawaz Sharif. India has not hesitated to conduct surgical strikes against terrorist training camps inside Pakistan while threatening to pull out of key agreements such as the Indus Waters Treaty. But the combined strength and determination of China and Pakistan will eventually force even the proud nationalist Modi to accept the status quo, perhaps ceding a Kashmir settlement in exchange for China's reducing its damming of the headwaters of the Brahmaputra River, on which so much of India's northern and eastern population depends. The more India wants secure access to Iran's natural gas resources, the more it will have to cooperate with Pakistan rather than shun it.

India's immediate priority remains bolstering its influence in Afghanistan, where it is the second largest investor after China. India recently completed construction of Iran's multiterminal Chabahar port near the Pakistani border, from which an Indian-built highway speeds delivery of Indian wheat to Afghanistan, helping the country import and export goods without depending on Pakistan. Even though Pakistan is suspicious of any Indian activity in Iran and Afghanistan, it still wants to move forward with the long-overdue Turkmenistan-Afghanistan-Pakistan-India (TAPI) natural gas pipeline, which is already under construction and which even Bangladesh wants to join.

In Bangladesh, Chinese and local engineers are working just south of the capital, Dhaka, to complete the new Padma Bridge, which will speed the country's garment production to southern ports such as Mongla and Chittagong, the latter being actively developed by India and Japan to gain a toehold in the country's market. Similarly, after Myanmar's decades of isolation ended in the late 2000s, China began upgrading the country's roads and ports to accelerate access to the Andaman Sea without having to rely on the strategic Strait of Malacca. Now India—which had scarcely engaged with Myanmar since the two were both part of the British Raj—is racing to develop the Sittwe port as its commercial bridgehead. Japan, too, has made Myanmar a strategic investment priority, expanding the Thilawa port near Yangon.

China's moves have thus awakened India, Japan, and others to invest in cross-regional integration and inspired the Myanmar government to renegotiate terms on certain Chinese projects to bring down their exorbitant costs and reduce Myanmar's debt burden.

This logic applies not just to Bay of Bengal countries but also high in the Himalayan mountains. After China crushed the 1959 Tibetan uprising, Bhutan accepted thousands of Tibetan refugees but also closed its borders to China for fear of suffering the same fate. In 2017, as China neared completion of a highway across southern Tibet—meant to connect to the CPEC corridor in Pakistan—it carved into disputed valleys at the intersection of China, Bhutan, and India's state of Sikkim. The 2017 Doklam plateau standoff was significant because China instigated an intrusion into disputed terrain, but India held its ground and China backed down. However, despite a meeting between Narendra Modi and Xi Jinping in 2018 during which they agreed to resolve the situation diplomatically, the dispute could still escalate and spread into nearby contested zones. China could make incursions into neighboring Arunachal Pradesh, militarize the disputed Aksai Chin terrain on its border with Kashmir, and distract India through joint naval drills with Pakistan in the Indian Ocean. This scenario clarifies why India is so paranoid about China but also highlights how many active theaters China must coordinate to shift the overall status quo.

Yet both China and India will benefit from linking China's east–west axis to the emerging Bangladesh-China-India-Myanmar (BCIM) Economic Corridor, bringing much-needed development to India's long-neglected northeastern region. Knowing that China will ultimately move forward with its trans-Tibetan highway (including a railway to Nepal's capital, Kathmandu), India has decided to redouble its efforts to influence its eastern neighbors by advancing the Bay of Bengal Initiative for Multi-Sectoral Technical and Economic Cooperation (BIMSTEC), which excludes China but includes a wide set of countries from Sri Lanka to Nepal to Thailand. The bet is paying off. In Nepal, a canceled Chinese dam project in 2017 opened the door for India's National Hydroelectric Power Corporation (NHPC) to move in.

The passing of the Dalai Lama will produce another significant moment of tension in bilateral relations. India is home to the Dalai Lama as well as the vast majority of the Tibetan Buddhist diaspora. As China moves to install the Dalai Lama's Beijing-designated successor, the potential for unrest in Tibet and pressure on India to support some notional Tibetan autonomy could spark significant escalation at the Sino-Indian border. India and China have two broad choices in how to resolve these confrontations. The first is to argue in circles about the provisions of the 1890 Anglo-Chinese Convention (signed nearly seventy years before India's independence and Tibet's absorption into China), which demarcated the border between Sikkim and Tibet. The other is to recall that this is the same terrain of the ancient Nathu La Pass, a passageway for Buddhist pilgrims and traders that was reopened as a trading post in 2006—which both countries declared India-China Friendship Year. It should be clear which path better represents the Asian way.

Many Western and even regional analysts perceive China's, Japan's, and India's maneuvers in Asia's mountainous frontiers and tropical coasts as a zero-sum contest. In reality, they reveal a complementary division of labor. The reason is that China's projects have inspired an infrastructural arms race by which India, Japan, Turkey, South Korea, and others are also making major contributions to building Asian connectivity. From Afghanistan to Myanmar, China finances and builds heavy infrastructure, while India and Japan train manpower. Taken together, all these investments help Asians deepen their ties to *one another* as much as to China. China is thus kick-starting the process by which Asians will come out from under its shadow. In the long run, both China and India's preferred corridors will emerge, overlap, and even reinforce each other, ensuring that inner-Asian goods will make it to the Indian Ocean, deepening intra-Asian connectivity for Asians' greater benefit. Geopolitical rivalries will only speed the Asianization of Asia.

From Forgotten Corner to Growth Driver: Southeast Asia Comes of Age

Only one postcolonial region has managed to bring about the kind of cross-border integration and stability reminiscent of the early decades of the European Union: Southeast Asia. The achievement of these dozen countries, with a combined population nearing 700 million, is even more remarkable given that it is the most ethnically, religiously, and linguistically diverse corner of the planet. After millennia of migration from India, China, Arabia, and Europe, the Association of Southeast Asian Nations (ASEAN) countries[16] are home to 240 million Muslims, 130 million Christians, 140 million Buddhists, and 10 million Hindus. The cultural diversity is also profound, with Hindu rituals widespread in Muslim Indonesia and Buddhist Thailand. Generations of family businesses have maintained tight cross-border linkages such as Muslim *hawala* networks and the ethnic-Chinese "bamboo network." Even with the layered heritage etched into the region's archaeological monuments and the mixed ancestry visible on its faces, Southeast Asia's postcolonial borders track to ancient kingdoms and linguistic groups, making its modern societies as discrete as they are diverse.

After centuries of colonial suppression followed by devastating (anti-)Communist wars, the founding of ASEAN a half century ago set the stage for the region to emerge today as a core pillar of Asia's future. Even though ASEAN as a diplomatic body is weak, the region's internal and external dynamics point to accelerated integration. Two decades on from the 1997 financial crisis, trade and investment liberalization and supply-chain integration have spurred robust economic growth on the back of record volumes of foreign investment with global linkages spreading beyond India, China, Japan, and Australia to the Gulf countries, Europe, the United States, and even Latin America.

ASEAN's members have committed to a 2025 master plan to harmonize standards for banking, telecoms, and e-commerce, by which time Indonesia, Thailand, and Vietnam may change their time zone to align with Singapore, Kuala Lumpur, and Manila. Air Asia and a dozen other low-cost carriers have made intraregional travel affordable for the masses, leading to waves of tourists visiting one another's countries and taking cross-border jobs with the growing number of large pan-Asian companies. In the coming years, major new transport and trade corridors such as a high-speed railway network from Kunming in southern China through Laos, Thailand, and Malaysia to Singapore will knit China ever more closely to Southeast Asia. China has positioned Kunming to be the capital of the Southern Silk Road, designating it to host pan-Asian cultural festivals and stonemasonry expositions that lure Afghans, Sri Lankans, Burmese, and Vietnamese.

The poorest ASEAN members, such as Laos and Cambodia, have already exchanged their strategic autonomy for Chinese cash. In both countries, Chinese companies have large and even controlling stakes in everything from electricity to factories, and both have canceled joint military activities with the United States and Australia. In Laos's northern district of Ton Pheung, Mandarin is widely spoken, clocks are set to Beijing time, and the yuan is the most common currency.[17] Chinese gamble and traffic in wildlife in designated zones in Laos, while Chinese dam projects along the Mekong River, combined with the usage of pesticides to boost fruit output, have polluted the land and endangered the health and livelihood of millions of farmers who depend on its fish. China's incursion is the reason Laos is using the growing interest in its market to attract Japanese, Singaporean, and other investors who can help Laos become more than just a Chinese vassal.

In Myanmar, China has the built-in advantage of consistently supporting the military junta through decades of isolation. Even as the country has liberalized in the past decade, China still dominates the trade and investment landscape. Myanmar's army has prosecuted a genocidal ethnic cleansing campaign against Rohingya Muslims, mercilessly quarantining and pushing them across the Naf River into Bangladesh, with smugglers sending tens of millions of yaba methamphetamine tablets with them. The Rohingya who have fled in the other direction to Thailand—which itself has waged a decades-long pacification campaign against its restive southern Muslim population—have wound up as bonded laborers in Thai fisheries. Democratic Thailand reverted to junta rule in 2014 after a coup that ousted the ethnic Chinese brother-sister act of Thaksin and Yingluck Shinawatra. Though Chinese make up about 20 percent of Thailand's population, the coup only increased China's influence, for the junta turned to China for new tanks and other military hardware. China has remained silent on the ethnopolitical instability of these two militant Buddhist regimes.

China has asserted itself into Southeast Asia's nexus of drugs and militants only when its own interests have been threatened. For decades, the notorious Golden Triangle spanning the mountainous confluence of the Ruak and Mekong rivers across Myanmar, Laos, and Thailand has been a leading center of opium production. In late 2011, after thirteen Chinese fishermen were murdered and dumped into the Mekong in a massacre masterminded by a Burmese drug kingpin, China insisted on joint river patrols involving Yunnan border police. Perpetrators from Myanmar, Thailand, and Laos were apprehended, extradited to China, and sentenced to death. The Hong Kong action filmmaker Dante Lam's muscular retelling of the events in *Operation Mekong* was one of China's top-grossing films of 2016.

Another pair of significant countries—Malaysia and the Philippines—have historically been strong US allies but more recently have tilted toward China. In the Philippines, the last president, Benigno Aquino III, lodged an international legal case against China over its South China Sea island occupation, a move viewed as a betrayal by China given Aquino's Chinese heritage. (While pure ethnic Chinese make up only 2 percent of the Filipino population, millions more have partial Chinese ancestry.) Conveniently for China, Aquino's successor, Rodrigo Duterte, also had a Chinese grandfather and sees China differently, hence China's financial support for his presidential campaign. Duterte—like all other Asian leaders—prefers multidirectional alignment to reliance on the United States alone. While the United States (at least pre-Trump) had been critical of Duterte's brutal tactics in his war on drug cartels and Islamist rebels, China has rewarded his threats to close US bases with $24 billion in cheap loans for infrastructure projects as well as fresh arms deals. Duterte also effectively ceded to China the South China Sea islands it had already fortified and militarized in exchange for a lucrative joint oil exploration deal between the Philippines' PXP Energy Corporation and a Chinese oil company.[18] Yet Duterte has not fully capitulated to China. He is correctly betting that settling a military dispute his country cannot win will entice ever more investors. The Philippines' biggest investors are actually the Netherlands, Australia, Japan, the United States, South Korea, and Australia—with China far behind. In 2018, Duterte traveled to India and secured more than $1 billion in new investment in the Philippines' tech and pharma sectors with the aim of creating 100,000 jobs. Geopolitical stability enables the growth Asia's second-tier powers need.

Malaysia demonstrates why getting too close to China can be politically costly. A middle-income country that shares no border nor has any outstanding dispute with China, Malaysia has long courted Japan, China, India, Australia, Korea, Saudi Arabia, the United States, and Europe, all for the purposes of bringing in valuable investment to finance economic diversification. The last prime minister, Najib Razak, however, leaned too much on China, especially to bail him out of a blatant corruption scandal and help him buy back ethnic Chinese voters who had deserted his party. The plan backfired, resulting in his spectacular defeat in the country's 2018 election and his subsequent arrest. China's projects in Malaysia—including a deepwater transshipment port at Malacca and an Alibaba logistics hub in the country's new Digital Free Trade Zone—are a boost to Malaysian enterprises, but citizens won't accept them at the cost of selling out their country's strategic autonomy. Even the most China-friendly countries in the region such as Malaysia are therefore renegotiating to bring down the cost of Chinese projects such as the eastern coast railway.

Vietnam stands up to China more pugnaciously than any other Southeast Asian nation. Despite their ideological fraternity and deepening economic ties—many refer to Vietnam as "Little China" for its industrious output—Vietnam is not afraid to send its navy to collide with Chinese vessels and oil rigs trespassing in its water or to partner with foreign energy companies such as ExxonMobil to extract gas in disputed regions. In 2016, the United States lifted its arms embargo on Vietnam in the hope of getting a foothold in the country's fast-growing defense market, which has traditionally been dominated by Russian tanks, air defense systems, and fighter jets. In 2018, the United States included Vietnam in the multinational Rim of the Pacific (RIMPAC) war-gaming exercises, while excluding China. Vietnam has also leased Japanese warships, purchased advanced Japanese radar systems, and opened its strategic port in Cam Ranh Bay to foreign vessels. China's fortification of islands in the South China Sea is intended to intimidate its peninsular and littoral neighbors, who all depend on the Strait of Malacca for trade in energy and goods—but Vietnam never backs down from a fight. Yet Vietnam also wants a modus vivendi with China and has agreed to suspend some of its own gas exploration projects in disputed waters. A grand bargain with Vietnam could be the strongest move China might make to weaken the United States' relevance in Southeast Asia, rendering moot the freedom of navigation operations the United States, France, and Great Britain have undertaken in the South China Sea waters. If the two agree to joint energy exploration and regulated fishing in the Paracels island cluster area, the likelihood of an uncontrolled escalation would be reduced.

The same scenario applies to Indonesia. As a founding member of ASEAN and a stalwartly nonaligned nation during the Cold War, Indonesia's strong economic growth has given it the confidence to refuse to cave in to Chinese pressure. Outsiders often portray a Sino-Japanese rivalry to "win" Indonesia, with China in the lead due to its successful bid to build a high-speed railway between Jakarta and Bandung. But the Jokowi government nonetheless renamed the portion of the South China Sea falling within its exclusive economic zone (EEZ) the "North Natuna Sea" and pushed forward with extraction from the East Natuna natural gas field even though it lies within waters claimed by China. It has also been impounding Chinese fishing vessels plying its waters. Indonesia knows that China and Japan are competing to profit from its modernization and thus does not have to sell its loyalty to anyone.

The archetype of this self-confident diplomatic behavior is Singapore. This surprises many outsiders because it is the only other country in the world besides China that has a majority ethnic-Chinese population. But owing to its strategic geography and financial wealth, Singapore has been the most confident of ASEAN countries, hosting US warships and carriers for long stretches of time. It has also become the region's neutral diplomatic hub, hosting important meetings between the leaders of China and Taiwan. After decades of China looking to Singapore for design and investment in its industrial parks, China recently began to voice its displeasure with Singapore over its support for international arbitration in the South China Sea dispute and its backing of the Trans-Pacific Partnership (TPP) trade agreement. The Chinese media took to accusing Singaporeans of being "Han traitors" and "forgetting their origins." Meanwhile, sophisticated Singaporeans are fed up with the more than 1 million immigrants from mainland China who have arrived since the early 2000s, both for their unwillingness to integrate into the country's urbane Anglophone culture and for their crowding of schools and public transport. The more Chinese Singapore has become demographically, the less comfortable it has become with China geopolitically. At the same time, Singapore has positioned itself to contribute to both the hardware and software of the Belt and Road Initiative (BRI). It has maintained privileged access to the most lucrative infrastructural investments in China, providing the high-quality engineering, and is also the conduit for more than 80 percent of the foreign investment flowing into BRI projects.

Though there is no single pattern to describe how Southeast Asians are coping with China's expansionist forays, wealthier countries are inversely beholden to China. None, however, accepts that China's seizure of disputed islands implies acceptance of its hegemony over waters that have for millennia belonged to them all. Each littoral state has a different name for its portion of the South China Sea, such as "West Philippines Sea" or "East Sea" (in Vietnam). And as the region's strategic confidence grows, its ability to withstand Chinese pressure does as well. Though bodies such as the ASEAN Regional Forum (ARF) are more cooperative accords than treaty structures, they have the potential to grow into genuine stabilization instruments tackling tough issues such as counterterrorism and maritime patrols. The more frequent these interactions become, the more Asians will develop the ability to self-regulate. Such large groupings also have the potential to be diluted: too inclusive to be decisive. But even if these bodies do not become supranational European-style institutions, they can serve as working forums to resolve disputes and build confidence in an Asia for Asians.

Australia Finds Itself on the Map

After the 2016 Brexit vote, some haughty Brits triumphantly speculated that the European Union would disintegrate further in the wake of losing a pivotal anchor. Instead, the rest of Europe rejected British populism, banded together to extract maximum concessions from the United Kingdom on its way out of the union, and continues to maneuver to capture its financial edge. The Brexit debacle is instructive for Australians, who have long thought of their country as the Great Britain of Asia, the avuncular white Anglophone leader of an unruly and underdeveloped region. But that's not how other Asians see it. Singapore's late founding father, Lee Kuan Yew, once warned that Aussies were destined to become the "poor white trash of Asia" if they did not reform their economy, something his comments helped jolt them to do. If Australia wants to be more welcome in Asia than the United Kingdom is in Europe, it needs to swallow the hard truth that it is not the center of Asia's solar system but merely a moon—one made of iron ore.

Australia's schizophrenia is simultaneously economic, geopolitical, and cultural. The country's leaders know they could not survive the economic consequences of alienating China. Furthermore, Chinese invest more than $10 billion per year in Australia in commercial real estate, infrastructure, health care, mining, energy, agribusiness, and other areas that help Australia's economy prosper even as commodity prices slump. Any blockade of Australia's exports to China, cooling of investment from China, or diversion of Chinese visitors from Australia would create an economic Armageddon.

It is this fear of "losing" Asia that reminds Australians just how strategically Asian they actually are and need to be. Australia remains deeply committed to preserving its role in Western security networks such as the Five Eyes intelligence-sharing initiative with the United States, Canada, United Kingdom, and New Zealand. But falling-outs between Australia and the United States over the sale of Darwin port—where the United States has a thousand marines stationed—to a Chinese People's Liberation Army–connected business, as well as over the resettlement of Syrian refugees, have strained the trust between the Anglophone allies. During their most recent joint exercises in 2017, Australia invited the Chinese military as a third partner, even at the cost of making the United States uncomfortable. Like other Asian countries, Australia is learning to say no to the United States in its effort to maintain a balance between the two powers.

Former Australian prime minister Tony Abbott once remarked that his country's ties to China are driven equally by fear and greed. Yet because Australia does not want to be too dependent on China economically nor the United States militarily, it has begun a new strategy of cultivating stronger economic and military ties with Japan, India, and Vietnam. ASEAN is Australia's second largest trading partner behind China, followed by Japan and Korea—and new trade agreements between all of them signal substantial growth not only in goods but also in services. Trade between Australia and India grew sixfold between 2000 and 2012, then stalled, with Australians complaining about the complexities of doing business in India. But given India's demand for commodities, improvements in infrastructure, and upwardly mobile population, there is a strong momentum behind Aussie-Indian trade growth.

Australia is learning to see Asia as not just a destination for commodities but a conduit for recycling capital into its own critical future industries. Whereas all its car-manufacturing plants have shut down due to lower-wage Asian competition, robust cattle exports to China fund major road upgrades as well as organic farms catering to Asian tastes. Australia is also reinvesting its iron-ore revenues into mining technologies that will be sold to Chinese at the new Sino-Australian Free Trade Industrial Park under construction on Zhoushan Island and to India, which needs to boost its own mineral production.

Most of Australia's 9 million annual tourist visitors also come from East Asia, and nearly 100,000 Chinese students are enrolled in schools across Australia, making education the country's third largest export. Australia has also set up dozens of technical institutes such as PSB Academy in Singapore, that lure Indian engineering students. Australia and New Zealand have among the highest rates of foreign student enrollment, and budget cuts at tertiary institutions make it that much more essential for them to recruit cash-rich, full-fee-paying Asians.[19] This growing services trade was a prime motivation behind Prime Minister Malcolm Turnbull's convening the Australia-ASEAN Special Summit in March 2018, at which, for the first time, leaders discussed Australia's joining ASEAN.

Concretely, if Australia joined ASEAN, it would encourage even more Asian immigration to Australia. For the better part of the twentieth century, various "white Australia" measures defined the country's immigration policy. The name says it all. Australia preferred European migrants in its labor unions and working its gold mines; the policy systematically restricted or penalized Chinese. Only in the 1970s were racial preferences in migration formally eliminated. Since then, the country's morphing demographics have set the stage for Australia's current Asianization. The country's most recent census reveals that from 2012 to 2017, Asians surged ahead of Europeans to become the largest source of foreign-born migrants, constituting half the country's new population. This gap is widening every year. Half of Australia's 1 million Chinese were born on the mainland, and Australia is the world's top destination for millionaire relocation—mostly the newly minted Chinese upper class. Today about 5 percent of Australia's population is of Chinese heritage and 2 percent of Indian heritage. About 15 percent of Australia's population is ethnically Asian. And although the aging population is white, the younger population is increasingly Asian.

Asians have come for the gold rush, pearl fishing, and gardening; they have fought in the Australian armed forces and built national roads and railways—but they are absent from the nation's grand story, as well as underrepresented in the country's Parliament, boardrooms, and media. After decades of political marginalization, these first- and second-generation Asian Aussies are finally becoming an organized voice and confronting the anti-immigration stance of the old white guard.

Given how much the Chinese have already invested in Australia, some have jumped the queue. In 2017, scandalous revelations—that wealthy Chinese businessmen with large agricultural and real estate holdings had been making donations to political groups and academic institutions to nudge them toward pro-Chinese positions on delicate issues such as the South China Sea—gripped the nation. The Chinese Consulate in Sydney has been the hub for supporting—or intimidating—local Chinese Australian politicians depending on their degree of friendliness toward China, while urging mainland Chinese store owners to fire Taiwanese. At the same time, scholarly books critical of China's penetration into Australian life have been pulled by publishers for fear of legal backlash from Chinese interests. The Australian government subsequently banned all foreign donations in its political system and is curbing foreign investment in strategic energy assets such as its power grid.

Australians' rite of passage to adulthood is the walkabout, either roughing it in the outback or wandering the world for a year or two—or sometimes a decade or two. Twenty percent of Australian students study abroad at least once. In the past, most would go to Europe and America, but the number of Aussie students heading to China has tripled since 2010 to more than 5,000. With many hypereducated Aussies idling in the country's traditional companies, some are being lured to work for Chinese tech companies. More Australian authors now have contracts with Chinese publishers than with American or British ones and feature well in literary festivals on the mainland.

The Singaporean businessman Calvin Cheng Ern Lee shows how wealthy Asians are capitalizing on the booming Chinese services sector. After spending several years in China licensing Western brands, he built a business setting up online training platforms for giant Chinese companies such as China Unicom and Ping An Insurance. His newest venture, now listed on the Australian Securities Exchange, takes gaming and other digital content made in Australia and delivers it to clients across China. Australia's leading-edge design and engineering companies are also jumping at the chance to profit from the urbanization and cross-border infrastructure boom under way to their north. The opportunity is both commercial and financial. Australia's Macquarie Group already manages the world's largest portfolio of infrastructure assets and is keen to construct new funds that take larger stakes in China and Southeast Asia. The Australia and New Zealand Banking Group (ANZ) has made a top priority of boosting lending for cross-border expansion for Australian businesses, while the country's largest insurer, QBE Insurance Group, has moved hundreds of jobs to the Philippines to save on costs and expand its business.

Australia is learning over time to embrace its Asian-ness. The Australian Open, the Southern Hemisphere's biggest sporting event, achieved a reputation equal to its Grand Slam tennis peers only in the 2000s, when it began to attract throngs of followers across Asia, especially Japan and China. As tennis has surged in popularity, today double the number of competitors are Asian versus five years ago, with many talented Asian youths training in Australia. Many of these realities were not part of the Australian conversation a decade ago. The more Asian Australia becomes, the less it can think of itself—and the less we should think of it—as a detached outpost of the West in Asia.

Japan Goes Global (Again)

In the decades after its surrender after World War II, Japan achieved such spectacular growth that it earned both admiration and fear. Even as Japan's economy plateaued in the 1990s, US policy makers and academics continued to imagine an East Asian order that could be designed around its leadership. But given Japan's offshore and insular culture, twentieth-century history of regional aggression, postwar pacifism, and growth rates barely reaching 1 percent amid skyrocketing debt and political rudderlessness (with eight prime ministers in ten years), even the return of Shinzo Abe as prime minister in 2012 and his attempt to introduce all-encompassing changes from the economy to the military have failed to restore Japan's confidence. Japan's political economy remains entrenched in a pattern most aptly described as democratic socialism overlaid on corporate feudalism. Yet this same Japan, wrestling with economic stagnation and demographic decline, is one of the world's most technologically advanced societies with an archipelago of pulsating metropolises.

Abe's so-called three arrows of economic reform were monetary easing, fiscal stimulus, and structural reforms (such as advancing deregulation and privatization and promoting entrepreneurship and female workforce participation). While Abe and his loyal Bank of Japan governor, Haruhiko Kuroda, initially succeeded in boosting export growth and reducing unemployment, they sent mixed signals on fiscal policy by raising consumption taxes and failed to raise wages or stoke inflation and domestic investment despite negative interest rates. Japan's debt continues to head into uncharted territory, with the Bank of Japan holding nearly half of it. Even a write-down of this debt is not expected to jump-start market confidence. Japan's corporate culture remains steeped in hierarchical traditions of obedience to management and sadomasochistic patterns of overwork—even to the point of death—known as *karoshi*. Japanese firms once towered over humble regional upstarts, but now many have fallen victim to them. In 2016, the Japanese electronics giant Sharp was bought by Taiwan's Foxconn.

But Japan should not be counted out. Contrary to much of the prevailing pessimism, global competition—and opportunities—are yanking Japanese companies out of complacency. With sluggish prospects at home, Japanese corporations had begun to look far beyond Japan for growth before Abe ever came to power. "Going global" has now become a progressive Japanese business mantra. More than half of Japanese merger and acquisition activity in recent years has been deals *outside* Japan. Japanese megabanks such as Mitsubishi Financial Group and Mizuho Financial Group have turned themselves into investment holding companies, financing Japanese firms pushing abroad to Southeast Asia as it displaces China as the new factory floor. From manufacturing Toyotas in Thailand and Indonesia to building ports in Myanmar, Japan is spending generously in the same countries it marched through rapaciously in the 1940s. Japan's high-quality agricultural products are also in growing demand across Asia as incomes rise and trade linkages expand. Japan has thus become much more vocal in promoting free-trade agreements (FTAs). It signed its first FTA with Singapore in 2002 and agreed to its biggest FTA with the European Union in 2017. As the Euro-Japan FTA comes into effect, more European and Japanese cars will cross the Indian Ocean, the Eurasian landmass, and even the Arctic to reach each other's markets, elevating Japan's incentive to throw its weight into the Belt and Road Initiative. Books Kinokuniya, the stylish Japanese bookstore chain, has become a prominent landmark in major Asian cities from Dubai to Singapore. In place of the old corporate culture known for seniority rather than meritocracy, new-economy companies such as the e-commerce pioneer Rakuten are promoting a more entrepreneurial and diverse workforce to match that of their investments such as Lyft and Pinterest in the United States and Price-Minister in France. Rakuten requires English competence, and at Uniqlo, English is the official workplace language. According to Rakuten founder Hiroshi Mikitani, "The greatest business risk [Japan] faces is that of staying at home."[20]

Japan is invigorating its already deep advantages in precision industries through new public-private alliances amounting to several trillion dollars devoted to the Internet of Things (IoT), big data, AI, 3D printing, robotics, biotech, health care, clean energy, enhanced agriculture, and other sectors—all ready for export to Asia's high-growth markets. SoftBank has become Japan's standout example of a bridge between Japan, Asia, and the world. SoftBank's Vision Funds—in which Saudi Arabia is the largest investor followed by the UAE—are the largest technology portfolio in the world, making aggressive investments in semiconductors, satellites, artificial intelligence, and IoT companies around the world. SoftBank also has stakes in e-commerce companies in India and a nearly 30 percent stake in China's Alibaba. SoftBank and Alibaba's partnership to capture India's e-commerce market is a powerful example of the emerging commercial triangle between China, Japan, and India. SoftBank will also invest $25 billion back into Saudi Arabia to stimulate innovation in the Gulf countries.

Given its aging demographics, Japan is at the cutting edge of technological approaches to managing elderly populations. It is already a world leader in factory automation; now it is automating daily life. At one of the newest amusement parks outside Nagasaki, the check-in staff in the on-site hotel are robots, as are the chefs and waiters in the resort's restaurant. Softbank's Pepper robot is now ubiquitous in shops selling everything from mobile phones to pizza. From furry mechanical seals serving as companions in nursing homes to robots with touch-screen faces gliding through hospitals and gathering patient data, Japan is at the forefront of building a hybrid human-robot civilization, liberally spreading its technological innovations across Asia.

But global Japan must avoid repeating the country's overly aggressive outward push from the 1980s. Its current buying spree has been considered indiscriminate, with nearly $20 billion wasted by companies such as Japan Post and Toshiba on failed acquisitions between mid-2016 and mid-2017.[21] Also, though there is an admirable vanguard of outwardly oriented Japanese companies, Abenomics has yet to awaken everyday businesses. One approach Japan is taking to shake up its entrenched conservatism is demographic: welcoming foreigners on a scale never before attempted. Japan's aggressive efforts to lure back overseas Japanese are a spectacle best witnessed at the annual Boston Career Forum (also held in Los Angeles and London), which attracts hordes of bilingual students gunning for jobs in Japan, including Chinese and Americans as well. Asians are flowing into Japan as migrants, workers, brides, and tourists. By 2016, Japan was home to a record number of foreign immigrants (nearly 2.5 million) and 1 million foreign workers. The number of Chinese has mushroomed from 150,000 in 1990 to more than 700,000 today, with many Chinese learning Japanese well enough to blend in relatively quickly. Japanese intermarriage has also risen, especially with spouses from China, the Philippines, Korea, and the United States. In the labor force, Vietnamese, Thais, and even Nepalis are growing in number.[22] In the run-up to the Olympics, thousands more construction workers will come from abroad. Across the board, Asians are plugging the low-skill end of Japan's widening labor gap, working in shopping malls and drugstores, where they service the millions of Asians who make up Japan's recent tourism surge. In Tokyo hot spots such as Shibuya, Shinjuku, and Ginza, the phenomenon of "explosive shopping by Chinese tourists" has been captured by the neologism *bakugai*, which was voted Japan's most memorable buzzword of 2015.[23] Furthermore, the weak yen has made Japanese real estate a popular buy among regional real estate investors. Chinese property dealers, US private equity firms, and Singaporean wealth funds are among the many investors betting on the long-term appeal of stable, sophisticated, placid Japan.

Surplus Asian engineering and computer science graduates are also a crucial remedy for Japan's shortage of white-collar tech talent, hence the government's recent pledge to fast-track permanent residency for highly skilled foreigners despite the cultural and linguistic obstacles. Starting in 2012, the authorities in Fukuoka, once a sleepy seaside city on the southern island of Kyushu, cut taxes on new businesses and launched a start-up visa to encourage the hiring of foreigners. In the three-year period to 2015, the city experienced a 20 percent growth rate in residents aged fifteen to twenty-nine, and in 2015 alone, 2,800 new companies were founded, the highest figure nationwide.[24] Fukuoka's mayor wants the city to become a Singapore-style "living lab" for IoT technologies. Though Japan still lags behind Singapore and South Korea as a start-up hub,[25] university labs and venture capital funds have sprung up around Keio in Tokyo, Nagoya, and Kyoto, with a particular focus on biotech and pharmaceuticals.[26] PeptiDream, one of Japan's leading biotech firms, sprang from a Tokyo University lab.

Despite Japan's technological inventiveness and cultural popularity in Asia, Japan's strategic posture in Asia has yet to fully recover from its history of imperial aggression there. To that end, it is trying to evolve beyond the antiquated 1990s logic that the US-Japan alliance could be a meaningful anchor of East Asian stability. Both countries have tried to revive the decade-old "Quad" of more frequent consultations and military cooperation with India[27] and Australia—a foursome that some liken to an "Asian NATO." At the same time, Japan is tilting toward revising its postwar constitution to allow it to strengthen its self-defense forces and even potentially go nuclear.[28] It is also fortifying its claims on certain Senkaku/Diaoyu islands by installing land-to-sea missile systems, raising the cost of any Chinese attempt to seize them. These moves go hand in hand with reducing its dependence on the semipermanent presence of US troops on its soil, for example by funding a new $160 million base on the US territory of Guam with the aim of relocating US marines there.

Yet neither Japan's army nor even its potent navy is sufficiently trained, coordinated, or willing to take on China without the United States' backing. Furthermore, Japan would face an economic tailspin given the likely Chinese embargo on Japanese goods and the ensuing capital flight, wiping out the rewards it has reaped from landmark investments such as Itochu Corporation's stake in CITIC Group and

SoftBank's in Alibaba. No country has better commercial networks across China's provinces than Japan—all of which would be at risk in the event of a serious conflict. The only upside to a Sino-Japanese war, then, would be if there were indeed a final settlement—in either side's favor—over the status of islands which have been used to inflame nationalism for several generations. Both sides will then have to close a chapter of history and move on. Somewhere between Japan as the "rising sun" and its slide into geriatric irrelevance is a more modest middle path as a pillar of the Asian system.

Geopolitical Jujitsu: The Future of the Asian Security System

Today all of Asia's empires and powers are seeking national revival; none will bow to the others. The future Asian geopolitical order will thus be neither American nor Chinese led. Japan, South Korea, India, Russia, Indonesia, Australia, Iran, and Saudi Arabia will never collectively come together under a hegemonic umbrella or unite into a single pole of power—neither bandwagoning with China or balancing against it. Instead, they are on high alert against excessive US *and* Chinese influence in their affairs.

Whether under the slogan of "peaceful rise" offered in the 2000s by President Hu Jintao or the more current "harmonious world" used by Xi Jinping, China is seeking to combine Ming Dynasty expansionism with Tang Dynasty cosmopolitanism. It seeks a world order in which either its principles sit at the core, as argued in the work of the philosopher Zhao Tingyang,[29] or Western hierarchy is replaced by parity among civilizations, as argued by the political scientist Zhang Weiwei.[30] Neither scenario allows for a long-term US military presence in East Asia, hence China's enormous investments in antiship ballistic missiles, stealth submarines, robotic warships, electromagnetic railguns, swarming drones, and militarized reclaimed islands and shoals in the South China Sea—all intended to push US forces east of the international date line. At the same time, China knows it is not omnipotent. Though it has enormous leverage over most of its neighbors, even military triumph in oustanding disputes may generate such adverse political and economic backlash that it is not worth the price. China cannot assure itself that seizing the multitude of disputed islands and mountains on its periphery would not lead to a blockage of its BRI projects or large-scale diversion of foreign financial and industrial activity. China has learned from Japan's hyper-aggression and the United States' overstretch to show restraint and caution, not pursue invasion and occupation.

Meanwhile, all Asians are pursuing greater strategic autonomy, making the region the world's largest arms bazaar. By 2020, total Asian military spending is set to reach $600 billion, double that of Europe and almost the same as that of the United States. Asians would rather spend these billions on their own militaries than underwrite the United States' global posture. From Saudi Arabia to Japan, Asians are building their own defense capacity so they can depend less on the United States to deter nearby enemies. Deterrence among Asians in turn reduces the need for extended deterrence on the part of the United States. Thus when Asians tell visiting US diplomats what they want to hear—that their role is essential to deter Iran, China, or some other threat—it does not mean they want US forces stationed on their soil forever. Rather, they want advanced weaponry for themselves and the ability to determine how and when, or whether, to use them—including to deter China. Furthermore, the more China itself exports advanced weaponry, from missiles to drones, the less likely it becomes that it could ever successfully force itself upon its neighbors. Blowback is as universal as empire. China is not interested in sharing Asia with the United States but will learn to comanage it with its fellow Asians.

Asia is thus not a set of dominoes but rather a dynamic strategic theater. During the Cold War, Americans failed to grasp that leaders from Iran's Mohammad Mossadegh to Ngo Dinh Diem in Vietnam were first and foremost nationalists pursuing their own cost-benefit calculations; their primary identity was not Western or Communist-leaning. China is learning the same today as regional powers such as India, Japan, and Vietnam stand up to China, showing that they are as proud of their history and as protective of their sovereignty as China is. These same Asian states are forging new geometries of cooperation. Some of these informal arrangements include the budding military cooperation among Japan, Vietnam, and India; between Australia and Japan; between India and Indonesia; among China, Malaysia, and Sri Lanka; and among China, Thailand, and Cambodia. Even those states that cooperate militarily with China want to be part of coalitions that are sufficiently robust not to fold under the weight of escalation with China. China and Russia have grown closer, but Russia tops the list of arms exporters to Vietnam, whose principal security threat is China. Those who are looking for either rigid lines of alliance or moral clarity among Asia's shifting partnerships will find themselves in an Escher painting. Consistent with Asian history, then, there is much more overlap across civilizational interests than there are discrete spheres of influence. This means less hot war and more jujitsu-like maneuvering in which competitors focus on defense and leverage, allowing an opponent to overextend so it can be knocked off balance.

Asians still have a long way to go in demonstrating regional solidarity. In addition to their military sparring, they willingly shelter and abet their neighbors' most nefarious militant groups: Hamas cells raise funds in Turkey, Indian Naxalite rebels hide in Nepal, Burmese Karen rebels hold a rear base in Thailand, and Pakistan's intelligence services provide refuge to the Afghan Taliban. At the United Nations, Arabs have sought condemnation of Israel and India of Pakistan. Meanwhile, China has denied India's bid to join the UN Security Council and the Nuclear Suppliers Group (NSG) while supporting Pakistan's nuclear program and shielding its terrorists from international sanction.

Still, Asians have thus far avoided the most catastrophic scenarios of international conflict. Though they still don't agree on their maps, they have been able by and large to separate their political and economic objectives. East Asians in particular have realized that their intense economic integration and rising prosperity require geopolitical stability. They do not want to derail the most remarkable mass economic uplifting in human history nor destroy the world-class infrastructure they are presently spending trillions of dollars building. In every instance of bilateral tension and escalation between China and its neighbors, this logic has prevailed. Whatever their differences, therefore, all Asians agree that these tentative moves toward a pan-Asian system are worth pursuing. The lasting solution to security dilemmas is not dependence on foreigners but regional cooperation. It takes decades to build a regional strategic culture and community—but it works.

As their internal diplomacy intensifies, Asian countries' outstanding disputes are much more likely to be solved as neighbors within the Asian system. By tying themselves together through infrastructure, trade, and finance, they are relearning how to share territory and resources as they did in previous eras of porous borders and soft sovereignty. The countries around the Caspian Sea—Russia, Kazakhstan, Turkmenistan, Iran, and Azerbaijan—are close to resolving all outstanding disputes related to the demarcation of the world's largest inland body of water, clearing the way for their shipping and undersea pipeline projects to move forward. Such functional integration makes possible further layers of mutually beneficial Asianization.

How will the United States fare in the next rounds of geopolitical jujitsu? Its historical posture across the region is fading, not least because US leaders and society want to avoid overstretch and entanglements. In West Asia, the failures of policy in Iraq, Afghanistan, and Syria have demonstrated the limits to US influence, costing the country substantial credibility. In East Asia, the "pivot to Asia" failed to materialize as a successor to the Cold War hub-and-spoke alliance system, especially as the United States abandoned the Trans-Pacific Partnership (TPP) trade deal. Asians still hold the United States to be important but also feel that it is unpredictable and even incompetent.

The United States' justifications for remaining tethered to East Asia are weakening due to the incremental reconciliations under

way. Since the 1990s, China has diplomatically cornered Taiwan, ensuring that almost no country in the world recognizes its independence as it becomes ever more dependent on the Chinese economy.
Though the Trump administration has promoted more official visits
and arms transfers with Taiwan, even the island's current nationalist
government has narrowed its political ambitions, focusing instead on
attracting foreign direct investment (FDI) and tourists from beyond
China, launching a new industrial policy around alternative energy,
and even fashioning itself as a Silicon Valley–like tech hub. As with
Japan, the outcome of a conflict with China, even in a scenario of a
US-backed stalemate, would be a severe loss of confidence in Taiwan's security. By the twentieth anniversary of Hong Kong's hando-
ver in 2017, a Taiwanese official commented to me that China had
really become "one country, *three* systems" given how strategically
straitjacketed both Hong Kong and Taiwan are.

Northeast Asia is another theater of reconciliation with major implications for the geopolitical landscape and the United States' role in
it. The US-sponsored dialogue to bring Pacific War antagonists Japan
and South Korea closer has been one of the genuine successes of US
Asian diplomacy. The two countries' shared fear of China also dwarfs
their historical animosity toward each other, nudging them toward
diplomatic closure over Japan's twentieth-century imperial brutality.
Their bilateral agenda has also broadened: Japan would like Korea
to join the TPP trade agreement, while Korea wants Japan to join the
AIIB infrastructure fund. Both moves would give new momentum
to their export credit agencies (ECAs), which push their engineering, computing, telecom, and other leading corporations aggressively
across the region. The next generation is also moving all three societies in the right direction. Several thousand Japanese students are
studying in Korea; they say K-pop has helped them get the hang of
the Korean language. They are joined by growing numbers of Chinese students who have also proved adept at learning Korean. When
the three nationalities encounter one another, they speak a mishmash

of Korean and English. This younger generation across China, Japan, and South Korea harbors only foggy national memories of foreign exploitation and shame, and their ongoing socialization counters the negative perception that the older generations have about one another. They also have no living memory of a United States that has greater claims to exceptionalism than they do. They would much rather work out their differences with their regional peers than depend on the United States to arbitrate them.

North Korea will be the true test of whether Northeast Asia can move from strategic suspicion to tactical adjustments. North Korea has been thought of as an isolated failed state, but the fact that its covert nuclear program has had links as far as Pakistan's A. Q. Khan nuclear-smuggling network, its chemical weapons program to Syria's Bashar al-Assad, its ballistic missile program to Iran, and its cyber-surveillance tools to Russia, are all evidence of the seedier side of the Asian system. Asian states can conspire to form an "axis of resistance" to perceived US hegemony.

South Koreans are largely in favor of reunification with the North, not least because of their proximity to the North and their sympathy for its citizens' plight. They supported both countries marching under a flag of unity (and fielding a joint ice hockey team) in the 2018 Winter Olympics and President Moon Jae-in's overtures to North Korea's Kim Jong-un, including their agreement to formally end the Korean War. Donald Trump's subsequent meeting with Kim Jong-un resulted in the United States' curtailing of military exercises with South Korea in exchange for assurances of North Korean denuclearization. (This has been called the "freeze-for-freeze" or "dual suspension" approach.) At the same time, to make progress with both China and North Korea, South Korean president Moon has been reluctant to move forward with deployment of the United States' Terminal High Altitude Area Defense (THAAD) missile defense system, echoing a Japanese mantra from the 1980s that Korea can "learn to say no" to the United States.[31]

The more North and South Korea, as well as China and Japan, cooperate to manage the emergence of a reunified Korean Peninsula, the less the United States' presence there becomes necessary. North Korean elites will accept reunification only if their security, positions, wealth, and other privileges are guaranteed. Unlike the lustration that purged many knowledgeable apparatchiks in Eastern Europe around the time of the Soviet collapse or the Iraqi de-Baathification after the 2003 US invasion, granting some degree of amnesty to North Koreans who served the regime under fear of execution would ensure that those with administrative backgrounds might continue to be useful.

Together, a unified Korea would go from being the historical kingdom "in between" China and Japan to an even more industrious economic power, rich in agriculture and minerals and with a low-cost labor force to produce Hyundai cars and Samsung phones as technology pours into its special economic zones. Air China flights from Beijing to Pyongyang are full of business opportunists. Both China and Russia have been building the country's ice-free port of Rason. Russia opened a ferry service to Rason in 2017, and China is laying a railway line to it. Even more ambitious, Russia would like to extend the Trans-Siberian Railway from Vladivostok through North Korea's capital, Pyongyang, to South Korea's capital, Seoul. Together, Russia and South Korea are planning gas pipelines, electricity grids, and other projects for North Korea as well. Singaporean urban planners have been consulted on how to resurrect the North's crumbling cities.

The new Asian diplomatic formations will require the United States to update its outdated bureaucratic cartography. Presently, the Pentagon divides Asia between Central Command and Pacific Command (or "Indo-Pacific Command") right along the border between India and Pakistan, but the Belt and Road Initiative and associated pan-Asian linkages render meaningless such arbitrary administrative divisions. The State Department, meanwhile, has at least three separate regional bureaus that cover various parts of Asia: Europe and

Eurasian Affairs, Near Eastern Affairs, and East Asian and Pacific Affairs. These silos were not known for robust coordination even before being gutted by the Trump administration. The most progressive US strategists have talked about the need to balance "heartland" (meaning core inner-Asian) and "rimland" (meaning Pacific maritime) strategies to avoid being overly China-centric, but no single policy move to back this up has been implemented.

Overall, the United States' financial position is weakening as Asians expand local currency borrowing and regional trade rather than depend on the US dollar and US markets. At the same time, the United States' energy and technology position is robust and growing. US oil and liqufied natural gas exports are major contributors to energy security for East Asian countries, while US military hardware and computing software are in high demand as well. US strategic influence in Asia is thus declining even as its economic dependence on Asia is growing. In the age of Asianization, Asia will shape the United States more than the reverse.

4

Asia-nomics

C hina watchers have often been polarized between two views: either China will devour the world or it is on the brink of collapse. Neither view is correct. Despite nonstop observation of China's inner political and economic workings, most outsiders lack a good understanding of China's political economy. Some predicted China's economic free fall after the Western financial crisis, failing to notice that its growing trade with other Asian nations and Europe cushioned it from such a fate. Others warned about its excessive credit to state-owned enterprises, ignoring the government's restructuring efforts and even investor demand to buy up shares in those firms. And those who criticized China for its excess steel capacity failed to catch its move to shift the supply onto its neighbors through the Belt and Road Initiative (BRI). These examples demonstrate that China is not a giant island floating above Asia. Rather, with more neighbors than any other country, it is deeply embedded in the Asian economic system in mutually dependent and beneficial ways. The future is Asian—even for China.

Asia's Third Growth Wave

China's gradual economic deceleration is not a cooling of the Asian story. As China decelerates, others are accelerating. We are entering the third wave of modern Asian growth that began with postwar

Japan and South Korea, followed by greater China (Taiwan and Hong Kong first, then the mainland), and now propelled by South and Southeast Asia. Each wave corresponds to a new set of countries in the demographic sweet spot of economic output, and each represents an ever larger share of Asia's enormous population. In the 1960s and 1970s, Japan and South Korea together had a combined population of less than 150 million. China in the 1990s had just over 1 billion people. Today the swath of high-growth economies from Pakistan through Indonesia encompasses 2.5 billion people, with another 300 million people in West Asia's growth zone spanning the Turkey–Saudi Arabia–Iran triangle. Asia's 5 billion people have an even longer—and larger—growth wave ahead than what they have experienced to date.

Asia's collective resilience represents the cumulative success of five decades of integration driven by Japan, followed by the tiger economies and China. Now another transition is under way as Southeast Asia takes on the mantle of "factory of the world"—a process driven by Japanese, Korean, and even Chinese firms outsourcing to the region. Japan, Korea, and China are high-savings societies, but as their populations get older and spend their savings, their consumption levels are climbing. Much as Japan, Singapore, and South Korea were the largest non-Chinese investors during China's rise, they—as well as China itself—remain the region's most important capital exporters, upgrading developing Asian countries through infrastructure, industry, and technology. Though East Asia still attracts more than half the region's total inbound investment, South and Southeast Asian economies such as India, Thailand, Vietnam, and Indonesia are climbing fast thanks to aging Asia investing in young Asia: South and Southeast Asian countries whose median age is under thirty. Asian growth is thus additive, not substitutive.

Asian wealth is also rising from one generation to the next. According to the HSBC's former chairman Stuart Gulliver, "The American dream of the 21st century is becoming the Asian dream of the 21st: A

MORE YOUNG THAN OLD: ASIA'S BALANCE OF YOUNG AND AGING SOCIETIES IS DRIVING ECONOMIC AND MIGRATION SHIFTS.

The median age in most Asian countries is below thirty, with the exception of aging societies such as Japan, Thailand, South Korea, and China, whose median age is forty or higher. However, owing to its large population, China still has the largest number of people below its median age, giving it and India very large young workforces well into the future. Increased migration from younger to older Asian societies is bridging labor shortages.

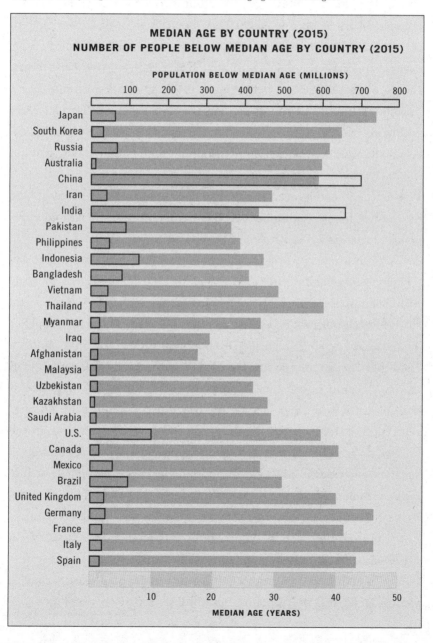

MEDIAN AGE BY COUNTRY (2015)
NUMBER OF PEOPLE BELOW MEDIAN AGE BY COUNTRY (2015)

POPULATION BELOW MEDIAN AGE (MILLIONS)

MEDIAN AGE (YEARS)

house, a car, a smartphone, travel, banking services, health care—the prospect of unfettered upward social mobility for many more families."[1] With greater domestic production of goods and services, weaker currencies, low commodity prices, controlled inflation, and rising intraregional trade, Asians increasingly buy things in their own currencies at much lower prices than Westerners pay in US dollars or euros. Asians can have a good life without being rich in American terms. Indeed, most Asians are not going to catch up to Western per capita incomes. China's per capita income is comparable to that of Russia or Brazil, not the United States or Britain. But that's not the point. Asian societies are focused on maintaining high employment, keeping the cost of living manageable, and promoting access to basic services. Western critics convinced themselves that slower growth would bring down the Chinese regime, but Xi has rightly pivoted the national narrative toward quality growth.

Twentieth-century material ambitions are represented by the American-invented statistical measure of GDP. But growth alone is insufficient to deliver overall well-being. In the twenty-first century, inclusive development has become a better measure of national progress. The recently devised Inclusive Development Index (IDI) takes into account not only economic size but also life expectancy, unemployment, median income, poverty level, inequality rate, household savings, carbon intensity, and other factors. In Asia, Australia and New Zealand rank highest, followed by South Korea and Israel, which rank in the top twenty as well. The next tier of emerging Asian countries is making substantial strides in most categories of inclusive development, including Azerbaijan, Malaysia, Kazakhstan, Turkey, Thailand, China, Iran, Vietnam, Indonesia, and the Philippines. Asia is also home to countries in the bottom tier such as Afghanistan, Pakistan, India, Bangladesh, Cambodia, Laos, and Yemen. According to the Asian Development Bank's Social Protection Index (SPI), South Asia, Southeast Asia, and Central Asia still only spend about half as much on assistance programs for the poor and unemployed as East Asians do. But as the Asian system grows together, so, too, will all its members learn how to pursue inclusive growth and help one another to achieve it.

ASIA BY AIR: THE WORLD'S BUSIEST SKIES

Nine of the ten busiest international airline routes are in Asia. While these are either within the Gulf Cooperation Council (GCC) or within East Asia, the number of daily long-distance connections between Asian subregions is growing rapidly each year.

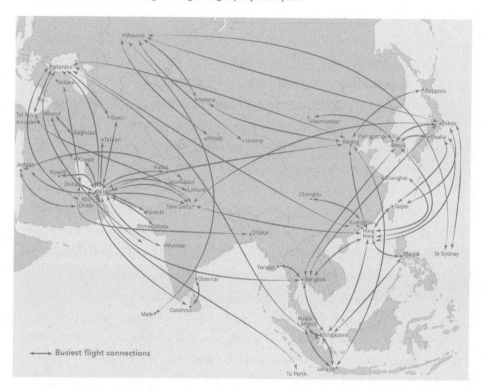

Fitting the Pieces Together

Today the Asian megasystem is coming together like an enormous jigsaw puzzle of dozens of large and small pieces, with economic complementarities creating a whole much greater than the sum of its parts. Since the 1997–98 Asian financial crisis, Asian countries' trade growth with one another advanced at a faster pace than the world economy as a whole. By the time of the 2007–08 Western financial crisis, intra-Asian trade was so robust that it cushioned the shock of falling exports to the United States and European Union. The "global financial crisis" was not actually global. In less than a decade since the crisis, Asia's internal trade as a share of its total trade nearly doubled from 29 percent in 2009 to 57 percent in 2016—nearly the same level as in Europe. Over those two decades, West Asian oil and gas producers were rapidly drawn into this Asian economic system to provide the fuel for East and South Asia's billions, first at high prices and now at lower prices, while also becoming a major market for East Asian goods and investment in their new manufacturing and logistics industries.

Trade has always been heavily regional even as it has globalized. By 2016, Europe still accounted for 30 percent of global trade due to its dense internal market, followed by Northeast Asia with 25 percent, North America with just under 20 percent, Southeast Asia with about 10 percent, and the rest of the world with just over 10 percent.[2] What is new is the extent to which non-Western regions have advanced their trade ties with one another, diminishing their dependence on exports to the United States and European Union. Over the past two decades, Asia's subregions (particularly Northeast Asia, Southeast Asia, South Asia, and West Asia) have gained the greatest share of global trade growth—with North America losing the greatest share. One of the biggest debates in global trade is whether or not developing regions can "decouple" from their historical dependence on the West as a source of investment and a destination for exports. The answer, increasingly, is yes. Asian economies are sufficiently diverse, supplying both mass-produced and high-end goods and services, and have great enough income disparities, that they have the most to gain simply from focusing on meeting one another's growing needs. The trade volumes between any pair of Asian subregions—Southwest Asia, South Asia, Central Asia, Southeast Asia, Northeast Asia—continue to grow faster than the average rate of global trade growth.[3] With major Asian trading nations such as China, India, and South Korea in the Trump administration's crosshairs, Asian countries are collectively accelerating their efforts to boost trade with one another. Indeed, with twenty-eight of the forty-four free-trade agreements proposed since 2013 being between Asian nations, all dyads of intraregional trade are set to expand further.

For several decades, Northeast Asia has formed Asia's main industrial conveyor belt, with a three-way division of labor between Japan, South Korea, and China.[4] Today still, East Asia's main five exporters— China, Taiwan, Hong Kong, Japan, and South Korea (just three countries, technically)[5]—account for $4.2 trillion in annual exports, almost the same as the European Union and North America *combined*. Taiwan's Foxconn was ranked as the third largest technology company in the world by revenue in 2015 and assembles 70 percent of all the world's iPhones, while the same country's Pegatron and Wistron do most of the rest. As China moves aggressively into high-tech areas, it is displacing some Japanese and Korean components with its own. In 2000, China accounted for less than 10 percent of Asia's tech exports; by 2014 it represented 44 percent.[6] Huawei, Lenovo, Haier, and BYD Automobile Company all rank ahead of their Asian peers and Western rivals in categories such as telecom equipment, laptops, appliances, and electric cars. But all three countries remain highly integrated, with China still importing large volumes of Korean and Japanese semiconductors[7] and South Korea still leading in the production of LED displays and memory chips. China is reducing the large deficit it has with both Japan and South Korea, yet all three are keen on passing a trilateral free-trade agreement as the trade volumes between them continue to climb.

Whereas this highly productive Northeast Asian triangle used to export mostly to the West, it is now providing ever more high-quality, low-cost electronics to the rest of Asia. What few outside Asia appreciate is something millions of ordinary Asians realize every day: that importing cheaper goods *from* China and exporting *to* China have raised productivity and competitiveness—so much so that Japan and South Korea have shifted huge volumes of their electronics manufacturing to the lower-wage Southeast Asia, allowing them to cut costs while diversifying into another huge high-growth market. An average Chinese factory worker earns nearly $30 per day, whereas in Indonesia and Vietnam workers still earn less than $10 per day. Japan has been the lead sponsor of ASEAN's industrialization since the 1970s and in recent years has doubled its annual foreign direct investment (FDI) into Southeast Asia to more than $20 billion, fully aware that it is the future market for Nissan's electric and flex-fuel (ethanol and other biofuel) vehicles. South Korea has further catapulted Southeast Asia into the top league of manufacturing by offshoring a broad range of electronics and automotive assembly work. Trade between South Korea and Vietnam is expected to reach $70 billion by 2020, and Samsung alone has $18 billion worth of investments in Vietnam from which its chip output will account for half the company's exports to China. More than 100,000 South Koreans now live in Vietnam. As part of Thailand's Eastern Economic Corridor (EEC) program initiated to boost industries in a historically underdeveloped region, Alibaba in 2018 committed $350 million to establish efficient logistics operations both in Thailand and across its borders with Laos and Cambodia.

Since 2014, as US, European, and even Chinese companies have joined Japan and Korea in outsourcing to ASEAN nations, the region has attracted more annual investment than China.[8] ASEAN's total annual trade amounts to nearly $2.2 trillion, one-quarter of which is within ASEAN, 15 percent with China, and 10 percent with Japan. Since the ASEAN-China Free Trade Area (ACFTA) went into effect in 2000—creating the largest free-trade agreement in the world by population—ASEAN has become China's third largest trading partner with $400 billion in annual trade. Overall, more than 60 percent of ASEAN's trade is within Asia.[9] As highly populous but poorer Asian subregions such as South and Southeast Asia—with a combined population of 2.5 billion people—attain higher incomes, they will take up an ever greater share of East Asian exports and displace Europe and North America as the primary destinations of East Asian goods.

India has bolted itself onto the East Asian growth story. Under Prime Minister Modi, India has embarked on a serious revival of its

"Look East" policy—now called "Act East"—sending commercial delegations to Northeast and Southeast Asia. India's trade with China has grown to $80 billion per year, though it imports six times as much from China as it exports to China. India's trade with ASEAN is growing far faster, projected to double from the present $70 billion annually within the next half decade. India also has nearly $20 billion in trade each with South Korea and Japan, with Modi and Shinzo Abe declaring the bilateral trade in technology goods to be a top priority. India's big push to renew its infrastructure, industries, and cities has spread business activity from traditional centers such as Mumbai, elevating second-tier cities such as Pune and Hyderabad into high-tech and manufacturing hubs. More than one dozen new port projects on India's coasts serve to boost Indian industry's efficient reach to West Asia and Southeast Asia.

AGING INTO COMPLEXITY: AS ASIAN SOCIETIES BECOME OLDER AND WEALTHIER, THEIR ECONOMIES CLIMB THE VALUE CHAIN.

Asia's wealthy and aging societies of Japan, South Korea, and Singapore also have the most complex economies in terms of the value added to their exports. Through their growing wealth and industrial policies, China, Thailand, and Malaysia are rapidly catching up.

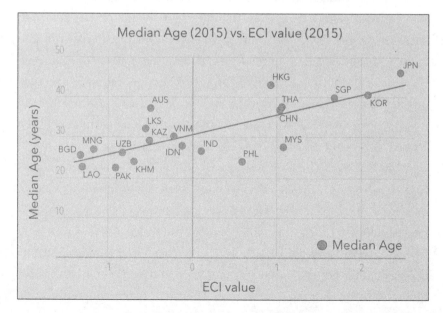

Asia's rapidly modernizing cities are also driving the region's accelerating connectivity. Each subregion of Asia has a growing number of thriving urban hubs: Abu Dhabi, Dubai, Riyadh, and Doha in the Gulf region; Istanbul, Tel Aviv, and Tehran in West Asia; Karachi, Mumbai, Bangalore, and Chennai in South Asia; and all of East Asia and Southeast Asia's metropolises from Tokyo and Shanghai to Bangkok and Ho Chi Minh City to Manila and Jakarta. Additionally, special economic zones from Vietnam to Oman serve as the designated entry and exit points for intermediate and finished goods. Like holes in a weaving board, these nodes enable the threads of commerce that tie Asians closer together from one end of the area to the other. Nine of the ten busiest international flight connections in the world are between Asian cities, with only the pairing of New York and Toronto in North America making it onto the list.[10]

All across Asia, one finds that Asians are now among the most prominent if not the very largest investors.[11] Since 2001, more than half of the $510 billion in foreign investment in Asia has originated within the region. Japan has caught up to and is overtaking Europe as the largest investor in ASEAN, and its investments in India have been doubling annually since 2015, now amounting to $4 billion per year and soon to surpass the United States'. Singapore leads all investors into India with $14 billion in annual FDI. China, too, has become a major investor in India into power, telecom, construction, and other sectors. Though China still lags behind Japan in total investment stock in Asia, it is catching up quickly—especially as it reduces its investments in the United States and raises its commitments in Asia.[12]

This is where the Belt and Road Initiative comes into the picture. China has been reserved about fixed investment in its own neighborhood—until now. Dan Rosen, a veteran China watcher, likens studying China's investment policy to spectrometry: watching the radiation sheds light on its inner character. To avoid having its savings overly concentrated in real estate and banks, China has acquiesced to further capital account opening, which spurred a wave of outbound flows peaking at $225 billion in 2016, at which point it suddenly cracked down on outward investment, instructing companies to end the pursuit of frivolous trophy assets and instead focus on Beijing's strategic priorities. In 2017, then, China's outbound FDI dropped below Japan's $170 billion—but with a much clearer focus on infrastructure in BRI countries. Funds in Beijing and Shanghai are sitting on tens of billions of dollars they have been mandated to invest in their neighbors' high-potential sectors from infrastructure and commodities to banks and telecoms. From Pakistan to the Philippines, China is laying down fiber-optic cables and setting up 5G mobile phone operators for hundreds of millions of people. Most of the world's largest engineering, procurement, and construction (EPC) companies are Asian, with giant contractors in China, South Korea, Japan, India, Turkey, and Saudi Arabia—and all of them want to build across Asia's jigsaw borders.

China already trades three times more with Asian countries than Japan does, making the renminbi ever more attractive as a currency for intra-Asian trade. At present, trade denominated in US dollars is four times greater in volume than the United States' actual share of world trade. Yet with the strong dollar making imports more expensive than they need to be, Asian countries have an incentive to shift away from the dollar. Though the Chinese renminbi is not likely to become a singular currency for Asia, Asian central banks are accumulating renminbi as their trade with China increases. China is intentionally pursuing internationalization to lock partners into renminbi-denominated trade prior to making its currency freely convertible. It aims to have half its trade denominated in renminbi in the near future—a goal that switching oil contracts to renminbi would advance rapidly. China is also strategically pushing blockchain-based currencies so that it can trade in ways that will evade the long arm of the US Treasury Department and its sanctions. Given the rapid advance of these blockchain instruments, it is more likely that all Asian countries will use them to denominate trade with each other than that they will all change to using the renminbi.

Whatever the currency, central banks such as those of Singapore, Australia, and New Zealand have established financial technology ("fintech") bridges to enable seamless cross-border payments with others quickly getting on board. In Asia, money knows very few borders.

Capitalism, Asian Style

Asian countries have no doubt that globalization has been their ticket to prosperity. Even as they become less dependent on Western economies, they are pursuing an "open regionalism" of integrating with one another while expanding trade ties far and wide. US backtracking on trade liberalization (even within its own region through NAFTA) has not diminished Asia's appetite to expand trade with every other world region as well as the United States. Throughout history, "free trade" has been advocated by rising powers with trade surpluses, notably Great Britain in the nineteenth century and the United States in the twentieth. In reality, however, they pursued a neomercantile strategy of import substitution and aggressive government-backed international expansion to achieve their superpower status. Asian powers are no different: they want economic globalization, not free trade.

Asians see the market as a partner, not a master. Asia became such a powerful economic region by applying lessons from the spectacular economic rise of Japan and South Korea through export-oriented, state-directed capitalism, as well as China's usage of special economic zones to attract foreign capital and technology, capital controls to prevent destabilizing short-term financial flows, incremental trade opening to protect key sectors, and industrial policy to stimulate strategic commercial niches and exports. From Russia to Saudi Arabia to Vietnam, state-backed companies ensure national control over critical industrial domains. There are also global champions in every sector. For every commodity China most requires—oil, steel, aluminum, lithium, and so forth—Chinese state-owned enterprises and holding companies have expanded globally and sought dominant stakes in local suppliers. Today the five largest banks in the world by assets are Chinese or

Japanese, led by ICBC, which now operates in sixty countries. Even in capitalist Japan and Korea, generations-old family-run business conglomerates (*keiretsu* in Japan and *chaebol* in Korea) enjoy protections for domestic incumbents.[13] In Korea, the ten biggest *chaebol* account for more than half the stock market's value, with Samsung and its subsidiaries alone representing a third of the market.

Though most Asian economies are more open than China's, they are taking lessons from China's decades of state-capitalist experiments. One major takeaway is that investment-led growth is a winning strategy, even as it flies in the face of Western economic dogma. After China joined the World Trade Organization (WTO) in 1999, its share of GDP derived from exports jumped from 25 percent to 66 percent by 2006. To many outsiders, China has overinvested in industrial output and infrastructure to a fault, generating wasteful overcapacity and littering the country with unnecessary megaprojects. Additionally, China's postfinancial crisis stimulus generated enormous debt, especially in the state-owned financial and industrial sectors, pushing total corporate debt to 170 percent of GDP.[14] But industry and services are not an either-or choice. In fact, hot sectors such as e-commerce depend on the high-quality transportation infrastructure China continues to build. Today exports again represent less than 20 percent of China's GDP and falling, while services represent more than half.[15] There have been and will continue to be many defaults of Chinese companies in nonfinancial sectors, but they are timed to minimize the overall economic and social cost. The government's interventions in credit and currency markets have thus delayed China's recognition as a market economy, but China has managed to achieve macroeconomic stability and maintained a cash pile to use for the next stimulus surge—likely in advance of the 100th-anniversary celebration of the Communist Party in 2021.

Even with the rise of a strong entrepreneurial class, collusion between business and government is common in Asia. In China, the chairman of Fosun International, one of China's largest conglomerates, headquartered in Shanghai and registered in Hong Kong, is an appointee to the Communist Party–run Chinese People's Political Consultative Conference (CPPCC). Even a bootstrapping entrepreneur such as Jack Ma has drawn much closer to the Communist Party, which he has praised as a "clean and honest government," even though it is widely considered the world's largest billionaires' club. In Asia's large capitalist democracies—India, Indonesia, and the Philippines—giant family-run conglomerates still anchor major sectors such as construction, real estate, shipping, commodities trade, banking, and telecoms. The corporate pyramid remains narrow at the top, and tycoons have enormous influence over policy. The Arab and Iranian approach is also a strong mix of the state-capitalist and family conglomerate models, with ministries all but running the industries they regulate and wealthy families controlling key niches in construction, import-export, agriculture, and other areas.

A major reason for this is that private family business remains the backbone of Asian economies. One-fifth of the world's five hundred largest family businesses are located in East Asia,[16] with China and India having the largest number. Eighty-five percent of India's companies are family businesses, representing two-thirds of GDP. The figures are similar for Malaysia and the Philippines. According to McKinsey, family businesses across the region have been growing at more than 20 percent per year over the past decade and using their strong cash positions to invest in joint ventures and new technology that raise the productivity of their home-based workers. Some might call this Confucian capitalism, recognizing the centrality of community—and it is as Chinese as the notion of *guanxi*, or having privileged influence through networks.

Asia now accounts for 30 percent of the world's billionaires, and India has more billionaires than any other country except the United States, China, and Russia. The Gulf countries, Iran, and Turkey add nearly one hundred billionaires to Asia's tally. With 85 percent of Asia's wealthy being first generation, the next two decades will witness one of the largest wealth transfers in history. Asia will soon have more billionaires and millionaires and a larger middle class than any other region. The wealth management industry is thriving in Asia as hundreds of new family offices set up in key cities, with banks often mere custodians. As one executive of a European bank put it, "In the US, American banks face little competition to service wealthy clients. In Europe, both European and American banks compete for the market. And in Asia, European, American, *and* Asian banks are all competing for wealthy customers. All our margins get squeezed, but at the same time it unlocks trillions of dollars of savings to be profitably invested."

Not all of these funds are wisely invested, however. High-growth markets are often the most corrupt, and Asia is no exception. Vietnam, Thailand, India, and Pakistan have the worst corruption rankings in Asia (along with the poorer Myanmar). But the combination of economic pragmatism, more disciplined leadership, and a desire to please investors has converged around significant anticorruption efforts across the region. Whereas in the United States a CEO might destroy corporate value and take his winnings home as a golden parachute and in Europe executives might have to pay fines from their own incomes, in Asia corrupt officials and executives are finally going to jail or being exiled. In China, Xi Jinping's anticorruption drive, despite its political motivations, has tightened the enormous leakage of capital stashed away by party officials and private tycoons. In South Korea, Samsung heir Lee Jae-yong was convicted and jailed in 2017 for making donations in exchange for merger approval, while president Park Geun-hye was impeached that same year and then convicted in 2018 on corruption charges and sentenced to twenty-four years in prison. Across ASEAN—most recently in Thailand and Malaysia—leaders have been sacking ministers for taking kickbacks, independent anticorruption investigative divisions are being allocated more resources, and corporate governance scorecards are being released to the public. India's prime minister Modi has cracked down on fuzzy accounting and offshore shell companies, while in Pakistan, the Panama Papers revelations forced Pakistan's prime minister, Nawaz Sharif, to resign in 2017.

As Asia gradually evolves from economies based on relationships to ones governed by rules and institutions, authorities will continue to steer markets toward national development. This is because Asians widely hold the view that markets should be subordinate to overall societal well-being, rather than held up as ends in themselves. Unlike in the West, Asian societies remain proglobalization *because* their governments are actively steering it in their favor. From India to Vietnam, surveys show support for globalization topping 80 percent (compared to less than 40 percent in the United States and France). The figures are similar when it comes to support for capitalism—which is ironic given the socialist history of major Asian nations. Rising antifinance and anti-high-tech sentiments in the United States are indicative of an ideological convergence toward the Asian point of view that banks and tech giants should not be allowed free rein to exploit consumers. Rather, they should be subservient to the state and serve broader societal needs, whether fiscal stability, job creation, infrastructure upgrading, skills training, or other objectives. The more Western governments bail out and prop up industries such as finance and manufacturing, the more their systems come to resemble Asian-style capitalism in practice, if not in theory.

Related to this, Asians learned in the 1990s to be suspicious of Anglo-American-style deregulated financial capitalism. Instead, they subscribe to the view that fiscal redistribution drives equitable growth, rather than the orthodox capitalist view that growth in itself results in redistribution. According to the IMF, reducing inequality requires higher taxes and more public investment, not less. Many Asian countries are therefore not hesitating to use macroeconomic levers such as lower interest rates, countercyclical investment, aggressive public spending, and higher taxes to promote greater equity and create jobs. Good public transportation, housing, electricity, sanitation, and other basics are crucial to a decent quality of life. Economic reforms cannot come at the price of high unemployment and social cohesion. China's government worries about the fate of workers displaced by robots and the profits that will accrue to firms that can cut head count while boosting output—but rather than let them offshore billions in profits, it taxes and takes shares in them to raise capital from their growth. Indonesia is steadily expanding its tax-to-GDP ratio to reach 20 percent by 2020.[17]

Asians have also taken on board IMF recommendations of "macro-prudential measures" such as the Basel III regulations that require high bank-deposit-to-lending ratios, sound loan-to-value ratios in property markets, and preferential lending to small and medium-sized enterprises (SMEs)—all steps that have helped Asians graduate from IMF support and protect themselves from the financial domino effects of crises generated elsewhere.[18] Meanwhile, the United States and numerous Western economies ignore the IMF wisdom they once dispensed. Yet Asian interest rates now move more in tandem with one another than with that of the United States, allowing them to push on with monetary and fiscal coordination. When Asian countries such as Turkey need strategies to contain inflation and stabilize their currencies, they look to India and Indonesia. The United States is gradually learning to move beyond its fixation on interest rates and focus more on boosting investment. In the words of the former UBS banker and LSE risk management professor Lutfey Siddiqi, "We are all Asians now."

From Underwriting the United States to Financing Asia

Foreign capital from the United States and Europe was a critical driver of Asia's economic ascent during the first and second waves of East Asian growth, from Japan's economic miracle to China's breakneck industrialization. East Asians then lent their prodigious savings to the United States and Europe in the form of buying their Treasury bonds. Asian capital thus became a driver of the US dollar's stability and status as a global reserve currency. China and Japan remain the two largest foreign holders of US Treasuries, with more than $1 trillion each, and Hong Kong and Taiwan also rank in the top ten with nearly $200 billion each in US dollar reserves. All of the top ten foreign holders of US dollar reserves—including Saudi Arabia, South Korea, India, and Singapore—are Asian economies, collectively holding more than 55 percent of US Treasuries.[19]

Furthermore, Asian foreign investment in the US economy, led by Japan, totals more than $1 trillion (compared to Europe's $2 trillion FDI in the United States), especially in industries such as energy, manufacturing, and real estate. Asian investors have helped keep oil pumping in the shale patches of Texas when prices slumped. Both the China Investment Corporation (CIC) and Korea Investment Corporation (KIC) allocate more than 50 percent of their public equity portfolios to US equities, and GIC Private Limited of Singapore (formerly known as Government of Singapore Investment Corporation) invests 34 percent of its assets in North America. Asian financing will also be essential to underwrite the long-term debt needed to fund the United States' infrastructure renewal. Saudi Arabia's Public Investment Fund (PIF) committed $20 billion to a $40 billion Blackstone fund devoted to US infrastructure.

Yet a great diversion of capital is under way as Asians refocus on investing in Asia (and Europe) rather than in the United States. Amid mounting bilateral tensions, Chinese investment in the United States fell by 90 percent in 2018. And as the United States' debt rises and Asian trade within Asia and with Europe grows far faster than that with the United States, Asians' appetite for US Treasuries is waning. As their societies age and their savings rates come down, East Asian countries' purchases of US Treasuries have plateaued. Arab central banks have been selling dollars to prop up their reserves, stimulate the domestic economy, and fund transitions away from oil dependence.

Instead of underwriting the US dollar, Asians are gaining confidence in investing in their own debt and capital markets. For decades, most Asian nations (with the notable exception of Japan) lacked sufficiently mature financial markets to absorb the region's enormous savings, which were instead recycled into London and New York. But the financial crisis laid bare how much US banks rely on financial engineering rather than underlying fundamentals to generate growth. For their part, Europeans feel burned by their purchases of US subprime mortgage debt and are less inclined to borrow short-term US dollars only to recycle them back into US consumer debt, plus they still need to worry about their own banking sector's solvency. Asian economies have managed to ride out the past decade of Western financial volatility and rising US interest rates. Each time the United States has raised interest rates, Western economists have predicted a "taper tantrum" in Asian currency markets. But these portfolio-capital outflows don't disturb the enormous and growing availability of capital for Asians to borrow.[20] Asians have spent two decades building currency swap lines to enhance their access to liquidity in the event of crisis.[21] These efforts have made available trillions of dollars' worth of liquidity for central banks to use as a cushion should the need arise.

To avoid the growing risk of high US dollar–denominated debt, many Asian governments are issuing large amounts of sovereign debt in their own currencies rather than US dollars, with investors lining up to buy. China accounts for about half of Asia's debt issuance.[22] Foreigners own only about 2 percent of China's sovereign debt, but China has indicated that it would be comfortable with about 15 percent foreign holdings and has given the green light to offshore renminbi "panda bonds" being issued by banks such as the United Kingdom's Standard Chartered. This could mean an additional $3 trillion in liquidity by 2025 to support China's continuing investments at home and abroad.[23] China's deleveraging is an opportunity for foreign investors: the crackdown on excessive bank borrowing, shadow banking, and even microlending has opened the door to foreign financial institutions to provide loans to Chinese customers. China's new central bank governor is pushing through reforms that will lift restrictions (with promises to eliminate them) on the percentage of joint ventures foreigners can own and caps on foreign stakes in Chinese financial firms, while allowing qualified foreigners to invest in A-class shares.

Saudi Arabia and the UAE have also raised tens of billions of dollars in bond offerings while cutting subsidies to trim their budget deficits. In 2017, the Philippines issued a popular twenty-five-year bond offering, nearly half of which was taken up by European investors, with one-third going to Asians and the remainder to Americans. Overall,

with Asian governments holding most of their own debt in local currencies rather than US dollars (except for Indonesia), they can keep interest
rates low and deleverage passively. And with high growth and savings,
most Asian economies can comfortably manage their current levels of
debt servicing. This is why most of Asia doesn't belong in the antiquated
catchall category of "emerging markets" with countries such as Argentina that are perpetually on international life support by the IMF.

Other significant measures are harbingers of deeper Asian financial
integration. Asia's cross-border portfolio investment surged fourfold
from $3 trillion in 2001 to more than $12 trillion in 2015, yet still only
20 percent of cross-border portfolio investment is intraregional (versus
60 percent in Europe).[24] Even though financial services remains a strategically protected sector in most of Asia, financial jurisdictions are
harmonizing regulations so that derivatives can be traded and cleared
on regional platforms, banks have greater access to operate in each
other's markets, stock exchanges are connecting, disclosure standards
are converging so companies can raise debt and equity more easily
across borders, and regulators are granting fund managers pan-Asian
"passports" to attract investment.[25]

These moves have supported an enormous expansion in Asia's
corporate bond markets. Traditionally, bond markets have provided
less than 20 percent of Asian corporate financing, far behind that provided by banks and equity. (Banks alone have represented as much
as 80 percent of total corporate debt in East Asia.) Furthermore,
Asians have preferred to invest in their own markets through "round-
tripping," meaning deferring to Western fund managers who allocated
far more to Western stocks than regional markets. But in the coming
years, Asian savings will flow far more into Asian investments than
into Western ones. The value of the US stock market doesn't reflect
underlying fundamentals of growth, nor does the weight of US companies in the MSCI World Index, which is currently greater than the US
GDP. Meanwhile, for Japan, China, and India, the ratio of equities to
GDP lies between 40 and 70 percent. Given the size of Asia's financial,

industrial, and technology conglomerates, there is enormous scope for them to securitize their assets. Asian bond markets are now expanding at a rate of 25 percent per year. Hong Kong's Hang Seng Index was the best-performing of 2017, while that same year the US Standard & Poor's 500 Index was only the thirty-third best-performing in the world. Most forecasters predict that Asian stock exchanges will deliver the highest growth in the decade ahead. Also, Asian ratings agencies have emerged in response to their Western counterparts' crisis of legitimacy, providing more robust data for investors looking to allocate more capital to Asia. Analysts project China's asset management industry to grow from today's $3 trillion to $15 trillion by 2025 based on the assumption that families will invest 10 percent of their household savings in financial assets (versus 4 percent today), while ASEAN's asset management industry should reach $4 trillion. From banks and breweries to construction companies and real estate, more and more ASEAN companies are launching IPOs.

Asian countries have eased their extreme caution about opening their capital accounts to foreign portfolio capital inflows, and Western investors are rushing in. Within two decades, Asian companies have gone from being dependent on borrowing from Western banks to becoming those banks' most coveted clients for their IPOs. Alibaba's 2014 IPO in New York was the largest in history at $25 billion, and Asian tech IPOs such as Singapore's SEA Group and China's Rise Education have become critical to generating the fees Wall Street banks crave. China now has more than fifty "unicorn" companies with billion dollar–plus valuations (slightly less than the United States), while India has about a dozen and ASEAN just under ten, with many more such pre-IPO companies gathering steam.

The global asset management industry is only about 5 percent exposed to Asia, something Western institutional investors—from asset managers and pension funds to family offices—are scrambling to correct as they search for high-yield fixed-income investments such as Asian currencies, sovereign debt, and corporate bonds. Tencent, Alibaba, and Baidu already rank among the largest companies in the world by market cap, but their rapid expansion of customer base and services makes them attractive as core elements of a Western retiree's portfolio to augment the struggling blue-chip companies such as GE and HP. Now that MSCI includes both Chinese and Saudi Arabian domestic shares in its emerging-markets index, trillions of dollars worth of active and passive funds will expand their Asian portfolios. China has launched Bond Connect and Stock Connect programs to encourage global investors to come into its financial sector. The Shanghai-based Lufax has opened an offshoot in Singapore specifically to partner with foreign investors seeking exposure to China's fintech market. With Saudi Aramco deciding to launch the majority of its listed shares on Riyadh's stock exchange (rather than in New York, London, or Hong Kong), many foreign institutional investors will raise their self-imposed limits on buying Asian equities.

The same goes for emerging- and frontier-market indices, which are dominated by Bangladesh, Vietnam, and other large-population Asian countries. When MSCI upgraded Pakistan from frontier-market to emerging-market status in 2016, the trading volume of MSCI's Pakistan ETF tripled and its value has been rallying steadily since. Then there was an intense competition to buy the Karachi Stock Exchange (now part of the Pakistan Stock Exchange), whose top one hundred companies have collectively returned 20 percent annually. The Shanghai Stock Exchange bought a 40 percent stake in the Karachi Stock Exchange (and a large stake in the Dhaka Stock Exchange as well). Asia is underpriced given rising demand and lower-than-perceived risk. Recent rating downgrades have spurred a necessary restructuring across Asian markets while also suppressing stock prices and price-to-earnings multiples, creating attractive buying opportunities. Across Asia, stock exchanges that have had only basic listings are now offering far more attractive public equities in telecoms, banks, real estate, technology, and other sectors. They also increasingly demand rigorous reporting on corporate governance, more independent directors, and compliance with environmental and social standards. Both shareholder and stakeholder interests are being taken into account.

Shifting toward flexible currency exchange rates has given Asian governments more room to maneuver and made their markets more attractive. Weaker economies used to try to control their currency value like a game of Monopoly in which the cash can't be used on any other board. When I first went to Uzbekistan nearly twenty years ago, both my jacket and pants pockets were stuffed with wads of the nearly worthless soum. Now the currency is convertible and stable, and Uzbekistan's growth rate of 8 percent is one of the world's highest. Arab and Asian investors are flying into and out of Tashkent weekly, looking to invest in real estate and other sectors. The demise in 2016 of the country's Soviet-era strongman, Islam Karimov, has been followed not by chaos but by economic pragmatism in the mold of its larger but less populous neighbor Kazakhstan. From India to Vietnam to Mongolia, numerous Asian countries have recently put themselves through painful currency reforms that have paved the way for economic stability and heightened investor interest.

This surge of Asian and global capital into the region will bridge the large gap in lending to "Main Street" businesses serving billions of Asians. So, too, will nontraditional or alternative lending models such as peer-to-peer (P2P) and balance-sheet lending. China's 2,200 P2P lenders (led by Dianrong, the Lending Club of China) comprise a market valued at $100 billion. In India, P2P lending is estimated to reach $8.8 billion by 2020. Similar operations are growing fast in Southeast Asia. But with Asian banks, nonbank financial institutions, and fintech representing a rapidly growing share of global financial assets and new regulations relatively untested, Asia could be the next epicenter of a global financial crisis. Westerners therefore need to better understand how Asian regulations and restrictions operate. Many Western fund managers scrutinize Asian corporate investor calls just as closely as they monitor Warren Buffett's Berkshire Hathaway shareholder meetings.

Asian governments have realized that privatizing state-owned companies will also lead to substantial new inflows of investment into Asian assets, bringing in capital to serve the needs of burgeoning populations in ways they can no longer afford alone. Countries are selling off assets to compensate for low oil prices, demonstrate the discipline necessary to attract greater foreign investment, or both. They are recycling assets, leasing old infrastructure to private investors and using the revenues to finance new infrastructure, thus avoiding raising taxes. The Gulf economies still depend on oil revenues to finance their spending, but to provide the capital necessary to boost their economies they need to fund long-term economic diversification. Saudi Arabia's national oil, mineral, and engineering companies have crowded out the private sector since the country's 1970s oil boom, paying wages so high that nobody wanted to be an entrepreneur. But as the country cracks down on the royal family's profligacy and strategizes a shift from merely pumping oil to producing exports, private enterprise will grow. Iran, too, is privatizing as it seeks to reduce the dominant role of corrupt and inefficient Islamic Revolutionary Guard Corps–linked companies. India, Thailand, and the Philippines are privatizing everything from airlines to dairies to casinos to raise capital and stimulate commercial activity in industrial and services sectors. As in China, India's very high levels of corporate debt (both financial and nonfinancial) are forcing the government to relax foreign investment regulations and accelerate privatization, which together should lead to better corporate governance. India is also reforming outdated policies such as bankruptcy laws by setting a timeline for liquidating failed companies so the private sector can restructure without government delays or devoting resources to unnecessary bailouts.

Even in state-capitalist systems such as China, Russia, and Vietnam, inefficient state-owned companies are being restructured to list shares for investors and be more independently run. China has successfully used its State-owned Assets Supervision and Administration Commission (SASAC) to restructure many state-owned entities (SOEs) in shipbuilding, steel, machinery, electronics, and other areas into functional (and even profitable) entities. The result is not fully private companies but rather Singapore-style government-linked companies (GLCs) in which state-financed investment funds have large stakes. Asia's mixed capitalism is evolving from backstopping inefficient behemoths to supporting firms' acquisition of competitors and their technologies. The Chinese government has encouraged major companies such as Baidu and Alibaba to buy substantial stakes in China Unicom and other state-owned companies and bring in their technological know-how to retool them to be better performers. This is how Asia's oligopolies of oversized conglomerates are making way for a new generation of firms operating across the traditional boundaries of finance and technology.

Following the Singapore model, other Asian countries are wisely seeking investment and technology from foreign investors rather than tax revenues. FDI across Asia is creating hundreds of thousands of jobs annually in electronics, information technology, and automotive, real estate, and business services, raising productivity and adding value across the economy. There are many anchor tenants now in Asia's skyscrapers, from Riyadh to Shanghai. This has attracted the global private equity (PE) industry to Asia, which has already surpassed Europe as the second largest destination for private equity (just behind the United States), with one-fourth of all global PE capital devoted to the region.[26] Four of the world's largest PE funds are Asian—SoftBank's Vision Funds in Japan, China State-Owned Capital Venture Investment Fund, the Sino-Singapore Connectivity Private Equity Fund Management Company, and the China Internet Investment Fund—each with $100 billion–plus in capital to deploy. Baring Private Equity Asia (BPEA) is the regional veteran and the largest Asian PE fund fully based in Asia, with forty companies in its portfolio. US PE firms have been doubling annually the number of deals they complete in Asia. The American PE fund KKR has bought fifteen companies in Asia since 2016 across the education, financial services, health care, insurance, and hospitality sectors. TPG, another US fund, has expanded its Asia portfolio to thirty-seven companies in the same sectors as well as real estate, tech, and energy. Bain Capital also has significant investments in Asia, including Japan Wind Development Company (JWD). European funds such as EQT have been investing in Asia for over a decade, with the Swiss-based Partners Group raising its Asia portfolio to 17 percent of its total and rising with each new investment. Western and Asian funds are also collaborating to upgrade and expand regional businesses. In 2017, the New York–based Global Infrastructure Partners and China Investment Corporation (CIC) together bought a portfolio of Asian wind and solar energy projects from Singapore-based Equis for $3.7 billion. As the luster comes off post-Brexit London, Indian industrial magnates who sell their plants to Singaporeans or other Asian investors have been parking their huge payouts in Dubai.

As Asian companies professionalize and scale region-wide in logistics, tourism, real estate, and outsourcing, they are expanding well beyond their home markets. The fastest-growing vectors of sales are Asians to Asians. India's $100 billion software market caters to Western tech giants such as Microsoft and SAP but also competes with them as Tata Consultancy Services (TCS) and Infosys provide affordable quality IT services worldwide. Price and taste play important roles as well. McDonald's and KFC, for example, have enormously successful food outlets in the United States and worldwide, but in the Philippines, neither can dislodge the fried chicken chain Jollibee, which has three times as many outlets as KFC and lines stretching around the corners—all the while expanding across Southeast Asia and the Gulf, where it competes with both of them (as well as opening several restaurants in the United States). Vitasoy, a small Hong Kong company that began selling soy milk to combat malnutrition, now operates in forty countries. Western retailers salivate at the prospects of Asia's urbanizing middle-class consumers, but China's 400 million millennials aren't nearly as attracted to Western brands as their parents. The more than 1 billion South and Southeast Asians who aspire to own refrigerators are buying them from Haier, LG, and Godrej. Simply put: Asians are buying far more Asian goods.

Though this is worrying for Western companies, it makes Asia much more attractive for the venture capital (VC) industry. Though Silicon Valley is still a first mover in many domains, it represents only 17 percent of annual global VC spending. In 2016, US venture investment fell by $10 billion to $76 billion.[27] Meanwhile, according to PricewaterhouseCoopers, in 2017 Asia had more investment in tech start-ups than the United States did. US VCs are part of the reason why. Many of the biggest, such as Sequoia Capital and Accel, have planted roots in Asia to branch out beyond the mature and overhyped US market. Their presence has inspired Asia-focused VCs, such as Golden Gate Ventures and East Ventures, while government-backed Asian funds have taken stakes in Silicon Valley incubators and accelerators, as Abu Dhabi Financial Group has done with the San Francisco–based 500 Startups. This rise of ever more regional start-ups has compelled Asian sovereign wealth funds such as Singapore's GIC to increase their Asian tech portfolios beyond their superstar investments Alibaba and Xiaomi. The Boston-based tech PE firm TA Associates had zero international staff a decade ago, but now half its employees and investments are outside the United States, especially from Mumbai to Hong Kong.

Talent is also in ever greater circulation between the West and Asia and within the region itself. When Pavel Durov, often referred to as Russia's Mark Zuckerberg, moved the communications app Telegram out of Russia, he shifted operations to Dubai and Singapore. The Singaporean Yinglan Tan, a graduate of Carnegie Mellon, was until recently the venture capital fund Sequoia Capital's lead partner covering Southeast Asia and India before he left to launch his own frontier tech-focused fund called Insignia Venture Partners, for which he had more than $100 million in commitments within weeks. "Today the perfect pan-Asian tech company," Yinglan tells me, "has a Singaporean headquarters, Taiwanese engineers, Vietnamese UX designers, Indonesia as its target market—and IPOs in Hong Kong." By operating inside Asia, he also knows that even though the United States and China are leading deep tech innovation, the other Asian countries are not vassals. Instead, local joint ventures are crucial to harnessing big data and making it relevant for building new products and services. The Jakarta-based e-commerce company Sale Stock Indonesia is using artificial intelligence (AI) to figure out how to cut costs on products that don't sell well by screening out designs that an algorithm designates as likely to fail.

Though many Western economists have portrayed Asia's rise as merely catching up with the West, it could well be that Asia is leapfrogging it. Asia no longer faces deficiencies in the money, technology, or talent needed to fund and scale companies in any industry. An older generation of Asians has been accustomed to receiving Western technology and having to figure out how it could suit their needs. But today Asians are focused on finding Asian solutions to Asian problems. Rather than copying Silicon Valley firms, Indians now take lessons from Chinese tech companies. Shailendra Singh, the managing director of Sequoia Capital India, says that his industry has never seen wider or deeper investment opportunities for tech leapfrogging. The start-up CeeSuite has automated the investment banking lifecycle for the vast pool of regional SMEs that could never afford Wall Street banks. Its founders are also creating a virtual accelerator that digitizes the stages and lessons of the start-up process, from crowd-funding investment through initial coin offerings (ICOs) and blockchain-based business models. Cybersecurity companies are thriving in Singapore and expanding from there. Asians are learning and adapting as much or more from each other as from the West.

The ride-sharing industry is emblematic of how Western companies are losing out to local rivals for both strategic and cultural reasons. As recently as 2015, it seemed as though Uber was taking over the world. But thanks to SoftBank's consistent support for a suite of Asian car-sharing firms—Didi Chuxing (DiDi) in China, GrabShare in Southeast Asia, and Ola Cabs in India—Uber's valuation dropped below that of DiDi, which bought Uber's China operations (after which SoftBank bought Uber shares at a discount).[28] In Russia, Uber was subsumed by Yandex.Drive; in Southeast Asia, Uber sold its operations to Grab-Share, which took another $1 billion in investment from Toyota. Now DiDi is expanding into Brazil, Ola Cabs (in which DiDi has invested) is moving into Australia, and Careem leads in the Gulf region. These Asian firms collectively own the Asian space while challenging Uber everywhere else. In many Asian cities, Uber is no longer the market leader but a transport solutions partner for indigenous champions. In stark contrast to Uber founder Travis Kalanick, DiDi founder Jean Liu—one of fifty recently minted billionaire Chinese females—is considered a nurturing mentor to her regional peers. Grab CEO Anthony Tan has said, "There's this sense of brotherhood, that we're in this battle together. Let's show them the power of Asia."[29]

Feeding and Fueling Asia

Autarky, not conquest, is the holy grail of geopolitics. Countries and regions that achieve self-sufficiency in natural resources, agriculture, industries, and technology can liberate themselves from the risks of foreign dependency. North America is self-sufficient in oil and gas, while Europe is striving for alternative and renewable power to substitute for its dependence on Russia's hydrocarbons. The more Asian economies integrate, the better they, too, will be able to pursue autarky.

Energy has been one of Asia's greatest sources of both economic and geopolitical vulnerability. Yet even as Asia's energy consumption rises, the risk of energy competition sparking conflict has been reduced due to the diversification of supplies and the rise of alternatives and renewables. East Asia alone consumes 80 percent of the world's liquefied natural gas (LNG) but, lacking a natural gas production and distribution infrastructure, the region has paid prices twice as high as in Europe and four times higher than in the United States. But as Qatar's LNG flows eastward, Russian natural gas is delivered to China and the Pacific, and Australia (thanks to Japanese investment) is overtaking Qatar as the world's leading natural gas supplier, Asians will get more and cheaper energy. In late 2018, Shell, together with partners from Malaysia, China,

Japan, and Korea, announced the construction of a massive LNG facility on Canada's western coast that will deliver gas to Asia in just eight days, versus twenty from the US Gulf Coast. Singapore's Keppel leads the world in the construction of offshore oil rigs and in 2017 deployed the world's first floating gas liquefaction vessel to cater to growing global LNG demand. Asian countries are also ramping up investments in all energy sources from oil and gas to nuclear, wind, and solar power.

Since Asia consumes most of the world's fuel, minerals, and food, it is only natural that commodities are traded in Asia as well. Ten trillion dollars of the global economy is made up of commodities production and consumption, and Asia now consumes more than half the world's supplies of coal, aluminum, nickel, copper, and zinc, as well as cotton, rubber, and palm oil, and imports most of the world's iron ore and other key ingredients of steel production. In the 1980s, 80 percent of the world's gold trade took place between the United States and the European Union, whereas today most gold is traded within India and China.[30] In recent decades, Western firms and markets have dominated the commodities trade, especially in mining, where Western cartels held an oligopoly of both pricing and regulatory power. But the playing field is leveling. Singapore has become the second largest physical trading hub for commodities, handling bulk buying, shipping, and storage contracts. The regulatory environment has matured to handle derivatives for commodities futures and risk management, as well as debt markets to finance production and trading activities. This has given Asians more confidence to exercise legal leverage within the commodities industry. In a recent dispute between the mining giant BHP and China, Singapore was chosen as the site for arbitration.

Because the main fuel-consuming sectors in Asia are steel production, industrial manufacturing, and transportation, Asia on the whole is not yet anywhere near a green energy landscape. The Gulf states, Iran, and Russia are among the world's largest oil and gas producers, with Emiratis and Qataris annually releasing more emissions per capita from their jeeps and air-conditioning than nearly any other country in the world. Meanwhile, China and India are two of the world's top three aggregate energy consumers (the United States ranks second). China continues to build coal-powered electricity plants at home—fueled partly by US coal exports to China—as well as abroad in Pakistan and Iran. Most of the world's largest coal-producing companies (and coal power financing banks) are Chinese, while most of the world's most squalid cities—Karachi, Mumbai, Delhi, and Dhaka—are in South Asia. Calcutta now ranks as India's most polluted city, and nationwide more than 2.5 million deaths each year are attributable to pollution (versus 1.8 million in China).[31]

ASIA'S RESOURCE SYSTEM

Asia is the largest producing and consuming region of the world for both food and energy. As more efficient agricultural techniques take hold and infrastructure linkages expand, Asian countries will be better able to compensate for droughts and crop failure and meet one another's food import needs, as well as meet the region's growing energy demand.

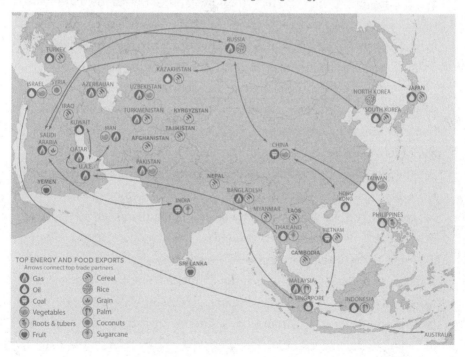

TOP ENERGY AND FOOD EXPORTS
Arrows connect top trade partners

- Gas
- Oil
- Coal
- Vegetables
- Roots & tubers
- Fruit
- Cereal
- Rice
- Grain
- Palm
- Coconuts
- Sugarcane

But Asia is also joining Europe in taking aggressive measures to reduce environmental degradation, though the challenge is on a far greater scale. In China, coal and oil are peaking as a share of energy production.[32] China is spending more than $100 billion per year on non–fossil fuel energy and is aiming at acquiring 15 percent of its total energy consumption from such alternative and renewable sources by 2020. Hydropower represents 80 percent of the country's renewable power and 70 percent of its new power-generating capacity. Wind power is a much lower share at 12 percent but growing fast.[33] More than 2 million people work in the solar-power industry in China compared with 200,000 in the United States, installing solar panels on buildings and even on new highway surfaces. In 2015, State Grid Corporation of China provided continuous power from only renewable sources to the 5 million residents of Qinghai province for a full week. With the help of Western architects and designers, China is deploying smog-eating towers that suck in smog and pump out purified air, recycling the captured waste into products such as jewelry, and smog-eating bicycles that release clean air with each turn of the pedal. China is also implementing European-style cap-and-trade carbon market schemes in the most industrialized provinces.

In addition to industrial output, transportation is among the first targets of any government serious about cleaning up its environmental footprint. China has set a target for 40 percent of the residents of its megacities to use public transportation by 2020, with slightly lower percentages targeted for big, medium, and small cities that have less congestion. It has also mandated that all automotive companies—foreign and local—sell electric cars or risk being banned from selling diesel vehicles. Just as Europe has done for decades in demanding high product safety standards to access its markets, China's powerful regulatory signals have jolted the global automotive industry. When the Trump administration pulled the United States out of the Paris climate agreement, California governor Jerry Brown led a delegation of states representing half of the US GDP to Beijing to sign a declaration pledging their commitment to the goals.

India's later start at industrialization has allowed it to focus on clean energy inputs into its growing manufacturing sector. Like China, India has plans for dozens of new nuclear reactors and solar farms. Renewable power grew from 2 percent of the country's energy supply in 2012 to 13 percent by 2015, with the industry on course to produce nearly 200 gigawatts of renewable power by 2022. For the 250 million Indians who still lack electricity or suffer from power outages during summer heat waves, the government is accelerating new solar-power and biomass projects.

The sooner China and India transition to alternative energy, the less fossil fuel they will import from West Asia. As oil and gas prices decline, therefore, Asia's largest energy producers are themselves accelerating their green transitions so that they can maximize their export revenues and spend less on domestic fuel subsidies they can no longer afford. With funding from Japan's SoftBank, Saudi Arabia and the UAE are investing in carbon-neutral eco-cities and 200-gigawatt solar farms. China and Malaysia have together captured two-thirds of the global solar panel market, reducing the price of production by 90 percent. Batteries are another area in which Asian dominance has brought down global prices. China, Japan, and Korea together account for more than 90 percent of the world's lithium-ion battery production, giving them an edge in powering their growing fleets of electric cars.[34] China's BYD Automobile Company is by far the largest electric car maker in the world and has recruited Warren Buffett as an investor and Leonardo DiCaprio as its poster boy. It is even making the next generation of double-decker buses for London. China is Tesla's second largest market, but its market share is minuscule and will be further challenged by start-ups such as NIO, whose models sell at half the price of a Tesla and offer battery-swap stations nationwide. Ultimately, Tesla will wind up like Apple in China, an accessory for the well-off rather than a mass-market vehicle. Looking forward, Japan's recent discovery of massive undersea rare earth mineral deposits will enable it to produce even lower cost batteries and other electronics for its customers worldwide—including Tesla, for which Panasonic is the main battery supplier.

All Asians now accept the evidence that "green growth" is not an oxymoron. One by one, Asian cities are making their way toward the virtuous circle of public-private financing for clean energy and transport, lower electricity costs and reduced government subsidization, and job creation in erecting eco-efficient buildings and deploying smart sensors and meters. China's Suning is building new low-energy data centers in all its business hubs. Hanoi, the city where today you are most likely to get hit by a motorcycle, plans to ban motorcycles and build a subway by 2030. The Philippines has begun to install tidal-power plants to harness oceanic wave energy that will allow entire islands such as Capul to be powered entirely off grid. And Adelaide, Australia, which over the past decade has transitioned to generating more than half its energy supply from renewables while promoting local agriculture through wastewater irrigation, has much to teach the rest of Asia about maximizing urban resources.

Asia is the world's largest food-producing and -consuming region, but few Asian countries use the modern machinery, irrigation techniques, and fertilizers required to get the most out of their farms. China's major agribusiness companies now have modern food-processing plants to raise production, setting the stage for their expansion across Asia. China is also erecting entire towns of Spanish-like greenhouses to produce fresh fruit year-round. Rudimentary land rights and farm cooperatives would also enable more of Asia's nearly 2 billion rural inhabitants to take out adequate loans to invest in better-quality seeds and tools for crop cleaning and packaging. India is using aerial surveys, satellites, and drones to complete a nationwide Digital India Land Records Modernization Programme (DILRMP) that will quickly qualify farmers for such services. With India's extensive investments in agricultural output and rural development—and the infrastructure to connect farmers to markets—Prime Minister Modi hopes to double farmers' incomes by 2022.

Asia's diverse fertile zones—from the Tigris and Euphrates to the Brahmaputra and Ganges to the Mekong and Yellow rivers—are being subsumed into a pan-Asian environmental system. The dry belt spreading from Iraq and Syria through Iran and Pakistan makes Western Asia increasingly reliant on food imports from as far away as Russia and South Korea. India has as much arable land as the United States (each 12 percent of the world's total) and more than China (which has 9 percent), making its agricultural modernization a key factor in feeding Asia. Yet China's diversions of the Brahmaputra River headwaters in Tibet have had significant consequences for the entire Gangetic civilization, much as its damming of the upper Mekong River has affected the agricultural production cycles of much of Southeast Asia. Meanwhile, China's overconsumption and pollution of its major rivers could speed up nascent plans to divert Russia's mighty rivers southward toward China's cities and farmland.

Asia has the largest number of megacities facing water shortages from overconsumption. Some Chinese cities are projected to run out of clean water by 2020.[35] India faces a crisis of water tables falling nationwide; Iranian protests have been spreading as taps run dry. Across the region, trillions of dollars of spending are necessary to fix leaky pipes and lay new ones, install efficient water management systems, and construct large-scale desalination facilities. Thus far, only in the wealthiest Asian cities such as Singapore has the combination of higher water tariffs, efficient utilities, and public awareness campaigns led to a decrease in average daily water consumption. Israel, which gets 55 percent of its water through desalination plants, will be selling its high-tech knowhow to most of its Arab rivals. Much more environmental knowledge must emerge if the megaregion is to stave off ecological catastrophe.

Asian cities from Dhaka to Jakarta also demonstrate the worst mismatches between vulnerability to rising sea levels and preparedness for coastal flooding. Should coastal inundations overwhelm today's defensive measures—such as building massive sea barriers, raising roads, and channeling seawater into underground aquifers—urban refugees will be forced to retreat inland to more hospitable elevations. Then there are the Pacific Islanders, for whom moving "inland" buys little time and incurs an exorbitant economic cost. For the peoples of Oceania, the sea has been as much of a resource as their land; their folklore celebrates the unity of humanity, land, and water.[36] The coming decades will test whether other Asians share this sentiment as a rising number of climate refugees from submerging Pacific island states such as the Solomon Islands, Fiji, and Kiribati arrive on firmer shores. Skyrocketing Asian greenhouse gas emissions have exacerbated their plight, and now Asian nations must decide how and where to relocate them. Equatorial Asians may have to become temperate Asians, changing the social fabric of Central Asia, the fertile borderlands between China and Southeast Asia, and eventually eastern Russia.

The landlocked Himalayan kingdom of Bhutan has been thrust into the strategic spotlight as a major source of glacial runoff flows into the Brahmaputra River, making it both a flooding hazard and a hydropower source. Steering water away from the former toward the latter will require new cross-border Asian investment in hydrotechnologies. In the Tian Shan and the Pamir Mountains, Kyrgyzstan's and Tajikistan's hydropower potential makes them crucial electricity providers for Xinjiang's growing Chinese population. Meanwhile, Australia wants to sell solar and wind power to Indonesia, and Mongolia is generating solar and wind power both for itself and to export to China. The more Asians invest in resource-sharing technologies, the more they will integrate into a regional ecological system to complement their economic system.

Asia's spiritual revival has been an ecological motivator across the region. As hyperspeed industrialization chokes Asian cities from coastal China to New Delhi, ever more Asians are opting for a slower life outside the megacities and lending their support to Buddhist and Taoist eco-activist movements that advocate sustainable living. At Mao Mountain, a sacred Taoist site in eastern China, the abbot Yang Shihua calls upon followers to revere the statue of Laozi as a "Green God." In 2018, the Buddhist Association of China successfully lobbied to block the IPO of a holy mountain site to prevent its overdevelopment. Even though religion is heavily regulated in China, Xi Jinping himself has called for China to return to its roots as an "ecological civilization."[37] Recent surveys suggest that all across Asia there is a strong willingness to pay more for sustainably sourced products.[38] Young Chinese are no longer fond of shark-fin soup.

Raising the Floor, Leapfrogging the Ladder

If Asia were a single country of nearly 5 billion citizens, its income inequality would be far worse than in any other region. Yemenis earn scarcely $2,000 per capita per year, while Qatar's per capita annual income has reached $125,000.[39] A similar disparity exists between the citizens of Myanmar and Singapore. But for Asians, poverty remains so extensive that it is a far greater concern than inequality. South Asian countries, especially India and Bangladesh, have extensive rural masses living in extreme poverty. Nearly one-sixth of Indians belong to the *dalit* caste of untouchables. Hundreds of millions of Indians are malnourished, have no working sanitation systems, and defecate in the open. About 500 million Asians—approximately one-tenth of the region's population—can be considered desperately poor. Still, from 1980 to the present, well over 1 billion Asians have been lifted out of poverty. Having achieved such spectacularly rapid gains in wealth in a single generation, Asians accept that inequality is an inevitable consequence of the tide that has lifted most boats. Their debates are thus not about lowering the ceiling for the wealthy but about raising the floor for the masses.

Asians view the remaining poverty in their midst as an opportunity to continue the mission of eradicating it through infrastructure investment, urbanization, economic growth, education, financial inclusion, and digitization. Ever more of Asia is joining in the largest-scale case of what economists call the advantage of late development, or "second-mover advantage": leapfrogging over traditional technologies and behaviors to the newest standards. Mobile phones come before landlines, digital banking before ATMs, cloud computing before desktops, electronic road payments before toll booths, and solar and wind power instead of oil and gas. Asian countries are going from no ID cards or taxes to biometric IDs and digital tax collection. The tidy historical sequence of catch-up growth as countries climb the ladder from agriculture to manufacturing to services has been disrupted by the sweep of financialization and digitization that has allowed even underdeveloped Asian nations to leapfrog through mobile banking, e-commerce, peer-to-peer services, and other innovations. In fact, both the old and new drivers of economic growth are prominent across Asia today.

Myanmar, one of Asia's poorest countries, is a good example of how the hard and soft aspects of late but accelerated development come together. Rather than fumbling through a thicket of haphazard regulations, Myanmar established a one-stop investment portal for rapid approvals. The country went from 1 percent to 90 percent mobile phone penetration in just five years. Given its archaic financial system, mobile banking is spreading before bank branches and ATMs—and eventually, once the whole population gets banking apps, demonetization (removing physical currency altogether) as its larger neighbor India has done. With their low wages, Myanmar, Cambodia, and Laos are also attracting their share of light manufacturing activity, helping them climb toward middle-income status.[40]

Consumption levels tend to take off once GDP per capita hits $3,000, which Pakistan has now crossed in terms of purchasing power parity (PPP). In Pakistan, the average disposable income doubled between 2010 and 2017, making the country the world's fastest-growing retail market, with the number of retail stores expected to double to 1 million between 2010 and 2020. Two-thirds of the country's 210 million people under the age of thirty, many of them joining the urban consumer class en masse, are benefiting Western brands from McDonald's to Dutch Boy paint. The overflowing street-side cafés of Lahore and Karachi represent the onset of what the Pakistani novelist Mohsin Hamid describes as "infinite demand." E-commerce is also growing along with 4G and broadband connectivity. Alibaba launched a national AliExpress.com shopping site for Pakistan in 2017.

The Hong Kong–based global supply chain manager Li & Fung is a superb proxy for South Asia's thriving logistics and retail sectors. In the words of the company's CFO, Spencer Fung, the company's size makes it a "bowling ball amidst grains of sand." As Li & Fung shifts from simple wage arbitrage (cost optimization) toward geographic arbi-

trage (speed optimization), it is becoming ever more a global company first and a Chinese company second. While China represents about half its production activity, it now has manufacturing activity in sixty countries and distributes through 8,000 retailers in a hundred countries. The more Li & Fung builds out its distribution network in India and Southeast Asia, the more Western companies such as Zara and H&M depend on it to penetrate those populous and rapidly urbanizing nations. Pakistan and Bangladesh are now its fastest-growing and highest-margin markets. From cotton fields to garment factories, Li & Fung helps turn analog countries into digital ones by applying efficien agricultural and manufacturing processes: digital games to train wor ers, 3D digital design to reduce the need for sending physical sampl to vendors via couriers, and drones for delivery. To take advanta of Pakistan's booming logistics industry, the United States' UPS teamed up with Pakistan's logistics leader, TCS, and Unilever made a fresh investment of $150 million in the country to cope the growing demand for its household products.

As Li & Fung has built out its range to sell everything from me devices to clothing direct to consumers online, it has acquired d of local Asian brands selling in more than three thousand stores Asia—putting it in direct competition with its own Western client depend on it for retail distribution.

After decades of neglect, India is now spending up to 20 of its budget on infrastructure, from railways to sanitation. A dollars in urban and transport investments has been proje 2015–2035, and in the first three years of Modi's administra million toilets were installed, mostly in rural areas. After d unchecked sprawl, India's infamous slums such as Mumbai's are shrinking dramatically as real estate developers have be zero tax on the construction of affordable housing. Much a has done, India is seeking to lure investment away from Ch its own coastal special economic zones for manufacturin Whereas for decades Mumbai was India's only significa

hub, today the states of Andhra Pradesh and Tamil Nadu are major commercial centers. The Bangalore-Chennai-Hyderabad industrial triangle in southern India has become the country's Pearl River delta, with 30 million people contributing 80 percent of the country's IT services, plus innovative clusters around biomedical engineering and digital finance. India's fastest-growing states in the past decade have been some of its most remote and backward, such as Sikkim and Bihar. Driven by construction, power generation, and manufacturing (and tourism in Sikkim's Himalayan region), both states have been growing by 12 percent to 25 percent per year. Goa has also grown by double digits on the back of mining and tourism.

India is expanding its tax base from the paltry level of 10 percent— just in time as its working-age population expands (and is not expected to peak until 2030). The combination of the goods and services (GST) tax and demonetization has formalized much of the gray economy and weakened the black market. With a stable currency and inflation in check, India has lowered its current account deficit to just 1 percent of GDP. Its stock exchange is one of the world's best performing, and Indians are pouring into it as much as foreigners, especially as the country weighs moving the rupee toward full capital account convertibility. India's per capita income has crossed about $7,000 in PPP terms, indicating that the phase of development consumption is complemented by financialization. While Indian citizens have historically been the world's largest hoarders of physical gold, the percentage of household savings represented by gold has dropped from 15 percent in 2013 to 5 percent in 2016 as families invested more in education, health care, and insurance products.[42] Asia's insurance market has witnessed enormous growth, with Asians buying life, property, automobile, and other insurance products.

The combination of digitization and demonetization has meant that Indians are becoming data rich before they are financially rich. Thanks to large-scale investments by corporates such as Reliance Jio Infocomm, all of India will be covered by 4G phone service by 2020.[43]

Jio's rival Airtel signed up 170 million new customers during a 100-day campaign in early 2018. Already 1 billion Indians (almost 100 percent of adults) have been issued the Aadhar universal ID card. Together with demonetization and the mandatory linkage of Aadhar IDs to bank accounts, well over $100 billion has been brought into the banking system in a year. Aadhar has also enabled rapid digital transfers of subsidies to the poor, with mobile wallets eliminating the need for bank branches and e-payments reducing transaction costs and corruption. Then there is IndiaStack, which brings together employment, medical, address, tax, and other records onto one platform accessed through fingerprints and, soon, retinal scans. India is set to export these digital innovations all across developing Asia. Bangladesh is now installing one-stop community centers to process everything from birth certificates to business licenses and minimize corruption. Such technological approaches to financial inclusion, especially for women, have pushed Bangladesh's growth rate higher than even India's or Pakistan's.

Indonesia is Southeast Asia's archetype of a country with a huge population, low income, and abysmal labor productivity—yet rapid growth. As in India, Singapore leads all foreign investors in Indonesia, where high-quality industrial parks make the country more attractive for global investors looking to diversify production away from China. Indonesia is also forcing foreign investors to transfer technology to its mining companies. Foreign investment raises labor productivity in both industrial and services sectors, such as telecoms and hospitality, that employ more than 60 million people and represent half the country's GDP growth. Taking advantage of Jakarta's 500,000 informal motorcycle taxis, Go-Jek leveraged Singaporean and US investment to professionalize into a full-scale logistics operation with integrated mobile payments (GoPay). Not only did the company beat its five-year growth forecast in less than a year, but a half-million drivers joined the formal economy and tax base. In 2017, Gojek was valued at $3 billion. In 2018, it announced plans to spread across Southeast Asia.

The key areas of Asia's digital integration—social media, payments, e-commerce, and ride sharing—have been on a steep ascent since 2015, growing by more than 30 percent per year in terms of user base and revenues. Given the significant cross-border population movements across Asia, migrant laborers have been among the first to benefit. Malaysia's Maybank has partnered with the Singapore blockchain start-up Crosspay to enable hundreds of thousands of unbanked Indonesian and Burmese migrants to receive payments. In Malaysia, nearly 100 percent of the population has bank accounts and mobile phones—and as in South Korea and China, mobile banking is far outpacing Internet banking in terms of subscriber growth. Across these middle- and low-income countries, the penetration of fintech products around lending and insurance is less than 5 percent, promising an enormous pool of nearly 2 billion customers ready to leapfrog. About $50 billion in fintech investment is expected every year until 2025 to upgrade Southeast Asia. Mobile banking is also taking off in Asia's poorest countries. By 2025, there may not be any more "unbanked" Asians.

China's fintech leadership is an important reason why. Chinese invest more than $100 billion per year in fintech products (far ahead of Americans at $35 billion).[44] The People's Bank of China (PBOC) already has a digital currency running parallel with the renminbi between government and banks to help scale traceable and secure financial transactions. And the $3 trillion in mobile payments made in China each year is far more than in any other country.[45] Chinese finance and lifestyle apps by Alibaba, Tencent, Baidu, and Ping An Insurance are more comprehensive than those of their Western counterparts Microsoft, Amazon, Facebook, and Google, providing payment, insurance, loan, and credit-rating services, as well as money market funds, wealth management, crowdfunding, and currency exchange. These Chinese platforms are also spreading more rapidly across Asia through joint ventures. Alibaba owns 80 percent of the Southeast Asian e-commerce marketplace Lazada Group, while Alibaba's Ant Financial has partnerships with Korea's KakaoPay, Thailand's Ascend Group, Mynt in the Philippines, Emtek in Indonesia, and Telenor Pakistan. Tencent's funding of the Singapore-based Garena (now Sea) has propelled its growth at faster rates in Southeast Asia than even Tencent achieved in its early years in China. Sea is now the region's largest gaming platform, its online marketplace, Shopee, leads the region in the number of vendors and buyers, and its Airpay branchless banking service dispenses mobile credits at nearly 200,000 locations. In 2017, SEA Group listed on the NYSE. China therefore is using technology not to conquer its neighbors but to finance their success.

Asian countries have no reservations about copying one another's best practices. As Japan and South Korea have gone cashless, China has followed suit. The UAE and Iran are both copying the contactless payment systems of Hong Kong, Taipei, and Singapore. The Jakarta One Card is a Chinese-style all-in-one identification card that supports public transport payment, retail banking, social security insurance, and car toll fees. Asia's enormous population size and economic growth mean that the commercial pie is growing. In China, only 15 percent of retail sales are through e-commerce, and only half of those are mobile. In the rest of Asia, the room for growth is even greater. Asian companies are most likely to capture Asia's digital upside given the massive customer base they have yet to fully integrate. Amazon and Alibaba each has about 40 percent market share in its home market— but Alibaba is growing far more quickly worldwide than Amazon is. Jack Ma points out that Alibaba is not just a company but an economy. Its electronic world trade platform (e-WTP) links suppliers and vendors around the globe in a borderless marketplace; its Tmall combines the marketplace of eBay with the infrastructure of Amazon, and its Alipay ecosystem keeps money within its orbit. Alibaba Cloud wants to take on Amazon Web Services in the global cloud computing market, with plans to leverage its hard infrastructure investments into "One Belt, One Road, One Cloud."

Building and Manufacturing Growth

Masses of farmers and peasants are moving into Asia's thriving cities. From Pakistan to Vietnam, another 1 billion Asians are expected to urbanize by 2040, equivalent to the entire urban population of Europe and North America today. Asia accounts for about 60 percent of the world's infrastructure spending, building out cities to absorb the influx of rural and migrant labor. Urban development in Asia is a self-fulfilling prophecy: the more cities are upgraded, the more people they attract, and the more that must be spent to upgrade them to accommodate yet more migrants. At the same time, urbanization promotes services instead of manufacturing as people's principal livelihood. Asia's cities are where the demand for construction workers, doctors, nurses, and teachers is the highest. Whereas China's elderly are concentrated in the countryside, its megacities are teeming with youths. The Philippines' "Build Build Build" Initiative has created a huge demand for skilled workers to manage construction projects and work in massive casinos, so much so that companies are raising wages to convince Filipinos not to go abroad for work. From Oman to Myanmar, rising tourism has created many new jobs in the hospitality industry, making it a crucial component of Asian countries' economic diversification strategies.

Across Asia, one sees jealous rivals actually copying each other in their urban and economic master plans. India wants efficient industrial zones like China's, Pakistan wants to be a tech hub like India, Uzbekistan wants shiny new cities like Kazakhstan's, Malaysia wants automated ports like Singapore's, Doha wants to be a glittering financial center like Dubai, and so on. The urbanization race is helping Asia build its way beyond the dreaded "oil curse," the historical phenomenon by which resource-rich countries stagnate politically and economically because they fail to invest outside their energy sectors. Asia already has a positive track record of beating the oil curse. Malaysia has diversified its economy and achieved relatively high income. Saudi Arabia and Kazakhstan are doing the same. Azerbaijan, the oil-rich Muslim republic on the western shore of the Caspian Sea, has spent the nearly three decades since gaining independence from the Soviet Union pumping oil to Europe via Turkey. But with oil prices (and its own oil reserves) declining, it is welcoming Chinese and Indian investors into its ports and other infrastructure to become a hub for Eurasian cargo transit. As Baku transforms from a city reeking of oil wells to a modern metropolis with a breezy corniche, Europeans, Russians, and Gulf Arabs have made it a tourism hot spot known for authentic Turkic hospitality, halal food, and therapeutic stone saunas.

STRIVING FOR SERVICES

Even as Asia remains the world's factory floor, its service sectors are growing far more quickly, representing an ever larger share of GDP for most Asian economies. This process is crucial in adjusting the rapid automation of factory labor.

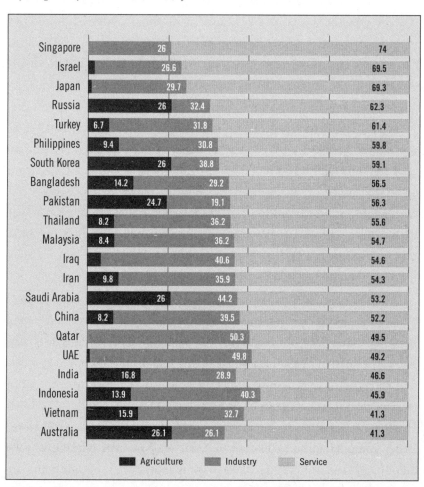

Asia's developing urbanization is evidence of one important strategy for confronting the threat of premature deindustrialization—the theory that not enough high-wage jobs are being created by the services economy to propel countries out of the so-called middle-income trap. But Asian industry is hardly disappearing, either. There may be fewer jobs in industry relative to the size of the labor force than a generation ago, but there are still more than 100 million manufacturing workers across Asia. Countries climbing toward middle-income status such as India and the Philippines are grabbing all possible industrial activity for their workers. As India allows greater foreign ownership in aviation, rail, finance, and construction, it has become the world's top destination for greenfield foreign investment, with more than $60 billion per year pouring into transport, information technology, electronics, and clean tech. The twin Invest India and Make in India campaigns direct investment into manufacturing and are coupled with a Skill India campaign that aims to train more than 2 million new labor force entrants every year for various industries. Importantly, in India services already represent 55 percent of GDP and industry only 30 percent. The country's trade-to-GDP ratio has fallen as rapidly as it has in China, from 55 to 40 percent. The Philippines, too, has plans to boost industries such as shipbuilding—and in 2017, industrial contribution to GDP was higher than ever. With Western and Asian companies pouring $150 billion per year in FDI into Southeast Asia (more than China), we have not seen the end of manufacturing outsourcing.[46]

Thailand is a good example of a middle-income Asian country where all of these forces are coming together. Thailand already has a strong manufacturing base, with exports growing in the double digits annually, but its productivity remains low. Realizing that a slowdown in exports to China has made its economy vulnerable, the military government cut red tape for investment so more foreign firms could come in and train a higher-quality labor force. It also loosened credit for SMEs so they can afford better computers and skills-training courses. Now it is offering its own automated "Industry 4.0" facilities to companies from the country that invented the mantra—Germany—so its engineering heavyweights can continue to save costs in Asia and be closer to their customers. As a result, Thailand's trade-to-GDP ratio has now climbed above 120 percent, while through similar strategies Vietnam's has climbed to 200 percent.

Though Asia remains the core of global industrial output, automation has become a far greater threat to employment than US tariffs and nearshoring (relocalizing production to America and Europe). Automation is unfolding in the West and Asia at the same time. Amazon and Alibaba both have robots sorting millions of products across their facilities. Universal Robots (UR), a Danish manufacturer of lightweight multitasking robotic arms, reports double-digit annual growth in Asia. GreyOrange, a robotics company based in Singapore and New Delhi, has two warehouse robots named Butler and Sorter that stock shelves and load hundreds of thousands of parcels per day, eliminating the cheap manual labor on which India's logistics sector has thrived for so long. GreyOrange's partnership with Flipkart (originally backed by SoftBank, Tiger Global Management, and Tencent but now owned mostly by Walmart) will help it survive against Amazon's aggressive incursion into India, allowing managers to focus less on head count and more on quality control. Rapid growth has meant that Asia's expanding sectors are not cannibalizing one another, as is happening in the West, where shoppers' move to Amazon is leaving shopping malls empty and Google and Facebook are crushing print newspapers. In Asia, e-commerce is surging but malls are full, and newspaper presses are churning despite fast-growing mobile advertising. There is a rising demand for everything, both physical and digital.

Asia thus has every intention of retaining the world's manufacturing supply chains, even if robots perform a growing share of the labor. South Korea currently leads the world in industrial robotics, with nearly 500 robots per 10,000 manufacturing workers compared to 300 in Japan and Germany and just 36 in China. South Korean workers can also wear exoskeleton bodysuits that allow them to perform more difficult tasks for longer periods with less physical stress. As its working-age population shrinks through aging from 1 billion people in 2015 toward 900 million by 2030, China is spending massively on industrial automation to plug its growing labor gap, buying both the machines and the foreign companies that make them. In 2017, the Chinese appliance giant Midea paid $6 billion for more than 85 percent of Germany's Kuka Robotics, one of the biggest makers of industrial robots in the world. Foxconn's spin-off Foxconn Industrial Internet, which automates factories, is now more valuable than Sony. Automation will enable China to save on labor costs, raise productivity, and boost its competitiveness against the very countries that have pioneered automation.

Even China's most open sectors such as automobile manufacturing have become emblematic of how local competition drives the market. For two decades, Volkswagen and Toyota led car sales in China, albeit through joint ventures that entailed substantial profit sharing. Today, the Hangzhou-based Geely designs and builds vehicles to European standards, not least because it owns Volvo, Lotus, and 10 percent of Daimler, which it brought in to build a $2 billion plant dedicated to high-end cars.[47] It is also spending 15 percent of its revenue on R and D—including a venture with the Dutch sensor maker NXP Semiconductors to develop in-vehicle telematics—accelerating its plan to displace foreign carmakers and increase its own car exports globally. Xi Jinping has promised that US carmakers will have greater access to the Chinese market, but why would Chinese buy American cars?

China's $300 billion Made in China 2025 initiative aims to upgrade Chinese industries to become self-sufficient in areas such as aircraft components, computer chips, and medical devices, while raising productivity in engineering, health care, food processing, and other sectors.[48] Episodes such as the Trump administration blocking the sale of equipment to the telecom giant ZTE in 2018 have only motivated China further to push for technological self-sufficiency. As China has become the largest market for semiconductors, it has launched the $20 billion China Integrated Circuit Industry Investment Fund Company to spur Chinese firms to achieve the ultrathin 14-nanometer chips made by firms such as Samsung and Intel. In 2017, Xiaomi abandoned Qualcomm chips and deployed its own Pinecone chipset, breaking its reliance on foreign providers. China's organic light-emitting diode (OLED) display maker BOE Display plans to deploy rollable displays by 2021. To the extent that China relies on high-tech imports, it acquires more advanced technology through trade with Europe, Taiwan, Japan, and South Korea than it does from the United States; hence the Trump administration's anti-China measures are not likely to meaningfully slow down the Made in 2025 initiaitve.

To maintain its edge over China, South Korea is training workers to deploy and manage high-end sensor networks. Such technical and business services represent the frontier of productivity in advanced economies, while their financial and industrial conglomerates generate substantial offshore revenues by aggressively exporting their innovations—especially to their Asian neighbors. According to the World Intellectual Property Organization's Global Innovation Index, Singapore and South Korea are two of the most competitive economies in the world, owing considerably to their deployment of technology in the workplace and their upskilling programs. In 2017, Samsung overtook Intel as the world's largest semiconductor supplier and edged out IBM for the most patents filed. In 2021, South Korea will open the International Science Business Belt in Daejeon, a complex encompassing eighteen universities, science parks, research centers, and a heavy ion accelerator.

Both the United States and the European Union are struggling to find ways to counter Asia's aggressive innovation strategies and commercial practices. Both have taken a strong line at the WTO against Chinese dumping of subsidized steel and chemicals on global markets and have become more restrictive about foreign investment in sensitive technology sectors. The US Congress (through its Committee on Foreign Investment in the United States) has blocked numerous Chinese attempted acquisitions of US high-tech companies (such as the semiconductor manufacturer Lattice Semiconductor and the memory chip maker Micron Technology), financial firms (such as MoneyGram), and the Chicago Mercantile Exchange and added stringent export controls on US companies selling advanced technology with military applications. Though this might slow down intellectual property (IP) acquisition by Chinese companies—whose IP thefts cost US companies an estimated $600 billion per year in lost profits[49]—it also reduces US exports at a time when Asian companies are aggressively promoting their own tech products. US companies thus want these mergers to move forward in order to enhance their market access to China and to piggyback on China's presence globally. MoneyGram thus plans to continue its partnership with Ant Financial to provide remittance and digital payment services internationally. It is too late to slow any of Asia's efforts at economic enhancement.

Asia.ai: Upgrading Societies

The history of technology flowing from Asia to the West is a reminder that science and technology don't belong to anyone. Western narratives have long derided Asian cultures as being merely copycats. But innovation is not just about scientific invention but about societal adaptation. Whether Asia is just catching up (as in life expectancy and nutrition) or racing ahead (as in mobile finance), it is adopting the latest technologies such as robotics, sensor networks, and synthetic biology. From blockchain to gene editing, success and advantage won't be determined by who is rich or poor, democratic or nondemocratic, but rather who best scales new technologies and business models.

As every society in the world faces varying degrees of technological disruption, one crucial factor Asians have in their favor is psychological: they are not afraid of new technology. They think of it not as a master but a service. Since the Meiji Restoration, Japan's rulers have been fascinated with technology, and today the Japanese are far ahead of other societies in human coexistence with robots in the home and workplace. For Japanese, robots connote the cuddly Astro Boy, not the destructive Terminator. From sensors embedded everywhere to bioenhancement, Asians are investing in the future without fearing that it will destroy them.

Asia's accelerating R&D spending is translating both into home market dominance as well as success abroad. China has ramped up its R&D spending to a level commensurate with its GDP size, contributing 20 percent of world R&D spending and accounting for a similar percentage of the global number of scientific researchers and publications. China represents about half of Asia's R&D expenditure by volume at $409 billion, with Japan at $190 billion and Korea at $120 billion, followed by India at $67 billion and Russia at $43 billion. Three of the world's top ten patent-filing hubs—Tokyo, Osaka, and Nagoya—are in Japan, ahead of Shenzhen and San Jose. Korea's bandwidth speeds are so fast that the country is effectively a cloud-first nation. And by mandating that download and upload speeds be equally fast (rather than privileging download), South Korea has become a nation not just of cultural consumers but of producers, with content spread and adapted across Asian language markets.

Seoul, Taipei, Singapore, Tokyo, Shanghai, and Shenzhen rank among the world's most high-tech cities. Each major Asian tech hub has a niche edge emerging from its ecosystems: Tel Aviv excels in cybersecurity, Singapore in fintech, Tokyo in robotics, Shenzhen in sensors, and so forth. Other places such as Dubai aren't scientific pioneers but make themselves regulatory test beds for everything from drones to driverless cars. Asia's cities lead the world in the deployment of sensor networks for the urban Internet of Things, lifting Korea's semiconductor exports 55 percent from 2016 to 2017. Now such sensor networks as well as energy-efficient LED lights are being installed in second-tier areas such as India's Bhopal. In China's Yinchuan, trash bins double as compactors run by solar power, with sensors alerting trash collectors when to empty them. Asia is also the site of important experiments in optimizing cities by size. Where cities have become too large and congested, such as Changsha, the government has attempted to motivate people to shift to second-tier cities to distribute the population better.[50] Now, instead of just four cities representing nearly half the country's middle class—as was the case with Beijing, Shanghai, Guangzhou, and Shenzhen in 2002—by 2020, inland China is expected to be home to 40 percent of the country's middle class.

Given the density of Asian cities, last-mile bike sharing and autonomous vehicles are other areas in which Asians are making strategic investments to navigate around the traditional path of universal vehicle ownership and crippling traffic congestion. Bike stations and dockless biking have been pioneered by companies such as Mobike and Ofo, which have spread from China across Asia and into Europe. As Asian cities prepare for driverless cars and buses on their street, policy makers, regulators, urban planners, and insurance companies are developing new frameworks to govern them. Even the Western firms ranked most likely to get self-driving cars onto the road first—including Ford, Renault, Daimler, Volkswagen, and BMW—will be looking to do so in Asia. In South Korea, Hyundai and Kia have partnered with Cisco Systems and other US IT companies to advance connected car communications. Baidu's open-source approach to driverless-car software development, called Apollo, has lured Intel, Daimler, and Ford to contribute resources. Baidu might be on a collision course with Didi Chuxing—or perhaps it will simply buy it. US firms are now copying Chinese innovations. LimeBike in California is copying China's dockless bike sharing as pioneered by Ofo and MoBike. DiDi has algorithms that predict which ride-sharing users will want a ride at certain times and locations and is designing driverless car interiors for shared augmented-reality experiences—programs that Uber and others will surely copy. Apple is conducting payments through the iMessage chat service, following what Tencent has done. Amazon now has a lending service similar to that of Alibaba. Facebook plans to follow WeChat by becoming a complete ecosystem of digital services. These examples demonstrate that the winners of a perceived competition between US and Chinese tech companies to innovate and compete for Asian markets are first and foremost Asians themselves.

Even in capital-intensive arenas such as particle physics and quantum computing, the combination of China's appropriation of US technology, luring Chinese American talent from Silicon Valley, and thriving enterprise culture have collectively driven Chinese innovation. Autonomous vehicles, energy-efficient power grids, and urban surveillance systems all rest on breakthroughs in AI such as neural networks, which Asians have developed at least a year ahead of their Western counterparts. Andrew Ng, a cofounder of Google Brain and Coursera who then became chief scientist at Baidu, argues that the complexities of Chinese characters and tones pushed Baidu toward advances in natural language processing (NLP) and voice recognition faster than its Western peers. Google's AI was built on text collected from computers, whereas Baidu from the start focused on location-based data and images collected from mobile devices. Large data sets are the fuel that powers the AI rocket. Alibaba has its customers' e-commerce and banking transaction data, while Tencent's data has expanded with its range of customer services while also integrating voice and facial recognition, a field in which the Beijing-based SenseTime is a global leader.

The contrasting approaches to AI have inspired significant Sino-American research collaborations. Google has invested more than $500 million in the Chinese e-commerce company JD.com and has opened an AI research center in Beijing. The United States' leading high-performance graphics chip maker, NVIDIA, has partnered with Baidu to enhance the company's efforts to deliver cloud-based services for home assistants and self-driving cars. At the same time, both Baidu and Tencent have funded AI labs in the United States, while Chinese investors more broadly have poured about $700 million into more than fifty AI start-ups in the United States—all of which want to advance their applications in Asia's largest markets. All of this helps to explain why, according to the Asian Development Bank, AI is creating far more jobs in Asia than it is destroying.

China's strides in AI have been so impressive that former Google chairman Eric Schmidt has said he expects China to surpass the United States in AI by 2025. But AI is not the arms race it is portrayed to be. Like many technologies, it is circulating and adapting to diverse contexts not dominated by any single power. Investments by Tencent and Hanwha in the Montreal-based Element AI will help expand that company's presence across Asia from Singapore to Tokyo. Japanese companies are applying AI to semiconductor manufacturing, helping them retain their edge in a critical components sector. India has dozens of promising AI companies. Its Fractal Analytics has a "consumer genomics" methodology that supports many of the world's largest retail companies. Indian AI companies will dominate the Indian market and compete globally in areas such as computer vision, medical diagnostics, legal contract analysis, and customer satisfaction surveys. Google is deploying ever more capital to fund and buy Indian AI companies. Pakistan also has one of Asia's leading AI outsourcing companies, Afiniti, which has more than three thousand employees and a valuation of $2 billion. Rather than one country or company dominating AI, then, the model of "AI as a service" is spreading across Asia, giving governments and companies a choice of whom to work with at the best price and on the most favorable data-sharing terms. If China engages in excessive data protectionism—using others' data through its investments and joint ventures but not allowing reciprocal access to Chinese data or the market—it will encounter pushback and lose out as local and foreign competitors offer more open platforms.

Spending Less to Live Longer

Another approach to boosting worker productivity is enhancing the workers themselves. Eugenics has a deservedly poor reputation given the Western experience with Nazism, but today in the United Kingdom and Scandinavia, Down syndrome has been effectively eliminated from the population by using prenatal screenings to terminate at-risk pregnancies. Japan, too, has a dubious history of eugenics due to its 1930s forced sterilization campaign targeting the mentally disabled. But Asia's regulatory environment increasingly enables the ambitious pursuit of applied biotech breakthroughs. China has used the same technology that Scottish scientists used to clone the sheep named Dolly in the 1990s to clone monkeys; CRISPR gene-editing technology was pioneered in the United States, but human trials are under way in Chinese hospitals while none has yet been launched in the United States. In 2016, scientists at Singapore's A*STAR developed a new protein that speeds up DNA editing, and the country's Temasek Life Sciences Laboratory has launched a large-scale synthetic biology incubator. It is likely that prenatal genetic interventions will become the norm in Asia.

More immediately, Asians are also benefiting from a global awareness about the importance of healthy lifestyles and the latest biomedical technologies and health care practices. Japan and Singapore have the world's highest life expectancies, which only some counties in California and Colorado can match. But from South Dakota to Kentucky to Florida, there are US counties with a lower life expectancy than that of the average citizen of Iraq, Bangladesh, and even North Korea. Smoking is in decline across Asia (except Indonesia) though Chinese and Gulf Arabs are now witnessing a significant rise in lifestyle diseases such as hypertension, diabetes, and obesity. In Southeast Asia, heart disease is projected to overtake pneumonia and tuberculosis (the region's previous leading killers) within a decade. Asian leaders know that with such large populations they cannot afford to replicate the large footprint of Western health care systems, which consume up to 20 percent of GDP. China's health care coverage has risen from 21 percent of the population in 2003 to nearly 100 percent today but total health care expenditure is less than 10 percent of GDP. Instead of the $9,146 per capita health expenditure in the United States or the $5,006 in Germany, Asian costs can remain closer to the current $4,000 in Japan or $1,500 in the Gulf region. More than 70 percent

202 The Future Is Asian

of Indonesians are now covered under the country's ambitious universal health care scheme, with Vietnam and the Philippines close behind.

In another major case of leapfrogging, telemedicine and cheap medical devices will reduce the cost of general medical treatments and elder care by localizing the point of diagnosis and treatment so patients can evade the need for hospitals altogether. Already more than 30 million Chinese use the Chunyu Yisheng app to pair them with appropriate physicians via live video, while Alibaba has begun online prescription fulfillment. The Indian start-up HealthCube provides comprehensive diagnostics and cloud-based digital records that any patient can access and share via smartphone with a network of doctors who can remotely prescribe treatments. For treatments local hospitals don't provide, Dubai and Singapore have become major hubs for medical tourism for elective surgeries, as have India and Thailand, which are also home to innumerable surrogacy clinics catering to Western families. Japan and India are already world leaders in pharmaceuticals, with Japan innovating low-cost medical devices that can support elderly health care across Asia and compete in the European and US markets. Even dentistry will become cheaper in Asia. In 2017, a Chinese robot performed the first fully automated dental implant surgery.

Learning for Life

Not all Asians have the same societal work ethic, but all are capable of the kind of consistent discipline necessary to push their nations forward. Over the years I've seen Palestinians and Jordanians toil to fix vehicles and build (and rebuild) entire towns, Indians and Pakistanis laboring on construction sites and carrying immense loads on rickshaw carts through choking traffic. East Asian professionals work interminable hours to save money for their children's education. They endure great suffering because they have to, because they see success in countries next door or nearby, and because they know their civilizations have been great before and can be great again.

ASIA'S GRAY MARKETS

Billions of Asians are accustomed to life in the informal economy, working either in sectors un-regulated by the state or for unregistered businesses. This gray economy represents anywhere from 12 to 50 percent of GDP and employment in Asian countries.

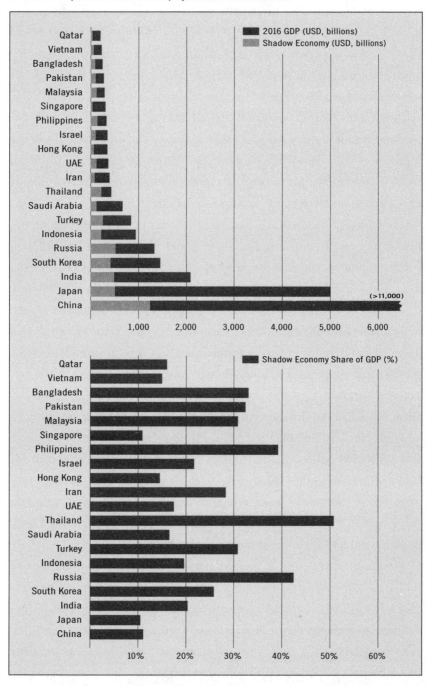

Hustling is nothing new to Asians. Westerners are only now be-coming accustomed to life in the gigonomy of multiple jobs in the formal and informal economy. But tens of millions of Indians and Pakistanis are used to working half the year in low-skilled industry and the other half in seasonal harvesting. Across Asia, the informal economy accounts for anywhere from 12 to 50 percent of GDP and employment.[51] But in another case of taking advantage of late de-velopment, most Asian societies have apps that allow people to be hired for part-time work based on their skills. In major Asian cities, new "homestels" (hotel hostels) are popping up that provide a mix of affordable long-term residency and coworking spaces.

Coworking spaces have become the hot real estate asset in nu-merous cities of southern India's tech belt. The reason is not only India's role as a global software hub but the large number of newly unemployed in the call center sector, with which India has become synonymous. Machine learning has caught up to Bangalore's chatty call center workers, automating customer service, data analysis, and other tasks. The IT industry remains India's largest employer—with 4 million workers and $150 billion in annual revenues in 2017—but net new annual hiring has plummeted from a peak of 400,000 toward zero. Top IT companies such as Infosys and Tech Mahindra will have layoffs of nearly 500,000 by 2020. Filipino back-office workers face the same risk to their call center jobs. Start-ups are absorbing some of the displaced while luring those who don't want to work in corporate behemoths. Bangalore is home to the world's largest start-up accelera-tor, founded by the Indian American serial entrepreneur Desh Desh-pande, where 1,200 entrepreneurs work under one roof.

Asian nations are in a desperate rush to convert their billions of bodies into productive human capital. South Asia has achieved a nearly two-thirds secondary school enrollment rate. The Philippines did not have a formal K–12 educational system and curricula until the past five years. Most Arab countries, however, still invest far too little in high-quality schools and professional training, but their high rate of youth unemployment has forced education to the top of the Arab agenda. The growing spending on secondary education is an early indication of how the next generation of Asians will be much more employable in the formal economy. India and Pakistan have hundreds of thousands of private secondary schools operating on roadsides and in villages. Rather than curbing this education entrepreneurialism, the government is issuing vouchers to subsidize enrollment while focusing on raising standards for certification. The results have been better student and teacher performance, as well as major cost savings to the government. Start-ups such as Zoho University take small-town high school dropouts and put them through coding boot camps so they can get programming jobs. At the tertiary level, countries across South and Southeast Asia are racing to double, triple, and even quadruple their university enrollment rates but making sure to subsidize tuition to avoid the United States' student debt crisis. The elite Indian Institutes of Technology (IITs) produce a small crop of world-class mathematics and engineering graduates annually, and some, such as IIT Delhi, are cofunding the conversion of PhD theses into start-up ventures.

To reach far deeper into India's bulging youth cohort and upwardly mobile middle class, a new breed of hybrid technical-professional academies has emerged. Rajendra Pawar, a cofounder of India's private education powerhouse NIIT, has scaled his on-site and online industry-linked skills programs to reach 500,000 students per year, training them on demand for Indian and global companies from oil rigs to tech parks, with curricular offerings expanding to service insurance, supply-chain management, programming, and other sectors. After completing one assignment, a student can return to be retrained for the next one. Hence NIIT's motto, which embodies the spirit of lifelong learning: "Anadi Anant" (Without beginning, without end).

East Asians are doing the best at preparing youth for an uncertain professional landscape. Much has been made of their hard-charging parenting style, which sociologists describe as interdependent—meaning being more involved in setting children's priorities and urging them to succeed as opposed to the more independent style of Western parenting. At the same time, the diminishing utility of rote learning in a world of automation has put a premium on creativity and teamwork, prompting Singapore to consider phasing out its dreaded Primary School Leaving Examination (PSLE), which requires intense study at the expense of a more joyful childhood. Chinese and South Koreans are also welcoming a new wave of schools focused on creative curricula. These and other Asian countries appear to be on the right track. According to the OECD's annual Programme for International Student Assessment (PISA), which tests students in dozens of countries on subjects such as science and math as well as reading and collaborative problem solving, Singapore, South Korea, Hong Kong, and Japan not only topped traditional subjects but demonstrated the highest aptitude in group teamwork as well.

Role Reversal: Western Dependence on Asian Growth

Asia has proved that it can grow even when the West does not, and as its consumption levels rise, it has also become the crucial growth driver for many Western multinationals. This is a remarkable role reversal. Asia used to mainly produce for the West, keeping labor costs down and profits high. Now the West must also produce *for* Asia, catering to its diverse income levels and tastes—and *in* Asia to meet government demands for local content and job creation as well as to be closer to their customers in hypercompetitive markets.

Even though the United States has a low dependency on exports as a percentage of its GDP, an estimated 40 million jobs are related to producing exported goods. Asia is also a crucial set of markets for the 20 percent of the US workforce employed in higher-end sectors such as finance and technology. Western businesses have long pinned their hopes on China's middle class, but the country's stringent requirements for joint ventures and data security have eaten away at their profits and technological edge. So, too, have the informal requirements whereby foreign companies are obliged to "pay to play," funding think tanks and government research that China can itself easily afford, only to not be granted the greater market access they expect in return. China has slowly begun to license foreign credit card companies to operate in the country, but only after UnionPay achieved 80 percent market share and WeChat Pay and Alipay gained acceptance in landmark tourist sites and other locations all over the world.

Recent Western business surveys of hot markets have thus revealed a shift in focus to India, Pakistan, Indonesia, and the Philippines—their combined population being just over 2 billion. Unlike in China, where foreign companies have no chance of achieving a dominant market share, these more open economies and democratic societies present Western firms with an opportunity to capitalize on Asia's next growth wave. From Vietnam to Myanmar, these fast-growing economies allow as much as 100 percent foreign ownership in lucrative sectors such as construction, real estate, finance, and retail. In other words, they are practically the anti-China.

Almost every sector of the US economy has benefited from Asia's rise. Since the US Congress lifted the four-decades-old ban on hydrocarbon exports, China has become one of the largest purchasers of US oil. US natural gas sales to Japan and Korea are also growing. In fact, the United States' trade deficit with Asia would be far higher today were it not for this rapid growth in US energy exports. Western firms are also making some of their largest energy investments in Asia. Chevron is leading a consortium to invest nearly $40 billion in expanding production in Kazakhstan's Kashagan oil field in the Caspian Sea. France's Total is poised to lead China's move into fracking to extract shale oil and gas. From soybeans to pork, North American food exports have also multiplied. The Chinese firm Shuanghui's acquisition of the American food producer Smithfield Foods has enabled far greater access to China's market. As soy displaces corn as the United States' most widely planted crop, North Dakota wants a new freight rail line connecting it to the Pacific Coast to speed its soy exports to Asia.

Asia is the foundation of price competitiveness and revenue prospects for the United States' largest consumer-goods companies. Seventy percent of Walmart's goods are made or procured in China. Though international sales are only one-third of its total revenue, Japan, China, and India are its fastest-growing markets. Despite big promises to nearshore production, Walmart has been tepid on US expansion while growing more aggressive on China through an investment in JD.com, buying Flipkart in India, and plotting Southeast Asia as its next major expansion target. Most Apple iPhones are also made in China, but 90 percent of mobile handsets sold in China are made by Chinese manufacturers, with Oppo and Vivo Global in the lead with double-digit market share, ahead of Samsung, Xiaomi, and Apple (which has at most 3 percent of the market).[52] Chinese handset makers are also moving faster toward high-performance 5G chips. As China's market has matured, smartphone sales have been declining. For both US corporate titans, therefore, the next strategic phase on which their earnings depend involves both producing and selling their housewares and gadgets aggressively beyond China.

America's leading tech companies are also racing to help Asia take advantage of its late development. Many Asian societies are grateful to Facebook, Microsoft, and Google for laying Internet cables along their coastlines and boosting their bandwidth. In India, Google Maps powers a $20 billion location services and marketing industry and is also aiding the country's goals of improving public sanitation by mapping the locations of public toilets. Google's Tez ("fast") leverages India's Unified Payments Interface (UPI) platform to allow the use of audio commands to make mobile payments, while its machine translation and speech-to-text apps will accelerate business communication in polyglot India and ASEAN. Google is also training 100,000 Indonesian software developers and translating Udacity courses into Bahasa. The United States' Internet and social media giants have long been focused on the greater Asia because of their lack of access to mainland China. Given Baidu's dominance of China's search engine market, it is in the rest of Asia that

Google, Yahoo!, and others need to gain market share in mobile ad revenue. Four-fifths of Facebook users are outside the United States, with the majority in Asia: India has surpassed the United States in the number of Facebook users, with Indonesia just behind the United States. Facebook's growing business units across the region support B2B and B2C businesses to scale. Just one of the thousands of examples is Ertos Beauty Care, founded by a down-on-her-luck Indonesian mother who turned her door-to-door cosmetics business into a multimillion-dollar enterprise through Facebook advertising and now competes with L'Oréal and other leading Western brands.

A more complex win-win story also explains how to succeed among Asia's tech-savvy consumers. The Los Angeles–based Riot Games surged in Asia by licensing its flagship League of Legends game to SEA Group. Riot Games' success in Asia paved the way for Tencent to buy the company outright, providing a capital influx that has allowed Riot Games to open more development offices in the United States and worldwide, hire more game coders, produce new e-games, and stage more championship events around the world—especially in Asia, where watching e-gamers compete on giant screens packs stadiums. Similarly, the Chinese drone maker DJI controls 80 percent of the world's consumer drone market, 80 percent of which is outside China. While it vanquished the US start-up 3D Robotics (3DR) in the hardware market, the two have partnered to integrate 3DR's Site Scan software into DJI drones. Partnering often works where direct head-to-head competition fails.

Western brands have long known that they can better reach Asia's masses by meeting them on price, which requires producing locally and in smaller quantities. Unilever's single-use shampoo pouches have become a well-known example of reaching the bottom billion. For the lower-middle and middle classes, which are poorer than their Western counterparts in dollar terms but active consumers of both discretionary and durable items, smaller cars and big-screen smartphones (since Asians tend not to want separate phones and tablets) have been important adaptations. Western pharmaceutical companies such as Merck,

AstraZeneca, and Eli Lilly are opening labs in China and India (in joint ventures with companies such as China MediTech and BeiGene) to develop "B" lines of lower-cost medicines for Asia's swelling populations and the rising incidence of cancer, diabetes, osteoporosis, and other ailments. Meanwhile, the United States' and Europe's largest insurers, from Prudential and MetLife to AXA and Aviva, are amassing assets through acquiring customers and raising premiums across Asia. Dyson, the British appliances company best known for its vacuum cleaners, employs more scientists in Asia than in the entire rest of the world, with R-and-D centers in Shanghai and Singapore and production facilities in Malaysia and the Philippines. Exposure to more Asian customers has led to product modifications such as different shapes for hair dryer handles and microprocessors that can handle volatile electric currents. Overall, Dyson's Asia revenues have risen by 40 percent in the past decade. At the top end, luxury-goods houses such as LVMH and Richemont are focused on Asia's swelling ranks of millionaires but are also buying start-up Asian brands by local designers who know their customers better.

Asia's consumer gravity is a fact of life not only for the biggest Western retailers but also for upstarts such as the sports apparel supplier Under Armour. Precisely because three-quarters of its sales are in the United States, where incumbents have stunted its growth, the company's only hope is to double down on Asia, where its sales continue to surge. A DHL client survey from 2017 showed that one-third of US SMEs prioritize Asia as a destination for their export growth versus only one-fourth that look to Europe. Indeed, Asia's annual retail market has reached $10 trillion, double that of the United States and triple that of Europe. China's 2017 "Singles Day" broke its own record as the world's biggest retail spending day, with more than $25 billion in goods purchased within twenty-four hours. Forty percent of the brands selling on the Alibaba marketplace were non-Chinese. In India, Amazon leads India's e-commerce market with more than $450 billion in annual sales, providing more opportunities for US vendors to reach India's digital consumers. Indonesia's Tokopedia is the country's largest e-commerce marketplace and is wide open to Western goods as well. The more e-commerce expands in Asia, the easier it becomes for foreign companies to get access to Asian customers.

Much of Asia needs a major boost in capital stock to raise productivity, creating huge opportunities for exporting high-quality industrial and technological goods to Asia. For chip manufacturers such as Qualcomm, Asian companies' rise in the handset market is a huge opportunity: most of its revenue comes from selling chips and technology licenses in China, and its chips are boosting the processing power of Samsung phones, enabling the company to offer new augmented-reality features. Similarly, the United States' few remaining industrial titans, such as General Electric and Honeywell, are more reliant than ever on gas turbines, nuclear power plants, and aircraft components sold to Asian markets. GE has two-thirds of its revenues outside the United States. After China, Saudi Arabia, and Turkey, India and Pakistan are large, fast-growing markets for GE. GE and Siemens are also building dozens of R-and-D facilities and plants across India to experiment with affordable ECG, MRI, X-ray, and blood analysis instruments, first for the Indian market and then outward from there.

The aviation industry also relies on Asia. The British Rolls-Royce has an entire supply chain for jet engine production spread across Southeast Asia. Since the Commercial Aircraft Corporation of China (COMAC) is still a long way from competing with Boeing and Airbus, both Western aircraft manufacturers depend heavily on rising orders from Gulf carriers such as Emirates and Asia's other large carriers such as Turkish Airlines, Singapore Airlines, and Chinese and Japanese carriers. China will surpass the United States as the world's largest domestic aviation market by 2024, with approximately 1.3 billion travelers per year versus 1.1 billion in the United States.[53] By that time, India is projected to reach 450 million annual air travelers, Indonesia will account for 250 million, and Vietnam 150 million. In the automotive sector, while the United States' domestic car sales

Effectively, Europeans and Asians have enticed US companies to shift their headquarters and technology to their own markets, where they also pay lower corporate taxes. Americans have been all too happy to oblige, a response that is sure to continue despite President Trump's ambitions to the contrary. The United States' recovering economic growth, rising interest rates, and reduced corporate tax rate have led to the repatriation of hundreds of billions of dollars in corporate cash, but only some of it will be invested at home. Top US companies are likely to use their cash piles for global acquisitions, buying undervalued Asian companies that have a large customer base, and for sourcing cheap skilled manpower. The evidence is visible at the Manila campuses of the Canadian-owned Telus Corporation, where more than fifteen thousand staff provide data analytics services for US tech giants as well as banks such as JPMorgan Chase and Wells Fargo. Similarly, professional services and consulting firms such as McKinsey & Company, Deloitte, KPMG, Accenture, and Ernst & Young have all expanded their Asia-based practice areas from infrastructure advisory to fintech to help Asian clients improve their corporate governance and consumer offerings.

The growing adoption of 3D printing for designing and producing auto components, medical devices, and various consumer products on a large scale might replace large volumes of goods mass-manufactured in Asia and reimported to the United States and Europe. But since most such goods are sold in Asia anyway, more and more companies are positioning these technologies as much abroad as at home. The San Francisco–based Flex (formerly Flextronics), one of the world's largest and most technologically sophisticated supply-chain managers, is deploying advanced design and tailored manufacturing solutions for clients ranging from Cisco Systems to Nike—especially in Asia, where the customers are.

Not only are Americans selling in Asia, but their travel as professionals and tourists to Asia helps US companies as well. As Asian consumption of entertainment surges, American pop singers, rock bands, and sports teams spend weeks touring Asia, selling out stadiums. Forty percent of American overseas tourists go to China (including Taiwan and Hong Kong), while nearly 20 percent visit India and 15 percent Japan, followed by the Philippines, South Korea, Thailand, Vietnam, and Singapore. Western travel magazines continuously regale their readers with dispatches from the Philippines and Indonesia, whose beaches perennially top the rankings. Marriott International has more than a hundred hotel properties in China and the same number in India, where it has overtaken the Taj Group, and more than thirty in Southeast Asia with a dozen new hotels under way. Airbnb has partnered with Alibaba and Tencent to promote seamless home-sharing bookings in China. But Western travel and hospitality companies have learned to be cautious about Asian sensitivities. In 2018, both Marriott and Delta Air Lines issued profuse apologies to China (and Marriott's China website was shut down for a week) after they identified Tibet and Taiwan as independent countries. The more Westerners and Asians mingle, the more they will learn to adapt to each other's preferences.

5

Asians in the Americas and Americans in Asia

The United States was founded by migrants from across the Atlantic, but in the nineteenth century Asians streamed in from across the Pacific. Filipinos were the first to arrive; their numbers steadily grew during the Philippines' time as a US colony. The Chinese became the largest foreign-born Asian population, settling mostly on the West Coast, until the 1882 Chinese Exclusion Act. Fast-forward more than a century, and in 2010, Asia officially outstripped Latin America as the largest source of new immigrants into the United States.[1] At the same time, Indians are the fastest-growing number of illegal immigrants, whether by overstaying their visas or by trying to enter the United States via Mexico.

Today 21 million US residents claim Asian heritage, the largest groups being Chinese (4.8 million), Indian (4 million), Filipino (4 million), Vietnamese (2 million), and Korean (1.8 million).[2] There are also an estimated 3 million Americans of Arab descent. Arabs have been migrating to the United States for more than a century, with the metro Detroit area attracting the first wave of Lebanese, Syrian, Iraqi, and Yemenis, who worked first as shopkeepers and eventually in Ford's automobile plants. The 1970s–'80s Lebanese civil war, the Persian Gulf War of 1990–91, and the invasion of Iraq in 2003 all continued to drive Arabs to Michigan even as the automotive industry declined as a major employer. Though the total number of Asians is just under half that of Hispanics, the gap is closing.[3] Immigrants from Asia are granted twice as many green cards per year as those from any other region and are becoming citizens at twice the rate of other regions as well.[4]

Nearly half of all Asians in the United States live in the West, with California alone accounting for one-third. California has by far the largest number of Asians at nearly 7 million, followed by New York with 2 million.[5] As a proportion of state populations, Hawaii leads the way with more than half (56 percent) of its residents of Asian heritage (primarily Filipinos and Japanese), followed by California (16 percent), then New Jersey, Nevada, and Washington, each of which is 10 percent Asian.[6] Asians also have the highest rate of intermarriage (29 percent) of any ethnic group.[7] By 2050, Asians are projected to displace Hispanics as the largest immigrant group, even though Latinos will still comprise a larger share of the total population.[8]

In recent decades, Asians have become much more visible in the American economy.[9] But Asians' incomes are as diverse as their ethnicity. Indians have the highest median household incomes, followed by Filipinos and Japanese, then Chinese, Pakistanis, and Koreans.[10] As a whole, Asians have a median income approximately $19,000 higher than that of whites, who are the next most prosperous group. Arab Americans also have a higher median income than the general population, and Syrian refugees are quickly joining the labor force.

Given the size and wealth of the Indian diaspora, the Indian wedding industry alone contributes an estimated $5 billion per year to the US economy (more than the annual spending on weddings in India itself). Even though second-generation Indians may be uncomfortable with religious rites they don't fully understand, they are drawn to the pomp of weddings involving horses and drummers. The University of Pennsylvania professor Devesh Kapur has termed this hybrid of American and Indian rituals a "big fat Indian wedding."[11] To capture Asian Americans' consumption power, department stores such as Macy's now actively celebrate Asian and Pacific American Heritage Month each May with a lineup of events featuring Asian chefs, fashion icons, and social influencers.

The United States' academic achievements have been furthered by the country's Asianization. From the Scripps National Spelling Bee to the Regeneron Science Talent Search competition, a substantial majority of winners are first- or second-generation Asian immigrants. Top New York high schools such as Stuyvesant High School and Bronx High School of Science were three-quarters Caucasian in the 1970s and are now majority Asian. The emerging emphasis on STEM (science, technology, engineering, and mathematics) education in the United States is due in part to a recognition of the competitive achievements of Asian societies in science as well as the demands of Asian parents in the United States. So, too, is the rising academic stress manifest in the elevated teen suicide rate. Asians' superior academic standing in college admissions has generated major lawsuits against prestigious universities such as Harvard, with aggrieved whites claiming that Asians benefit from affirmative action policies that whites now seem to need to guarantee sufficient representation in universities and Asians demanding that admissions criteria be more meritocratic rather than artificially limiting their enrollment through racial quotas.[12]

It is safe to say that Silicon Valley would not be what it is today without Asians. With their level of educational attainment, Indian immigrants (72 percent of whom arrive in the United States with a bachelor's degree or higher) now account for 70 percent or more of the United States' annual quota of H-1B visas. The influx of hundreds of thousands of tech workers from southern India has made Telugu the fastest-growing language in America. According to the researcher Vivek Wadhwa, from 1995 to 2004, 53 percent of tech start-ups in the Valley were founded by at least one foreigner, overwhelmingly Asians.[13] The campuses of Google and Facebook are tech equivalents of UN headquarters, with canteens offering cuisines from Arabic to Japanese.[14] Indians in particular are not only powerfully represented in the tech workforce but also highly networked through organizations such as The Indus Entrepreneurs (TiE).

Asians have also become prominent on the US athletic scene. From China's Yao Ming in basketball to Japan's Ichiro Suzuki in baseball, individual Asians have achieved legendary status in American sport. The Taiwanese American NBA star Jeremy Lin is considered a marketing dream for his jersey sales among Asian Americans and the popularity of clinics he holds during tours around Asia, while Japan's Shohei Ohtani of the Los Angeles Angels is already being hailed as the next Babe Ruth for his pitching and batting abilities. Almost every American figure skater on the 2018 US Winter Olympics team was Asian, as was the Korean American Chloe Kim, who won the snowboarding gold medal.

Americans have become ever more attuned to Asian belief systems and spirituality. In the late nineteenth century, the Indian monk and philosopher Swami Vivekananda elevated Hinduism in global consciousness through his speech at the World Parliament of Religions in 1893 and lectures across the United States, giving rise to numerous Vedanta centers teaching Hindu ideas. Fritjof Capra's 1975 bestseller *The Tao of Physics* popularized Hindu and Buddhist mysticism while elevating their status in the West by claiming that their insights were complementary to those of quantum mechanics. Karen Armstrong's books on Buddha and Muhammad and Deepak Chopra's books, which repurpose Vedic philosophies for a modern age, have also been bestsellers. The thirteenth-century Persian mystic Rumi is the United States' bestselling poet.[15] The number of self-identified Muslims in the United States is rising at the rate of nearly 100,000 per year, a mix of converts from Christianity as well as immigrants from Pakistan, Bangladesh, and India. The number of Muslims in the United States has more than tripled since 2000 to 3.3 million, despite the precipitous rise in anti-Muslim sentiment and hate crimes against Muslims since 9/11.

The prevailing stereotype of Asian minorities celebrates their academic and economic achievements but assumes their political impotence. That, too, is changing. Though Asians have been active in US politics for two generations, they are gaining greater prominence today. Hawaii has had several Asian American governors, beginning with George Ariyoshi in the 1970s. Former Louisiana governor Bobby Jindal ran for president in 2016. In 2017, a record number of Asian Americans were sworn into the 115th US Congress, including representatives Ami Bera and Ro Khanna, both of California; Stephanie Murphy of Florida, the first Vietnamese-born member of Congress; and Tammy Duckworth of Illinois, the first Thai member of the Senate.[16] The half-Indian Kamala Harris is the junior senator from California, and since 2013, the half-Samoan Tulsi Gabbard of Hawaii is the first practicing Hindu congresswoman. She was sworn into the House using a Bhagavad Gita instead of the Bible. From state legislatures to school boards, Asians are also climbing the ladder of local politics with ever more confidence. In 2017, Hoboken, New Jersey, elected its first Sikh mayor, Ravi Bhalla, despite a campaign of flyers that labeled him a terrorist threat. There one also finds the recently opened Shri Swaminarayan Mandir, one of the largest Hindu temples in the world, made entirely of hand-carved marble. At the federal level, the Nobel Prize–winner Steven Chu served as President Obama's secretary of energy, the Indian-born Preet Bharara was a high-profile US district attorney prosecuting white-collar crimes in New York, and former South Carolina congresswoman and governor Nikki Haley, of Sikh parentage, now serves as the Trump administration's ambassador to the United Nations.

With its centuries of history as a global immigration magnet, the United States has always been a place where the internal politics of foreign lands plays out through diasporas. More than one-third of

Americans have some Irish heritage, and many Irish Americans provided cash for the separatist IRA to purchase weapons in the 1970s and then supported the 1990s peace initiatives of the Clinton administration. The global Jewish diaspora, 70 percent of whose 5.2 million members reside in the United States, have also practiced a form of long-distance nationalism evident in their political and financial support for Israel. More recently, the United States has been thrust into the center of Turkish politics for serving as the home of the moderate Islamist preacher Fethullah Gülen, whose movement Turkish president Erdoğan considers a terrorist organization.

The presence of South and East Asians has added a new layer to the United States' international ethnopolitics. In 2014, while the US-based Sikhs for Justice petitioned Congress to label the Hindu-nationalist Rashtriya Swayamsevak Sangh (RSS) a terrorist organization, its political party, the Bharatiya Janata Party (BJP), was ramping up fund-raising across the United States for the campaign of Narendra Modi, who was himself banned from entering the United States due to his alleged complicity in anti-Muslim riots in his home state of Gujarat in 2002. Modi's global grassroots campaign ultimately carried him to India's highest office, and the ban was lifted given his diplomatic immunity. Indian Americans today are as divided about their party loyalties in India as they are in the United States: tech superstars are cozy with Democratic elites, while many doctors, real estate professionals, and small-business owners have backed Trump for his muscular antiterrorism talk and tax cuts.

China, which in the 1990s often found itself on the wrong foot diplomatically as the United States criticized its human rights record and frequently demanded the release of political prisoners, has turned the tables worldwide, punishing countries that host the exiled Tibetan spiritual leader the Dalai Lama. As Chinese dissidents spread around the world, so, too, do China's domestic politics. In 2017, the fugitive Chinese real estate mogul Guo Wengui gained notoriety with his accusations of corruption at the highest levels of the Communist Party. The Chinese diaspora—amplified through social media—was torn between those who aggressively disseminated his claims and those who declared him (and his supporters) to be traitors and Party spies.

Canada already finds itself in a very advanced state of cohabitation with Asian domestic affairs. When it liberalized its immigration policy in the 1970s, it welcomed waves of immigrants from Hong Kong, South Korea, the Philippines, and Taiwan, as well as refugees from Vietnam, Cambodia, and Laos. Since the 2000s, however, mainland Chinese and Indians have far outstripped other Asians except for Filipinos, while in total Asians represent well over 50 percent of all migrants into Canada.[17] Canada has for years offered foreign students a direct path to citizenship, with the countdown beginning the day they set foot on any university campus. Already almost one in every seven Canadians is of Asian heritage.

Vancouver is now North America's most Asian city. In recent years it has superseded Los Angeles as the top destination in North America for flights outbound from China, with nearly 120 direct flights per week from ten Chinese cities. At the same time, intra-Chinese rivalries have become part of daily life as the number of immigrants from mainland China has outstripped those from Hong Kong, meaning that "Hongcouver" has lost its Cantonese edge to a new Mandarin-speaking majority.[18] As if in lockstep with this process, Canadian deportations of Chinese refugees or illegally smuggled migrants have been steadily rising, while undercover Chinese state security operatives have entered Canada to intimidate former employees of state-owned enterprises into repatriating themselves and the funds they've allegedly embezzled. Now Ottawa is facing pressure from Beijing to sign an extradition agreement so China can expeditiously haul back economic fugitives and dissidents—in exchange for a free-trade agreement that Canada covets. Meanwhile, Prime Minister Justin Trudeau's close ties to Canada's Sikh community proved embarrassing during his February 2018 visit to India, where memories of the Sikh separatist movement has not faded. All of this ethnodemographic-diplomatic drama could be just the beginning given the high-level Canadian government discussions on how to increase the country's population from the current 35 million to potentially 100 million by the end of the century.

Anchors or Opportunists?

In many towns across the United States, home prices have been driven upward by an influx of Asian families. Real estate investment schemes such as the EB-5 program have attracted more than 50,000 Chinese, Vietnamese, and South Korean investors, who since 2015 have contributed approximately $30 billion per year to the US economy in exchange for residency, which paves the way for potential citizenship. In the wake of the Trump administration's reduction of H-1B visas, Indians have also begun to take up the EB-5 "golden visa." Real estate developers are preparing ever more materials in Chinese to speed up the deal making. In 2017, Berkshire Hathaway launched a partnership with the Chinese property site Juwai.com to reach an even larger Chinese audience.[19] By some estimates, a similar number of Asian "anchor babies" are born each year in the United States to women engaging in birth tourism.[20]

Students constitute the largest flow of Asians into the United States. Chinese lead the way with nearly 100,000 new arrivals each year, and a total of about 300,000 Chinese are currently enrolled in US educational institutions. India, South Korea, and Saudi Arabia are the next three largest sources of foreign students in the United States, with each sending more than Canada. In total, Asians have surpassed Europeans as the largest share (more than half) of the more than 1 million international students currently studying in US universities.[21] The single most pan-Asian spot in the United States on any given day might be a West Coast US college cafeteria, where Asians gravitate toward one another—and tend to vote for one another in student council elections.

Education is already one of the United States' largest economic sectors, with public and private spending nearing 10 percent of GDP. Tuition payments in the United States by Chinese students alone amounted to nearly $10 billion during the 2014–15 academic year.[22] As Asian student numbers have swelled, new cottage industries have arisen to funnel Asians into community colleges and provide tutoring services to get them up to speed in English or other subjects. The University of Illinois pays commentators to broadcast its football games in Mandarin, Purdue University has hired Mandarin-speaking counselors for its mental health center, and the University of Iowa's business school has hired instructors to coach professors in how to pronounce Chinese names.[23] Assimilating Asian students is itself a new cultural economy. Asian students' presence in the United States also has far-reaching economic effects in the rental market, the food and beverage industry, and tourism. If Asian students were gone, the United States would miss them dearly.

Yet a sea change is under way in the Asian student flow. As US universities cut budgets and raise tuition, while the number of student visas issued has declined precipitously since 2015, many Asian students have been choosing to go to Canada, Great Britain, Australia, and other countries. Indian student visa applications fell 30 percent in just the first year of Trump's presidency. Suspicions about loyalties also play a role. The FBI claims that all of its regional bureaus have encountered cases of Chinese students in particular doubling as amateur spies, collecting information that is then indirectly reported back to Beijing. In early 2018, the University of Texas at Austin terminated funding from the state-supported US-China Cultural and Educational Foundation, and the Trump administration imposed restrictions on Chinese students pursuing master's degrees in high-tech fields. If Chinese government agencies reduce scholarships for Chinese students to come to the United States, their numbers will decline proportionately as well.

Certainly, over the past two generations, millions of Asians have settled in the United States and become proud Asian Americans. Most of their children—whether American-born Chinese (ABC) or American-born confused *desi* (ABCD) for Indians—think of themselves simply as American—no ethnic prefix hyphenation needed—and will only ever have American passports.[24] Chinese and Koreans continue to take Western and Christianized names such as Thomas, John, and Andrew for boys and Vivian, Lucy, and Amy for girls. A previous generation of Asians concentrated in ethnic ghettos wherever they went. Today Asians want to fit in everywhere.

But unlike previous generations from China and India, who were leaving behind poor and stagnant countries, today the percentage of international students who return home upon obtaining degrees is rising steadily; for Chinese it grew from 72 percent in 2012 to 82 percent in 2016.[25] Given the tightly knit Asian collegiate communities, in which many students often socialize only among themselves, it seems as though many Asians studying in the United States, if not the majority, wind up networking mostly with one another, building relationships that result in entrepreneurial collaborations executed back home in Asia. A degree from MIT or Stanford and a brief stint in Silicon Valley are now predictably followed by a return to Asian tech hubs such as Bangalore and Hangzhou. Rather than remaining in the United States and contributing to the US economy—as immigration liberals argue should be encouraged and rewarded with immediate green cards for foreign graduates—Asians are increasingly taking their US educations back home.

This contradicts the common view in the United States that the large numbers of Asian students are a symbol of the United States' eternal appeal and centrality in the global cultural order, as if studying in the United States were the primary (or only) path to self-fulfillment and automatically confers a lifelong adoption of American values. Clearly, most Asian students do not come to the United States to become American, absorb American values, and disown their homelands but rather to acquire an important, but not essential, feather in their pedigree cap to prepare for global professional life—most likely back in Asia.

Asia is teeming with "repats"—Asians who have returned home. Both China and India have attracted several hundred thousand returnees (or "reverse diaspora"), including notable success stories such as Robin Li, who started Baidu after studying in Buffalo and working for Infoseek. Even weaker Asian societies such as Pakistan, Uzbekistan, Indonesia, and the Philippines are luring back talent. Up to 2 million Uzbeks working in Russia may return as the country launches a new phase of modernization. When expats become repats, bringing back skills and cash, they establish themselves as heads of large companies and start-ups, advise governments on major reforms, buy up properties to redevelop, and start schools and hospitals for underserved populations.

The majority of Asians coming to the United States for education are therefore not new Asian anchors but rather opportunists, taking the best of American academic expertise and entrepreneurial culture back to their homelands, where they can be among extended family and make a greater difference to their national futures. With or without racial profiling in the United States, this is what is happening. Additionally, Asian governments are rolling out the red carpet to lure back émigrés to lead R-and-D projects in hundreds of new industrial parks.[26] Chinese think tanks also have taken on the American-style revolving-door approach to active policy advisory, luring back the country's social scientists based abroad.[27] Building on the previous generation's pedigree, a growing number of elites in inner leadership circles from Riyadh to New Delhi to Beijing have Western MAs or MBAs (including former Indian prime minister Manmohan Singh and China's new vice premier, Liu He) or enjoyed sabbaticals and visiting scholarships in the United States or United Kingdom, bringing the best of Western knowledge home to adapt to their own societies. Interestingly, though overseas returnees are accustomed to favorable treatment in the job market, they are increasingly facing competition from talented students who have never left China.[28] Indeed, two decades ago, China launched Project 985, pledging to invest more than $2 billion to upgrade nearly forty universities to help them earn a place in the top tier of global academic rankings. In 2017, Tsinghua University and Peking University landed spots in the top twenty, with eight other Chinese universities in the top one hundred.[29] India, however, still lags behind with only two universities in the global top two hundred.

Meanwhile, working for Asian companies is no longer uncommon in the United States. Americans have worked for Japanese car companies for decades, and Tennessee, Kentucky, Alabama, and other states continue to compete for Toyota or Hyundai to locate plants in their states.

have been contracting since 2016, Asia's car market nearly quadrupled from 2009 to 2016. General Motors' sales in Asia are growing between 5 and 15 percent per year. Asia also accounts for nearly 50 percent of Volkswagen's sales. And from Abu Dhabi to Singapore, the defense contractors Lockheed Martin and Raytheon are rolling out their best weaponry at Asia's air shows, hoping to win large contracts for drones and missiles from modernizing militaries in the Gulf region, India, and East Asia. China will not be a major market for their wares, but much of the rest of Asia already is.

Asia's rapid urbanization has inspired Western networking hardware giants such as Cisco Systems and IBM to deploy their most advanced technologies in Asia. Singapore offers such companies a "living lab" for demonstration projects in using sensor networks to efficiently manage everything from traffic to security for large populations. In Singapore, France's Dassault Systèmes has created the world's most advanced 3D geodata platform, where it designs customizable and energy-efficient bridges that it hopes to sell across Asia. Western know-how is therefore accelerating Asia's claim to be home to the "smart cities" of the future. The Los Angeles–based AECOM, one of the world's top engineering and design firms, has three thousand staff in China, another three thousand across Southeast Asia, and a growing number in India, with Saudi Arabia and the UAE its fastest-growing offices. The legendary Chicago architecture firm Skidmore, Owings & Merrill designed Dubai's Burj Khalifa, while Gensler of San Francisco designed the Shanghai Tower, currently the world's second tallest building.

Even as Washington looks askance at the Belt and Road Initiative, US banks see it as essential to their Asian positioning. Citibank recently launched a strategy called "Asia to Asia" (A2A) that identifies a half dozen of the most rapidly intensifying intra-Asian trade relationships (South Korea–Vietnam, Japan-Thailand, and so forth) and aims to finance or advise as many of those cross-border transactions as possible. Asia's share of global mergers and acquisitions activity rose from 16 percent in 2005 to 40 percent in 2016, with China's share ranging from 30 to 60 percent.

Numerous states jockeyed to lure Foxconn with billions in tax breaks and cash rebates, a contest eventually won by Wisconsin. US workers, like Asians, care much more about their paycheck than where their employer comes from. This should come as no surprise given the deteriorating economic health of many American families. Sectors such as banking, insurance, housing, real estate, health care, and entertainment make the United States a gargantuan economy, but financial problems have eaten away the American dream of home ownership on both ends: financially insecure millennials can't afford to buy their first homes—and may never buy a home as the family unit shrinks in size[30]—while struggling elderly families sell their homes to cash-rich Asians and live out their final years in more modest rental properties. Meanwhile, e-commerce has decimated the United States' retail sector, with shopping malls closing weekly nationwide. Sixty percent of the US economy is consumption, but 60 percent of the population is struggling economically, with 80 percent of US jobs low-skilled and low-paying. Rising inequality has become a hot-button political issue, with the top 10 percent claiming an ever larger share of national wealth. The rich have gotten richer and the poor poorer: the country's median income actually fell by 5 percent between 2010 and 2013, to $46,700, while middle-class incomes continue to stagnate.

All of this makes Americans the perfect mass market for cheap Asian goods—just like billions of other customers around the world. Indeed, tens of millions of poor Americans don't have smartphones that would allow them to access lower-cost mobile banking and instead pay high fees for low-balance bank accounts, debit cards, check-cashing services, or payday loans. They would all be better off with cheap Asian smartphones and WeChat, not to mention low-cost Indian generic medicines, which already represent one-third of the US market. Americans' binge consumption has meant not only endless shopping for largely unnecessary merchandise but also binge eating at all-you-can-eat restaurants that are fueling the nation's obesity crisis. Even a shift from bingeing to an "experience economy" will benefit hard-working

Asians, who push themselves overtime in the gig economy, have lower rates of drug addiction, and can thrive in hot entrepreneurial areas such as selling coding courses or Chinese lessons.

Even if the number of Asian real estate investors, birth mothers, and college students coming into the United States and Canada plateaus, the demographic Asianization of North America will continue to a considerable degree. This is generally for the greater good. From San Francisco to Pittsburgh, educated Asians are a key ingredient in what makes some American cities more cosmopolitan and desirable as places to live in. Vibrant and populous cities with ethnically diverse residents (such as Vancouver and Toronto) rank at the top of the tables when it comes to livability and creativity.[31] Americanization has been a boon for Asians seeking a stable life and liberal education. Now Asianization is breathing vitality into American communities—and giving Americans global opportunities they cannot get at home.

From Asian Americans to American Asians

In addition to the return of Asians to Asia, what is also new—and deeply significant for Western attitudes toward Asia—is the rising numbers of Americans who are consciously exposing themselves to Asia from an early age and then traveling to study and live in Asia itself. Americans are traveling en masse to study Mandarin in China, launch start-ups in Singapore, and backpack around Vietnam and Myanmar. The difference between today and a generation ago is that it is not clear whether today's Western millennials decamping for Asia will ever return.

The Asia bug bites as early as kindergarten, with Chinese immersion programs growing in popularity in major American cities—and even as alternatives to overcrowded, low-quality public schools. New York City's sticker-shocking Avenues school promises Chinese fluency before graduation. In Colorado, Mandarin has displaced Spanish as the most popular second language to study. In 2015, then president Obama launched the 1 Million Strong program in an effort to have 1 million American students learning Mandarin by 2020—an impressive figure, except when compared with the estimated 400 million Chinese who are learning English.

For the majority of Americans not deeply exposed to Asia before college, the pull of Asia takes hold during freshman year as romantic aspirations to study Italian give way to larger and more lucrative Asian linguistic opportunities. Asian studies departments and Asian language teaching are strengthening nationwide. Asian thought also holds a growing allure as an entry point into an Asian future. Harvard's most popular class after economics and computer science is Classical Chinese Ethical and Political Theory. Adding to the roster of American scholars who have developed a strong competency in Asian languages and history, more universities are hiring Asian faculty members and awarding fellowships to Asians who bring authentic perspectives and enhance the training of Western academics.[32] From Edward Said's manifesto *Orientalism* to the rise of postcolonial studies—with its critical views on the legacies of imperialism from Asian luminaries such as Gayatri Spivak, Sara Suleri Goodyear, and Homi Bhabha—the migration of Asian scholars to the West has spurred essential debates about the dynamics and norms of global society. For established academics, long-standing and fruitful intellectual exchanges such as the Harvard-Yenching Institute's collaboration with Beijing University are being reinforced with ever more platforms for scholarly sharing.

Once seduced by this rigorous exposure to Arab, South Asian, or East Asian affairs, undergraduates then go through the ritual of studying abroad, with the number of students doing so doubling in the past decade. Europe still receives half of US study-abroad students each year, but Asia has now overtaken Latin America for second place.[33] China is the world's third most popular destination for study abroad—and would easily surpass the United Kingdom were it not for all the Chinese themselves who are studying there. India, Japan, and Korea have also been growing steadily as major study-abroad destinations.[34] Nearly 15,000 Americans head to China each year, and the rest of Asia pulls in a nearly equal number. Anglophone programs in the Philippines and Australia are witnessing up to 10 percent growth per year in American participation.

Asian countries welcome not only American students with open arms but also American university campuses. Particularly after the September 11, 2001, terrorist attacks, when Asian students began to experience difficulty in getting their student visas approved to matriculate in the United States, US colleges raced to expand their international presence. Georgetown, Cornell, and Northwestern have campuses in Doha; New York University has campuses in Abu Dhabi and Shanghai; Yale has already graduated several cohorts of students from its campus in Singapore; and Duke has a full-fledged undergraduate program near Beijing. The emergence of top-tier Western centers of learning in Asia may have significant consequences for the number—and caliber—of Asian youths who travel to the United States for their tertiary education. Singapore's top graduates, known as government scholars, are accustomed to spreading themselves across Stanford, Harvard, Oxford, and Cambridge but now have the option of attending NYU Shanghai or Yale in their own backyard. Additionally, leading Chinese, Japanese, and Korean universities have in the past decade launched all-English curricula with a mix of faculty including repatriated Asian PhDs and Western academics seeking well-paid opportunities abroad.[35] Asians increasingly have the luxury of getting their top-tier English-language education delivered in their home country, meaning that a decade or two hence, Asia's best and brightest may well remain in Asia for their entire educational journey.

A growing number of Americans are doing the same. Because many such Asia-based programs offer subsidized tuition and accommodation, state-of-the-art facilities, and other perks, many top-tier American high school graduates are choosing at the outset to get their "American" education in Asia. Suddenly, instead of just one year abroad, their entire undergraduate education is spent overseas. Think about what this means. Each year, thousands more Western students are not imbibing a standard Western narrative and the presumptions of superiority that come with it. They remain open-minded, and Asian ideas become part of their intellectual foundation moving forward.

After college, Asian opportunities abound. Each time I have lectured at Beijing's Tsinghua University in the past decade, I have noticed ever more Western faces among the graduate students taking advantage of its high-quality, competitively priced MA program, which is taught in both English and Mandarin and offers robust networking opportunities with multinationals and Chinese companies. The year 2016 also witnessed the launch of the Schwarzman Scholars program, a generously endowed scholarship branded as the twenty-first-century equivalent of the Rhodes Scholarship— but drawing top talent to Asia, not Europe. Chinese commentators have long complained that China sends its best students abroad to study but does not get other countries' best minds in return. Now that is changing.

Also at the graduate level, business schools and their executive programs have put down stakes in Asia. Harvard Business School's most recent curricular innovation—known as "global immersion"—requires students to tackle challenges for partner companies and then travel and embed themselves in their headquarters, most of which are in Asia. France's INSEAD, which has long had a campus in Singapore, is being copied by other Western business schools such as the University of Pennsylvania's Wharton School, which opened the Penn Wharton China Center in Beijing in 2015.

For the West's educated, professional, and mobile class, no region is better placed than Asia to capitalize on Brexit, opposition to Trump, and Western elites' revulsion with their own politics. There is already an older stratum of American bankers, English teachers, and missionaries who are deeply familiar with the advantages of expat life in Asia. Legendary investors such as Mark Mobius and Jim Rogers have strategically located themselves in Asian hubs in order to gain local insight into how to capitalize on Asia's breakneck growth. Now a new generation of expats is following in their footsteps, taking advantage of Asia's mix of opportunity and comfort and enjoying the hallmarks of expat life such as low taxes, high quality of life, public safety, rigorous education, and efficient governance that one finds in key Asian hubs that also rank among the world's safest cities: Tokyo, Osaka, Singapore, Hong Kong, Melbourne, and Sydney.

Particularly since the financial crisis, the number of American expats has ticked up substantially. The number of US citizens living abroad was only 4 million in 1999 and 6.8 million in 2013 but reached 9 million in 2017.[36] Among Asian countries, the Philippines, Israel, South Korea, and China have the largest number of American residents, with China and India the fastest growing destinations for Americans heading abroad. According to the industry-standard HSBC Expat Explorer survey, expats in Asia are three times more likely to earn over $250,000 per year as they would at home.[37] Asian airlines have a nearly unlimited appetite for US-trained pilots, offering them salaries of up to $300,000 per year.[38] With salaries at that level, it is no surprise that thousands of American and British financial professionals and consultants have chosen to retire in Asia rather than return to dead-end middle management, cutthroat competitive positions, or mandatory retirement in New York or London. Instead, they shrewdly manage their taxes and housing and health care costs and leverage their regional networks to continue working in private equity, wealth management, or merchant banking. American teachers can also circulate among the many new international schools popping up in Asian cities and earn about triple their home salaries—with better education for their own kids.

The combination of the financial and energy downturns has affected many expat families whose breadwinners were recalled or laid off by banks and oil and gas companies. But the story that doesn't make Western headlines is how many more expat families have remained in Asia and gone local by taking jobs with regional companies and putting their kids into local schools. Switching from high-pressure Western employers to more creative and ambitious Asian companies has gone from an outlier choice to a desirable career move. This in turn has helped overcome the long-standing social divides between expats and locals in places such as Hong Kong and Singapore, where expats increasingly see themselves not as separate and superior but as very much part of the community. Rather than detaching expats from Asia, then, the economic troubles in the West have largely encouraged expats to become *more* Asian in their lifestyles. And the more rapidly Asia modernizes, the broader the range of destinations in which Western expats are planting roots. Bangkok, Jakarta, and Ho Chi Minh City are poaching experienced Americans already living in Hong Kong, Taipei, and Singapore. Phuket and Bali now have well-connected airports and high-quality international schools, resulting in a growing resident population of digital entrepreneurs.

Asian governments know that in the short run it makes sense to import brains to stimulate innovation. The Gulf countries have been attracting British, German, and American talent for decades. In Saudi Arabia, the King Abdullah University of Science and Technology (KAUST) offers sizable salaries to American academics to relocate to the desert near Mecca and work on pressing challenges related to the country's energy industry and other sectors. Westerners are also being drawn by entrepreneur visa schemes offering stable long-term residency in exchange for hiring and training locals in cutting-edge areas ranging from metallurgy to artificial intelligence. Thailand has launched a four-year visa for entrepreneurs who want to start a business in the country. China is not content only to lure back overseas Chinese but has also launched the Thousand Talents Plan, which has attracted more than six thousand non-Chinese entrepreneurs, scientists, and innovators to take up residency in China. Almost every Asian country is doing the opposite of the West: opening its arms to attract talent from far and wide.

Asia has never looked so enticing for American millennials, 80 percent of whom believe that Asia is the most important foreign region for their future. American engineers and English teachers are in high demand across the region, young American actors and stuntmen are trying their luck in Hong Kong's thriving film industry, and Americans are approached on the street to adorn commercial ads targeting Asian customers. American basketball and soccer players are earning solid seasonal paydays staffing teams from China to Thailand. Importantly, it is not just any young Americans that Asia is attracting today but the clever, adventurous, risk-taking, entrepreneurial ones. Over the past two decades of intensive traveling across Asia, I've witnessed a surge in the number of young Americans making the leap over the Pacific—often indefinitely. Whether or not they have a concrete plan, it takes both courage and brains to make it in alien countries operating in exotic tongues. Just two of the hundreds I have gotten to know are a young Canadian, J. T. Singh, who bounced between Singapore, Hong Kong, and Shanghai before establishing a lucrative niche as a cinematographer making viral branding videos for Asian cities and companies, and Benjamin Joffe, an energetic French investor and tech mentor who runs one of the largest start-up incubators in China. In the age of global social media, each such success story inspires five—or five hundred—more. And with the rise of nomad-friendly short-term housing from Tokyo to Bangkok to Bali, ever more Westerners are trying their luck in Asia—with no plans to return home. Asians settling in America are called Asian Americans. Will we call this new caste of Americans settling in Asia "American Asians"?

6

Why Europe Loves Asia but Not (Yet) Asians

A sia's relations with Europe are long-lasting and intense. From Greek armies to the Crusades to European colonization, greater Asia has for millennia been on the receiving end of European fascination and imperial designs. In the reverse direction, Phoenicians ruled the Mediterranean, Mongols plundered eastern Europe, Arabs preserved classical Greek learning, and Chinese goods and inventions inspired the Silk Road. Most Western knowledge of Asian civilizations, languages, and religions comes from European explorers and missionaries such as the English navigator James Cook, who mapped the South Pacific islands, and philologists such as Max Müller, the German professor at Oxford who romanticized the East, particularly India, in the mid-1800s, while mining it for transcendental wisdom. Or consider Nicholas Roerich: as he wandered Tibet and the Indian Himalayas, the Russian mystic and spy believed that the region's ancient symbology provided a rational structure to reconcile art, science, and religion. Europe's persistent obsession with Asia has been essential for Asia's own self-discovery: It was French archaeologists who stumbled upon the great temples of Angkor Wat in Cambodia's dense jungle, unearthing the Khmer civilizational heritage that attracts millions of tourists every year.

Although the very term *Asia* is a European coinage meant to designate the "other" in lands beyond, the rapid blending between Europe and Asia unfolding today portends a continental superfusion. Washington's conventional wisdom has been that the United States should put the declining Europe on the back burner to focus on the rising Asia. Now it appears that the declining United States and its failed Asia policy have put Euro-Asian convergence front and center. From London to Shanghai, networks of high-speed railways, trade hubs, and Internet cables are underpinning a Euro-Asian commercial axis that even shows signs of evolving into a Eurasian *system*.

As an exchange student, undergraduate, think-tank analyst, and doctoral candidate throughout the 1990s and 2000s, I would frequently travel between the United States and Europe as part of transatlantic delegations aimed at extending the bonds between the twin pillars of Western civilization. For Americans, it was a strategic investment in a Western alliance necessary to manage Russian volatility, Arab instability, and the "global war on terror." For Europe, the United States still represented its primary security umbrella and economic partner, as well as Europe's key political ally in promoting human rights and democracy. Europe, simply put, saw hope to the west and fear to the east.

Today the situation seems almost reversed. Under presidents Bush and Obama, the fallout over the disastrous Iraq War, and revelations that the United States was spying on its closest allies left Europeans feeling alienated from the United States. During the Trump administration, the rift has only deepened as Washington has called for uncomfortably high levels of defense spending by Europeans, threatened the region's core industries with tariffs, and dropped out of the Paris climate agreement. To Europeans, then, Asia has suddenly begun to appear a more stable long-term value proposition than the United States. And just as suddenly, my invitations to Europe shifted from requesting a perspective on Washington to seeking insight into Asia.

Asia has become a wedge issue between the United States and Europe. The United States sees Europe once again as a frontline region against an expansionist Russia and a collapsing eastern Mediterranean. But these are crucial geographic bridges in advancing the Eurasian agenda. While the United States banned almost all contact with Russian officials and reneged on its agreement to engage with Iran, European countries were hosting Iran investment conferences every month and speaking to Vladimir Putin weekly about settling the Ukraine crisis and restoring energy cooperation. One might even claim that given the stagnation in European-American relations—a dull but steady marriage not immune to tantrums—Asia is increasingly what animates the household chatter. Indeed, Asia is being invited into the dining room. At the elite Munich Security Conference, traditionally a transatlantic gathering of foreign ministers and defense officials taking place each spring, the growing presence of Russian and Chinese officials is what has kept the forum from becoming a moribund ritual—and what has kept US vice presidents, secretaries of state, and leading senators returning each year.

Europe's pivot eastward is proving to be much more successful than the United States'. Europe has been leading the way in eastward expansion since the 1990s, with the EU doubling its membership by absorbing Eastern European countries and deploying funds such as the European Bank for Reconstruction and Development (EBRD) to modernize them. The Council of Europe includes Russia and the Caucasus countries, while the Organization for Security and Co-operation in Europe (OSCE) includes all other former Soviet republics as well, including those of Central Asia. The Asia-Europe Meeting (ASEM) already represents the world's largest global economic group, accounting for more than half of global GDP and more than 60 percent of world trade. Asia-Europe trade is expected to reach $2.5 trillion by 2025, about double the current trade between Europe and North America or between North America and Asia.[1]

There is no question that Europe will prevail over the United States in the race to profit from Asia's rise. Since both Europe and Asia fear the creeping protectionism of "America first" policies, their mutual desire to substitute the United States with new Eurasian ties has only grown. The end result of the United States' protectionist measures has been damage to US workers and exports, with Europe grabbing every opportunity to capture markets that Americans have been closed out of through reciprocal tariffs.[2] With Europe's trade surpluses being absorbed by Asian demand, Germany's ministers openly rebuff the US Treasury's calls to rein them in.

Europeans and Asians agree that their main collective priority is to connect the Atlantic to the Pacific. A century after China declared war on Germany, Germany has thriving relations with China and other Asian nations. China has replaced the United States as Germany's top trading partner outside the European Union. All European leaders travel more to Asian countries than to the United States, and German chancellor Angela Merkel visited China eight times between 2004 and 2018. The German and Chinese cabinets meet annually for a joint session. During Merkel's 2018 visit to China, Xi Jinping promised to "open the door even wider" to German business. The German engineering giant Siemens has thrown its weight behind Belt and Road precisely because it has been active in the markets lying between Germany and China far longer than Chinese companies have—and China also needs its high-tech products to achieve its Made in China 2025 goals. Another example is Germany's Manz, which sells an advance thin-film coating to Chinese solar panel makers such as Shanghai Electric Group. Hamburg has a three-decades-long sister city partnership with Shanghai that has gained steam as their ports exchange ships ever more frequently. Berlin's city government has launched a StartUp AsiaBerlin program that sends delegations of tech entrepreneurs to Bangalore, Manila, and Jakarta, helping companies such as Coolar—which makes solar-powered refrigerators ideal for tropical Asian countries that still lack electricity—to expand far from home. Meanwhile, the annual Asia-Pacific Weeks Berlin brings Asian entrepreneurs in the other direction to survey and procure technologies from German tech innovators.

China has thus far been the most aggressive in selling its wares in Europe. Inside the enormous hangars of the Messe Berlin grounds, there are ever more frequent expos featuring the latest Chinese flat-screen TVs and household appliances to stock European department stores. Even if you don't wander around the convention grounds, you can tell the Chinese sales teams have descended on Berlin through the announcements in Mandarin at Tegel Airport. But the more Eurasian infrastructural connectivity expands and reduces the costs of travel and marketing, the more Asians will set up shop in Europe as well.

The most significant episode in European countries' accelerated reorientation to Asia is their joining the Asian Infrastructure Investment Bank (AIIB) over US objections, putting their diplomatic and commercial weight behind a Chinese-sponsored institution. But their move was perfectly logical, for the European Union—not the United States—is China's largest trading partner.[3] With the European Central Bank ramping up its purchases of renminbi for its reserves and allowing offshore renminbi clearing centers across Europe, the expansion of Sino-European liquidity is paving the way for even more commercial integration.[4] Related to this, European countries are now focused on copying the German model of driving exports in high-growth markets, especially in Asia. Because European countries see the enormous potential of Belt and Road to benefit their major exports, they are sending warnings to Beijing to make sure they get their fair share of the work.

The massive EU-Asia trade volumes already achieved are even more remarkable given the lack of any major trade agreements across Eurasia and the long-distance shipping on which most transcontinental trade depends. Now, with the launch of more than fifty new freight rail lines linking a dozen Asian countries to a dozen major European cities, corporate Europe is even more enamored with the Asian opportunity. Kuehne + Nagel, one of the world's largest freight-forwarding companies, is expanding its Asia operations while also deploying its knowhow in digital logistics to speed up intra-Asian logistical throughput between dozens of Asian ports and urban hubs. As trains run from Yiwu to Madrid, Chengdu to Duisburg, Belt and Road conferences are popping up in London, Milan, and Berlin on a monthly basis.

Duisburg, Germany's largest inland port, is the site of extensive Chinese investment in transport and logistics operations and also the point of departure of twenty trains per week headed for China. In 2017, a German-Chinese cultural exchange commission organized a Kazakhstan Day in Duisburg at which more than a dozen countries set up pavilions and hosted speeches, concerts, art exhibits, and food trucks celebrating the many countries lying along the iron Silk Roads linking the two ends of Eurasia. The centerpiece of this Blue Container festival was the trains. For the first two years of continuous freight service, many of the railcars painted with the bright blue logo of China Railway Express were full of cargo heading from east to west—brimming with laptops and mobile phones—but relatively empty for the long return back to Asia. But by 2017, Europeans realized that the same insulation moderating the temperature inside containers full of Chinese electronics could also protect refrigeration units storing French wine, Iberian ham, and Belorussian milk.[5] As Asian demand soars for high-quality European frozen foods, trans-Eurasian railways will transport them to Asian grocery stores ever more efficiently.[6] Even Western Europe's biggest food companies, such as Nestlé and Unilever, earn no more than 20 percent of their revenues in Europe. Asia is already their fastest-growing and in some cases their largest market.

Europe's retail industries are aggressively penetrating all Asian markets. The German sporting goods titan Adidas sells more shoes in Shanghai alone than in all of Switzerland and Austria. Both Germany's multinationals and its SMEs have ever smoother access to business-to-consumer (B2C) platforms such as Alibaba's Tmall (formerly Taobao Mall). As European pharmacies such as dm-drogerie markt tie up with Alibaba, they can seamlessly export high-quality baby care products such as milk powder formula on trains reaching Asia in days rather than weeks. France, too, has sought to boost its trade with Russia, China, and India. In 2016, its trade with those three countries alone amounted to nearly $100 billion, still less than its $142 billion with the United Kingdom and United States but increasing much more quickly. The 2018 World Cup witnessed a record profit for the Fédération Internationale de Football Association (FIFA), which lured one-third of its sponsors from China versus none in 2014, even though China itself didn't even qualify (though South Korea knocked the reigning champion, Germany, out of the competition). Three straight Olympic games are being held in Asia—Korea 2018, Japan 2020, and Beijing 2022—which will boost sales for European manufacturers of everything from soccer balls to skis.

Europe's awakened corporate focus on Asia is unmistakable. In recent years, the Dutch telecom operator Veon has run networks covering more than 200 million people from its hubs across Russia and Kazakhstan. In 2018, Norway's Telenor sold off its Eastern European operations in order to double down on its Asian operations in Bangladesh, Myanmar, Pakistan, Thailand, and Malaysia, which together represent a market nearly fifty times as large. The United Kingdom's Cross-Government Prosperity Fund, the government's nearly $2 billion annual development assistance investment program, gives its largest allotments to Turkey, India, China, and Indonesia. Even some of the most well rooted European industries have globalized to Asia. English, Spanish, and Italian football clubs pack Asian stadiums for off-season exhibition games. Many Michelin-starred European chefs have expanded into Dubai, Singapore, Hong Kong, and Shanghai (where Jean-Georges Vongerichten has his most profitable restaurant). Italian private banks that for two centuries had only domestic operations now earn half their revenue in Asia.

Given the breakneck pace of Asian urbanization, one of Europe's chief exports is its model of sustainable cities to Asia's teeming megacities. Entire European countries, including Germany, Italy, and Spain, are at or near grid parity, meaning that the cost of installing wind, solar, and other renewable power now pays for itself in operational savings to citizens and businesses. Once known as a "garden city," Bangalore today is often called the "garbage city" due to its outdated urban planning and impenetrable congestion. For choking New Delhi or congested Manila to live up to their potential, they need to adapt the bicycle lanes, public parks, affordable housing, green architecture, and vertical agriculture of cities such as Paris, Vienna, and Berlin. As Asia grows wealthier and older, its citizens want not just factory towns but walkable communities. German city planners designed the Tianjin Eco-city in China and are under way with a similar master plan on the Mongolian steppe. Siemens has built Bangkok's elevated light rail and is expanding Kuala Lumpur's while bidding to implement a dozen more across Asia. The European Union's International Urban Cooperation (IUC) program works with more than thirty pairs of cities bridging Europe and Asia to fund sustainability projects. European and Asian cities now share guidance and case studies on platforms such as Metropolis, which also convenes city officials to establish direct city-to-city policy transfer relationships across Eurasia. The German architect Ole Scheeren has designed award-winning East Asian buildings such as the Interlace in Singapore, the MahaNakhon tower in Bangkok and, in Ho Chi Minh City, the Empire City project, where green design will meet the natural green of Vietnam's tropical flora. British architect Norman Foster designed an entire new sustainable capital city, Amaravati, for the Indian state of Andhra Pradesh. And for Asia's masses, a dozen European companies have developed low-cost 3D printed homes made of snap-together parts.[7]

Another valuable service Europeans have to offer Asians is moving money across borders. HSBC, Standard Chartered, and other banks with colonial origins have been operating in dozens of Asian markets for generations and have broad regional networks that most national Asian banks haven't yet built. Standard Chartered has effectively become a Silk Road bank, focused almost exclusively on outbound Chinese and pan–Indian Ocean BRI-related projects. It is British only in name.

Asian countries' investment in Europe is substantially higher than in the United States. Chinese investment in Europe reached $40 billion in 2016 across sectors such as consumer goods, entertainment, utilities, and telecoms, and will continue to rise as China diverts investments away from the United States.[8] The China National Chemical Corporation (ChemChina)'s purchase of the Swiss-based agrochemical company Syngenta alone was worth $40 billion and is China's largest overseas acquisition to date.[9] After a decade of mergers and consolidation, the Indian-led ArcelorMittal is Europe's largest steelmaker, followed closely by India's Thyssenkrupp Tata Steel. In 2015, Saudi crown prince Mohammed bin Salman purchased the rebuilt Château Louis XIV in Louveciennes, France, for $300 million, an eye-opening transaction that shed light on the cottage industry of financiers, lawyers, and other professionals kept gainfully employed by Arabs' luxury investments across Western Europe.

The United Kingdom remains the top European destination for Asian investors, followed by the Netherlands, France, and Spain. The recently retired Hong Kong tycoon Li Ka Shing's Hutchison Whampoa is the largest foreign investor in the United Kingdom, and China's ABP Group has been developing east London's Royal Albert Dock as a special commercial zone, effectively a portal for Asian companies seeking a bridgehead in the United Kingdom. In 2017, two Chinese navy frigates docked in London on a goodwill tour, symbolic perhaps of the reversal of imperial fortunes since the Opium Wars. With Brexit weakening Great Britain's economic profile, Asian funds have been quick to take advantage, now dominating new commercial real estate transactions. Qatar holds $50 billion worth of UK assets, including stakes in flagship British companies such as Sainsbury's and British Airways, and also owns more property in London than the British royal family does.[10] Post-Brexit Britain is desperate for financial and trade agreements with Asia, especially in the services arena which accounts for most of its exports. The Financial Conduct Authority (FCA) has proposed a new set of rules intended to lure major Asian IPOs to London's stock exchange rather than to its competitors in the United States. Former prime minister David Cameron wasted little time after leaving Downing Street in taking over a $1 billion fund dedicated to enhancing the United Kingdom's trade links with Asia. A London-Singapore "fintech bridge" helps new companies raise money seamlessly in either jurisdiction and particularly benefits UK companies that want to access Asian banking markets. Eight commercial Chinese banks have offices in London to facilitate European investment in China and Belt and Road projects. The sentiment heard so often in London is truer than ever: "Britain is for sale."

China Dividing Europe, Europe Rediscovering Asia

In the 2000s, it was fashionable for US foreign policy elites to distinguish between an "old Europe" that recoiled at the United States' muscular foreign policy (in particular the invasion of Iraq) and a "new Europe" of countries that shared Americans' realism about global dangers and supported higher defense spending and foreign interventions. Arabs have also used their financial clout to tilt European foreign policy. Now China has begun to exploit the old/new Europe divide with the same "new" eastern European countries that support Chinese investments, including construction of a Budapest-Belgrade railway, power plants and steel factories in Serbia, and oil refineries in Romania, even if they might not meet European standards on procurement transparency and environmental quality. Countries such as Romania and Bulgaria are becoming depopulated, postindustrial farmlands. Given Asia's rising food demand, China and other Asian countries continue to buy up European agricultural land and lay the corridors that will transport its products back to their hungry region for decades to come. For countries that just one generation ago were locked in the Soviet sphere of influence, to be courted with military hardware from the United States, modernization funds from Europe, and new investments from China is a propitious reversal of fortune.

China has even created a new diplomatic grouping called the 16+1 forum with its own secretariat and annual meetings to coordinate various Chinese investments in Eastern Europe and matchmaking between Chinese entrepreneurs and local SMEs.[11] The crossover from commerce to politics has had its intended effect: large investments in the Greek port of Piraeus and in Hungarian industries and think tanks have led to Greece and Hungary watering down EU statements critical of China's human rights record. Hungary—whose people sometimes refer to themselves as the "Asians of Europe" given their ethnic history and linguistic structure—has even proclaimed "Eastern opening" as a new pillar of its foreign policy. Eastern European socialist parties

are also keen participants in China's Progressive Alliance of Social-
ists and Democrats, showing how China builds political ties across the
spectrum, not just with heads of state. This stands in stark contrast to
the failure of the US-sponsored Alliance of Democracies Foundation
during the Clinton administration, which in the 1990s sought to have
Poland as the key anchor of a global liberal movement. In 2012, Poland
was the host of the inaugural 16+1 summit.

Despite a half decade of frosty ties following the awarding of the Nobel
Peace Prize to the Chinese dissident Liu Xiaobo in 2010, Sino-Norwegian
commercial ties have resumed, much to the delight of Norway's salmon
farmers, who suffered under Chinese boycotts. China Oilfield Services
Limited (COSL) is again gaining contracts with Norway's Statoil, and
Chinese and Korean gas exploration in the Arctic has resumed. Chinese businesspeople have attempted—thus far unsuccessfully—to buy
scenic but strategic Arctic real estate in Norway and Iceland. Finland,
meanwhile, has branded itself as an Arctic hub for Asian investors, and
25 percent of its exports go to Asia.

European regulations are catching up to commercial realities. Previously, Europe lacked strong market advisory services and watch-
dogs for Asia, but now groups ranging from the Asia-Europe Business
Forum (AEBF) to the European Chamber of Commerce in China to the
Mercator Institute for China Studies (MERICS) in Berlin provide up-
to-the-minute guidance for European companies, policy makers, and
intelligence services. The European Union still denies China the one
blessing it most craves—"market economy" status—despite a combined
thirty trips to Europe by Xi Jinping and Premier of the State Council
Li Keqiang. Because China's playing field is far from level for foreign
entrants, Europe is demanding reciprocal access to China's consumers
and stronger protection for European businesses before it will grant
China an upgrade. And, like the United States, the European Union is
growing much more cautious about approving Chinese acquisitions of
sensitive technologies with potential military applications—hence Ger-

many's blocking of Fujian Grand Chip Investment Fund's attempted purchase of the semiconductor equipment manufacturer Aixtron SE. Mistrust of China remains high, especially in countries where Chinese investment is the highest.

But unlike the tension between the United States and China, Europe's conflicts with China are better described as competitive friction: Europe's high-quality goods and strict regulations clashing with Asia's intellectual property theft and asymmetrical market access. As European countries run up against slowing growth and intellectual property risk in China, they are diverting investment to elsewhere in Asia. With labor costs competitive and skills improving, German industrial powerhouses such as Bosch have begun to shift their production of advanced antilock braking systems and other auto components to Vietnam, where they are installing the latest technologies and training engineers. There are already 1,800 German companies in Singapore, with 100 more on average adding a presence there annually. With more than $20 billion in annual investment flows into ASEAN, the European Union is Southeast Asia's largest investor, its cumulative $85 billion in foreign investment larger than that of any other region. And with more than $250 billion in annual trade, the European Union has already surpassed Japan as ASEAN's second largest trade partner behind China—and ASEAN is the European Union's third largest trade partner after the United States and China.[12] Switzerland has had a free-trade agreement (FTA) with China since 2014 and is now negotiating similar access with multiple ASEAN countries. Where the nimble Swiss go, Brussels usually follows, and indeed, the European Union is negotiating an FTA with ASEAN based on an existing arrangement with Singapore.

European horizons now encompass all of Asia. After South Korea and Japan, India is the next major economy poised to sign a free trade agreement with the European Union. At the 2017 India-EU Summit, the European Investment Bank (EIB) made its largest commitments ever to flagship Indian initiatives such as Skill India and Digital India, with contracts given to European companies to promote Indian "smart cities" through renewable energy projects. At the same time, both Germany and France are selling military hardware such as new submarines to India. Fresh on the heels of British prime minister Theresa May's visit to India in 2017, London mayor Sadiq Khan followed with a large delegation to both India and Pakistan. This is how Europe plans to get the upper hand in the race for two of the world's fastest-growing economies—no longer as colonizers but as trade partners.

A similar dynamic is unfolding in the Arab Gulf markets, where Europeans are preferred partners to guide the high-stakes process of economic transformation to a postoil future. France's EDF, for example, is leading the national rollout of solar power across both Saudi Arabia and the UAE so they can reduce their oil and gas consumption, cut fuel subsidies, and export more hydrocarbon energy. European engineering firms dominate the Gulf region's megainfrastructure projects, with the German architectural firm SL Rasch's design for the Mecca clock tower (six times taller than Big Ben) as only the most symbolic example, while Volocopter is supplying Dubai with drone taxis. Great Britain has aggressively ramped up its sale of missiles and other hardware to Saudi Arabia for its bombing campaigns in Yemen.

Among the Arab Gulf nations, Saudi Arabia is particularly resentful of Europe's rushing into Iran, even canceling pending contracts with Germany. But frustrated with the United States' reneging on its commitment to lift sanctions on Iran gradually in exchange for a freeze of its nuclear program, Europeans are more explicitly breaking with the United States and Saudi Arabia. While the United States threatens to deny access to the US market to European companies doing business with Iran, European countries have quietly restructured their presence in the United States to allow them to legally transact more business with Iran, while developing a parallel financial network that evades American interference. Europeans have also allowed Iranian investment funds to purchase pharmaceutical and machinery companies, helping Iran stock up to weather the sanctions downturn. In the posh Kish Island free-trade zone lying off the coast of Iran, local European banks out of reach of UN sanctions sign deals with companies in countries from Belgium to Turkey to Indonesia to finance investments in Iran.

Sanctions have at best delayed the inevitable flood of investment that will absorb Iran into the Eurasian commercial system. IranAir has purchased Airbus planes, European energy companies are developing Iranian gas fields in consortia with Asian partners, Norway's Saga Energy is building $3 billion worth of solar power facilities in Iran, and Mercedes-Benz has sold a fleet of new buses there. The train has literally left the station, with luxury trains carrying Europeans from Budapest to Tehran for lengthy sightseeing holidays around the country's resplendent historical treasures. Tourism into Iran is doubling year over year, with more than 6 million foreign visitors in 2016.[13] After Brexit, the United Kingdom can scarcely afford not to pursue every option to expand trade in and procurement of British goods and has been pushing for Iran to contract with British businesses in energy, infrastructure, and other sectors.

Europe's history of trading on the Silk Road stretches back to well before the colonial era, and as the new Silk Road era unfolds, European countries know they have to earn their footholds in the Asian marketplace. The British no longer have a commercial edge in India, nor the French in Vietnam, nor the Dutch in Indonesia. One by one, European cities are also coming up with their own strategies to compete for Asian cash. In the maritime hub of Venice, business federations are congealing together into larger metropolitan and provincial groups, realizing that they need to represent not just 250,000 people but at least 5 million if they want to impress their visiting Chinese and Indian counterparts. At the same time, the province of Veneto wants more autonomy from Rome, partially so that it can cut out the federal bureaucracy from its budding relationships with Asian trade partners. Asianization thus means that European cities are clustering together more seriously even as it leads to more devolution within European countries.

Asians March West

From Afghans claiming Greek descent to the German minority in Kazakhstan, small settlements and slight traces of European lineage can be found dotted around Central Asia. Across nearly six thousand years, Indo-Aryan migrations brought Indus civilizations into sustained contact with northern and western Eurasian peoples. To this day, Lithuanian retains a high number of cognates with ancient Sanskrit. But these historical curiosities pale in comparison to the flows in the reverse direction. In just the past several generations, Asians have formed large settled communities in Europe. Postcolonial migrations brought substantial numbers of South Asians to Britain. Today there are nearly 2 million Indians and 2 million Pakistanis in the United Kingdom alone, together (along with Bangladeshis) accounting for more than 5 percent of the British population. As of 2015, the name Mohamed (in its various spellings) has overtaken Oliver as the most popular name for baby boys in England. Since the 1950s, Turkish *Gastarbeiter* ("guest workers") have become a significant demographic feature of Germanic Europe as well. Today an estimated 4 million Turks constitute nearly 5 percent of Germany's 82 million people. With the relaxation of citizenship laws in the 1990s, many now hold German nationality. There are also 1 million Turks in France and 600,000 in the Netherlands. While Arabs (and Africans) have long been a prominent postcolonial presence in France, in the 1990s Arab populations also began to rise in Germany followed by growing numbers of Chinese, Vietnamese, and Indians in the 2000s. Düsseldorf, whose sister city in central China is the megalopolis of Chongqing, hosts the largest Chinese and Japanese populations in Western Europe. As the reunified Berlin rapidly absorbs immigrants from far and wide into its thriving cultural scene, it is fast becoming Europe's most Eurasian city, with Turkish doner kebabs, Arabic falafel, Indian lassis, and Chinese wok noodles available in its numerous hip neighborhoods. In an ironic twist of history, the further into the past Europe's colonization of Asia fades, the more Europe is becoming a scene of demographic Asianization.

Asians in Europe are no longer just a needy underclass; they are climbing the political and corporate ladders. In Great Britain, there have been about a dozen MPs of South Asian origin and a similar number of peers in the House of Lords. In 2018, Sajid Javid, whose parents came to England from Pakistan, became the United Kingdom's home secretary. Born in Dhaka, Lord Sushanta Kumar Bhattacharyya came to Birmingham in the 1960s and upon completing his PhD founded the Warwick Manufacturing Group, which was responsible for the British Midlands' manufacturing renaissance. Jitesh Gadhia, an investment banker made a lord in 2016, was sworn in using a copy of the Hindu epic Rig Veda. Asians have even become more visible in European countries without deep colonial histories. In Germany, the politician Cem Özdemir was the first (in 1994) Bundestag member of Turkish ancestry and has been chairman of the Green Party, while the ethnic Vietnamese Philipp Rösler served as minister of health in Angela Merkel's cabinet. Indian-born Anshu Jain served as co-CEO of Deutsche Bank for three years. Two percent of Swedes are of Iranian origin, with many achieving national prominence in sports, arts, science, media, and politics. And Norway has more than 50,000 Pakistanis, including Hadia Tajik, the country's youngest ever cabinet minister (of culture), and a number of MPs. Asian athletes have also gained high-profile visibility, including the boxer Amir Khan and cricketer Moeen Ali in the United Kingdom, while Arab, Japanese, and Korean footballers have broken into the English Premier League and the German Bundesliga.

Asian tourists are swarming to Europe in steadily growing numbers. Chinese tourists favor the United Kingdom, Germany, and Italy, while Indians visit Eastern Europe as much as Western Europe, especially cities such as Prague and Budapest, where Bollywood scenes have been filmed. GAP stores in central Paris have large posters featuring cuddly Chinese-looking kids in cute outfits. Asians also love packing cruises, from Scandinavia to the Adriatic, with Norwegian Cruise Lines and Italy's MSC each recently ordering ships with room for some 7,000 passengers, nearly double the previous capacity.

Wealthy Arabs have long been avid visitors to the United Kingdom and France, spending lavishly in London and Paris hotels and keeping many horse stables in business. Lavish Indian weddings, long visible in the United Kingdom, have even come to France: the steel magnate Lakshmi Mittal rented the Palace of Versailles (and hired the singer Kylie Minogue) for his daughter's engagement party—not to mention shelling out for fireworks over the Eiffel Tower.

Living in Germany in the mid-1990s, I never thought I'd see the day when German-speaking Indians wearing lederhosen would be serving beer on Munich's fabled Marienplatz. Yet today, according to surveys conducted by the European Commission's Eurobarometer, South and East Asians overwhelmingly have positive views of Europe for its political stability and protection of rights. But many Europeans don't share the same liberal outlook about Asians, especially Central Asian gangs using Lithuania's lax border controls to enter the twenty-six-country Schengen area, within which people and goods can travel freely. More recently, the rising presence of Arabs, especially more conservative Arab Muslims, has elicited significant responses. France, the Netherlands, and Belgium are among the European countries that have implemented full or partial bans on women wearing a *burqa* or *niqab* in public, while Switzerland banned the construction of minarets on mosques. Austria has banned the construction of foreign-funded mosques altogether. In 2017 elections, Germany's right-wing and frequently anti-Islam Alternative für Deutschland (AfD) party won slightly more than 10 percent of the seats in the federal parliament, and an anti-immigrant conservative coalition took power in Austria.

These political events are symptoms of deep tensions building up as once homogenous European societies grapple with assimilating the migrants, refugees, and asylum seekers who have flooded in, spiking with the Arab uprisings that broke out in 2011 and the Syrian civil war. Germany accepted more than 1 million refugees in 2015 alone. On Sonnenallee in Berlin's Neukölln district, every other shopfront sign is in Arabic. Sweden has more than 120,000

Syrians, most of whom arrived after 2011. Their presence has inspired deep soul-searching in the immigrant-friendly country about how to maintain its liberal culture.

Blowback on European soil from West Asia's ethnic and sectarian turbulence is not new. It has been three decades since the Iranian *fatwa* against the Indian British author Salman Rushdie, who was accused of blasphemy for passages in his novel *The Satanic Verses*. In the 1990s, Turkish and Kurdish gangs played out their civil war with reciprocal bomb attacks on each other's restaurants and gas stations in Germany. Al Qaeda's devastating attacks on Madrid (2004) and London (2005) underscore how Europe has for some time been unable to escape West Asia's instability. Each ISIS-affiliated terrorist attack in London, Paris, Brussels, Berlin, or Barcelona shines a spotlight on Europe's immigrant underclass while worsening its ostracized status. In eastern Europe, anti-immigrant sentiment has given broad license for Hungarians and Slovakians to drive Roma gypsies—an ethnic Indian people numbering in the millions across Central and Eastern Europe—from their homes. Slovakians harass even wealthy Arab tourists dining in public squares. But as Europeans get serious about migration restrictions, even with a steady degree of Muslim immigration, by 2050 Muslims will represent only 7 to 8 percent of the European population. The Asian demographic challenge for Europe thus remains much more cultural than numerical.

In fact, Europe desperately needs *more* Asians to plug its massive labor shortages. Across Europe, hotels and facilities are so understaffed that they cut back on services (yet resist automating them). Many of Germany's industrious provinces require thousands of workers that could come only from southern Europe or Asia. Nationwide, Germany is seeking 200,000 nurses by 2020 and is actively recruiting Filipinos to care for its elderly. At the same time, Indian tech workers have become highly sought after to staff European companies. Even after establishing an institute in the United Kingdom to train more

British engineers, Dyson still needs at least three thousand engineers for the company's flagship manufacturing center in England. In the war for talent, Asians are being snapped up.

Then there are students. The United Kingdom remains the most popular destination for Asian students, but with post-Brexit cuts to the country's education budget, the country will require even more full-tuition-paying Asian students than ever before. In parallel with US colleges, dozens of elite and second-tier European universities have set up parallel campuses across Asia.[14] With subsidized tuition costs and a practical focus on preparing for management roles in multinational industries, Asian students see serious long-term value in European training. So, too, do Europeans shuttling between their home and Asian campuses. France's Institut d'Études Politiques de Paris (Sciences Po), Italy's University of Turin, and numerous other European universities are running special programs for their students to learn Mandarin and Chinese corporate governance on the ground and connect students to jobs with leading Chinese corporates such as Huawei and ICBC, for which they might work as managers when they are back in Europe. Both Asians studying in Europe and Europeans studying in Asia are thus becoming the pioneers of a future common Eurasian understanding; what they are building together is going to be more powerful than Europe's paroxysms of populism.

European governments are belatedly, but systematically, stepping up efforts to elevate the greater Asian realm more broadly in the public consciousness. Since 2000, the Asia-Europe Foundation (ASEF) has hosted sizable annual editions of its Creative Encounters series among artists. The Louvre in Paris has a standing partnership with Qatar's resplendent collection of Islamic art. The Humboldt Forum, Berlin's newest and most centrally located cultural monument, will make an extensive collection of Asian Silk Road artifacts its main standing exhibition when it opens at the end of 2019. For decades, Turks and Arabs have resented Europe's vast collections of their cultural treasures, but now these are seen as reminders of the historical greatness they might once again achieve with European support.

Both Europeans and Arabs have realized the semipermanent nature of the latter's involuntary arrivals. The German government has committed several billion euros to an immediate, large-scale program aimed at refugee assimilation. The European Union has launched a regionwide program to help universities match new migrants with jobs on campuses, a reminder of how much more generous European refugee policy has become than the United States'. Europe today is the wealthiest region in the world, with the best average quality of life, but there is no scenario under which it will not increasingly Asianize. In the decades ahead, the European Union may eventually expand its commonwealth to bring in new Asian members such as Turkey and Azerbaijan, and European nations may also assimilate more migrants (even if at a slower rate) to compensate for their low fertility and to care for their aging populations. Or they could do neither—in which case Europe will become depopulated and poorer and then have little choice but to open itself even further to Asian investors in its real estate and companies. Europe can choose its own path, but all roads lead to the same destination.

7

The Return of
Afroeurasia

E urope, Russia, and Turkey are all turning to the east—and so is Africa. For centuries, the combination of European colonialism and Cold War manipulation kept the West in the driver's seat of African strategic affairs. Although the Soviets backed Marxist revolutionary parties in Angola and Sudan and Chairman Mao pledged China's solidarity with fellow developing nations, ultimately Great Britain, France, and the United States dictated Africa's fortunes. Since the early 2000s, however, Africa has rapidly reoriented toward Asia. The most salient driver of this shift was the commodities supercycle of 2002–2012, during which trade between Asia and Africa grew by nearly 2,000 percent (yes, 2,000 percent). During that time, nearly half the world's fastest-growing economies were in Africa. Africans would be much worse off today if Europe had remained their only major destination for food exports. Instead, today more than half of Africa's trade is with Asia. The broader Indian Ocean realm from East Africa to Oceania is to some degree decoupling from the West on the back of its rising internal trade and financial flows. Instead of Paris and London, Dubai has become Africa's leading offshore hub. Emirates has displaced Air France as the largest carrier of passengers to and from Africa.[1] Dubai Ports World is expanding port facilities and logistics centers in Senegal, Algeria, Egypt, Rwanda, and elsewhere. Chinese, Indian, and other Asian traders and bankers meet most frequently with their African clients in Dubai.

Scholars of the precolonial world refer to the robust interconnections spanning the greater Indian Ocean as the Afroeurasian realm, indicative of just how historically rooted today's rekindled Afro-Asian kinship is. While Western media and economists ignore Africa, Asian strategic interests in the continent are surging. As if to compensate for the Ming Dynasty's failure to capitalize on its naval prowess, China has aggressively sought to strengthen its positioning in East Africa as a gateway to the continent's interior resources and markets. Egypt, Ethiopia, and Kenya are Africa's anchor members of the Belt and Road Initiative. In Africa, China is Asia's talisman, its presence a sign that opportunity is coming. Wherever China goes, other Asian countries are sure to follow, bringing their wares and their deal making. Asian infrastructure from ports to Internet cables has laid the foundation for underdeveloped African countries to be much more efficient participants in the world economy, diversify their economies, and boost their consumption. Africa's slowly emerging urban middle class is visible in the giant new shopping malls popping up in Lagos, Nairobi, Johannesburg, and the next tier of cities such as Kigali, Kampala, and Dar-es-Salaam. If Western firms are pleased with their growing sales in Africa, they have Asia to thank.

But it is Asian firms that are really capturing these opportunities. In Ethiopia, more than $10 billion in Chinese loans and $100 million in investment have gone into industrialization programs in textiles and pharmaceuticals. After a change in Ethiopia's foreign investment laws, Chinese firms went into the leather industry and now employ hundreds of times as many Ethiopian workers as any local firm. In Lesotho, Chinese and Taiwanese firms have made clothing production (such as Levi's jeans and Reebok shoes) the country's largest sector.[2] Helen Hai, the founder of the Made in Africa Initiative, has relocated Chinese garment production and other light manufacturing to countries such as Senegal and Rwanda. BYD Automobile Company is setting up a large-scale electric-car production facility in a Moroccan free-trade zone in order to reach both the African and European markets.

As China's commercial presence in Africa has increased, the presence of Chinese *xinyimin* (immigrants), who number an estimated half million, has also become visible in many African cities. Most are not employees of state-owned enterprises but rather independent migrant workers following state employees and importing cheap goods from China for the overseas Chinese and local communities. Among those who head overseas on state-sponsored visas, many stay abroad permanently and start their own businesses in retail or manufacturing.[3] On top of this, a new class of skilled, English-speaking Chinese managers is seeking out African experience through programs run by the Sino Africa Centre of Excellence Foundation.[4] Though falling commodities prices, stronger local competition (including African businesses with their own connections to Chinese imports), and xenophobia have led to well over 150,000 Chinese returning home from Angola alone, there has also been a surge of Chinese manufacturing and greenfield investment in countries such as Kenya. Such businesses will bring a more diverse Chinese workforce to Africa.[5]

Stories about China's vast African footprint, misplaced largesse, and neocolonial exploitation are piled high in Western media, taking impressive facts but leaping to speculative and dubious conclusions. Every railway, fuel refinery, sports stadium, and shopping mall is portrayed as a strategic ploy to advance the Chinese occupation of the continent—especially China's new military base in Djibouti, where it has also taken over Dubai Ports World's operation of the country's key container port and planned naval support facilities in Namibia and Angola. Then there is China's own propaganda, such as the recent blockbuster *Wolf Warrior 2*, in which benevolent Chinese troops and aid workers give a beat-down to ragtag US mercenaries trying to depose a legitimate African government.

African countries' debts to China are mounting. China now owns more than half of Kenya's external debt, with Zambia rapidly catching up.[6] China has a sophisticated menu of options for responding to repayment problems. The most common is debt restructuring: rolling over payments to a longer time horizon—and sometimes redenominating debt in renminbi instead of US dollars or Kenyan shillings. China can also convert debt into greater equity in local enterprises and new investments in other sectors such as banking and telecoms. These multifaceted financial and commercial ties provide ample leverage for China's escalated military presence. Beyond Djibouti, China has negotiated with Mozambique, Angola, and Nigeria for upgraded naval access.

It is far too soon, however, to project a path toward Chinese imperial gunboat diplomacy in Africa. China did not set out in the 1990s to colonize the planet. Rather, it grew so quickly that it found itself becoming the world's largest importer practically overnight. Even as it seeks to secure the resource flows on which it depends, China's primary objective is to *diminish* its dependence on unstable and far-off areas such as Africa. As some African nations default on their debts, it could well be that rather than seeking compensation through occupation—and invite an anti-Chinese backlash that would make twentieth-century anticolonial movements look tame—Chinese banks may simply sell their bad loans to other Asians such as Indians, who are still interested in those markets.

Indeed, Africa is a crucial showplace of how Asianization is far greater than China. China has been the first mover in terms of upgrading African ports, railways, and mines—but those assets make it easier for other Asian countries to participate in African markets. Where China opens doors, other Asian countries stream in to pursue their own agendas. As China's imports of African commodities slow down, India's and ASEAN's imports are rising. China is buying less Congolese cobalt for mobile phones, but India is buying more. Indian trade with Africa has reached $100 billion per year and is growing at 35 percent annually, and 20 percent of Indian foreign direct investment is directed toward Africa.[7] For decades, India's corporations and tycoons have used Mauritius as a tax shelter, but now Indians are establishing businesses across Africa, from oil to hotels to breweries. Where Chinese infrastructure projects and technology acquisitions fail due to political backlash, Indians are already coming in as the new preferred partners. Numerous Ethiopian factories taking Chinese capital have turned to Indian consultants to boost their workers' productivity.[8]

During the early postcolonial decades, India supported African countries by bartering with them for goods rather than trading in their scarce holdings of dollars. Today Nigeria is India's largest trade partner in Africa, and Indian companies are forging into the country on the back of the $10 billion credit scheme the Modi government has offered. As Nigerian tannery workers are displaced by the overwhelming competition from China's synthetic leather dyes, many may wind up repairing Tata cars, which drive all over Africa, or work for India's Bharti Airtel, the telecom market leader in eighteen African countries and the second largest telco on the continent. From their work in Afghanistan and the Himalayas, Indian road crews also know how to cope in harsh environments; India's Infrastructure Leasing & Financial Services (IL&FS) has been awarded a growing number of construction contracts in strategic countries such as Ethiopia.

When it comes to Asian migration to Africa, the presence of Chinese is novel, but it is only a small percentage of the total number of Asians in Africa. Since the nineteenth century, when the British brought Indians to build the Kenya-to-Uganda railway, the number of Indians in Africa has swelled to over 3 million, concentrated in South Africa, Mauritius, and East African countries such as Kenya.[9] Durban, South Africa—where Mohandas K. Gandhi lived in the early twentieth century and launched his nonviolent campaigns against discrimination—is today the largest Indian city outside India.[10] Africa's two youngest homegrown billionaires, Dubai's Ashish Thakkar and Tanzania's Mohammed Dewji, are from Indian immigrant families. India's NIIT educational system is the most prominent foreign educational force in Africa, bringing its model of aligning curricula to industry needs across the continent.

Japan, too, has decades of experience across Africa through lending by the Japan International Cooperation Agency (JICA). Its current agenda pledges $40 billion toward infrastructure and development projects.[11] Japan and India enjoy a warmer image across Africa than China does. They have also partnered in pledging more than $200 billion toward a new Asia-Africa Growth Corridor in partnership with the African Development Bank.[12] Malaysian, Korean, and Singaporean companies are increasingly visible in the African business landscape as well. Despite accusations of "land grabbing," Asian agribusiness investments help boost agricultural productivity, which is currently far lower in Africa than anywhere else in the world even though Africa is home to 60 percent of the world's arable land. A much-needed green revolution may finally come to Africa through Asian investment in everything from hybrid seeds to rural roads to efficient trading.[13] Indeed, as African harvests come under strain from climate change and rising consumption, African nations are importing ever more food from Asia.

The long-term implications of renewed Afro-Asian synergy across the Indian Ocean are thus overwhelmingly positive. Asians are paving the way for Africa to cope with populations now triple (or quadruple) their size during the colonial era and to participate in the global economy on an equal footing. Though Western chatter about Chinese neocolonialism is inevitable given the West's own history in Africa, a much better analogy (if a Western parallel is needed) would be a continental-scale Marshall Plan. The ultimate irony—and hypocrisy— of labeling China a neocolonial power is that China's investments in cross-border infrastructures such as the East African Railway, spanning a half-dozen countries, are actually enabling Africans to overcome the artificial and restrictive boundaries they inherited from European colonialism. The fact that Asians are scrambling around Africa does not mean that Europe's nineteenth-century "scramble for Africa" is being restaged. Asians are racing to connect Africa, not to divide it, building modern infrastructures that both Western multilateral agencies and African governments have been neglecting for decades. Afro-Asian linkages date back many centuries but have never been stronger.

Aggressive courting of developing countries by major powers is often assumed to be a "race to the bottom," but as African countries' economies grow and their leaders become more pragmatic, shrewd diplomacy among various suitors can drive a race to the top where the winners accrue the most benefits from foreign interests. After all, Asians are buying African resources at a high price, not plundering them, providing revenues that governments can use to invest in economic diversification. African corruption is rife, especially in the mineral and infrastructure sectors—but it long predates Asia's return to Africa: colonialism, the Cold War, and kleptocracy are the most significant factors. When it comes to bribery of African leaders, Europeans are unsurpassed. Indeed, only in the past several years have major European governments actually enforced (though not fully) the OECD Anti-Bribery Convention. There is much that Asian powers and investors can do to tame African corruption, but there is much more that Africans will have to do themselves. The combination of Asia's continued dominance in global manufacturing and low-cost robotic automation means that Africa may never attract large-scale manufacturing, even at rock-bottom wages. Africa will therefore have to efficiently capitalize on its minerals to invest in livable cities, services jobs, and education of entrepreneurs to tailor products for African markets. The more Africans observe and partner with Asian investors, the more they will learn how to protect their key industries and pass laws that require joint ventures, technology transfer, and local worker upskilling—exactly the formula Asia took to spark its own ascent.

Some African leaders have spoken of their admiration for the so-called China model, which they take to mean economic reform without political change. Yet Africa's patchwork of fifty-three postcolonial states with highly divergent regimes most resembles postcolonial South Asia. India alone has nearly thirty states, representing a staggering multiethnic mix of civil war–ridden basket cases and bootstrapping growth champions. In both India and Africa, agriculture employs far more citizens than industry, business-government relations vary between collusion and conflict, and tycoon industrialists provide much-needed services for vast swaths of the population. One leading light of stable African development, Rwanda, has consciously modeled itself on Asia's most successful city-state, Singapore. President Paul Kagame, a long-time admirer of Lee Kuan Yew, has delivered more than fifteen years of high growth while making large-scale social investments. Rwanda today ranks alongside Mauritius as Africa's leader in competitiveness, government efficiency, and access to credit and leads the world in the percentage of parliamentarians (64 percent) who are women. Whatever African countries' role models are for governance, they are all Asian. At the 2015 Forum on China-Africa Cooperation in Johannesburg, South Africa, President Xi said he supports allowing "Africans to solve African problems in an African way."[14] But in truth, the best thing for Africa would be to learn the *Asian* way.

8

The New Pacific
Partnership

There are many similarities between the Asianization of Africa and the dynamics transpiring across the even larger Pacific Ocean separating Asia from Latin America. Once firmly in Europe's colonial orbit, then subservient to US hegemony, Latin American countries are connecting to Asia with ever greater efficiency. Commodities flow in one direction; investments in infrastructure, utilities, and industry in the other. Commercial relations intertwine, debts mount; migration accelerates, mistrust rises. China-centric ties gradually dissipate into much broader and more fruitful Asia-wide engagement.

The fundamental differences between the African and Latin American circumstances, however, make the latter's Asianization profoundly new. Consider that the Pacific Ocean has historically been Earth's greatest barrier to regular contact between continents. Though ancient humans crossed the Bering Strait land bridge from Asia to the Americas more than 17,000 years ago, there is no thousand-plus-year history of regular trading relations between Asian and Latin American civilizations as there has been in the Afroeurasian realm. Furthermore, the United States' dominant position in Latin America has scarcely been threatened since the Monroe Doctrine was articulated in the early nineteenth century. Neither Fidel Castro's Cuba (despite the 1962 missile crisis) nor Venezuela under Hugo Chávez spawned regionwide resistance, and the region's nearly total economic depen-

272 The Future Is Asian

dence on trade and investment with the United States has imposed strict limits on Latin American geopolitical flirtations.

This time really is different. Europe's economic slowdown, North America's energy revolution, and President Trump's combative stance toward Hispanic immigration have been unfolding just as Asia's ties with Latin America have blossomed. For most Latin American countries, China is already the largest trade partner, especially due to their export of beef, soy, oil, and lithium. The fast-growing Pacific Alliance nations from Mexico to Chile have been pursuing enhanced trade with Asia for years. Thus, even though the United States pulled out of the Trans-Pacific Partnership (TPP) negotiations,[1] Chile went ahead with convening all the Latin and Asian participants just weeks after Trump's inauguration—with the addition of China as an observer.[2] When trade tensions between the United States and China threaten soy exports, South America benefits: Brazil and Argentina now export more soy to China than the United States does.[3] The trade bloc Mercosur, which includes Argentina, Brazil, Paraguay, and Uruguay, is pushing for a free trade agreement with Japan, which even the United States does not have.

Because Asia is such a lucrative destination for Latin exports, pushing westward is a strategic imperative, as evidenced by the fact that Chile and Peru have almost twenty free-trade agreements with Asian countries. Forty percent of Peru's exports go across the Pacific, and Asia is the only region with which Argentina has a trade surplus. As difficult as penetrating Asia's densely competitive business landscape is for Latin American companies, pioneers such as Brazil's Vale, the world-leading iron ore and nickel producer, as well as Mexico's baked goods supplier Grupo Bimbo, have made the leap to scale across Asia and encouraged others to follow suit.[4]

Not just South America but the entire Western Hemisphere now differs from the United States on how to manage rising trade with Asia. US trade with China amounts to nearly $600 billion per year but has decelerated to under 2 percent annual growth, with the United States imposing tariffs on various Chinese goods (including solar panels and steel) in an attempt to reduce its swelling deficits. Though Canada also has a large deficit with China, it is pushing for a free-trade agreement to boost its exports of commodities, machinery, and services. Mexico, too, is seeking freer trade with China as its exports of copper, circuits, and cars steadily grow. Similarly, while the United States, Canada, and Mexico have trade deficits with Japan, only Canada and Mexico are liberalizing trade with that country. Since the Japan-Mexico Economic Partnership Agreement went into effect in 2005, Mexico has steadily cut its deficit with Japan as its exports have grown, even as it benefits from importing high-quality auto parts for its fast-growing car factories. ASEAN has now surpassed Japan as the United States' second largest trade partner in Asia, and the United States' combined trade with ASEAN, Japan, South Korea, and India substantially exceeds its trade with China. But without joining the TPP, the United States' leverage over all these markets weakens. According to the Peterson Institute for International Economics, not joining the TPP will cost the United States more than $130 billion in lost trade and investment until 2030, with Canada and Australia displacing the United States' market share in beef, pork, dairy, and grain sales and Singapore and Australia eating into the United States' strong position in finance, consulting, and communications.[5] Given the damage tariffs inflict on US industries by raising the cost of imports and killing jobs, the Trump administration's regret at pulling out of TPP is logical.

As with Asian countries' ties to Africa, Asian–Latin American trade and investment volumes continue to grow even as commodities prices decline. China continues to make large pledges to Latin America, targeting $500 billion in trade and $250 billion in investment between 2015 and 2019.[6] Together, the China Development Bank and Export-Import Bank of China provide more annual financing to Latin America than do the World Bank, Inter-American Development Bank, and Andean Development Corporation combined. On top of this, another $30 billion is coming from Asia in industrial and infrastructure cooperation funds.[7] As depreciating currencies and price controls sent

Brazilian utilities companies tumbling, Chinese power conglomerates bought more than twenty electricity companies there between 2015 and 2017. Chinese-backed funds are also making $20 billion in new investments in Brazilian ports, logistics, mining, technology, and agribusiness ventures. In Argentina, a $17 billion loan issued in 2017 will fund two nuclear power plants and solar energy projects and hydroelectric dams.[8] In Mexico, the Chinese automaker JAC Motors is building a large plant that should employ six thousand workers. Like Tokyo and Seoul, Beijing and Guangzhou now have direct flights to Mexico City.

Not unlike their counterparts in Africa, Latin American manufacturers often view Asian companies as unfair competitors and the resent informal barriers to entry in the Chinese market.[9] They also fear that further opening could make it difficult to hold on to certain industries. In 2015, for example, Costa Rica lost its flagship Intel plant to Vietnam. China's loans in South America face similar criticisms to those leveled about its financing of African governments. China's massive loans to Venezuela have temporarily kept the kleptocratic regime of Presdident Nicolás Maduro afloat but have done nothing to enhance the country's creditworthiness. Ecuador, too, owes alarmingly high sums to China, which it must pay with oil shipments until about 2025.[10] China's $100 million per year in arms exports to regimes such as Venezuela, Bolivia, Peru, and Argentina also raises eyebrows in Washington. While the United States has slashed the budget of its flagship International Military Education and Training (IMET) program, China has ramped up its equivalent, courting senior Latin American military officers. Then there are the social and environmental concerns over Brazil's trans-Amazonian railway project, which China strongly supports; it may accelerate deforestation while mistreating indigenous peoples.

Yet, as in Africa, this is not a neocolonial age. The leverage cuts both ways, and linear projections based on the past have little relevance. For example, rather than turning Venezuela into a bridgehead for its continental forays, China realized it was throwing money down a sinkhole and cut off additional loans. Venezuela subsequently defaulted on $160 billion of debt, much of which was owed to China and Russia. Brazil would not allow China to dictate a major electricity price hike, nor would China want to alienate hundreds of millions of Brazilians by doing so. China is learning that stability and openness serve its interests better than do hegemony and resentment.

As South American economies work through their dynamic relations with China, they are also moving forward without inhibition to build ties with other Asian powers. For most Latin American countries, India has overtaken China as the fastest-growing export destination. Despite the distance, the region already provides 20 percent of India's mineral imports and is a growing source of food as India gradually opens up its protected agricultural sector. In the reverse direction, Asians view the 650 million population of Latin America and the Caribbean as a huge market of fast-growing customers for all kinds of hardware from tractors to televisions. Latin America is a large destination for Indian car exports and represents more than $1 billion in annual Indian pharmaceutical exports. Twenty-five thousand Latin Americans work for Indian IT companies.[11] Currently, India exports more to Mexico and Brazil than it does to Indonesia and Russia. The Japanese carmaker Honda, the Korean electronics juggernaut LG, and Vietnam's key telecom services provider, Viettel Group, are all investing and growing across the region. The timing could not be better for the recent publication of a guide for Asians doing business in Latin America, *Understanding Latin America: A Decoding Guide*, by the veteran Venezuelan diplomat Dr. Alfredo Toro Hardy.

Asians actually have a long history of assimilation in Latin America that is promising for future ties. In the mid–nineteenth century, nearly 225,000 Chinese "coolies" were taken to Cuba to work on plantations and Peru to work in the mines. By the early 1900s, many of those manual laborers were running businesses in townships across the Andes. Today, the Wang and Wu families are among the richest in Peru, and central Lima's Chinatown is home to a thriving and successful community of Chinese business families. Over the past century, Japanese went in waves to Brazil, first to substitute for the declining numbers of Italian migrants, but quickly became established professionals. Japanese Brazilians have become the largest Japanese diaspora, their population of 1.5 million larger than the number of Japanese in the United States. The Japanese Peruvian Alberto Fujimori served as the country's president for a decade from 1990 to 2000, and his daughter Keiko narrowly lost the presidential election in 2016. Arabs have also assimilated well throughout Latin America, with Lebanese trading families establishing a succcessful presence from Mexico (the home of the billionaire Carlos Slim) to Colombia to Brazil. Indians, too, have circulated in the Caribbean and South America since the mid–nineteenth century, when they arrived as indentured workers of the British Empire in the East Indies. Indians make up the majority of the populations of Trinidad, Suriname, and Guyana, where Cheddi Jagan served as the premier in the 1960s and president in the 1990s.

With its long history of Asian ties, South America's largest economy, Brazil, has the biggest bilateral economic footprint with Asia as well, despite not having a Pacific coastline. Brazil's experience is instructive for the future of Latin America's ties to Asia. The Japan International Cooperation Agency (JICA) has been supporting Brazilian industrialization since the 1960s and helped make Cerrado the breadbasket region responsible for 70 percent of the country's farm output.[12] Though Japan's trade with Latin America is much smaller than China's, its investment portfolio is larger and far more diversified across industries such as shipbuilding, textiles, steel, and automobiles. There are lessons to be learned from the Japanese experience for Latin America as it deals with China—and for China as it deepens its presence in the Western Hemisphere. Japan, too, began with a focus on acquiring commodities and exporting manufactured goods but soon began transferring its technical and managerial know-how across Brazil's economy.[13] Over the course of the past decade, during which China has been Brazil's largest trading partner, Brazil has turned a massive deficit into a $12 billion surplus. In fact, Brazil has a trade surplus with all Asian countries except Korea.

For ambassadors from Brazil's vaunted diplomatic training academy the Rio Branco Institute, Asia is the new destination of choice. Flávio Damico, currently serving as Brazil's ambassador in Singapore, puts it plainly: "We are an Atlantic country, but the future is in Asia." As with other Latin nations, China is its largest trading partner, India the fastest growing, and ASEAN surpassing Japan. Indonesia is the home of Brazil's largest single foreign investment in Asia, a nickel-mining operation on Sulawesi island. For Brazil and other Latin American nations, there is no tension with China as they refocus their energies on the rest of Asia. There is only upside. As Damico puts it, "We have the resources, they have the people."

Latin American countries need to ensure that they use Asia not just for hardware but also for software, making the most productive use of their resources. Countries such as Singapore are playing an important role in this regard. As Mexico develops special economic zones in the country's south, it has turned to the Singaporean firm Surbana Jurong to build world-class industrial parks. Singapore is also investing in raising productivity in the country's energy and hospitality sectors. Each year, the Latin Asia Business Forum in Singapore attracts dozens more companies from both sides of the Pacific that are looking to ramp up commercial ties. Latin American construction and architecture companies are starting to use the Singaporean VRcollab's virtual reality software for site development, and Singapore's Educare is rolling out its math curriculum in Colombia's schools. Meanwhile, Singapore's e-government services leader, CrimsonLogic, is deploying its customs clearance software solution in Chile, Bolivia, Peru, Trinidad, and Panama, whose newly expanded canal has enabled a far higher volume of container ships from Asia to efficiently reach the US East Coast, and LNG tankers from the East Coast reach Asia. One Panamanian ambassador sums up the country's ambition as this: "We want to be the Singapore of Central America."

9

Asia's Technocratic Future

Democracy is widespread in Asia, but it covers a vast spectrum of countries from those ranked higher than the United States in their democratic quality to those that give the term a bad name. Asia has top-ranked democracies such as Australia and New Zealand (which inherited British parliamentary government traditions), Japan and South Korea (whose postwar political systems were designed by the United States), and Taiwan, whose democratic model is watched closely by China (even if it is not followed). Both South Korea and Taiwan rank in the top tier of the Bertelsmann Stiftung's Transformation Index, which measures the strength of a country's democratic consolidation and state effectiveness. The rule of law is so strong in South Korea that the country impeached a sitting president and jailed him for more than two decades and is now implementing strict term limits. Meanwhile, India, Indonesia, and the Philippines are evolving as democracies, while democracy in Pakistan, Bangladesh, and Myanmar is still fragile. Asians do not lack an interest in democracy or the ability to sustain it. But they do have a no-nonsense bias in favor of pragmatic government and are culturally cautious about becoming collectively undisciplined. Mindful of the excesses of history, they are on guard to balance the progressive ambitions of stronger governments with the potential abuses of stronger leaders. They want to be more inclusive, but not at the price of effectiveness.

The term *democracy* tells us ever less about how—or how well—a country is run. From Mexico to Italy, democracies today are the places where surveys show that populations have the least trust in and respect for politicians and for democracy. In Russia, Turkey, and Iran, elections are merely instruments of pacification, release valves that buy breathing space for regimes. Rule of law, meaning that laws are above the executive, looks more like rule *by* law, in which governments abuse the law as a tool of power. In recent years I have noticed that even when Western analysts and commentators are speaking to each other on panels or debates and are asked point-blank which countries they feel have an admirable vision and strategy for their future, they almost always answer China, India, and Singapore. The same appears to be true of the global general public. According to a twenty-five-country survey in 2017, India (53 percent) and China (49 percent) both ranked ahead of the United States (40 percent) as countries perceived as having a positive global influence.[1]

Today the debate over what constitutes the best form of government and how to achieve the right balance between individual freedom and collective duty has been blown wide open. The universal challenge facing all societies is intensifying complexity at the intersection of geopolitical turbulence, economic volatility, technological disruption, socio-economic inequality, and environmental stress. This is a tall order—and there is little evidence that Western governments are best suited to adapt to these demands. As in natural evolution, success and failure are determined not by preconceived theories but by adaptability.

The Anglo-American Failure

There is a difference between an alignment of the stars and a gift from God. The United States' twentieth-century ascent was the former. It built the world's largest economy and military while Europe plunged itself into decades of warfare and Asian and African colonies remained suppressed. In the postwar decades it maintained the most dynamic and innovative economy and had a sense of purpose in leading the free world through the Cold War. Even as political parties changed, there was continuity in governance and a strong national ethos. The past generation has witnessed a significant departure from those heady days. Deregulation, deindustrialization, financialization, and politicization have combined to tear the American societal fabric. By 2014, a Gallup survey found not only that the majority of Americans are fed up with the performance of their government but also that 65 percent of them have have lost faith in their *system* of government.[2]

The complacency with which many Western politicians continue to view the world makes no sense to millennials, who aren't animated by the fading spirit of Western Cold War triumphalism. Common citizens of all ages have lost trust in their institutions, whether the White House, Congress, political parties, the Supreme Court, big business, or the church. They have good reason to believe the US system is "rigged"—something both Trump and the country's more liberal scholars agree on. Prominent research underscores how the United States has reached the perverse state of democracy without governance and rights without democracy.[3] The former connotes enfranchised citizens for whom services are considered a privilege rather than a right, and the latter implies a society of freedoms whose laws are not made in the public interest. On top of this, pervasive gerrymandering allows politicians to choose their voters rather than the reverse. And these conclusions were drawn *before* Trump's election, which exposed how the United States' style of democracy is as much a tool of division as of unity. Two decades ago, in the aftermath of the Soviet collapse, Western intellectuals confidently presumed that Asian strongman rule would break down amid economic empowerment and rising demands for political accountability. Now they fear that their own systems are regressing into either strongman rule or rudderless democratic chaos.

If economic growth is the foundation on which liberal democracy is built, the West's chronically slow growth foretold today's populism—despite its illogical and counterproductive arguments and consequences. Yet the phenomena of Brexit and Trump show how poorly the Anglo-American elites who dominate English-language debates understand their own societies. They further conflate the United States and Great Britain with the Western liberal order itself. That is not how most Europeans see it. Western civilization contains a range of regimes from US presidential republicanism to Nordic constitutional monarchies to Western European multiparty parliamentary democracies to Eastern European illiberal regimes. It is not an ideological bloc. Despite shared history and overlapping interests, there are palpable divides between the Anglo-American and continental European governance systems, with Canada much closer to Western Europe than to its US and British cousins. Recall how Americans and Brits confidently predicted that after the twin shocks of Brexit and Trump, a populist wave would sweep through Europe. But the Dutch, French, and German elections of 2017 showed precisely the opposite: despite populist pressures, conservative and social democratic parties aligned behind agendas of reform and solidarity. Continental Europe has maintained a larger middle class and lower inequality.[4] European countries have had to raise their retirement ages and make their labor markets more flexible, but they have not dismantled their welfare states. The German system of multiparty consensus is a world apart from the US Congress. It has found compromise on immigration, social spending, infrastructure, and other issues on which parties disagree but know they must demonstrate progressive results to get reelected. The common Western predicaments of aging populations, rising debt, eroding industrial base, wealth concentration, low trust in institutions, and weakening social fabric are thus neither evenly distributed nor similarly managed across the West.

The US political system is not the West's leading model of good governance. Over the past decade, the US standard of living, as measured by median income, has actually fallen, while education, health care, public safety, and other areas are weakening. According to the social psychologist Steven Pinker, the United States is "backward" compared to most of the rest of its Western peers. The exorbitant privilege of controlling the world's leading reserve currency affords the US monetary stability despite twin deficits, but it cannot mask either the country's deep inequalities or the lack of meaningful remedies for them.[5] In politics, the United States suffers from an abundance of representation and a deficit of administration. There is a great excess in the power of representatives—congressmen and senators—and a deep shortfall in the power of administrators—governors and mayors. There are too many officials trained in law and not enough in policy: Too much time is spent arguing rather than doing something. As a result, politics has gotten the upper hand over policy: "We're getting nothing done!" the late senator John McCain lamented angrily in the summer of 2017.

Not long ago it was said that Chinese people prefer material stability to democratic instability. Now the same seems to be true everywhere. Pew Research Center surveys conducted worldwide suggest that people do not want democracy at the price of corruption and incompetence. Rather, there is a surprisingly high willingness to consider nondemocratic forms of government not only in Asian countries (including democracies) such as Japan, South Korea, and India, but also in Western democracies, including Great Britain, France, and the United States, each of which reports more than 50 percent of respondents favorable to the notion. A prominent survey reveals that from World War II to today, the percentage of Americans who feel it is "essential to live in a democracy" has fallen from three-quarters to under one-third.[6]

Global political discourse is shifting onto a postideological terrain where performance—based on measurements of high-quality governance and citizen satisfaction—is the arbiter of success. All societies want a balance of prosperity and livability, openness and protection, effective governance and citizen voice, individualism and cohesion, free choice and social welfare. Everyday people don't measure these things by how democratic their country is but by whether they feel safe in their cities, can afford their homes, have stability in their work, have a plan for growing old, and can remain connected to friends and family. As the Anglo-American political constellation veers off course, it could learn from Asia's leading systems, which focus on long-term vision and collective benefits rather than short-term hyperindividualism and narrow special interests. Indeed, in the aftermath of Brexit, numerous British ministers and economists offered hope in the notion that the United Kingdom would become the "Singapore of Europe"— never mind the irony of looking up to a former colony as a role model. Perhaps, however, the United States and Great Britain could both learn some lessons from Asia's leading technocracy.

Singapore: A Technocratic Role Model

The idea that too much democracy can be dangerous is not an Eastern idea. The ancient Greek philosopher Plato articulated a range of possible regimes from aristocracy to tyranny and described democracy as the penultimate phase of degeneration. For Plato, the essential ingredients of a successful *polis* were an educated and engaged citizenry and a wise ruling class: democracy combined with political aristocracy. Democracy with neither of these attributes, he felt, would lead to a free but dangerously anarchic society vulnerable to tyranny. To ward against such decay, his preferred form of government was led by a committee of public-spirited "guardians." Today we call such a system a *technocracy*.

Technocratic government is built around expert analysis and long-term planning rather than narrow-minded, short-term populist whims or private interests. It is meritocratic (elevating competent leaders) and utilitarian (seeking the broadest societal benefit). Technocratic leaders are selected more by IQ test than by popularity contest. They are extensively educated, trained, and experienced professionals, not just pedigreed elites. Technocratic politics is not just ad hoc and reactive. Rather, technocracies are where political science starts to look like something worthy of the term: a rigorous approach to policy.

The modern usage of the term *technocracy* dates to France's humiliating defeat by Prince Otto von Bismarck's Prussia in 1870, after which the elite École Libre des Sciences Politiques (now the Institut d'Études Politiques de Paris, or Paris Institute of Political Studies) was founded to train political and diplomatic leaders in the hope of turning the Third Republic's fortunes around. In the late nineteenth century, though admiring the German state's organizational design, future president Woodrow Wilson pleaded for Americans to take seriously the "science of administration."[7] Americans have forgotten that it was twentieth-century technocratic interventions that propelled the country to the peak of its greatness: the Gilded Age gave way to the Progressive Era through far-reaching policies such as housing settlements for the poor and curbs on corruption in federal agencies and Congress, President Franklin D. Roosevelt's post-Depression New Deal created large professional bureaucracies such as the Social Security Administration, and President Harry Truman's post–World War II Federal Highway Administration completed the nation's transportation infrastructure. Silicon Valley became the epicenter of innovation not through the accidental comingling of sunny weather and venture capital but with strategic support from the Pentagon to develop industries from radar to semiconductors to the Internet and GPS. These are the technocratic foundations of America's strength, even as they are now held in disdain by those who label professional bureaucracies a "deep state."

If there is anything about the United States today that Asians want to emulate, it is not Washington's politics but Silicon Valley's story of "managed innovation." Billions of people around the world are rightly amazed by the United States' dynamism and resilience: no other nation in history, democracy or otherwise, has created such a high standard of living for 300 million people. But countries without its geographic size, depth of capital markets, generations of industrial innovation, and scale of talent—which includes every other country in the world—cannot afford to experiment arbitrarily with their precious limited natural or human resources until they get lucky. When countries fail to live up to their strategic ambitions or their citizens witness democracy failing to deliver on its promises, they turn to technocracy to get things done right.

Across Asia, from Moscow to Muscat and from Dubai to Beijing, the most admired and closely studied government today is that of Singapore.[8] Many Asians can relate to its colonial inheritance of a parliamentary system. Numerous Asian nations also had one very strong postcolonial leader who shepherded them through the vulnerable early decades, though none as charismatic and effective as Singapore's Lee Kuan Yew. Lee believed that the phrase "law and order" has the terms reversed: order matters first and foremost, then law. In its early years, Singapore's town hall meetings featured Chinese, Tamils, and Malays bickering with one another in their own languages, so Lee imposed English on them. Bandits used to kidnap and extort both locals and foreigners; Lee made those crimes punishable by death. Today Singapore has no private ownership of guns, virtually no crime, and total public safety. It ranks as one of the world's richest and best-educated countries, has the highest-quality infrastructure and most effective government, and is one of the easiest places to start a business. According to Save the Children, only in Slovenia do children grow up in a social environment as safe and healthy as Singapore's. It was well-deserved when, in 2005, *Time* magazine hailed Lee Kuan Yew as a "philosopher king" for the success of his transformation of Singapore into a first-world entrepôt and an inspiration to China. There is a standard retort that the lessons of small countries cannot be applied to large ones. But today some of the largest and most populous countries on Earth are trying to make themselves into big Singapores.

Asians far and wide look to Singapore's technocratic approach to responding efficiently to citizens' needs and preferences, learning from international experience in devising policies, and using data and scenarios for long-term planning. Though Singapore institutionalized its technocracy before allowing democracy to unfold fully, today the government tries to marry the virtues of democratic inclusiveness with the effectiveness of technocratic management. Democratic feedback is crucial for governments to ensure that they are on the right track, but democracy is not an end in itself. Many Western commentators celebrate the theater of politics as if it were the embodiment of pure democracy. But democracy does not guarantee achievement of the higher goal of effective governance and improved national well-being. Indeed, too much politics corrupts democracy, and too much democracy gets in the way of policy. Politics is about positions, policy about decisions; democracies produce compromises, technocracies produce solutions; democracy suffices, technocracy optimizes.

A proper technocracy is far more flexible than dogmatic regimes and more capable of changing course than democracies. Lee Kuan Yew originally had socialist pretensions before pivoting in the 1970s to less regulated Hong Kong–style labor markets. Paradoxes thus appear that make perfect sense in practice, if not in theory. Singapore can be described as freewheeling—it has no trade restrictions and prostitution is legal— but also as a nanny state: it has the world's most robust government-subsidized home ownership scheme, mandatory savings for retirement, and a universal and cost-effective public health care system. It is a top-ranked free market, yet the government manages half the economy through state-backed companies. In other words, it is a libertarian nanny state in which capitalist self-reliance fuses with redistributive handouts and a large official role in the marketplace to ensure the stability of government revenues. It is big government but also lean government.

A Singaporean civil servant, Peter Ho, differentiates between blame-seeking and problem-solving cultures.[9] Whereas Western democracies today have wish lists, Asian technocracies have strategies. Democracy guarantees neither that good ideas will emerge nor that they will be implemented. Good technocracies are equally focused on inputs and outputs. Their legitimacy comes both from the process by which the government is selected and from the delivery of what citizens universally proclaim they want: solid infrastructure, public safety, clean air and water, reliable transportation, ease of doing business, good schools, quality housing, dependable child care, freedom of expression, access to jobs, and so forth. The technocratic mind-set is that delay in getting these things done is itself a form of corruption. Instead of playing perpetual blame games, good technocrats are always out to solve problems.

The technocratic playbook that Singapore follows focuses on building societal agility through strategies codeveloped between government, industry, and academia. For such a small country, it has a highly diversified economy. The unemployment rate is nearly zero. The SingPass system puts all official documentation and functions within reach online. The government sets reasonable key performance indicators (KPIs) that are tracked at regular intervals to assess progress. In no other society is the delivery of public services so diligently monitored through KPIs. From passport checks and public toilets at the airport to banks and university administration buildings, Singapore is populated with touch-screen tablets asking you to rate the service you've received—and the government actually pays attention to the results. The government is also transparent about its own performance. The annual audit of all public and publicly financed institutions, from banks to universities, is an open naming and shaming exercise, putting online and on the front pages of the *Straits Times* any lapses in fiduciary or other standards.

This opens the door to appreciating that Singapore has a very strong democratic culture even if there is limited democratic choice. Voting is mandatory—as it is in Australia, Belgium, and some other democracies. (Given the low voter turnout in many Western societies, their electoral outcomes can hardly be considered democratically legitimate unless they, too, adopt mandatory voting.) Politicians hold weekly dialogues in public housing courtyards and function rooms. Parliamentary debates and budget hearings are open to the public and televised. Citizens comment vocally on everything from taxes to transportation to health care spending. If the national pension fund's portfolio returns just 1 percent lower than expected, citizens start to howl. The government also organizes hundreds of deliberative consultations, conducts extensive surveys on all major policy questions, and channels online petitions to a parliamentary committee. Some caricature Singapore as the French diplomat and historian Alexis de Tocqueville's "good despotism," a regime that seeks to gratify the people's desires and "spare them all the care of thinking and all the trouble of living." But, as Plato foresaw, only an educated population can responsibly assume democratic rights.

Despite all of this inclusive dialogue, Singapore does not overconsult. Deliberation never degenerates into paralysis. Citizens armed with real-time information want a voice in policy—but they also want action. Because Singapore's leaders enjoy the trust of the public, they have the capacity to autonomously weigh diverse factors and make comprehensive decisions. In short-term-oriented electoral democracy, the future has no constituency; everything has to be "sold" to the people as a quick high. But as the political psychologist Philip Tetlock has demonstrated, full transparency over political deliberations can lead to decisions aimed at being popular rather than correct.[10] Hence democracy must be supplemented by technocratic instruments that assess the long-term implications of decisions and offer correctives.

Tetlock's work also demonstrates the failure of experts to correctly predict a range of political and economic events. This is not a knock on technocracy. Governance is not about predictions but about decisions. Technocrats aren't supposed to compete in prediction markets but listen to them, as well as to subject-matter experts and the public, and craft holistic policy. Indeed, there is ample evidence that Singapore's ruling party, even though it faces little electoral competition, responds to citizens' concerns and even reverses course on policies when necessary. For example, when rapid immigration overstressed the transport system, the public outcry led to significant immigration restrictions. When foreigners were allowed to invest in the public housing market, it caused price volatility that angered locals; the policy was changed overnight. Concern about adequate elder care for the rapidly aging population and the high cost of living has prompted substantial increases in welfare and social spending. Being self-correcting is more important than being correct in any one thing.

The technocratic backbone of any successful government is a professional civil service. Civil servants are stewards of governance who know how to administer federal agencies. They should possess intellectual know-how, robust capacity, and bureaucratic autonomy. According to research by the Hertie School of Governance in Berlin, which emphasizes impartial hiring and promotion, statistical diagnosis of social and economic data, and the number of advanced degree holders employed, Singapore's civil service is second to none. It is run like a spiral staircase: with each rung a civil servant learns to manage a different portfolio, gaining firsthand experience and building a broad knowledge base. By contrast, US politics is like an elevator: one can get in on the bottom floor and go straight to the top, missing all the learning in between.

Just as important as what the civil service does is how it does it. Scenario planners are embedded in every ministry. These "foresight officers" conduct their own research and global case studies to frame impartial scenarios for leaders to consider on an ongoing basis. Singapore's Civil Service College (CSC) has invested more than $10 million in simulations that resemble Pentagon war gaming. Scenarios are designed to pull leaders far out of their comfort zone and develop robust strategies to maintain the country's relevance. To create the most realistic scenarios and plans, the civil service recruits for expertise in economic strategy, infrastructure, environmental stewardship, defense, and social services. Urban planning, for example, is handled by teams meshing architects, economists, demographers, ecologists, and many other experts. Rather than building more vertical bureaucracies, such horizontal mechanisms pool resources and apply them to functional challenges such as monitoring borders and aviation, tracking supply chains, ensuring food security, and protecting critical infrastructure. Along the way, generalists become specialists and vice versa. Collectively, Singapore's civil servants are a well-rounded team of humble perfectionists.

Lee Kuan Yew stressed the importance of an effective administrative bureaucracy that would enforce the rule of law and be impervious to corruption. One successful antibody against corruption is having highly paid ministers whose visibility demands that they view government service as a trusteeship rather than as a pathway to later wealth. Even after the salaries of cabinet ministers and other senior officials were slashed by one-third to one-half in 2012, Singapore's public servants are still the highest paid in the world. Civil servants earn high salaries and also receive modest bonuses tied to national economic performance. Each year, several hundred of them are selected by competitive evaluation as "administrative officers" who earn double the standard salary.

Max Weber, the father of modern government science, would have been gravely worried by the state of the United States' federal service, which has been in decline since the Ronald Reagan administration in the 1980s. The more than 2 million US civil servants (including half a million postal service workers) across more than four hundred agencies are underpaid and overworked, often use archaic software, and are subject to periodic government shutdowns. They have no mandate and little incentive to learn from other countries. Institutional memory—the accumulation of historical knowledge—fades as professionals retire and politicians consult neither the repository of experience nor the experts who have lived through it. The Congressional Research Service (CRS) of the Library of Congress and the Government Accountability Office (GAO) have been essential to providing policy evaluations and recommendations independent of industry lobbyists, but today the GAO's work is often ignored, while the CRS shies away from tackling politically controversial issues. Great Britain, too, has suffered immeasurably since the Margaret Thatcher era of dismantling the once vaunted civil service. Instead of David Cameron consulting the civil service to produce scenarios on the impact of a potential Brexit for public consideration *before* the infamous 2016 referendum, the unprepared successor government of Theresa May hastily cobbled together a committee to help chart the country's path into the unknown. This is neither the process nor the outcome any sensible Asian nation would wish to emulate—whether technocracy or democracy.

Finding and executing on the best ideas is far more likely in a meritocratic system. A meritocracy is not just about intellectual achievements but about tangible experience. It promotes good people from within rather than circumventing them with political appointees. Meritocracy mitigates revolutionary demands because there is a sense that higher social standing and leadership are open to all based on their skills and hard work. Producing a pipeline of skilled leaders requires an unshakable commitment to public education. Singapore's current prime minister is a computer scientist, and serving a term as education minister is an essential stepping-stone to higher office. Like its technocrats, teachers in Singapore are respected and paid well.

American-style political oligarchy is neither technocracy nor meritocracy. In a meritocracy, declaring a candidate "unfit" or "unqualified" is not merely a campaign epithet but a measurable proposition. Trump won the election even though most voters felt he was unqualified to be president. In the United States, "electability" clearly refers to being capable of winning an election, whereas in a meritocracy it would mean one's deservingness to do so. Furthermore, saying things that are unconstitutional and unethical doesn't make you just figuratively disqualified but literally disqualified.

Even a meritocratic technocracy like Singapore needs to be careful not to slip into an oligarchy alienated from its people. In 2011, long-standing parliamentarians from the ruling People's Action Party (PAP) lost elections for appearing elitist during campaigns. In 2017, many citizens were excited to have a chance to elect their (ceremonial) president only to find out that the qualification criteria were narrowed to favor only one. (This was done in the name of promoting a minority-race female, Halimah Yacob.) Some people simply want to see unexpected faces with unconventional backgrounds appear in the country's top ranks. The trends suggest that this will happen. The PAP's share of the popular vote has dropped from nearly 90 percent in the 1970s to less than 70 percent today. For the first time in 2015, every single parliamentary seat was contested by multiple parties. Nonetheless, in that election, the PAP actually gained back numerous seats it had previously lost simply by taking on board the opposition Workers' Party's platform of investing more in new transport infrastructure and public housing and curbing immigration. No matter what the parliamentary balance, a half-dozen nonconstituency MP seats are allotted to prominent voices from business and civil society who regularly make conscientious and critical statements on government policy.

Owing to its British inheritance and one-party dominance, Singapore's parliament is a mix of Oxford Union and consultative assembly. In a technocratic system, the purpose of parliamentary democracy is not simply to elect representatives but to have parliaments be a mechanism for constant consultation with the citizenry. Remember that elections are retroactive: they often punish rather than prescribe. Because they are a referendum on individuals as much as issues, they don't provide citizens guidance on specific policies. Voting by itself is therefore far from the best means of capturing popular sentiment on an ongoing basis. For that, we need data: qualitative data, such as surveys, polls, and social media, and quantitative data, such as demographic and economic trends. The combination of social and sensor data can be more comprehensive than election results, for it is broader in scope (covering the full spectrum of issues rather than being hijacked by hot-button topics) and fresher (collected more regularly than infrequent elections). Scaling technology is easier than scaling trust, but the former can be a path to the latter.

Westerners think of data tools as aiding democracy, but in Singapore, democratic deliberations, whether elections, initiatives, surveys, or social media, contribute data sets that help technocrats steer policy based on all available evidence. For example, data that represent the poor, elderly, or youth—such as their financial behavior and education status—are essential inputs for leaders to ensure that they are taking everyone's needs into account. Singapore is not a slave to the data it gathers but balances data and democracy so they complement each other: data can determine which policies are necessary, while democracy can modify and ratify them. That is precisely what is happening as the country raises health care spending and increases subsidies for the poor. Data-driven technocracy is thus superior to representative democracy alone because it captures the specific desires of the people while short-circuiting the distortions of potentially corrupted representatives and special interests.

There is an acute irony in the pace at which Asian technocracy is adapting to modern technology and calls for "digital democracy." Western polemicists used to argue that communication and social media technologies would make Chinese authoritarianism obsolete once everyone had access to mobile phones, satellite TV, and other information channels. But in fact these technologies and the transparency they bring about are putting the heat on unresponsive democratic leaders while *reinforcing* the legitimacy of technocratic regimes that are responsive to public needs.

Prime Minister Lee Hsien Loong has said that Singapore is becoming a "normal" country with democratic "toing and froing." But make no mistake: Singapore's people are far more interested in tangible delivery outputs than in democratic inputs for their own sake. They want a credible intellectual check on authority, not partisan gridlock. There is a slippery slope from technocratic consultation to democratic populism—and the former should never be sacrificed for the latter. Today no country can afford the kind of short-term, narrow-minded populism that targets electoral outcomes rather than national performance and wastes months or years on "lame-duck" preelection paralysis.

That is why the Singaporean public is so fixated on the next generation of rising leaders several years before the next election. Unlike rule-for-life authoritarians, Lee Kuan Yew stepped down as prime minister in 1990, twenty-five years before he died. His son Lee Hsien Loong wants nothing more than to ease into retirement by 2021. He can sleep soundly knowing that a dozen ministers in their late forties and early fifties are building a collaborative transition team years in advance. The fact that nobody descended from Lee Kuan Yew is likely to lead Singapore anytime soon (if ever again) bothers almost no one. Instead, Singapore is evolving toward a far more sophisticated collective presidency, a democratic-technocratic committee with a broad and deep knowledge of all aspects of governance.

With stability anchored and generational change in leadership at hand, Singapore is coming to terms with harsh laws that have their origins in expired conditions and outdated norms. There are active and heated public debates about revising the Internal Security Act (ISA) to limit the government's power of preventive detention, initiating a freedom of information act, curbing restrictions on political assembly, decriminalizing homosexuality, and abolishing caning as a form of official punishment. For each such law, there is a historical and cultural context, whether British colonial rule, fear of Cold War Communist insurgency, or the values of an elderly Christian population. Singapore is not afraid to evolve its ethical codes, but it rightly remains paranoid. Even as the government learns to trust the public ever more with the responsibilities of freedom, it would be foolish to expect a country even more ethnically diverse than when it was founded to tolerate, in the name of free speech, reckless abuses of liberty such as inciting communal hatred.

As the Singaporean sociologist Chua Beng Huat demonstrated in his book *Liberalism Disavowed*, Singaporean policy choices in matters of public housing, multiracialism, and state-directed capitalism all exemplify its unique, non-Western path.[11] Singapore is an example of how objectives such as racial equality have to be engineered to guard against tribalist proclivities. There is a difference between diversity and inclusion. Theoretically, democracy provides the crucial instrument to keep multiracial societies at peace because all are given equal voice. But this alone does not eliminate racial factors in social, economic, and political decision making. Indeed, the existence of race-based and religious parties in India and Malaysia only hardens a competitive mind-set among ethnic and racial groups. Successful management, or transcendence, of such tensions demands both a higher sense of unity and policies that actively bring diverse groups together. This is why Singapore requires that public housing blocks be cohabitated by substantial percentages of Chinese, Malays, and Indians and that every slate of political candidates be made of up individuals reflecting the country's racial diversity. Even though the leadership does not yet feel comfortable having a non-Chinese prime minister—though the most popular politician is a Tamil Indian—it has had many Indian presidents and justices and a Malay female president, and Indians make up a disproportionate share of the present cabinet.

Technocracy is well suited to Asia's more deferential cultures, but technocracy should not abuse its cultural privilege by remaining aloof. It should be civil rather than military, inclusive rather than a clique, data driven rather than dogmatic, and transparent rather than opaque. Technocrats are good at weighing means and ends, costs and benefits, causes and effects. But to avoid veering into elitist indifference, technocrats must blend democracy and data, foresight and feeling. They must learn to lead not just with the "head" (aptitude) but also with the "heart" (compassion) and "hands" (experience)—not just ticking boxes on dashboards but getting out enough into the streets.

The creed of a good technocracy must therefore be utilitarianism, allocating resources to achieve maximum social mobility and public benefit. The government's objective should be not only wealth maximization but also welfare maximization—a mix of Adam Smith and Jeremy Bentham—both the flourishing (and protection) of individual liberty as well as the promotion of fair and equal opportunity. There need not be a tension between democratic means and utilitarian ends; technocrats have to heed the former and deliver the latter. Utilitarian governments know that the tide will not necessarily lift all boats; most boats, in fact, will need an added lift through policies such as affordable housing and transportation, low-cost health care and education, and minimum wages and social insurance. An informed public may respect and trust its leaders for their competence, but it will judge them by their performance, not their credentials.

European countries' austerity policies in response to the financial crisis have been painful examples of nonutilitarian thinking by national leaders and financial lobbies. Extreme spending cuts have been both inhumane and counterproductive: tightening the belt on the poor has only served to contract economies and increase insecurity. Austerity does not create jobs, raise incomes, generate taxes, or boost consumption. The United States, too, has suffered from a deficit of utilitarian thinking. The Wall Street bailout engineered by Federal Reserve chairman Ben Bernanke and Treasury secretary Tim Geithner is credited with saving the financial system, but no correspondingly robust policy was engineered for Main Street. Only utilitarian thinking can bring about another Progressive Era in America.

When I travel to countries such as Oman, Georgia, the UAE, Kazakhstan, or dozens of other aspiring Asian nations, I am always presented with a sleek binder whose cover features some variation on "Vision" or "Strategy" for 2020, 2025, 2030, or beyond. The pages are full of bold language and the imagery of glass towers, driverless cars, vertical farms, and knowledge workers. In other words, they are all copied and pasted from Singapore's master plan. After decades of importing intellectual capital, Singapore's model has become its own best export, raking in billions of dollars annually from contracts to build dozens of Singapore-style industrial parks in China, Vietnam, India, and now the Arab countries and Africa, followed by corporate services to manage facilities and build local skills. Singapore's governance model is open source. Each year, the Singapore Cooperation Program brings thousands of foreign officials to study its institutions. At the same time, delegations of mayors and officials from all across Asia arrive weekly on the campus of the Lee Kuan Yew School of Public Policy for executive training programs, in which they learn technocratic techniques they can take home and implement. The state builders, urban planners, and economic strategists of the twenty-first century all take their inspiration from Lee Kuan Yew, not Thomas Jefferson.

China's Technocratic Evolution

Before technocracy had a name, Confucian bureaucrats practiced it in the Han Dynasty of the second century BC—indeed, perhaps the ancient world's closest analog to Plato's ideal republic. But more recently, Mao's dogmatism and Soviet communism were derisively labeled "technocratic" for their disastrous central planning, throwing the term into disrepute. Despite their socialist pretensions, those regimes proved not to be particularly utilitarian, willfully ignoring evidence contradicting their policies and failing to adapt to the international economic environment.

After Mao, China recovered some of the virtues (old and new) of technocratic theory and practice. Deng Xiaoping's admiration of Singapore's success inspired his pragmatic opening of the economy, unleashing its potential through a mix of shock therapy and small-scale experimentation. Since that time, China has gained four decades' worth of experience with markets, making many adaptations and course corrections. Successive generations of leaders beginning with Deng and continuing through Jiang Zemin, Hu Jintao, and now Xi Jinping have not only built on the accomplishments of their predecessors but also brought diverse backgrounds in engineering and management to the upper echelons of leadership.

China continues to live by Deng's counsel to "cross the river by feeling the stones." The Party remains Communist in name but continues the tradition of studying a wide range of models, including Western capitalism and social democracy, to learn lessons for its own benefit. Whereas outsiders fear that China is exporting its authoritarian model to the rest of the world, the country is much more focused on *importing* best practices from abroad, as the now-favored phrase "socialism with Chinese characteristics" (now enshrined in the Chinese constitution) suggests.

As a result, the government is far more self-correcting than earlier iterations, demonstrating policy agility in the handling of internal and external crises. Provincial chiefs, business executives, and academic experts are actively consulted to chart the country's economic restructuring, resulting in proentrepreneurship reforms across the country.[12] The scholar Jessica

Teets calls this model "consultative authoritarianism."[13] President Xi has been described as chairman and CEO, a combination of Mao's ideological reign and Hu's administrative centralization.[14] By formalizing the merger of the presidency and party chairmanship, he has completed the union of party and state, making the Chinese political system even more unified before he retires from both positions after perhaps one or two more terms.[15] He has inserted his doctrines into China's official ideology, but his first priority remains the preservation of order. Unlike other long-term rulers, Xi is not dismantling the state but strengthening it so that it will long outlast him. Entrenched despots could potentially benefit from aspects of the China model if that means focusing on infrastructure, education, health care, technology, and all the other things China has done right.

In *The China Model*, the Canadian political theorist Daniel Bell rightly pointed to how meritocracy, experimentation, and decisiveness have catapulted Chinese modernization in ways democracy might well have hindered. Not dissimilar to the ancient Confucian emphasis on rule by princes, Chinese Communist Party policy requires anywhere from one month to one year of training at the Central Party School of the Communist Party of China every five years, while the leadership goes on annual retreats to different provinces to study progress and challenges in towns, villages, and the countryside. Bell advocates a further evolution toward a "vertical democratic meritocracy": democracy at the bottom (since municipal leaders are actually popular and can respond to rapid feedback); experimentation in the middle (such as provinces attracting investment and supporting industries that suit their natural resources and human capital); and meritocracy at the top (so that there can be consistent long-term policy implementation). Bell also calls a "compassionate meritocracy" one in which officials are rewarded for demonstrating corruption-free behavior and actions taken in the public interest.[16] This is arguably the right model not just for China but for any sensible country.

China is the only country in the world in which about forty years of training are required before one is allowed to wield federal authority. Xi has purged rivals but not talent. Thousands of officials meritocratically work their way up the ladder and build significant administrative experience. Despite Xi's power consolidation, therefore, he still relies on the six other members of the Politburo Standing Committee and many other high-level officials who have equally deep governance experience across many portfolios. Compare this to the United States' executive branch, where each new president replaces the entire cabinet and the top four thousand positions with his or her political appointees, some (or many) of whom lack a basic understanding of the scope of their own responsibilities. Chinese citizens, not surprisingly, have far more respect for their government than Americans do. As one Chinese scholar remarked, "Chinese people don't love their government, but they trust it."

Graduating from Democracy to Technocracy

For decades, Western intellectuals touted India as "the world's largest democracy." Meanwhile, other Asians saw it for what it was: a squalid, overpopulated, quasi-socialist third-world morass; big but not important. Seen from the inside out, democracy in much of Asia has been more an exercise in vote banking than in political progress. Parliaments have not been the embodiment of genuine democracy but rather the junction points of local corruption and federal politics. This is more or less the role of legislatures across South and Southeast Asia to this day. India's parliamentary elections have been described by scholars as little more than auctions, with everything from sacks of rice to televisions bartered for votes. Pakistani political parties live and die with their patron family or dictator. Bangladeshi democracy is little more than a poker game between two rival families who use ministries and courts to undermine each other at every turn—agreeing only to pass laws that curb judicial independence and press freedom. Thailand's parliamentarians don't run the country but rather give handouts to their constituents and help organize funerals. Myanmar has formally turned to democracy, but the military still controls 25 percent of the parliamentary seats and has an effective veto on all legislation. Indonesian factory owners and landholders buy parliament seats to shape regulations to their benefit. Beneath the veneer of democracy, then, many Asian parliaments have been little more than public-private racketeering operations.

CAN ASIAN GOVERNMENTS BE BOTH EFFECTIVE AND INCLUSIVE?

Most Asian countries made steady or significant improvements in their government effectiveness rankings between 2010 and 2016. In cases of slight decline, such as in South Korea and the Philippines, recent changes in government portend a return to a more positive trajectory.

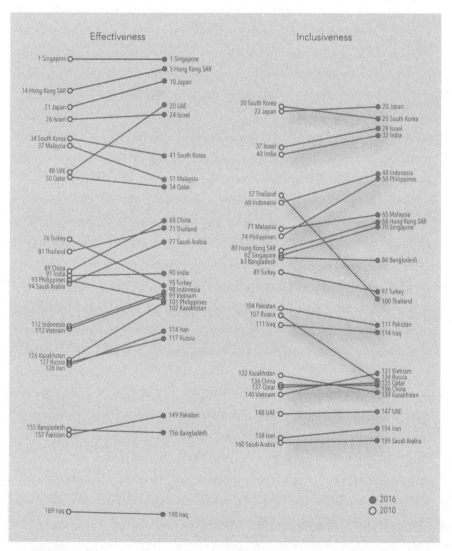

Asian publics know all too well how long their mafia politics
has masqueraded as democracy. Because India, Indonesia, and the
Philippines has each endured decades of forgettable or regrettable
governments, they have all in recent years elected leaders with explicitly *technocratic* pretensions. Indians, Indonesians, and Filipinos
are no longer content to be part of a vibrant commercial society with
a dysfunctional government. Fed up with patronizing clichés about
how they thrive despite their governments, they have voted in leaders with no-nonsense agendas focused on accountability in public
affairs and a less corrupt environment for business, as well as major
investments in infrastructure, jobs, education, and health care. At
the same time, these three countries have climbed the most places
among Asian countries between 2010 and 2016 in the Economist Intelligence Unit's Democracy Index for their growing political inclusiveness. But make no mistake about the causality: they have become
more inclusive because of the technocratic steps they have taken, not
because of any changes in their electoral practices.

Here, then, is a key reason to pay attention to technocracy: because it is Asia's future. Technocracy becomes a form of salvation
after societies realize that democracy doesn't guarantee national
success. Democracy eventually gets sick of itself and votes for technocracy. Think about it: these three countries have had functional
democracies for at least a generation, but only now is the world paying attention to their progress in introducing digital ID cards, cutting
red tape, and establishing special economic zones—all ideas that have
come from technocratic leaders. Daily political life in many Asian
countries is consumed by concerns over subsidies, security, construction, currency, and other nuts-and-bolts issues—issues the public
wants to see better managed. The 1.7 billion citizens of Asia's three
largest democracies rightly want to balance their unruly politics with
technocratic discipline. They are sufficiently democratic already—but
they are not nearly technocratic enough.

For those who view countries first and foremost by differences in their political systems, it is surprising that India is one of the chief advocates of Chinese-style top-down economic reform. But divergence among regimes doesn't preclude learning across borders. After all, the average person in "Communist" China leads a far better life in almost every possible dimension than the average person in "democratic" India does. What Prime Minister Modi has realized is that, unlike China, India went through a political devolution prior to building national unity, meaning it remains much less than the sum of its parts. Successive governments have perennially made payouts to the provinces to purchase loyalty, which only encouraged further fragmentation. At independence, India had only fourteen provinces; today it has twenty-nine. Modi is not out to reverse democracy but to compensate for this debilitating sequence of devolution before modernization by harmonizing national infrastructure, taxation, and investment regulations. He replaced the outdated Planning Commission with a federally structured think tank called the National Institution for Transforming India (NITI Aayog) to steer national economic transformation. He is also trying his best to become an Indian version of his hero Lee Kuan Yew by ruthlessly tackling corruption.

The rise of elected technocrats comes not a moment too soon for Asia's masses. India's Modi, Indonesia's Joko Widodo (Jokowi), and the Philippines' Rodrigo Duterte all have backgrounds as provincial governors or mayors in which they confronted local needs and tested ideas. They are a reminder that even poor, nonelite leaders who actually have experience governing are almost always a superior choice to well-heeled representative politicians. It is all too easy to lump such unheralded leaders into the category of "elected strongmen" alongside Erdoğan and Putin, as many Western commentators like to do. They need to get out more. India has gone from a country in which for decades what limited economic and social progress occurred was in spite of government to a nation where the government is one of the chief drivers of innovation and the main source of confidence both domestically and internationally. Until Modi's election, only a narrow slice of Indians truly benefited from the 1990s liberalization policies. He has brought a technocratic mind-set and utilitarian ethos to a country that truly needs it. Despite his unhealthy cultural illiberalism and dangerously populist political partners, his technocratic mantra is a big step forward for India: "Minimum government, maximum governance."

India and Indonesia rank at the top of a 2018 survey of countries whose citizens believe their democracy is working well, with greater than 70 percent satifaction (as high as in Germany and Canada). Both Jokowi in Indonesia and Duterte in the Philippines also have illiberal strains. Both have resorted to extrajudicial means in their antidrug wars but are widely supported by increasingly well-informed publics. Duterte is an example of the polarizing nature of debating the merits of strict Asian leaders. In Western media he is derided as a Hugo Chávez of Asia, a gruff quasi-socialist strongman with blood on his hands. Meanwhile, at home, he is wildly popular for taking on drug lords and cleaning up the streets. Singapore's tough gun and drug laws show that it is possible to win the war on violence despite a turbulent background involving transnational criminal gangs. Not only do Asian publics support their governments' tough policies, but Western criminal justice is beginning to resemble certain Asian codes with its stiffer penalties for drug and handgun offenses, to say nothing of the treatment of suspected terrorists.

Asia's leaders are rightly more focused on state capacity than on parliamentary proceduralism. Boosting capacity doesn't mean building bloated bureaucracies; Asian governments already have those. It means creating a leaner and more effective government, from streamlined tax policy to online portals for business licensing and procurement.[17] Governments are shrewdly calculating the benefit multinational partners will bring in terms of investment and taxes, jobs and wages, skills and technology. They are getting tougher on domestic incumbents as well, taking a hard line on companies that don't deliver on time by not paying until construction projects are complete. In the Philippines, officials now speak not just of public-private partnerships (PPPs) but add a fourth P: public-private partnerships for the people.

The term *Asian values* used to imply deference to authority by a condescending government. But since the 1980s, Asians have demonstrated that even entrenched elites can be confronted and ousted once the population is sufficiently fed up with their rent-seeking profligacy. Asians have traded in their infatuation with the gilded class for single-minded demands for quality governance. Becoming more liberal and democratic does not mean that they will fail to toss out ineffective elected leaders in favor of technocratic doers. Thailand's military junta, which took power in 2014, has found strong support within a highly liberal society for its management of the country—for the time being. Modi has already suffered electoral defeats in some states. It is refreshing that upstart political movements—from the cricket star Imran Khan's Pakistan Tehreek-e-Insaf (PTI) party to the millennial-driven Future Forward Party in Thailand—have been holding leaders' feet to the fire, demanding greater transparency and accountability in government, and motivating throngs of youths to become politically engaged. To deserve to be elected, however, these new parties need meaningful policy platforms and talented managers capable of implementing them. Even though countries once referred to as transition democracies—Georgia and Mongolia—continue to have competitive elections, more significant to the quality of their governance is that they, too, are bringing in technocrats to manage the economy, pensions, infrastructure, investment, and other critical areas so that important long-term policies can withstand electoral flip-flops. The faces headlining Asian politics will constantly change, but the technocratic policies should endure.

There is a Western idea that holds that populations in single-party-dominated states are docile lemmings accepting a social contract that exchanges basic handouts for political freedom. But as Duke University professor Edmund Malesky has shown in the case of Vietnam, citizens don't support the government out of fear of the ruling party but rather out of fear of the unknown alternative. Indeed, they are pragmatically and even sincerely supportive of the government even if presented with hypothetical alternatives whose agendas appear sound but whose credibility and competence is unproved.[18] Vietnam's rapid economic progress and social opening, even if not coupled with radical political change, have made it a model most developing countries want to emulate.

All of this means that when Westerners look at the future of Asian governance, they need to jettison the comforting liberal democratic prism of Japan, Taiwan, and South Korea, governments strongly shaped by US postwar influence, and start looking at the new vanguard of more cautious and maturing democratic technocracies. What has enabled Thailand to progress despite dozens of coups and changes of government over the past century is its strong tradition of monarchist loyalty and centralized bureaucracy. Both order and reform in Thailand emerge from the country's technocratic spine, not its democratic organs. Similarly, even as Malaysian power rotates among politicians who have been on the scene for decades, a sufficient array of technocratic bodies managing foreign investment, infrastructure, technology, and other key areas carries forward. None of these is a fully free democracy, but each is seeking an appropriate balance between political openness and goal-oriented technocracy.

According to the independent watchdog organization Freedom House, more than half of Asia's governments are ranked "not free." The countries with the highest execution rates in the world are in Asia: China, Iran, Saudi Arabia, Pakistan, Vietnam, and Iraq. Alongside China and Russia, Southeast Asian nations such as Vietnam, Thailand, Cambodia, and the Philippines have some of the world's most harsh and violent prisons. Asian governments have been shamefully brutal toward minority populations: Palestinians in Israel, Kurds in Turkey, Rohingya in Myanmar, Tibetans and Uighurs in China, and Tamils in Sri Lanka, to name a few terribly victimized Asian peoples. Those countries' regimes either explicitly seek ethnic, religious, or racial purity—or simply pursue it in the name of political stability. At the same time, steady gains have been made in overall political rights and civil liberties, with greater diversity of political parties and greater freedom of association. More and more Asian states are thus moving in the direction of becoming hybrid regimes, mixing democracy with strong executives. They cannot be easily dismissed as authoritarian when there is broad support for steady leadership.

The bottom line is that across Asia, rising incomes, technological penentration, and generational change are enabling greater social and economic freedom—but politics remains fairly controlled, because regimes like it that way and, to a large degree, people do as well. The desire for stability and social order is as natural to humans as the desire for freedom. Large, diverse, fragile postcolonial Asian countries have no desire to adopt American-style democracy if it will put at risk the stability on which societal progress and successful democratization depend. This is why one should not expect an increasingly liberal social culture to be attended by governments' becoming any less strict. Asians realize that there is such a thing as too much freedom and that responsibility is just as important a word in healthy societies.

Asia's Top-Down Revolutions

Almost all Asian countries today share a restless impatience to get things done. Rather than delivering wild swings in government, Asians now aim for continuity across administrations on core issues such as economic and judicial reforms, investments in infrastructure, and safety nets. As INSEAD dean Ilian Mihov has demonstrated by correlating variables of the World Bank's Worldwide Governance Indicators (WGI) with economic growth, it is the rule of law, not democracy, that most strongly drives economic performance. Asians have realized that the protection of private property, a liberal entrepreneurial culture, and responsive government are the crucial drivers of their current upward trajectory. Rising middle classes everywhere demand these institutions and practices—or threaten revolution.

These lessons are particularly appropriate for Asia, where there are numerous leaders whose rule is effectively total: Mohammed bin Salman in Saudi Arabia, Recep Erdoğan in Turkey, Bashar al-Assad in Syria, Vladimir Putin in Russia, Ilham Aliyev in Azerbaijan, Nursultan Nazarbayev in Kazakhstan, Gurbanguly Berdimuhamedow in Turkmenistan, and Xi Jinping in China. Since none will democratize executive power by choice, we should look instead to see whether they and others can become more progressively technocratic.

The oxymoronic notion of "top-down revolution" is a reality across Asia, and it rests both on the credibility of the vision and the depth of trust people have in their leadership. According to the 2018 Edelman Trust Barometer, only Asian countries have high levels of trust in government: Singapore, China, India, Indonesia, and the UAE have the highest scores.[19] When governments enjoy trust, they can not only pursue long-term transformation but also act decisively in crisis, whether an economic downturn or a sudden geopolitical shock. Because such Asian leaders think in generational rather than electoral terms and lines of authority are clear, everyone knows exactly where the buck stops. Neither political nor corporate leaders can slip into anonymity and wash away their sins. Failures may be forgiven, but they are never forgotten.

At the same time, because Russians know they cannot change their government, they focus instead on tangible outputs, the content of good governance without the form of democracy. Vladimir Putin has imposed and maintained stability in Russia, helping the country weather regional turbulence (some of his own making) and low oil prices while rehabilitating some industry, building shopping malls and vocational schools, and restoring a sense of pride. Starting in 2015, he appointed several competent technocrats to run state-owned companies and manage far-flung regions.[20] Despite engineering a comfortable victory for himself in Russia's 2018 presidential election, one should not be surprised if he spends his current term expanding this bench of professional administrators so that he can retire (or semiretire) in 2024.

At the same time, appointing a few technocrats is not the same as creating a technocratic system. Because we hear more and more countries touting their technocratic credentials, we should be careful not to take it at face value—lest the term come to be as unconvincing as democracy is. Always beware the oligarch in disguise. In Russia and Turkey, strongmen declare themselves to be technocrats while running elaborate patronage-based regimes (a polite way of saying mafia states). They may call in economists with Western degrees to help shore up their currencies and stave off balance-of-payments crises, but they are not meritocratic or utilitarian nation builders. Real technocrats are not Gucci-wearing thugs, nor are they Islamist wolves in sheep's clothing. They aren't in a hurry to get rich quick or hoard executive powers. The essence of technocracy is improving governance, not preserving one's own rule.

Yet as the case of Russia demonstrates, the leaders of many countries will entertain a shift from crony power to technocratic decision making only once their own power is firmly entrenched. These are Asia's transition technocracies, countries in which leadership has been seized or inherited and democracy is weak or pliant—but a new crop of young and often foreign-educated experts is relieving the old guard of its duties. They defer to the ruler who appointed them, but their loyalty lies with the state. In countries such as Azerbaijan, Kazakhstan, and Uzbekistan, I regularly encounter this new guard of technocrats. None of these countries is likely to have a competitive election in the next decade or more, but in the meantime, much of their policy is moving in the right direction.

Even the Arab Gulf region's rigid monarchies are finding ways to modernize their systems and societies. Saudi crown prince Mohammed bin Salman has pursued a radical agenda of economic transformation, education investment, affordable housing, reduced corruption, and curbs on the influence of the country's Wahhabi clerics—all at the same time. As his liquidation of any critics demonstrates, however, political reform is not yet on the agenda. Though the UAE is also a monarchy, it more resembles Singapore in its attempt to use its sovereign wealth to spur economic diversification and build a technocratic caste capable of overseeing key policy areas and monitoring key performance indicators. It now ranks seventh in the world in competitiveness. Whereas governments such as that of the UAE used to hire foreigners to operate many of their agencies, now there are enough talented and eager young Emiratis competing with one another for top government jobs that that is unnecessary. The annual ASDA'A Burson-Marsteller Arab Youth Survey, conducted across twenty countries, revealed in 2018 that the UAE ranks as the most desirable place in which to live, ahead of any Western country.

Across Asia, youths are a large part of the restless wave either supporting transformative governments such as Saudi Arabia's or opposing defunct ones such as Iran's. Indeed, Iran's youths don't go to the mosque to bide time; they go out on the streets to protest against corruption and an out-of-touch, geriatric theocracy. The same is true in Georgia and Armenia, where each new government is given at most a year to prove it will embrace good governance before citizens rise up and foment a much-deserved political crisis. Nationalism cannot substitute for rule of law or efficient public service delivery. Asia's wayward regimes such as Turkey and Iran are living on borrowed time.

Then there are the countries that have hit rock bottom. In Iraq, the Western focus on democracy rather than state building led to the perpetuation of factionalized sectarianism, with Shi'a replacing Sunni atop the hierarchy. For Asia's most war-torn and fragile states, such as Yemen, Syria, and Afghanistan, SWAT teams of Indian bureaucrats training civil servants would be much more useful than democracy activists. With today's unparalleled accumulation of historical knowledge about what works and what doesn't in all policy areas, coupled with the ability to assess and adapt those policies in real-time, even Asia's most challenging corners can be turned around with the technocratic toolkit.

Asia's "Civic" Societies

Across most of Asia, civil society is neither as independent nor as politically vocal as in the West. Taiwan, Hong Kong, and South Korea are important exceptions. In Hong Kong, civil society groups took center stage in political upheavals such as the 2014 "Umbrella Revolution" and continue to agitate against Beijing's political encroachment. In South Korea, social groups flooded the streets to demand the ouster of President Park Geun-hye in 2017. In Singapore, NGOs are generally volunteer groups dedicated to civic causes but not permitted to undertake political activities. The Chinese government imposes strict controls on lawyers, activists, and all manner of "social organizations." In 2017, it passed a law requiring all foreign NGOs to register with the government and allow their activities to be closely monitored and regulated. In West Asia, Iranian civil society takes great risks to mobilize for political and social causes, while in its Arab neighbors, such activity is all but impossible and is becoming increasingly so in Turkey. By contrast, in Uzbekistan, where the police state once mercilessly tortured political activists, a regime change has meant that Human Rights Watch has been allowed back in and a new television station publicly challenges the government.[21] India has long been considered the "NGO capital of the world" given an estimated 2.5 million civil society organizations active across the social, health, religious, and political domains, not least the Hindu-traditionalist Rashtriya Swayamsevak Sangh (RSS) movement, which provides the ideological underpinnings of the ruling Bharatiya Janata Party (BJP) and has sought to impose a narrow ethnoreligious narrative nationwide from textbooks to media.

Traditional television and print media are still censored to varying degrees across Asia. Press freedom is severely curtailed in China, Vietnam, Laos, Cambodia, and Myanmar. Countries such as Iraq, Syria, Russia, India, Pakistan, and the Philippines account for the highest numbers of journalists murdered in recent years. In some of these countries (such as India), it is a highly free and vocal press that is being punished by political agents. In West Asia, even the most politically unfree countries now have more variegated and opinionated television discourse. The Qatar-based Al Jazeera International altered the media landscape in the Arab world with its critical coverage of the region's regimes (except, of course, its own) and early support for the Arab uprisings in 2011, and it has inspired imitators such as Al Arabiya.

Especially among youth, I find that more and more people across Asia openly speak their minds on all subjects except for the narrow range of issues on which a roll of the eyes or suggestive glance—or customized emoji—suffices. The rise of social media has provided a major release valve for almost all Asian societies, with websites and commentators often located beyond the reach of insecure governments. Their governments have seized on the digital domain in ways that create greater space for personal and entrepreneurial freedom but also make it a new zone of political control by actively censoring Internet content. China is representative of both. The rise of the blogging site Sina Weibo and Tencent's WeChat have burst open the digital public sphere and given Chinese people a voice on social policies and corruption. The government listens, takes constructive comments on board, and cracks down on criticism—all at the same time.

Conservative Asian cultures have been slow to liberalize in terms of women's rights, but generational and technological changes are leading to a sea change in social norms. Though India, Pakistan, and Bangladesh have all had female heads of state (such as India's Indira Gandhi and Pakistan's Benazir Bhutto) and many women in parliament, backward religious customs still enable widespread abuse, subjugation, and rape. With India's male preference causing a horrendous gender imbalance—35 million surplus males facing social .alienation and a brideless future—the situation may get worse despite government decrees and activist outpouring. The poorest Arab and Central Asian states such as Yemen and Afghanistan report the most appalling rates of sexual harassment and discrimination in schools and public life. In Arab states such as Jordan, cultural inhibitions continue to prohibit educated females to work, leading to a large number of unemployed female university graduates. Even in the most advanced Asian nations, such as Japan and South Korea, women still lag behind in terms of pay. In China, women are empowered economically and play major roles in the private sector; they make up 40 percent of Alibaba's management. Politically, however, a renewed push to brand women as child bearers—part of the effort to boost the population after the termination of the one-child policy—reflects the minimal role women still play in politics. One economist caused a stir by suggesting that several men share one wife.

But there are some indicators of progress. From Jordan to Pakistan, honor killings have been criminalized. By taking to Twitter and YouTube, Saudi women created a publicity storm that led to an edict allowing women the right to drive (though some of the movement's leaders were subsequently arrested). Crown Prince Mohammed bin Salman has further allowed women to attend sporting events and go to movie theaters. In the UAE and Qatar, women have been socially prominent for two decades, especially in education, where the majority of teachers are female. The UAE's cabinet has more women than the United States', about half of them Western-educated. Already about one-third of Arab start-ups are run by women, and as oil wealth dwindles, educated women will be crucial to raising household incomes, further modernizing gender norms. In Iran, where women are publicly casting off their head scarves, universities are full of women, including in traditionally male-dominated areas such as computer science.

The better educated and wealthier Asians become, the more demanding they will be that their voices be taken into account—irrespective of whether their governments become more or less formally democratic. The current spate of crackdowns on civil society in numerous Asian countries is a reflexive response to a more confident media and a new educated class of entrepreneurs, youths, and women who despise corruption and elite impunity. The tide of history remains with these people: governments know that suppression is not the way to make their countries worth living in.

Can Asia's tycoons and upwardly mobile purchase the solidarity that colonialism, social inequality, and poor governance has taken from their societies? Charity is enshrined in the teachings of the Buddha and in the Koran but is less systematized and publicized than in the West. According to the World Giving Index, since 2014 the country with the most consistently high rate (90 percent) of charitable giving is also one of the poorest, Myanmar, due to its devout Buddhist beliefs. Similarly, owing to the principle of *zakat*, an alms tax that constitutes mandatory giving and is one of the five pillars of Islam, nearly 90 percent of Arab Gulf citizens made charitable donations in 2016.

From Li Ka Shing to Saudi prince Alwaleed bin Talal, some of Asia's highest-profile billionaires have endowed professorships and centers devoted to their region's affairs, their names adorning buildings at leading American and European universities. At home, however, cultural traditions urge them not to be boastful about wealth but instead to give discreetly and humbly. What is changing is both the scale of giving and its formality, with charity becoming more formalized and visible in order to inspire others and create a greater impact. Between 2010 and 2016, China's top one hundred philanthropic donors tripled the size of their commitments to $4.6 billion. No single Asian country has as vast a demand for welfare as India. Mohandas K. Gandhi influenced an early generation of Indian industrialists, such as the Tata and Godrej families, to donate 10 percent or more of their annual earnings to a range of causes such as education. More recently, a far larger set of India's wealthy has stepped up, with charitable donations rising sixfold between 2010 and 2016, overtaking foreign sources in value. Asian business leaders are increasingly recognized in the West for their efforts at financial inclusion, such as ICICI Bank CEO Chanda Kochhar, who received the Woodrow Wilson Award for Global Corporate Citizenship in 2017.

At the same time, Asian philanthropy will not follow the same path as in the West because of an abundance of caution about the trustworthiness of civil society groups that lack substantial track records and oversight. As a result, most Asian billionaires (with the exception of some Arabs and Indians) aren't jumping to sign on to Bill Gates and Warren Buffett's Giving Pledge to donate most of their wealth. Instead, they invest in operational charities. The Ayala Foundation in the Philippines has, since the 1960s, focused on programs in education, youth leadership, arts, and culture. In China, forty-six of the country's wealthiest two hundred individuals have now established such foundations. Private banks such as Credit Suisse have assisted dozens of clients to set up such foundations. In 2015, Laurence Lien, the chairman of Singapore's Lien Foundation, founded the Asian Philanthropy Circle to foster collaboration among regional donors. Also in 2015, China's first independent philanthropic training center, the China Global Philanthropy Institute, began operations with the support of philanthropists from China and the United States. Asians cannot donate to change makers until they produce more of them.

Given the importance of education in almost all of Asia's rags-to-riches stories, it is no surprise that spreading and enhancing educational opportunities are a leading focus of philanthropists such as Abdulla bin Ahmad Al Ghurair, the founder of Mashreq Bank, who has donated $1.1 billion to educational causes. Azim Premji, the chairman of Wipro, has given $8 billion to charities, and his eponymous foundation focuses primarily on improving rural education. Tencent cofounder Charles Chen left the company in 2013 to devote himself full-time to a $320 million fund for transformational ideas in education and gave $300 million to upgrade the liberal-arts-focused Wuhan College. This new vanguard of Chinese tech billionaires also has the advantage of deploying the very technologies that created their wealth. Both Alibaba's and Tencent's foundations have set up websites for the donation of discarded mobile phones and desktop computers, together raising hundreds of millions of dollars for local technology distribution programs. Tencent "charity boxes" in stores and airports have payment platforms that allow donations of less than $1 using its popular e-payment system. *Zakat*, too, has gone digital: an online UNHCR appeal that ran during Ramadan in 2013 raised $700 per donor.

Impact investment has become a major new thrust of Asian philanthropists. The Emirates Foundation, the Arab Foundations Forum, and Islamic Development Bank have all raised funds and directed them toward social enterprises delivering innovative health care models, both alone and with Western partners such as the Bill & Melinda Gates Foundation's Lives and Livelihoods Fund, a $2.5 billion initiative to combat illnesses such as polio and river blindness, which has become the largest such fund based in the Arab world. But wealthy and conscientious Asians need to do much more to address the consequences of poverty, inequality, and social stress. India, Pakistan, and the Philippines have millions of homeless people and street children. Sri Lanka, Mongolia, and Kazakhstan have among the world's highest suicide rates. Porous borders and fragile societies also help explain why Asia's human trafficking, from Saudi Arabia through Pakistan and India and across Southeast Asia, surpasses the rest of the world by a wide margin.[22]

Asia's swelling populations and large-scale challenges have elevated the role of technology in societal governance. Across Asia, one finds leaders fluent in the language and application of the latest digital technologies. The UAE has appointed a minister devoted to AI, is putting all government data and services on blockchain platforms, and is rolling out a fully digital currency, em-Cash, by 2020. In China's Jiangsu province, one-meter-tall robots in government offices scan, review, and administer the sentencing of tens of thousands of standard cases such as traffic violations or unpaid bills. The Seoul municipal area's mVoting system allows millions of residents to effortlessly evaluate and vote on initiatives relevant to their district or interests. Meanwhile, the United States is still fighting over net neutrality and Italy can't figure out how to deploy broadband Internet.

China is at the forefront of using big data as a tool to encourage behavioral conformity. Drawing on data from Alibaba, Tencent, and other platforms, authorities use the new social credit system (SCS) to determine which citizens have committed dishonorable acts and issue penalties. Some have been denied loans, cannot buy airline or train tickets, have had their passports suspended, or temporarily lose their Internet access. Though seemingly Orwellian from the outside, many (if not most) Chinese want greater transparency into what the government monitors—and now, for better or worse, they know. Importantly, the social credit system also cracks down on restaurants that sell contaminated food and vendors selling counterfeit goods. Reputation has long been an important currency in Asian societies, and now it applies to everyone in the social and commercial marketplace.

Asian countries are simply doing first what Western governments would do more of if they were allowed to deploy such technologies without being outed by whistle-blowers. Given the revelations about the United States' National Security Agency (NSA) and other intelligence agencies' unconstitutional breaches of citizens' privacy, the lines are blurring between the notions of Western rule of law and Eastern abuse of power. As Chinese companies deploy their surveillance technologies, including facial scanning and mobile app tracking within China (especially in the restive Muslim Xinjiang province), as well as export them across Asia and to countries in Europe, the lines will blur ever further.

Asians have watched as digital technologies have destroyed jobs, warped politics, and ruptured societies in the West—and they don't want to follow the same path. Their governments are demanding that Western tech companies such as Apple remove VPNs from their apps and location data about their citizens on their territory. Most of the largest Facebook-using populations besides the United States and Brazil are Asian—India, Indonesia, the Philippines, Vietnam, Thailand, and Turkey—but those countries, democracies or not, also represent the largest share of requests to censor content deemed offensive to the state. Asian leaders such as Narendra Modi and Jokowi Widodo have huge followings on Twitter and Facebook that have been crucial platforms for citizen engagement, policy messaging, and campaign mudslinging across Asia. But after observing Russia's manipulation of Facebook in the 2016 US election—and viral videos sparking riots in India and Myanmar—Asians have recruited Facebook and WhatsApp to actively screen and counter viral hoaxes in order to ensure that "fake news" does not destabilize communal harmony. As the economist Danny Quah puts it, free-for-all populist cultures resemble the comments section of online newspapers: they get hijacked by ranting trolls. A better model might be liberal societies in which officials act more like Wikipedia editors who ensure veracity and a sense of order.[23]

Across Asia's vast array of cultures and regimes, societies generally appear to be comfortable with certain norms such as mixed capitalism, technocratic governance, and social conservatism. It is not likely that Western ideas will triumph over this Asian mind-set. To the contrary, in the coming decades, global competition will punish the sentimental. For societies to prove that they are capable of confronting the complexities arising from the intersection of social, political, economic, technological, and environmental stress, they will need capable leaders with a utilitarian mind-set. Asian technocracy is already proving that it is as well—and perhaps better—suited to the task as Western democracy is.

Governing the World the Asian Way

Asia's rise is also rebalancing the narrative of global governance. Governance is the provision of order and rules, not just regulating but even supplying public goods. Asia has long been on the receiving end of global governance, but now it is very much a shaper of norms and provider of public goods. When the United States was spending heavily on its global military presence and others were able to keep their budgets down, it was called a security umbrella. When China recycles its trade surpluses and reserves into low-cost infrastructure for dozens of countries, why don't we call it a development platform? When the United States requires that all dollar transactions be cleared by US banks so the US Treasury can sanction financial flows, it is considered to be upholding the financial system. But when Alibaba provides a platform for millions of SMEs to seamlessly trade with one another worldwide, why is it not called a breakthrough in global peer-to-peer commerce?

Westerners don't want to hear that Asians are taking on greater leadership in setting global rules any more than they want to hear that the United States is disengaging from crucial aspects of global governance—but both are happening nonetheless. Rather than Western conversations about some vague Eastern authoritarian challenge to their systems, it is much more fruitful to look at the tangible contributions Asia makes to regional and global order and governance.

The provision of global public goods is, like world order itself, multipolar. The United States does provide the world's leading reserve currency and polices the oceans. However, Asians (and many others) not only view the United States as having abused its strategic and financial weight, but they can fulfill ever more of these functions themselves. In the military domain, Asian powers already undertake their own joint sea-lane patrols. They are, as India terms it, "net providers of global security." In the global economy, Asia has been the key source of countercyclical spending and demand during the prolonged Western economic downturn, keeping entire sectors from commodities to consumption afloat. About half the G20 is made up of Asian states, whose central banks are crucial for global economic policy coordination.

As with Europe, Asia's great-power stability is the region's biggest contribution to global governance. But there are further essential public goods that Asians are taking the lead in. It is useful to contrast the ways in which the public goods of security and infrastructure are deployed. Military alliances are exclusive in nature. The United States supports countries that buy its hardware and protect its interests. By contrast, the provision of infrastructure is much more a platform service for anyone to use. In addition to all the roads, railways, and ports China builds—which will remain in use even if China no longer actively needs them—China has become one of the world's largest shipbuilders, reducing the cost for developing countries to reach global markets. It also installs electricity grids and fiber-optic Internet and launches satellites that help with everything from fishing-vessel navigation to bike sharing. These investments may facilitate Chinese trade, but that does not change the fact that they are also elevating entire economies into the twenty-first century. When China buys up global lithium supplies to make cheap batteries for electric cars and sells affordable solar panels worldwide, it brings revenue to Chinese companies but also contributes to reducing global greenhouse gas emissions. Indeed, China, Japan, and India are all major exporters of the solar, wind, nuclear, and other energy technologies that reduce our global carbon footprint.

This is a reminder that while China makes many contributions to global governance, these join a long history of Asian activity. Japan has been one of the world's largest foreign assistance donors, providing more than $300 billion in aid to 185 countries. It continues to be second to none in its generosity as a contributor to human development. India has provided more than 200,000 troops for more than fifty UN peacekeeping operations. (China has provided barely

2,000.) Japan and India have together launched more than two hundred satellites for other countries, reducing the cost for their national telecommunications systems. For the first seventy years of the Nobel Peace Prize, almost no Asians were recognized internationally for their humanitarian or peacemaking efforts. But since the 1970s, more than a dozen Asians have been awarded the prize, from Japanese prime minister Eisaku Sato for committing to the country's denuclearization to the microfinance pioneer Muhammad Yunus to Pakistan's teenage activist Malala Yousafzai.

Yet the measure of Asian countries' contributions to global governance is not their obedience to Western-led bodies that have little relevance to their lives. That idea is both arrogant and meaningless. It is not for Asia to adapt itself to what have become effectively transatlantic organizations but rather the reverse. As the world becomes more multipolar, the rules of the system must adjust or the old order will simply collapse. The International Monetary Fund, World Bank, and UN Security Council do not actually govern global finance, development, and military activity, respectively. Rather, these organizations, and the powers behind them, are competitors in a much larger marketplace of global financial, economic, and security services—with Asians equally capable of devising institutions that better suit their needs. The Regional Comprehensive Economic Partnership (RCEP) trade agreement and the Asian Infrastructure Investment Bank (AIIB) are just two major examples. If the UN Security Council fails to expand to include more Asian powers, they will simply ignore it.

Rising powers both shape global norms and selectively ignore and undermine them—much as the United States has done time and again. The United States has circumvented and violated World Trade Organization (WTO) rules with its unilateral tariffs, while China has undermined the same organization through its exemptions and noncompliance. India leads developing countries in WTO negotiations to protect food subsidies against Western corporate pressures. It is impossible to imagine the Western agenda of strengthening intellectual property protection moving ahead without significant changes to the way in which Western companies have defined and protected it.

Already we can see many other examples of what will happen—for good and for ill—as Asians get more involved in global governance. In the UN Human Rights Council, most Asians—whether Israel, Arabs, or Chinese—are not interested in Western countries' (or one anothers') efforts at annual reviews of their records. They would just as soon shut the Council down—though it was the United States that quit the body altogether in 2018. The World Bank has sought to make itself more relevant in Asia by pushing critical units out of Washington and expanding its offices from Istanbul to Singapore. Those Asian hubs do not simply carry out the headquarters' agenda; rather, they serve Asia's priorities of infrastructure and clean energy. The international police federation Interpol has established a twin Asian headquarters in Singapore to focus on tackling cybercrime, but China and Russia are using the organization to issue more politically motivated "red notices" to apprehend enemies of the state—including the head of the Interpol itself, Chinese Meng Hongwei, who vanished during a visit to China in September 2018. The growing number of Asian banks participating in the SWIFT interbank network has increased the organization's ability to facilitate global financial flows, but these new participants are taking a tougher line against excluding Iranian banks, which the United States has tried to do. In partnership with the World Economic Forum, Japan, China, and India have set up centers to help design the future of regulation of AI, blockchain, drone, and other technologies. At the International Telecommunications Union (ITU), where the future of Internet regulation is taking shape, Asian officials go toe to toe with Americans and Europeans on matters of data privacy and e-commerce regulation.

The future landscape of global regulation appears to be a hybrid of conventional Western rules and Asian practices. Investments by Asian sovereign wealth funds will be robust, but much more scrutiny of deals will create greater transparency. The United States and European Union will ever more confidently block Chinese investments in their territories unless their companies are granted reciprocal access—and have protections for their innovations. All the while, other Asian powers will be building their technological and financial foundations, snapping up assets where Chinese are rejected and building their own global portfolios. The only new global rules that will be accepted will be those that Asians agree to.

10

Asia Goes Global: The Fusion of Civilizations

To describe something as "Asian" can often have opposite connotations: elegant or unsophisticated, precise or chaotic, risk averse or bold. Not only do outsiders have divergent understandings of "Asian," but so, too, do Asians. The vast diversity of Asian tongues from Arabic, Turkish, and Farsi to Chinese, Vietnamese, and Bahasa is a salient reminder that Asians will always struggle to speak with one voice. European colonialism also had a lasting impact on the construction of national identity, warping it from inclusive to exclusive. Asians identify themselves to one another by their country of origin—and do the same when they go abroad: Indians, Chinese, and Koreans don't travel the world saying they are "Asian." The notion of "Asian" thus appears to be an artificial construct. Among Asians, there is no longer any common understanding of what it means to be Asian. Europe may have invented the term for Asia's geography, but it has robbed Asia of Asian identity. It does not help that Western media accounts of intra-Asian relations can be summed up with one predictable word—nationalism—usually modified by adjectives such as toxic and virulent.

Though no doubt Asian societies, like European ones, have deeply ingrained preferences for racial purity and even strains of xenophobia, the ground-level story points toward an accelerated intermingling across the region. Asians already share cultural and material affinities that date back to the ancient Silk Roads, and colonialism forged a common Asian spirit of resistance against Western empires. Despite economic stasis and political lethargy, postcolonial affinities blossomed as well. Since the 1950s, each successive Asian Games has garnered expanded commitment and ever larger national teams, as well as sporting spirit of fans and the media. Today, cross-border education and labor opportunities combined with intermarriage are changing the complexion of Asia—even though its enormous population sizes make it harder to notice.[1] Asia's layering of peoples and cultures is far too textured for Asian states to be racially defined as European societies have been. Rising intra-Asian connectivity has also launched new conversations that are nourishing regional understanding. Asians are finding that their preferences for technocratic governance, social order, and conservative justice bind them together in an era when Western societies no longer serve as role models for their future.

Asia today is more a sponge than a bloc. The Turkic former Soviet republics of Central Asia have ditched Cyrillic for Latinized scripts so they can communicate more easily with Turks and Indians. Meanwhile, Afghanistan's main foreign television content comes from India and Turkey. Asian expats are mingling and intermarrying in Mumbai, Seoul, Hong Kong, Sydney, Shanghai, and Singapore (whose official languages are English, Malay, Mandarin, and Tamil). The more mixed up Asians become, the more they might find "Asian" to be an easier identifier than the complex hyphenations of their multinational origins. Asia is recovering its Asian-ness.

Branding Asia

Asian countries are at very different stages of branding themselves to the outside world. China's image mobilization has included sponsoring lunar New Year's festivals and setting up more than five hundred Confucius Institutes around the globe. China also spends lavishly on advertorial supplements in Western newspapers and China-focused documentaries on the BBC, Discovery, and other channels. From 2009 to 2013, a high-level presidential council deliberated how to promote

Korea's brand, leading to the country's increasing its contributions to global aid agencies. Arab countries spend lavishly on Washington and London lobbying firms to burnish their images among politicians and investors. The rise of Al Jazeera International, Russia Today, and China's CGTN—all in the English language—represents a major shift in how Asians and the West consume "global" media: Not only have Asians ceased to defer to Western news to interpret their own affairs, but intellectually curious Americans and Europeans increasingly flip to foreign channels for a global perspective and an alternative to their own programming.[2] Branding budgets aside, a survey by Portland Communications and the USC Center on Public Diplomacy found that Japan holds the highest ranking (sixth) for global appeal among Asian countries,[3] while Singapore tops the Asian Barometer Survey (ABS) among Asians as the model Asians would like to see their country emulate.[4]

India still lags well behind its Asian peers in active self-promotion, but its passive approach is paying dividends. Post-Independence India fascinated Western hippies, poets, and writers. The "hippie trail" carried streams of European wanderers overland to India in the 1950s and 1960s, during which time Allen Ginsberg toured India for fifteen months seeking wisdom, while Jack Kerouac parroted his readings in Indian philosophy in *Dharma Bums* and wrote a posthumously published biography of the Buddha. The time of the Beatles' late-1960s retreat to India to study Transcendental Meditation is widely considered to have been one of the band's most productive periods. In the mid-1970s, Steve Jobs wandered India barefoot wearing only a *lungi*, an ascetic seeking purity and Buddhist inspiration, before returning to California to apply his quest for inner perfection to computing hardware by cofounding Apple. Marc Benioff similarly took a meditative sabbatical around India after leaving his job at Oracle, resulting in the birth of the cloud software giant Salesforce, whose offices have ample meditation rooms.

More recently, hit novels such as Elizabeth Gilbert's *Eat, Pray, Love* have further popularized visits to India's many yoga ashrams. Bollywood has not only infiltrated global film culture but also spawned dance classes, DJ music mixes, and wedding themes around the world. There are few more famed musicians than India's sitarist Ravi Shankar or maestro conductor Zubin Mehta, who has directed philharmonics in Montreal, Los Angeles, New York, and now Israel.

Referring to the rich history of Buddhist exchange between India and China, the noted twentieth-century Chinese scholar and diplomat Hu Shih claimed that India had conquered China for two thousand years without ever sending a soldier over the border. In 2011, China even donated $1 million toward India's ongoing effort to revive the once great Nalanda University, the ancient world's greatest center of Buddhist learning. Today India's spiritual heritage and practices are gaining far broader global appeal. India's most significant cultural coup has been the designation of June 21 by the United Nations as International Yoga Day, now celebrated by millions of people in hundreds of cities. Since 2012, the number of yoga practitioners in the United States has climbed by 50 percent to nearly 40 million, with most reporting improvements in strength, balance, dexterity, and mental clarity. Yoga is complemented by the practice of mindfulness—a mix of reflection, gratitude, and living in the moment, loosely derived from Buddhist meditation—which has swept Western homes, universities, and corporate campuses (which are increasingly designed by Chinese *feng shui* consultants). The Art of Living Foundation (AOLF), founded in 1981 by Ravi Shankar, has become a global mindfulness and peace movement spread over 156 countries. Mindfulness courses are part of career enhancement at Google and General Mills, and Microsoft CEO Satya Nadella credits mindfulness with his turnaround of the company's strategy. Mindfulness apps such as 10% Happier have been downloaded millions of times. Could it be that the next Enlightenment will come from adopting the teachings of ancient Asian cultures?

Given that numerous Asian civilizations can draw on more than five thousand years of cultural heritage, reviving their distinct historical wealth naturally concerns them more than generating a unified pan-Asian identity. Even with their deference and respect for one another, there cannot be a singular Asian cultural resurgence across such a vast and diverse domain. But there is a renaissance of sharing under way among Asian societies that rising wealth and integration is enabling. Asians are ever more favoring Asia, a trend reflected in shopping, eating, arts and entertainment, and migration and tourism. It is only a matter of time before someone launches an "Asia-vision" song competition.

Asians Crisscrossing Asia

As in the nineteenth century, Asia's pattern of migration, intermarriage, and demographic blending is repeating itself but on an ever larger scale. Indeed, Asia's own Asianization may be the most significant demographic megatrend of the twenty-first century. Asian enclaves in other Asian countries are not a new phenomenon by any means. The Spanish colonial government in the Philippines established the first Chinatown in the Binondo district of Manila in 1594. Today, Asia is the origin of nearly 40 percent of the world's migrants, and according to the United Nations' 2015 International Migration Report, between 2000 and 2015, Asia added more migrants to its own population than did any other region, with 26 million international settlers across the region (ahead of Europe's 20 million). Asia, then, is both the world's main source and main destination of international migrants.

China's diaspora of more than 50 million people is found mostly across Southeast Asia, where their roles have evolved from plantation farmers and merchant traders to construction workers and bus drivers to corporate executives and athletic coaches. Though China's diaspora is larger than India's, the 30 million members of India's diaspora are more widely dispersed. Within India's immediate neighborhood, the 4 million Indians in Nepal constitute 15 percent of its population, and the nearly 1 million Indians in Sri Lanka account for 5 percent of its population. In Southeast Asia, the 2.5 million Indians in Malaysia make up 10 percent of its population, and the 350,000 in Singapore make up 9 percent. And in the Gulf region, the 4 million Indians in Saudi Arabia make up 15 percent of its population and the 3.5 million Indians in the UAE make up 40 percent of its population.[5] Indians based in the Gulf countries send home more than $12 billion in annual remittances; elections in Indian states such as Kerala sometimes hinge on the Gulf remittances that fill campaign coffers. There are also 4 million Pakistanis around Asia, 3 million of whom are in Saudi Arabia and the UAE alone. Another 2 million Bangladeshis reside across the Gulf region.

As South Asian populations ballooned in the Gulf region from the 1970s through the 2000s, they were mostly laborers in construction and low-level clerical functions. Today Indians and Pakistanis continue to fill the majority of those roles, but, especially in the UAE, Oman, and Bahrain, they have also formed a class of managers, executives, industrialists, and entrepreneurs who are playing important social roles—and even political ones advising the monarchies. Over time, technology could do away with the need for a substantial percentage of lower-end Asian workers: Dubai is mandating that one-third of homes and offices be constructed using 3D printed materials, meaning easy-to-assemble modular construction requiring much less labor, and Oman wants to use drones rather than Bangladeshis to water its parks. Many unskilled South Asians will therefore return home to India and Pakistan, where construction wages are rising on the back of massive infrastructure investment. At the same time, yet more skilled South Asians may continue to flow to Gulf Cooperation Council (GCC) countries as they seek managers for their many new special economic zones and logistics hubs.

From Dubai to Hong Kong, millions of Filipinos and Indonesians continue to work as maids, cleaners, nannies, clerks, and drivers and in other low-wage services jobs. Along with South Asians, these Southeast Asians form a semipermanent community that is graduating from exploitation toward acceptance. For decades, South Asian construction workers have had their passports confiscated by Arab contractors, while one-third of Southeast Asian maids have reported being overworked, underpaid, and humiliated. But the Filipino government has begun to use its diaspora as a lever, temporarily banning its nationals from working in countries where employers abuse them, such as Kuwait, until they are allowed to keep their passports and guaranteed timely salary payment and insurance. The Indian government has begun to deploy its own insurance scheme covering its blue-collar workers in the GCC and a dozen other countries. From Dubai to Singapore, local movements have sprouted (with government support) to encourage sharing meals and stories with guest workers to show appreciation.

Middle-income countries making large investments in modernization, such as Thailand, are magnets for foreign labor. Thailand has an estimated 5 million migrant workers, mostly from Myanmar, Cambodia, and Laos. A crackdown on undocumented labor in 2014 forced 200,000 Cambodians to scramble for the border—but the resulting paralysis in the construction sector forced the Thai government to immediately reverse course and offer amnesty. Malaysia also depends on foreign labor from Thailand, Indonesia, and Myanmar, boosting its GDP while serving as a major source of remittances for rural families across its borders.

The staggering demographic mismatch between Asia's old and young countries means that youthful Asians will continue to be pulled farther from home to meet labor demands. Even large countries such as China, Russia, South Korea, Japan, and Thailand have huge labor shortages—up to 30 percent of their current working-age labor force between now and 2030—while Pakistan, India, Indonesia, and the Philippines have enormous surpluses of labor to export both within and beyond Asia. If aging China has exported so many people around the world, imagine young India and Pakistan, whose combined population is larger than China's and whose citizens already speak English or learn it much more quickly.

Rising migration is notable even in Asia's historically most impervious cultures, Japan and South Korea. To this day, it is not uncommon to see signs outside Japanese bathhouses, shops, and pubs declaring restrictions against foreigners. Yet although Japan and South Korea have the lowest rates of foreign-born residents among advanced economies, the numbers are growing rapidly.[6] In 1990, foreigners made up 0.1 percent of South Korea's population; today they are 3 percent and climbing toward an estimated 10 percent by 2030, a level comparable to some Western societies that have been experiencing foreign immigration for many decades longer.[7] In South Korea, the rate of international marriages has also skyrocketed, from just over 1 percent in 1990 to 14 percent by 2014. Just one generation since their Cold War hostility, Vietnamese women now make up the largest number of international brides for South Korean men, followed by Chinese, ethnic Korean Chinese, Japanese, Filipino, and Cambodian women.[8] The number of multiethnic families in Korea now stands at nearly 1 million, double the number of just a decade ago, with the highest rates—nearly 40 percent—in towns such as Wangok near Ansan, which has declared itself a "borderless village" due to its two-thirds non-Korean population. Korean media use the term *Kosean* to capture the Korean-Asian mixed-race future.

In Korea and Japan, assimilation has gone from a taboo topic to a necessary reform. Though integrating "New Koreans," as they are known, presents formidable cultural challenges, their inclusion in local voting and councils indicates that the country is ready to revise its citizenship laws, which have long been tied to ethnic bloodlines and ancestry. Even in Japan, which has gone out of its way to treat foreigners as temporary industrial interns, surveys suggest that youths are less wedded to ethnicity as a marker of identity.[9] Rather than being the rigid ethnonationalism portrayed from the outside, Asian identity is clearly under construction.

Asians are also pouring into China due to its economic growth, demographic imbalance, and widening labor shortages.[10] In recent decades, thriving coastal China has relied on its vast pool of rural labor to serve as low-wage construction and factory workers, cooks, and cleaners. But even the 200 million Chinese who have been part of this domestic labor force will not be enough as China's population ages. Officially, the number of foreigners taking up residence in China has increased by 10 percent per year since 2000, according to the 2010 census. Unofficially, there are countless more already spread across China. The Filipino Consulate in Hong Kong estimates that more than 200,000 undocumented Filipinas work as domestic helpers and nurses in China. Each spring, an estimated 50,000 Vietnamese illegally cross the border into Guangxi province to harvest sugarcane. Since 2015, the provincial government has even formalized a program to attract Vietnamese to work in Guangxi's factories. Women from neighboring countries are also being imported to marry China's 35 million surplus males. With a total foreign population under 1 million, however, it will be some time before non-Chinese make up even 1 percent of China's enormous population. China will therefore never become a "melting pot" but rather something of a salad bowl in which foreigners are a sprinkling of pepper.

Migration and intermarriage are already hallmarks of Asia's most diverse cities such as Dubai, Hong Kong, and Singapore. For many years, Singapore's national ID cards allowed a "CMIO" choice of ethnicity: Chinese, Malay, Indian, and Other. But as the rate of intermarriage nearly tripled from 7 percent in 1990 to 25 percent in 2017, the government now allows citizens to choose two races. Singapore is already home to a large number of "Ch-Indians," including prominent ministers. One generation hence, the government will surely have to

338 The Future Is Asian

allow three races to be chosen on each ID card. In the Gulf, legal, religious, and cultural restrictions prevent any significant rate of marriage between Gulf Arabs and South or Southeast Asians,[11] but that does not prevent Indians and Filipinos from marrying in cities such as Dubai and raising a new generation of "Indi-pinos."

The next generation of Asian identity is also being formed in Asia's schools and universities. In 2016, there were 400,000 foreign students in China, a 5.5 percent increase over the year before. There are four times as many Southeast Asian students in China as Americans and three times more South Korean students as Americans, as well as growing numbers of Indians and Russians. Pakistan's government plans to make Chinese-language study mandatory after sixth grade, meaning that a decade hence, the number of Pakistani students in China could be many times higher than the current 20,000. Japan comes in second with more than 150,000 foreign students, and the number is growing at nearly 10 percent annually, with the largest numbers coming from China, Vietnam, and South Korea. In 2016, South Korea crossed 100,000 foreign students on the back of growing numbers of Chinese, Vietnamese, and Japanese students. India, too, saw a 7 percent increase in the number of foreign students, to about 42,000, with the largest cohorts coming from Nepal, Afghanistan, and Bhutan. Malaysian universities attract large numbers of students from Iran, Indonesia, and China, while Thai students spread across Japan, China, and South Korea. ASEAN is approving the mutual recognition of member states' academic certifications, which will allow for the subregion of 700 million to advance toward its own version of Europe's popular Erasmus Programme. In recent years I've met many cross-border ASEAN couples hailing from Malaysia to Laos who met while studying in Japan and migrate together pursuing careers in multiple countries. The more Asians study in one another's countries, the more they will socialize into a pan-Asian generation with greater regional understanding and shared identity. This now stretches to the Arab Gulf, with cities such as Dubai increasingly popular among Russians and Chinese seeking internships in a fast-paced business environment. Across the Gulf region, affiliate campuses of Western MBA programs such as that of the London Business School make going to London itself unnecessary.

In generations past, when Asians set their sights on the West, they might have heard of or visited New York and California, but they normally didn't go to Goa or Guangzhou. The United States and Europe have been major beneficiaries of the desire of the Asian middle class to vacation at Disney World and in the Big Apple, take selfies at Big Ben and atop the Eiffel Tower, or splurge on skiing in Zermatt or Whistler. Las Vegas casinos advertise themselves months in advance as destinations for Asian holidays such as Chinese New Year. Each year record numbers of Asians travel abroad, led by more than 130 million Chinese, with India recently overtaking Japan and projected to reach 50 million outbound tourists by 2020. Global revenues from Chinese, Japanese, Korean, and Indian tourists amount to more than $350 billion annually, triple the spending of American tourists.[12]

But a new generation of Asians has balanced out regional and global travels. Today the world's most visited cities are Hong Kong, Bangkok, Singapore, and Dubai—all Asian. (Only London ranks alongside these Asian cities.) One reason is that the top eight destinations of Chinese tourists are Asian countries, followed by the United States and Italy. Since 2016, Paris has actually declined as a destination for Asians. South Korea remains the top destination for Chinese tourists (despite the recent ban on Chinese visiting the popular Jeju Island), while Chinese also swarm through Japan and Australia and sent a record 1.5 million tourists to Russia in 2017. With visa restrictions drastically reduced and low-cost airlines flourishing, Asians are discovering their own region in record numbers. India's inbound tourism is growing by double digits annually and just crossed 10 million visitors. It's hard not to spot Japanese and Israelis from Himachal Pradesh to Goa. Indian destination weddings are a business boon for Dubai, Bangkok, and Bali. Iran grants simple on-arrival visas to woo

Chinese and Japanese, nearly 5 million Russians visit Turkey annually, and Arab intellectual and business elites, feeling less welcome in Europe, increasingly spend their downtime in Istanbul and Antalya. Islands such as Hainan have branded themselves a mix of Hawaii and Dubai and attract throngs of Asians looking for safe low-cost holidays and a first contact with China.

As Asia becomes a more attractive tourist destination, it is also learning not to destroy the habitats the world is so eager to visit. Bhutan has pioneered high-value, low-impact eco-tourism. On Bali and other Indonesian islands, visitors often spend a day working with cashew growers or learning about fragile shark habitats. Thailand and the Philippines have also developed a sustainable tourism culture to support local communities. In 2018, the Duterte government announced a six-month closure of the popular island of Boracay to give resorts time to modify their infrastructure to minimize the pollution caused by the constant crush of tourists. A sustainable Asia is one that both Asians and the world are far more likely to continue to appreciate.

Recycling Asian Culture

True to their syncretic history, Asians continue to absorb Western influences, often as a means toward bridging diversity in their own societies. Language is one example: listen to speakers of Hindi and Tagalog today, and you are hearing "Hinglish" and "Taglish." American English as a global language has become an important cultural bridge within Asia. Microsoft's recent breakthrough in instantaneous translation of complex Chinese into English will significantly enhance communication among Chinese, other Asians, and the world at large.

The recirculation of Asian culture through global media and commerce is accelerating Asia's self-discovery. Mixed martial arts is an unmissable story in this regard. For many years, outside of their rustic *dojo*s, Chinese, Japanese, Koreans, and Thais had almost exclusively national martial arts cultures, with only low-level fight cards across

Asian boundaries. But suddenly, with the arrival of America's Ultimate Fighting Championship (UFC), mixed martial arts (MMA) trainers, and TV networks, the fusion of boxing, wrestling, muay thai, judo, and other Asian specialties became sellout events with a huge pay-per-view TV following. The Thai national Chatri Sityodtong returned from a career on Wall Street to found the hugely successful ONE Championship mixed martial art (MMA) series in Singapore, bringing together dozens of Asian competitors in frequent events across the region. In the process, Asians have become much more aware—and proud—of their warrior traditions. At the same time, the rise of MMA has elevated Americans' consciousness of these Asian martial arts. Karate, judo, and taekwondo gained popularity in America in the 1970s and 1980s, but now muay thai kickboxing gyms have popped up across the United States. Entertainment based on Asian martial arts is now big business as well: *American Ninja Warrior* is just one of the global spin-offs from the Japanese original, Shaolin monks, with their kung fu stunts, regularly tour all continents, while kung fu academies have sprouted up from Europe to South Africa.

Asians have also benefited from global recognition of their contemporary artistic output. Two decades ago, only a few Asian artists, such as the Japanese abstract painter Yayoi Kusama and the pop art maestro Takashi Murakami, drew widespread recognition. But by 2008, the Guggenheim's major retrospective of the Chinese artist Cai Guo-Qiang's installations and a record-fetching sale in Hong Kong of a Zeng Fanzhi painting placed Asian contemporary artists on the global map, with museums and galleries seeking out their works not purely for an exotic complement to Western collections but in reverence of their creative qualities. In the arts, too, global circulation has been crucial. A number of the most prominent Japanese and Chinese artists learned to express themselves fully during long stints in the West, especially New York, where Ai Weiwei began his career as both an artist and a prolific political critic; he now resides in Berlin.

Asia's leading cities are ramping up investments in becoming cultural hubs. Tokyo is already an architectural mecca for students and admirers of the buildings of Kengo Kuma, Tadao Ando, and Toyo Ito. Hong Kong's annual Art Basel week has attained a stature equal to its counterparts in Switzerland and Miami. Now other Asian metropolises are undergoing an artistic renaissance as dilapidated industrial sites are converted into lofty ateliers as in Taipei's Songshan Cultural Park, Beijing's lively 798 Art Zone, and Shanghai's M50 Creative Garden. Sharjah and Jeddah have emerged as hubs for cultivating Arab artistic communities in avant-garde galleries, while Doha and Abu Dhabi have marked the beginnings of an Arab cultural renaissance with spectacular architectural landmarks such as Doha's Islamic Art Museum and Abu Dhabi's branch of the Louvre. Singapore has opened both a stately new national gallery that contains the world's largest collection of Southeast Asian art and converted a former army barracks into an open-air village of interactive galleries. Singapore Art Week and Art Stage Singapore have stoked the demand for art by the region's nearly one hundred billionaires and growing upper class. As poorer Asian countries such as Indonesia have stabilized politically and liberalized culturally, they, too, have allowed art schools to flourish, not only in hot spots such as Bali but also in lesser-known hipster cities such as Bandung and Yogyakarta. The respected Sundaram Tagore Gallery now promotes Filipino photographers, sculptors, and street artists.

All of this points both to Asians themselves paying more attention to—and spending more money on—Asian art. Chinese billionaires and cultural institutions are scouring the world for Chinese artifacts held abroad for centuries to bring them home. Whether Arabs looking to park money or East Asian tycoons seeking collections to show off, Asians from the Gulf states to Japan are stocking up their collections of both Western and Asian art, driving double-digit growth in revenue for auction houses such as Sotheby's and Christie's, which are ever more on the lookout for the next Asian art wave to elevate for their Western clients, just as they have promoted South Korean minimalism (*dansaekhwa*), Indian sculptors such as Anish Kapoor, and Indonesian pop art.

Similarly, Asia's music scene has benefited from adopting Western rituals such as wild dance festivals and viral YouTube videos. A decade ago, there were only a handful of events, such as the Fuji Rock Festival. Today, there are also Summer Sonic in Japan, Pentaport Rock Festival in Korea, Electric Zoo Shanghai, ZoukOut in Singapore, and the global Ultra Music Festival across nearly ten locations in Southeast Asia alone. After importing these Western habits, Asia's cultural exports have fanned outward. The Korean Wave (Hallyu) is the most obvious example. While the satirical rapper Psy's hit "Gangnam Style" was the first video to reach 1 billion (and then 2 billion) views on YouTube, he is the tip of an iceberg whose foundation includes K-pop groups that have thousands of fan clubs as far away as Hungary and Peru, with K-pop competitions being held in the United States and France. In May 2018, the Korean boy band BTS reached number one on the US *Billboard* top 200. The rap singer Nichkhun stars in one of Korea's most popular boy bands—even though he is Thai and grew up in southern California. With his fluency in Thai, Korean, and Mandarin, Nichkhun is one of a growing number of truly pan-Asian stars appearing in commercials and movies across the region. To capture ever more global entertainment mind share, the Korea Foundation for International Culture Exchange (KOFICE) has become a powerful agency dedicated to promoting Korea's lucrative cultural exports.

Asian food, too, has become a global sensation, from fast food to haute cuisine. Broadly defined, Asian cuisine is a vast collection of ingredients and culinary styles, from Mediterranean chickpeas to smoky grilled Central Asian lamb to Southeast Asian coconut milk and spices to Pacific Rim soy sauce. Each reflects a distinct cultural blending that has evolved over centuries, mostly with Asian neighbors. Colonial influence on Asian cuisine is far less prominent than the reverse. Though

Vietnamese enjoy *banh mi* sandwiches resembling French baguettes (but made with rice flour) and one finds mayonnaise on salads in Laos, Western food has barely made a dent in Asian tastes. Only Japan and China have more than one thousand McDonald's outlets, with other large Asian countries having around two hundred to five hundred each. More important, McDonald's menus across Asia look nothing like those in the United States; they feature masala dosa burgers in India, shrimp burgers in Japan, and McNoodles across the region. The dozens of items on McDonald's menus in Asia that one cannot get in the United States are a reminder that even though there are aspects of Western life to which Asians aspire, to truly succeed in Asia, one must become Asian.

By contrast, Asian culinary traditions are very much and ever more part of Western life. Tea, of course, originated in China and was taken to India by the British in order to compete with China's dominance in the tea trade. Ketchup comes from the Hokkein *kê-tsiap* and derives from a Vietnamese fermented fish sauce that British traders took back to England (where tomato was substituted as a base) as far back as the early eighteenth century. In 2018, the Swedish media confessed that their country's famous meatball recipe had been borrowed from Turkey in the eighteenth century by King Charles XII. Across the West, rice is now stocked in wide assortments, from Indian basmati to Thai jasmine to Korean short grain.

Across the board, over the past two decades, Asian food has gone from diaspora staple and cheap takeout to mainstream fast food and upscale cuisine. Japanese sushi is ubiquitous in both low-cost malls and high-end restaurants and hotels, and ramen noodles, once nothing more than a late-night fill-me-up for college students, are now a feature of menus nationwide. Alongside the usual Chinese retaurants serving General Tso's chicken, Korean barbecue and kimchi-laden *bibimbap* bowls have popped up in many US cities. (Wherever Kia opens an automotive plant, kimchi is sure to appear on menus nearby.) Panda Express generated $2 billion in 2014 alone, and Taiwanese bubble tea—milky with lemongrass and tapioca jelly pearls—is gaining a foothold across the United States with hundreds of new shops nationwide. In Europe, Euromonitor International reports a 500 percent growth in sales of Asian fast-food restaurants since 1999. Indian curry houses in England employ more workers than the country's combined iron, steel, coal, and shipbuilding industries, and Indian chicken curry sells in greater volume in Great Britain than does fish and chips. In London, Hakkasan, which blends Cantonese cuisine with fancy cocktails, has earned a Michelin star.

Fusion across culinary cultures is producing innovation and success. China-India fusion cuisine is popping up in Mumbai and Shanghai, as well as New York and London. At the annual superstar chef gathering Madrid Fusion, Indian and Thai chefs such as the Blue Elephant's Nooror Somany have been feted. After his training at the Culinary Institute of America, the Korean chef Yim Jungsik rocketed to stardom by adapting molecular gastronomy to produce a new Hansik (Korean) style. His exotic concoctions have earned his New York restaurant two Michelin stars, while his more traditional outlet in Seoul has only one star. One of the latest trends spreading across American food trucks and malls is "Ko-Mex" (Korean-Mexican) fusion, which began with Korean Americans in Seoul longing for the Mexican flavors of their American childhood, another testament to how reverse migration and ethnic intermingling produces novelty.

In the world of fashion, Asia is now holding its own and expanding—both alone and through smart partnerships with European incumbents. The Japanese icon Issey Miyake began his career with Givenchy in Paris before launching his own labels, which brought Eastern styles to global prominence. Today Asian fashion is prominent from streetwear to haute couture. Uniqlo is a widely known Japanese label that has earned a large and loyal global following, while Shanghai Tang, which revives Chinese styles from a century ago, was bought early on by the Swiss luxury group Richemont and carried worldwide. Superdry is a highly successful British brand that uses gibberish Japanese characters on its clothing to enhance its unique appeal. The more the phenomenon of "Fashion Week" spreads from Dubai, Mumbai, and Shanghai, the more aggressively local designers compete to gain attention and customers in Asia, Europe, and beyond. Until recently, the nearly two-hundred-year-old high-end Lane Crawford department store chain in Hong Kong carried only four Asian labels, given its clientele's Western aspirations. Today it boasts thirty Asian brands across its collections. H&M's profits have been down substantially since 2015 as Asian brands capture Asian tastes. All Western apparel brands want more visibility among India's urban elites, but dozens of Indian designers, including Manish Malhotra, Tarun Tahiliani, Ritu Kumar, and Neeta Lulla, have already reached such paramount status that they will have to Indianize themselves to compete. Simply put: Asian is now cool. Just ask Lady Gaga, who regularly wears Roggykei outfits, a label created by graduates of the Osaka College of Design.

Asian fashion models have also broken through on the global stage. Though South Asian models such as Padma Lakshmi and Yasmeen Ghauri graced Western fashion magazines nearly two decades ago, it was China's Liu Wen who became the first Asian to earn a spot on the *Forbes* list of highest-paid models in 2013 upon becoming the first international spokeswoman for Estée Lauder. Since then, Japanese, Korean, and other Asian models have made strides in the industry as well. In the cosmetics industry, Korean beauty products are the new global standard, with brands such as Dr. Jart+, Missha, and Etude House opening US outlets and global e-commerce sites. With Chinese ladies closely following the Korean trends, Unilever leapt to purchase the Korean beauty product maker Carver Korea for $2.7 billion in 2017. Between K-pop and cosmetics, Korea has become the most sought-after destination for European nannies seeking positions in Asia.

And then there is cinema. Asian themes are not new to Hollywood, not least because of 1980s classics such as *Gandhi*, *The Last Emperor*, and *A Passage to India*, as well as notable films from the 1990s and

2000s set in Asia including Tom Cruise's *The Last Samurai,* the Clint Eastwood–directed *Letters from Iwo Jima*, and the all-Asian casts of *The Joy Luck Club* and *Memoirs of a Geisha*. Many Western moviegoers have also become familiar with the Taiwanese-born, American-educated, Oscar-winning Ang Lee for his melancholic *Brokeback Mountain,* the erotic *Lust, Caution*, the special-effects pioneer *Crouching Tiger, Hidden Dragon*, and the sympathetic 3D drama *Life of Pi*. Hong Kong's Wong Kar-wai has earned global acclaim for his films of repressed desire such as *In the Mood for Love* and its sequel, *2046*. Numerous other Chinese film directors have also achieved global standing, including Zhang Yimou, who adapted Mo Yan's *Red Sorghum* to the screen and also directed the spectacular opening and closing ceremonies of the 2008 Beijing Summer Olympics. Jia Zhangke's film *Still Life* won the Golden Lion at the 2006 Venice Film Festival. Wang Bing, whose acclaimed documentaries confront sensitive social issues such as labor camps and Burmese minorities, embodies how Asian film-makers are confidently bringing local themes to global audiences with a humanistic appeal. All of this was before *Crazy Rich Asians* conquered American cinemas in the summer of 2018.

For Hollywood, China's economic heft has cut two ways. On the one hand, China's opening of two dozen new movie screens every day (including with immersive architectural environments catering to 4D experiences) has Hollywood studios salivating over surging ticket sales. Asia as a whole and China in particular have helped numerous franchises from *Jurassic Park* to *Star Wars* to *The Fast and the Furious* and the *Marvel* superhero films to reach $1 billion in global revenue in ever shorter time spans. China's commercial and political tentacles, however, have insinuated themselves into Hollywood, both helping the industry finance more films and compromising its artistic freedom. Dalian Wanda's purchase of AMC in the United States and Odeon in Europe, as well as the production studio Legendary Entertainment, has capitalized ambitious productions and ensured penetration into China's massive audiences. But access has come at a price, with plotlines shifting to favor pro-Chinese narratives such as China's space agency conducting an interplanetary rescue in *The Martian* or replacing a mystical Tibetan in *Doctor Strange* with a Nordic-looking character.

Other Asian film industries have taken a more commercial and less editorial approach. The Abu Dhabi–based Image Nation has also financed Hollywood films such as *Men in Black 3* and *The Circle*, while the government has lured New York University to establish a film academy alongside its academic campus there. South Korea has taken a purely commercial approach. Its film exports increased by 82 percent in 2016 alone on the back of Yeon Sang-ho's zombie thriller *Train to Busan* and Park Chan-wook's *The Handmaiden*, with multiple Korean films picked up for distribution by Netflix and Amazon—both of which are competing vigorously in India, with Netflix launching several original Indian series, such as *Sacred Games*, starring Bollywood A-listers.

Hollywood is seeking ever more crossovers with Asian cinema. The success of *Slumdog Millionaire*, which swept eight Oscars in 2009 (including one for the English director, Danny Boyle, and the Indian composer, A. R. Rahman), kicked off a broader thrust to bridge American and Asian cinematic cultures. But the biggest shift in Asian cinematic tastes is the enthusiasm for cross-Asian collaborations. Cultural sensitivities have prevented major crossovers among Asia's major cultural markets, despite notable exceptions such as the half-Japanese, half-Taiwanese Takeshi Kaneshiro—sometimes called the "Johnny Depp of Asia"—who has starred in both Chinese and Japanese movies. In 2006, the Thai production *Invisible Waves* featured a Japanese lead actor, with other cast members from Hong Kong and Korea, and was shot in Macau. Chinese and Korean studio executives have put out a raft of joint productions such as *A Wedding Invitation* and the 3D sports action drama *Mr. Go*. An even trickier but more lucrative act is Bollywood's crossover with Chinese cinema. Jackie Chan's 2017 movie *Kung Fu Yoga* features stars from

China and India who manage to speak each other's languages when they need to (plus lots of subtitles), with English and Arabic thrown in across sets spanning Dubai and the Arctic. The film is designed to have pan-Asian appeal well beyond the two major driving markets, and despite the cultural complexity of the undertaking, it earned about $200 million worldwide. In 2016, Image Nation and China Intercontinental Communication Center launched a $300 million fund to promote joint productions such as Chinese- and Arabic-language content in the countries lying between Saudia Arabia and China. Some now speak of a pan-Asian "Asiawood" industry.

Commercial Hindi cinema has been no stranger to global outreach. As far back as 1946, Indian cinema achieved global acclaim with the Cannes Film Festival's grand prize awarded to Chetan Anand's Hindi-Urdu film *Neecha Nagar*. The Bengali filmmaker Satyajit Ray was revered by Martin Scorsese and received an honorary Academy Award in 1992; Wes Anderson dedicated his 2007 film *The Darjeeling Limited*, which was set mostly in India, to Ray. Non-Indian audiences across Asia have been enthralled by Bollywood for decades. As early as the 1950s, Raj Kapoor films were the rage in the USSR, where they were seen as an antidote to Hollywood poison. Bollywood remains popular across Central Asia and the Caucasus. In the 1980s, Bollywood films were so popular in Egypt that they threatened local film revenues, leading to the government limiting Indian film screenings. Today there are more than thirty Arab TV channels that show Bollywood films, with talk shows devoted to interviews with their stars. On the back of Bollywood films that achieved international acclaim such as Shah Rukh Khan's *Kabhi Khushi Kabhie Gham* and Aamir Khan's *Three Idiots*, Bollywood fan clubs have sprouted around Europe. In 2010, the University of Vienna hosted a three-day international conference on Shah Rukh Khan and Global Bollywood.[13] Aamir Khan's 2016 biopic *Dangal*, about female wrestlers in India, earned more revenue in China than in India itself. As Saudi Arabia has opened movie theaters again (including to women), Pakistani films have been among the first to be screened, with "Lollywood" (Lahore's Bollywood) planning new productions aimed at the Saudi market.

Bollywood's North American audiences have been largely limited to the Indian diaspora, though that is large enough to fill entire stadiums in New Jersey when Bollywood stars tour the United States performing entertainment ensembles. Still, from the caricature cartoon character of Apu in *The Simpsons* to the slapstick Asian stereotypes of the Korean Indian *Harold & Kumar* duo to the full Asian cast of *Fresh Off the Boat* (based on Eddie Huang's memoir), each decade has brought a rising number of Asian stars into mainstream American television and cinema and mainstream Asian issues onto the American social agenda. The Bollywood starlet Priyanka Chopra was brought in to headline ABC's prime-time action drama *Quantico,* and the Taiwanese singer Jay Chou was cast in *The Green Hornet* to draw a larger Asian audience. Most major American TV networks now have a plethora of South and East Asian anchors.

India's cultural exports have reached as far as Latin America, where self-styled Indian gurus lead large crowds in meditation at "yoga raves" and Indian rock bands tour Brazilian music festivals. After the Mexican actress Bárbara Mori's breakthrough in the 2010 Bollywood action drama *Kites*, a cottage industry has been spawned of Latina actresses seeking success in India's film industry.[14] More than a dozen Bollywood films have been screened at the Bogotá International Film Festival, while Rio de Janeiro hosts an annual festival dedicated to Bollywood films. Ever since an award-winning 2009 Brazilian soap opera was set in Jaipur, with Brazilian actors dancing to Bollywood hits, upward of 30 million Brazilians have watched Indian films while Brazilian tourism to India grew eightfold by 2016. Each Indian film shot in Bangkok or Dubai, Switzerland or Spain, Iceland or New Zealand brings throngs of Indian tourists to the country a year later. It is no wonder that government agencies from Finland and Poland to Israel and Fiji are offering major tax rebates to Indian film studios.

It cannot be overstated to what extent Bollywood has been a moral medium for Indian society, whose polyglot nature has most persuasively been bridged through cinematic drama rather than newspaper translations and government edicts. Today the most hot-button issues, from gender stereotypes to government corruption to caste resentment, are aired through film first and foremost. Film has artfully stirred national pride by re-creating epic mythologies and celebrating anticolonial uprisings big and small, as in Aamir Khan's *Lagaan* about a ragtag group of Indian villagers who learn cricket well enough to defeat a team of seasoned British colonial officers, earning relief from their crushing tax burden. Importantly, whereas national politics has succumbed to religious chauvinism, Bollywood has remained a club of secular solidarity, with an estimated one-third of star actors being Muslim (double the Muslim percentage of the population). Aamir Khan and other leading film personalities have evoked the spirit of one's "duty as a citizen" to carry the torch of tolerance.

There are other ways in which ethnocultural pride are supplanting long-ingrained deference to colonial norms. Local languages are again flourishing, not just in cinema but also in literature. Also, South Asia's (and Southeast Asia's) obsession with skin whitening is being challenged by a nascent "brown is beautiful" movement. Asians are realizing that neither remaining stuck in, nor blaming the past for present social ills is of any use. They are no longer being divided and ruled and should stop finding more ways to continue to divide themselves from one another.

What Asians Think

A century on from the pan-Asian idealism of Okakura Tenshin, Rabindranath Tagore, and Liang Qichao, Asians are rediscovering their intellectual synergies and composing narratives that seriously challenge the West's uncritical self-appraisal and tenants of modern Western political history and thought. Why does the West brand itself as the defender of human rights globally when it has backed so many dictatorial regimes? Is unrestrained individual freedom truly the essential foundation of commercial innovation and success? Isn't capitalism essential for democracy rather than democracy being essential for capitalism? Should meritocratic training be more important than democratic popularity in selecting political leaders? As was the case with Asia's Cold War nationalists, educating Asians in the West produces not pro-American stooges but rather intellectuals able to stand up to the West in a language it understands.

Pan-Asian intellectual convergence today is nothing like the Nehruvian brotherhood envisioned during the insecure postcolonial years, but something much more constructive. Today's leaders don't aspire to a fanciful "United States of Asia" but a more humble yet productive commonwealth of commerce and learning. Even though very few Asians born, raised, and educated in Asia have found a prominent voice in the West, they have been proven right by events because they have not lost their authentic understanding of their region's rhythms and dynamics.

But Asians still need to read much more about one another. Though Asians share interrelated histories, differences in culture and language have limited the penetration of pan-Asian ideas. Western publications have filled the gap.[15] In the West, geopolitical occurrences from 9/11 to China's rise have boosted funding for Arab and Asian studies. Well-funded North American universities and scholarly outlets such as *The Journal of Asian Studies*, the flagship publication of the Association for Asian Studies, based in Ann Arbor, Michigan, continue to lead the field. Publications edited by Asian scholars at Asian universities such as the *Asian Journal of Social Science*, published by the National University of Singapore, have decisively less reach both within Asia and certainly in the West. Asia now has many academic centers that now produce rigorous scholarly output that Western academics should pay more attention to rather than citing one another in self-referential loops. In just the past few years, I have noticed a change in tone: American "experts" now come to Asia to be schooled, not to lecture.

There have been numerous Asia-centric efforts to report Asia from the inside out. From the 1940s to the 2000s, the *Far Eastern Economic Review* (*FEER*) enjoyed a wide following in Asia for its extensive local coverage of the Asian business scene. In the 1970s, two former *FEER* correspondents founded *Asia Week* with the explicit intent to deliver "Asia through Asian eyes." By the 1980s, competition for eyeballs on Asian newsstands intensified as Western magazines launched Asian editions such as *Time Asia, Fortune Asia,* and *Asian Geographic,* but these remained effectively imports from the West with limited indigenous content. *Asia Times,* founded in Bangkok in 1995, markets itself as the "only all-digital, pan-Asian site aimed specifically at English-speaking users." Its readership is half Asian, half European and North American. For the Sinophone world, there is *Yazhou Zhoukan* (Asia Weekly), focusing on international affairs from a Chinese perspective. On the whole, though, these pan-Asian publications have fallen far below the reach of domestic media in local languages.

Asians have had far more success in the global literary than journalistic scenes. Owing to their shared linguistic and cultural heritage, East Asians have centuries of familiarity with each other's literary traditions. *The Tale of Genji,* written by the Japanese noblewoman Murasaki Shikibu in the early eleventh century, is widely considered the world's first psychological novel and has inspired many writers through the ages including Jorge Luis Borges. China's four great classical novels spanning six centuries—*Water Margin, Romance of the Three Kingdoms, Journey to the West,* and *Dream of the Red Chamber*—are read and taught across South Korea and Japan.

The past two generations have witnessed a great acceleration of awareness of Asian literature. China, Japan, and India have produced a raft of writers who have risen to global acclaim. Rabindranath Tagore was the first Asian to win the Nobel Prize in Literature in 1913, but then came a void until Yasunari Kawabata of Japan in 1968. Kenzaburo Oe won the prize in 1994, Gao Xingjian of China in 2000, Mo Yan of China in 2012, and the Japanese British writer Kazuo Ishiguro in 2017.

From Western Asia, the Israeli Shmuel Yosef Agnon won the Nobel in 1966 and the Turkish novelist Orhan Pamuk in 2006. The prestigious Man Booker Prize has gone to numerous Asian writers such as Salman Rushdie, Aravind Adiga, Kiran Desai, and Arundhati Roy, all of whom have made Asian themes more familiar to Western readers, and the prize's international award went to the Korean novelist Han Kang for her multipart drama *The Vegetarian*.

Indian and Japanese authors in particular have attained mass global audiences, notably Haruki Murakami (*Norwegian Wood*) and Amitav Ghosh (*The Glass Palace*), as well as the Afghan-born Khaled Hosseini (*The Kite Runner*). In popular culture, Asian-Western crossover literature that tackles issues of social stress at ethnic intersections has caught fire with the success of Amy Tan (*The Joy Luck Club*), Jhumpa Lahiri (*Interpreter of Maladies*), Celeste Ng (*Everything I Never Told You*, *Little Fires Everywhere*), and Kevin Kwan (*Crazy Rich Asians*). American writers who delve deeply into exotic Asia such as Lisa See (*The Tea Girl of Hummingbird Lane*, *Shanghai Girls*) have also proved their staying power on best-seller lists. Jin Yong's fabled Condor trilogy, often likened to a Chinese *Lord of the Rings*, has taken decades to translate into English but has gained a huge following.

Asians have also achieved prominence in the sciences, often by directly focusing on the most pressing societal needs. Japanese scientists have long led the way in Asia's contributions to global research, winning numerous Nobel Prizes in medicine and physics, as well as the prestigious Shaw and Lasker prizes in life sciences. Japan's Shinya Yamanaka, the winner of the 2012 Nobel Prize in Physiology or Medicine, tops the *Asian Scientist* list for revolutionizing the field of stem cell research, and in 2016 Yoshinori Osumi won the Nobel Prize for his research on autophagy (cellular decay). The 2015 Nobel Prize in Physiology or Medicine was awarded to the Chinese pharmacologist Tu Youyou for her discovery of the malarial treatment artemisinin, shared with the Japanese biochemist Satoshi Omura. Importantly,

Tu Youyou received all of her education and conducted all of her research exclusively in China at the Academy of Traditional Chinese Medicine (TCM). The award is just the latest in a string of prominent public and clinical recognition of the success of TCM and ancient Indian medical practices such as Ayurveda, which argues that holistic healing must place equal emphasis on the mind and spirit in addition to the body. There is more to Asia's fusion of science and spirituality: The global medical and environmental communities increasingly converge around the physiological and ecological benefits of a vegetarian diet. In other words, if everyone ate like a Hindu, the world would be a more sustainable place.

Epilogue: Asia's Global Future

Asia dominated the Old World, while the West led the New World—and now we are coming to a truly global world. There is no turning back from today's multipolar, multicivilizational order. There is also no turning back the clock. The Western world order no longer exists and will not return. It was as contingent as any other era, and we are better served by aspiring to a more inclusive and stable horizon. Be wary of those who believe that history repeats itself or even rhymes. The cumulative turnings of the historical wheel yield movement in new directions. Never before has there been a global system so strongly imprinted by multiple civilizations, regions and poles of power spanning all continents, a world order in which the success of each depends on a healthy degree of globalization among them. The task before us, as Henry Kissinger noted in his book *World Order*, is to channel "divergent historical experiences and values . . . into a common order."[1]

Globalization has created a global society, but in recent centuries, as Duke University philosophy professor Owen Flanagan points out, the default compass of morality has derived from the views of the most unrepresentative group: Western Educated Industrial Rich Democracies (WEIRD). Meanwhile, the Asian majority of the global population, according to the social psychologist Richard Nisbett, has very distinct cognitive processes, especially East Asians, who do not draw sharp distinctions between subject and context. Eastern philosophy advocates the unity of self and other, man and nature, while Western philosophy elevates the distinctions between them and places the individual rather than family or community at the center. While Western approaches seek true or objective knowledge, the cultural scholar Prasenjit Duara argues that Asia's transcendental faiths are open-ended: knowledge does not have to have an immutable form but can change according to circumstances, and its purpose can be to pursue universal goals such as harmony. This seems a sophisticated relativism appropriate to today's times.

Global thought requires more than just creating space to hear others' ideas or juxtaposing cultures. Asia has reached a full reckoning with the impact of Western history on its present. Now the West must reckon with the rise of Asia on its future, immersing itself in the Asian worldview in an effort to rise above both self and other in search of synthesis on matters as wide ranging as international law and scientific ethics.

There is some positive evidence that these more syncretic conversations are taking place. The Buddhist Dalai Lama has demonstrated that he is quite an empiricist, stating that if science refutes certain Buddhist beliefs, then science should prevail. Pope Francis has opened up dialogues with Islamic authorities and the Chinese government, looking for common ground. The pillars of the global religious establishment are clearly aware of the world's irrevocable spiritual multipolarity; they must accept one another's unwavering strength and find mutually acceptable ways forward. In all spheres of global life, there is a need to graduate from dialogue to synthesis: Western atomism and Eastern holism, humanism and scientific materialism, freedom and harmony, democracy and technocracy—all enriching our shared experience.

Global order is not passed down by divine mandate; it is a complex, ever evolving process. Asia today is reviving the ethos that enabled its earlier eras of greatness: confidence in its values and open to knowledge. It has even crossed the threshold from learning to application, generating innovations that are being shared around the world. The relations among the world's centers of gravity involve recycling capital, refining ideas, and adopting technologies in ways that have enriched them all. Europe amassed great power and profit from colonizing Asia,

Asia has grown stupendously from American and European outsourcing, and now the United States and Europe are being buttressed by infusions of Asian investment and talent. This, not multipolar competition, is the true nature of a global system.

We are only in the early phases of global Asianization; hence we must continue to explore how the coming decades will transpire. How will Asia manage the current wave of geopolitical, economic, social, and technological transformations? Will mixed capitalism, social conservatism, and technocratic governance remain a magic formula, elevating those societies that have not yet adopted it? How will Western and other powers respond to Asia's rise, and what adjustments will Asians make to those reactions?

A new chapter of global history is being written before our eyes, one in which Asian and Western civilizations, the North American and Eurasian continents, all play profoundly important roles. Today Westerners prefer the phrasing "global rules-based order" while Asians favor the Chinese phrase "community of common destiny." Tomorrow we will realize that they are two sides of the same coin—and that both the rules and the destiny must be made together. That is where we are on the wheel of global history.

Acknowledgments

Moving to Singapore in 2012 was the beginning of a wonderfully deep immersion into contemporary Asia. Despite two decades of traveling for long stretches across the region, finally I have spent these past years seeing it—and the world—from the inside out. The result, I hope, is a prism in which all Asians are both comfortable and inspired.

I would like to thank my highly respected colleagues from the Lee Kuan Yew School of Public Policy for their marvelous support and insights for this project, especially former dean Kishore Mahbubani and professor Kanti Bajpai, director of the Centre on Asia and Globalisation, whose generous financial support enabled valuable research assistance for this book. Danny Quah, Razeen Sally, Yuen Foong Khong, Tan Kong Yam, Siddharth Tiwari, James Crabtree, Francesco Mancini, Blake Berger, Byron Chong and numerous other colleagues have been an outstanding sounding board for the ideas presented here.

The next generation of scholars has also been invaluable source of research and fresh ideas. Adnan Ahmad and Ian Reinert, both Lee Kuan Yew School graduates, were superb in gathering and analyzing data related to trade patterns and fiscal policy. Allen Cho masterfully pieced together the Northeast Asian industrial landscape. Aditya Ramachandran's fluency in Asian and American worldviews reminded me just how global the next generation of Asians truly is. I owe extra special thanks to Xiao You Mok, a Singaporean native with a degree from Japan and now earning a PhD in the United States, whose pan-Asian aesthetic sensibility, meticulous research skills and effortless intellectual grace made a genuine imprint on this undertaking. These Asian millennials give me great hope for the region's future.

Friends in Singapore, who always have their finger on the pulse of Asia, have been a regular souce of insights across the board: Pavel Bains, Beh Swan Gin, Alexander Bernard, Umej Bhatia, Ernesto Braam, Chan Chun Sing, Sangeet Paul Chaudary, Calvin Cheng, Eng Cheong Teo, Brooks Entwistle, Shaokai Fan, Nick Fang, Mark Fogle, Amol Gupte, Peter Ho, Tarun Kataria, Ron Kaufman, Gaurang Khemka, John Kim, Joshua Kuma, Ann Lavin, Frank Lavin, Lien Chen Lien, Joseph Liow, Kevin Lu, Eddy Malesky, Aaron Maniam, David Marx, Law Chung Ming, Daniel Lee, Adam Levinson, David Mann, Sopnendu Mohanty, Vignes Sellakannu, Caesar Sengupta, Satvinder Singh, Michelle Tan, Yinglan Tan, Sudhir Vadaketh, Sriram Vasudevan, Michael Vatikiotis, Ravi Velloor, Karsten Warnecke, George Yeo, and Mikhail Zeldovich. Special thanks to Aussie tech entrepreneur Philip Lutton for his wide-ranging thinking on how exponential technologies will unfold in the Asian domain, Neeraj Seth for his inexhaustible knowledge of Asian economies, and Ravi Chidambaram for his big-picture thinking on what makes Asia tick. For their counsel on how Latin America views Asia's rise, I am grateful to Flavio Damico, Mauricio Baquero-Pardo, Braz Baracuhy, Federico Barttfeld, Manuel Talavera Espinar, Fredesman Turro Gonzalez, Alfredo Toro Hardy, Alfonso Murillo, James Sinclair, and Natan Wolf.

A great many experts on the history, philosophy, politics, and economics of Asia and global thinking about Asia have provided very useful information and insights: Graham Allison, Arjun Appadurai, Zubaid Ahmad, Richard Allen, Ali Aslan, Genevieve Bell, Karan Bhatia, Penny Burtt, Cliff Coonan, Patrick Cordes, Jack DeGioia, Prasenjit Duara, Jack Dwyer, Casper Ellerbaek, Andrew Field, Gordon Flake, Spencer Fung, Mishaal Gergawi, Alison Gilmore, Brad Glosserman, Martin Gray, Michael Green, Steve Grubb, Guoliang Wu, Blair Hall, Nat Hansen, Jonathan Hausman, Rupert Hoogewerf, Ann Julian,

Kosmo Kalliarekos, Robert Kaplan, Gerry Keefe, Kevin Kelly, Claudio Lilienfeld, Peggy Liu, Manish Kayshap, Suat Kiniklioglu, Udai Kunzru, Wolfgang Lehmacher, Scott Malcomson, Anna Marrs, Avinash Mehrotra, Simon Milner, Pankaj Mishra, Siddharth Mohandas, Yascha Mounk, Alexandre Parilusyan, Safdar Parvez, Chris Patten, Joseph Phi, Kai Poetschke, Noah Raford, Julia Raiskin, Laurent Ramsey, Sean Randolph, Rahul Reddy, Gideon Rose, Dan Rosen, Jim Rowan, Manuel Rybach, Richard Samans, Rana Sarkar, Jonas Schorr, Elliot Schrage, Chris Schroeder, John Seely Brown, Reva Seth, Clara Shen, Philip Shetler-Jones, Lutfey Siddiqui, Ben Simpfendorfer, Sarita Singh, Lauren Sorkin, Shantanu Surpure, Didi Kirsten Tatlow, Richard Threfall, Vijay Vaitheeswaran, Hal Varian, Andy Ventris, Steve Walt, Wang Gungwu, and Justin Wood. Scott Malcomson once again deserves special thanks for his intellectual and editorial counsel.

During the research and writing of this book, I enjoyed an invigorating semester-long sabbatical at the Robert Bosch Academy in Berlin, and wish to thank for their warm hospitality the wonderful team of Sandra Breka, Jannik Rust, Korbinian Bauer, and Madeleine Schneider. I'm also grateful to the roundtable participants they assembled to discuss Europe's relations with Asia, as well as other German dignitaries and experts with whom I spent time during my stay: Thomas Bagger, Laurence Bay, Bjoern Conrad, Patrick Donahue, Wolfram Eilenberger, Mark Hauptmann, Sebastian Heilmann, Julian Hermann, Hanns Guenther Hilpert, Wolfgang Ischinger, Josef Janning, Alex Kugel, Undine Ruge, Eberhard Sandschneider, Ulrich Sante, Wolfgang Schmidt, Frank-Walter Steinmeier, Tan Tah Jiun, and Jan Techau.

I would also like to thank other Europe-based experts for their thoughts and analysis: Valerie Amos, Giovanni Andornino, Ricardo Borges de Castro, Peter Burian, Carlotta Clivio, Norbert Czismadia, Peter Eigen, Theresa Fallon, Enrico Fardalla, Alex Fox, Giuseppe Gabusi, Thomas Geisel, David Giampaolo, Christoph Goeller, Nik Gowing, Jan-Friedrich Kallmorgen, Sebastian Kaempf, Daniel Korski, Taavi Kotka, Leah Kreitzman, Christin Kristofferson, Mark Leonard, Bruno Macaes, Stanislav Matejka, Ann Mettler, Helmut Morent, Martina Poletti, Ulrich Schulte-Strathaus, Jeremy Shapiro, Kristin Shi-Kupfer, Francesco Silvestri, Pawel Swieboda, Irene Tinagli, Paul Unschuld, Taleh Ziyadov, and Felix Zulauf.

Every visit to Japan is special, and most recently I have learned a great deal from time spent with Shiro Armstrong, Tetsuro Fukunaga, Yoichi Funabashi, Daisuke Iwase, Tadashi Maeda, Gen Miyazawa, Hiro Motoki, Sachio Nishioka, Kazumi Nishikawa, Teru Sato, Akihisa Shioaki, Makoto Takano, Tatsuya Terazawa, Hirotaka Unami, and Takashi Yokota. During an auspicious visit to Mongolia, I had the pleasure of gaining the wisdom of friends old and new: Ariunaa Batbold, Khaltmaagiin Battulga, Lundeg Bayartuul, Zorigt Enkhbat, Tsetseglen Galbadrakh, Tuvshinzaya Gantulga, Dulguun, Nomin Chinbat, Ganhuyag Hutagt, Ben Moyle, Ogi Moyle, Baatar Navaan, Lundeg Purevsuren, Erdenebold Sukhbaatar, and Ganzorig Vanchig. I was also honored to participate in the Crawford Leadership Forum in Canberra in 2017 and wish to thank the organizers, participants and other friends in Australia who have provided the view from "Down Under": Stephen Bartos, Gareth Evans, Michael Feller, Evelyn Goh, Allan Gyngell, Greg Hunt, Sung Lee, Martine Letts, Jason Yat-Sen Li, and Peter Singer. And for hosting me (and my adventurous daughter) in the enchanted kingdom of Bhutan, I'd like to extend my deepest gratitude to Prime Minister Tshering Tobgay, Chewang Rinzin, Sigay Dem, and Adrian Chan.

As my travels have taken me many times to China, Russia, India, Pakistan, Central Asia, the Gulf, and all ASEAN countries, I have acknowledged many friends and contacts from these countries in my previous books. Here I would like to particularly thank the following people for more recent conversations that directly contributed to this book: Rashid Amjad, Aluf Benn, Daniel Bell, Bing Song, Azam Chaudhry, Brahma Chellaney, Alisher Ali Djumanov, Dong Wang, Michael Eisenberg, Hassan Fattah, Yasar Jarrar, Angelo Jiminez, Mishaal Gergawi, Karl Gheysen, Mallika Kapur, Anusha Rehman Khan, Nasrullah Khan, Eric X. Li, Mersole Mellejor, Afshin Molavi, Antonio Morales, Roland Nash, Ramon Pastrana, Lubna Qassim, Abhijnan Rej, Jorge Sarmiento, Irina Schwarzburg, Jen Zhu Scott, Shahbaz Sharif, Aditya Dev Sood, Dmitry Suslov, Mudassir Tipu, Dmitri Trenin, Antonio Ver, Chris Weaver, Brian Wong, Tarik Yousef, Saadia Zahidi, Artem Zassoursky, and Taleh Ziyadov.

I can no longer imagine books without maps and infographics, and for producing another crop of insightful imagery I am ever so grateful to Jeff Blossom at Harvard's Center for Geographical Analysis as well as Tanya Buckingham and Casey Kalman at the University of Wisconsin–Madison.

By now Jennifer Joel at ICM knows I would never make a strategic decision without her. That is because she is not only an agent but also a true friend. With her characteristically strategic deftness, Jenn guided me through a publisher transition that brought this book into the very capable hands of Ben Loehnen at Simon & Schuster, who, as fate would have it, has known me since my very first literary foray. Ben and his team have been absolutely delightful, utterly professional, and remarkably efficient.

Each subsequent book does not become any easier to write, but the effort provides plenty of fresh fodder for dinner table discussions with family wherever they may be. I'm ever grateful to my parents, Sushil and Manjula Khanna, my in-laws Javed and Zarene Malik, my brother and sister-in-law Gaurav and Anu Khanna, and of course my beloved wife, Ayesha, and our kids, Zara and Zubin, with whom I'm grateful to be building our Asian future.

Notes

Introduction: Asia First

1 Only the African Group in the United Nations has more members with fifty-four. Asia is home to 2,301 spoken languages, and Africa ranks second with just over 2,100 languages.

2 Branko Milanovic, "Global Income Inequality by the Numbers: In History and Now—An Overview," World Bank Policy Research Paper no. 6259, November 2012, http://documents.worldbank.org/curated/en/959251468176687085/pdf/wps6259.pdf.

3 Kishore Mahbubani, *Can Asians Think? Understanding the Divide Between East and West* (New York: Steerforth Press, 2001).

4 Asian Development Bank, *Key Indicators for Asia and the Pacific, 2015* (Manila: Asian Development Bank, 2015), https://www.adb.org/sites/default/files/publication/175162/ki2015.pdf.

5 Homi Kharas, "The Unprecedented Expansion of the Global Middle Class: An Update," Global Economy & Development Working Paper no. 100, Brookings Institution, February 2017, https://www.brookings.edu/wp-content/uploads/2017/02/global_20170228_global-middle-class.pdf.

6 Since most ancient cultures thought of themselves as the center of the world, Asian civilizations had names for one another but no word for "Asia." To this day, Chinese use the word "Yaxiya" and Japanese "Ajia" for the region.

7 The scholar of geography Harm de Blij presented a global cartography of twelve realms, half of which are explicitly Asian: Southwest Asia, South Asia, East Asia, Southeast Asia, Australasia, and the Pacific Islands. Russia was defined as a separate realm, though it lies mostly within Asia.

8 North and South America together have a similar number of large states: Canada, the United States, Brazil, and Argentina.

9 As the scholar P. K. Basu argued in *Asia Reborn*, "The umbrella of colonialism

and its post-colonial and Cold War effects masked the underlying unity of the Asian continent," Prasenjit K. Basu, *Asia Reborn: A Continent Rises from the Ravages of War and Colonialism to a New Dynamism* (New Delhi: Aleph, 2017.)

10 Barry Buzan and Richard Little, *International Systems in World History: Remaking the Study of International Relations* (London: Oxford University Press, 2000).

11 The United States is the top trading partner of Canada and Mexico, but for the United States, the European Union and China rank ahead of Canada and Mexico.

12 Yoichi Funabashi, "The Asianization of Asia," *Foreign Affairs* 72, no. 5 (November–December 1993): 75.

13 "GCC Trade with Asia Growing and Diversifying," *The Report: UAE: Dubai*, Oxford Business Group, 2015, https://oxfordbusinessgroup.com/analysis/gcc -trade-asia-growing-and-diversifying.

14 Xi Jinping, "New Asian Security Concept for New Progress in Security Cooperation," remarks at the Fourth Summit of the Conference on Interaction and Confidence Building Measures in Asia, Shanghai, May 21, 2014. Ministry of Foreign Affairs of the People's Republic of China. Retrieved from http://www .fmprc.gov.cn/mfa_eng/zxxx_662805/t1159951.shtml.

15 "Kevin Rudd, Toward an Asia-Pacific Union," Asia Society, June 4, 2008, https:// asiasociety.org/kevin-rudd-toward-asia-pacific-union.

1. A History of the World: An Asian View

1 Sebastian Conrad, *What is Global History?* (Princeton: Princeton University Press, 2016).

2 The Eastern Zhou Dynasty, by contrast, was more dispersed, with kings still dependent on feudal lords and rival fiefdoms to maintain power.

3 Another prince of the same period, Vardhamana Mahavira, also undertook journeys of self-sacrifice and meditation that inspired the system of nonviolence and spiritual liberation known as Jainism.

4 In search of manpower for their global colonial empires, the Portuguese and Spanish, together with the Arabs, expanded the existing slave-trading routes across the Sahara Desert, through Egypt and Ethiopia, across the Red Sea to the Indian Ocean, and soon after across the Atlantic Ocean from the Caribbean to Brazil. This sixteenth- and seventeenth-century slave trade morphed into rivalries among European powers to subjugate and partition Africa.

2. Lessons of Asian History—for Asia and the World

1 "The 112th Canton Fair Closes with US$30 Billion Turnover, Showing Stable Overall Trade Situation," PR Newswire, Nov. 12, 2017. http://www.prnewswire

.co.uk/news-releases/the-112th-canton-fair-boosting-trade-with-asia-pacific
-markets-170463406.html.

2 By 2050, Islam's world population is expected to match that of Christianity, with
more than 2.5 billion believers each.

3. The Return of Greater Asia

1 KinLing Lo, "US Take Note: Chinese, Russian Militaries Are Closer than You
Think, China's Defence Minister Says," *South China Morning Post*, April 4, 2018,
https://www.scmp.com/news/china/diplomacy-defence/article/2140301/us-take
-note-chinese-russian-militaries-are-closer-you.

2 The largest foreign group in Russia is Ukrainians, whose remittances make up 5
percent of Ukraine's GDP.

3 Margaret Coker, "Hoping for $100 Billion to Rebuild, Iraq Got Less than a
Third," *New York Times*, Feb. 14, 2018.

4 For the same reasons, Israeli start-ups have made Singapore their regional hub
to access the growing Southeast Asian market for advanced technologies.

5 Niv Elis, "Private Ashdod Port Building Ahead of Schedule, Says Ports
Company," *Jerusalem Post*, April 12, 2016, https://www.jpost.com/Business
-and-Innovation/Private-Ashdod-port-building-ahead-of-schedule-says-ports
-company-451039.

6 Benjamin Netanyahu, "Full Text: Netanyahu's Speech on Iran in Munich," Feb.
18, 2018, https://www.haaretz.com/middle-east-news/full-text-netanyahu-s
-speech-on-iran-in-munich-1.5826934.

7 The Shanghai Futures Exchange and its subsidiary International Energy
Exchange have already launched renminbi-denominated oil contracts.

8 "GCC Needs to Invest $131bn to Meet Five-Year Power Demand," Arabian
Business, Jan. 18, 2018, https://www.arabianbusiness.com/energy/387887-gcc
-needs-to-invest-131bn-to-meet-five-year-power-demand.

9 Carlotta Gall, "In Afghanistan, U.S. Exits and Iran Comes In," *New York Times*,
Aug. 5, 2017.

10 Ziad Haider, "Can the U.S. Pivot Back to Asia? How Trump Should Respond
to China's Belt and Road Initiative," *Foreign Affairs*, May 23, 2017, https://www
.foreignaffairs.com/articles/china/2017-05-23/can-us-pivot-back-asia.

11 Xi Jinping, "Secure a Decisive Victory in Building a Moderately Prosperous
Society in All Respects and Strive for the Great Success of Socialism
with Chinese Characteristics for a New Era," speech delivered at the 19th
National Congress of the Communist Party of China, Oct. 18, 2017, http://
www.xinhuanet.com/english/download/Xi_Jinping's_report_at_19th_CPC
_National_Congress.pdf.

12 In 2017, the United States suspended military assistance to Pakistan for noncompliance with its counterterrorism objectives in Afghanistan.

13 https://www.timesnownews.com/international/article/pakistan-elections-2018 -united-states-of-america-used-pakistan-as-hired-gun-pakistan-tehreek-e-insaf -imran-khan-nawaz-sharif-pakistan-muslim-league/257073.

14 https://en.dailypakistan.com.pk/pakistan/pakistan-should-not-become-scapegoat -for-us-policy-failure-imran-khan/.

15 James Leibold, "China's Minority Report: When Racial Harmony Means Homogenization," *Foreign Affairs*, March 23, 2016, https://www.foreignaffairs .com/articles/china/2016-03-23/chinas-minority-report; Sara Newline, "Growing Apart? Challenges to High-Quality Local Governance and Public Service Provision on China's Ethnic Periphery," Harvard Kennedy School Ash Center for Democratic Governance and Innovation, July 2016, http://ash .harvard.edu/files/ash/files/growing_apart.pdf.

16 The member states of ASEAN are Indonesia, Vietnam, Thailand, Singapore, Myanmar, Malaysia, the Philippines, Laos, Cambodia, and Brunei. East Timor and Papua New Guinea are expected to join in the coming years.

17 "Laos: On the Borders of the Empire," Al Jazeera, May 25, 2017, https:// www.aljazeera.com/programmes/peopleandpower/2017/05/laos-borders- empire-170522105221541.html.

18 Oil-rich Brunei has a small claim on the South China Sea due to its possession of the disputed Louisa Reef but has remained quiet as its exports to China have grown from nearly zero in 2003 to almost $2 billion in 2015 due to the establishment of the Brunei-Guangxi Economic Corridor.

19 As if to emulate East Asian countries' aggressive innovation promotion strategies, Australia's Department of Education and Training issued a directive in 2018 that universities receiving public funding must demonstrate the contributions of their research to the economy, society, or culture and will be ranked by panels to determine future funding.

20 Leo Lewis and Shunsuke Tabeta, "Japan Business Leaders Urge Real Globalisation," *Financial Times*, Jan. 12, 2016, https://www.ft.com/content /80bb0344-78d6-11e5-a95a-27d368e1ddf7.

21 Takako Taniguchi and Kazunori Takada, "Japan Notches $18 Billion of Soured Deals amid M&A Boom," Bloomberg, June 6, 2017, https://www .bloomberg.com/news/articles/2017-06-05/japan-notches-18-billion-of-soured -deals-amid-record-m-a-boom.

22 "Record 2.38 Million Foreign Residents Living in Japan in 2016," *Japan Times*, March 17, 2017, https://www.japantimes.co.jp/news/2017/03/17/national/record-2 -38-million-foreign-residents-living-japan-2016/#.W37WGooh2Uk.

23 Shusuke Murai and Tomoko Otake, "'Bakugai,' 'Toripuru Suri' Share Top Honors as This Year's Most Memorable Buzzwords in Japan," *Japan Times*, Dec. 1, 2015, https://www.japantimes.co.jp/news/2015/12/01/national/bakugai-toripuru-suri-share-top-honors-years-memorable-buzzwords-japan/#.W37WUooh2Uk.

24 Kate Springer, "Japan's Fukuoka Poised to Be the Country's Next Silicon Valley," CNN, Nov. 16, 2017, https://money.cnn.com/2016/11/16/technology/fukuoka-startup-city/index.html.

25 "Singapore, Korea and Japan Most Innovative Countries in Asia," HRM Asia, June 19, 2017, http://www.hrmasia.com/content/singapore-korea-and-japan-most-innovative-countries-asia.

26 Kenji E. Kushida, "Japan's Startup Ecosystem: From Brave New World to Part of Syncretic 'New Japan.'" *Asian Research Policy* 7, no. 1 (2016): 67–77.

27 Even though Japan has followed a nonnuclear policy since World War II, in 2017 its parliament approved an accord to sell nuclear reactor technology to India, which has long held out from signing the Treaty on the Non-Proliferation of Nuclear Weapons (NPT).

28 Doug Bandow, "Time to Let Japan Be a Regular Military Power," *The National Interest*, Oct. 29, 2017, https://nationalinterest.org/feature/time-let-japan-be-regular-military-power-22954.

29 Zhao Tingyang, "Rethinking Empire from a Chinese Concept 'All-Under-Heaven' (Tian-xia, 天下)." *Social identities* 12, no. 1 (2006): 29–41.

30 Zhang Weiwei, *The China Wave: Rise of a Civilizational State* (World Century Press, 2012).

31 China's ban on Korean cosmetics imports and halt of Chinese tourism to Korea's popular Jeju Island also pressured the Moon government.

4. Asia-nomics

1 Stuart T. Gulliver, "Seizing the Asian Opportunity," Speech at the Asian Business Insights Conference, Duesseldorf, Germany, February 7, 2017.

2 World Trade Organization, *World Trade Statistical Review, 2016*, 2016, https://www.wto.org/english/res_e/statis_e/wts2016_e/wts2016_e.pdf.

3 It is worth noting, however, that trade *within* each Asian subregion has not necessarily grown due to internal frictions or insufficient comparative advantage. India's trade with its neighbors within the SAARC group, for example, has been flat, as has trade within the GCC.

4 Indeed, because the demand for low-cost Chinese electronics is so high worldwide, the internal trade among China, South Korea, and Taiwan accounts for only 34 percent of their trade versus 70 percent in the European Union and

50 percent in the NAFTA zone. All data are from the World Trade Organization and International Monetary Fund.

5   For the purposes of economic statistics, World Bank data sets separate Hong Kong and Taiwan from China. Taiwan has intense trade ties with China, Japan, South Korea, and ASEAN totaling nearly $300 billion per year. Hong Kong's global exports amount to $500 billion per year.

6   Karl Lester M. Yap, "China Surpasses Japan as Asia's Top High-Tech Exporter, ADB Says," Bloomberg, Dec. 7, 2015, https://www.bloomberg.com/news/articles /2015-12-08/china-surpasses-japan-as-asia-s-top-high-tech-exporter-adb-says.

7   PricewaterhouseCoopers, "China's Impact on the Semiconductor Industry: 2016 Update," January 2017.

8   By 2015, ASEAN's top investors were in the European Union ($70 billion) and ASEAN itself ($65 billion), followed by Japan ($60 billion), then China (combined with Hong Kong) ($55 billion) and the United States ($35 billion).

9   Trade within the larger East Asian space is largely balanced: China has only recently begun to achieve a slight surplus of $40 billion in trade with its southern neighbors. Japan and ASEAN also have a balanced trade of nearly $250 billion per year, and South Korea is not too far behind with $130 billion in trade with ASEAN.

10 OAG, *"Busiest Routes,"* February 2018; https://www.oag.com/hubfs/Free_Reports /Busiest%20Routes/OAG%20Busiest%20Routes%202018-A4.pdf?hsCtaTracking= 5cf02a77-684e-42e5-aa7f-d56bbc799a4e%7Cd12dd304-c189-4484-9bf0- 590a339253db.

11 Wee Kee Hwee, Jaya Prakash Pradhan, Maria Cecilia Salta et al., *ASEAN Investment Report, 2017: Foreign Direct Investment and Economic Zones in ASEAN* (Jakarta: ASEAN, 2017), http://asean.org/storage/2017/11/ASEAN-Investment -Report-2017.pdf.

12 Japan's foreign direct investment stock in Asia (outside China) remains far larger than China's: $260 billion versus only $58 billion.

13 Japan's largest mafia group, the Yakuza, operates in a similar fashion, consisting of nearly two dozen groups with 53,000 members and an estimated $7 billion in annual revenue from its role in industries such as entertainment, construction, real estate, and finance.

14 China's debt-to-GDP ratio has climbed to 260 percent, and its capital output ratio (the amount of investment needed to generate additional income) has doubled since the mid-2000s.

15 The services sector has become the largest driver of employment as well (36 percent versus only 33 percent in industry and 30 percent in agriculture) and generates higher wages and profits than do state-owned enterprises. At the

same time, private consumption now represents more than half of GDP while investment has fallen to one-third.

16 David Bain, "The Top 500 Family Businesses in the World," in *EY Family Business Yearbook 2015*, Ernst & Young, 2017, 182–87, https://familybusiness.ey-vx .com/pdfs/182-187.pdf.

17 "IMF Sees Room for Rising Tax-to-GDP Ratio for Indonesia," Indonesia-Investments, February 8, 2018, https://www.indonesia-investments.com/news /todays-headlines/imf-sees-room-for-rising-tax-to-gdp-ratio-for-indonesia/item8577?.

18 Only the most fragile Asian economies such as Georgia, Iraq, Jordan, Afghanistan, and Kyrgyzstan have standby credit arrangements with the IMF.

19 Japan remains Asia's largest net foreign creditor with more than $3.5 trillion in overseas assets, but with China's annual surpluses of $1 trillion and foreign exchange reserves of $3 trillion, China is expected to catch up with Japan by 2020. Together, Japan and China hold nearly $7 trillion in foreign assets across foreign currency reserves, portfolio investment, and direct investment. In terms of total FDI stock, China's nearly $1.4 trillion ranks just ahead of Japan.

20 Gemma B. Estrada, Donghyun Park, and Arief Ramayandi, "Taper Tantrum and Emerging Equity Market Slumps," ADB Economics Working Paper Series no. 451, Sept. 2015, https://www.adb.org/sites/default/files/publication/173760/ ewp-451.pdf.

21 The Chiang Mai Initiative (CMI) and subsequent Asian Bond Markets Initiative (ABMI) facilitated local currency debt swaps among ASEAN and its main three trading partners, China, Japan, and South Korea.

22 Amy Lam, "China Drives Asia's Record International Bond Issuances for 2017," Nikkei Asian Review, Dec. 28, 2017, https://asia.nikkei.com/Business/Markets/ Nikkei-Markets/China-Drives-Asia-s-Record-International-Bond-Issuances-For-2017-Dealogic.

23 Foreigners can now buy into interbank lending (currently a market of more than $10 trillion) and local government, central bank, financial institution, and corporate bonds, as well as certificates of deposit- and asset-backed securities in the secondary market.

24 International Monetary Fund, *Regional Economic Outlook, April 2015: Stabilizing and Outperforming Other Regions*, April 2015.

25 Singapore, Malaysia, and Thailand established the ASEAN Trading Link in 2012 to provide a mechanism for transfer of orders across three participating exchanges, expanding into a mutual framework for clearing and settlement in 2014. Asian regulators are also adopting central counterparty clearinghouses (CCPs) as part of the G20 capital market reforms.

26 Preqin, "Preqin Special Report: Asian Private Equity & Venture Capital," Sept.

2017, http://docs.preqin.com/reports/Preqin-Special-Report-Asian-Private-Equity-and-Venture-Capital-September-2017.pdf.

27 Crunchbase, *Global Innovation Investment Report: 2016 Year in Review*, https://static.crunchbase.com/reports/annual_2016_yf42a/crunchbase_annual_2016.pdf.

28 Apple also made a $1 billion investment in DiDi in 2017.

29 Judith Balea, "Grab's Anthony Tan on His Unforgettable Meeting with Masayoshi Son, brotherhood with Didi," *Tech in Asia*, May 25, 2017; https://www.techinasia.com/grab-anthony-tan-on-his-unforgettable-meeting-with-masayoshi-son-and-brotherhood-with-didi.

30 India's trade in and consumption of gold is mostly private, while China's is mostly public, given that it is the world's largest producer and consumer of gold.

31 Philip J. Landrigan. Richard Fuller, Nereus J. R. Acosta, et al., "The *Lancet* Commission on Pollution and Health," *The Lancet* 391, no. 10119 (2017): 462–512.

32 Ye Qi and Tong Wu, "Putting China's Coal Consumption into Context," Brookings Institution, Nov. 30, 2015, https://www.brookings.edu/blog/up-front/2015/11/30/putting-chinas-coal-consumption-into-context/.

33 China projects 250 GW of wind power by 2020. See Daniel Cusick, "China Blows Past the U.S. in Wind Power," *Scientific American*, Feb. 2, 2016, https://www.scientificamerican.com/article/china-blows-past-the-u-s-in-wind-power/.

34 Due to spiking cobalt prices, all lithium-ion battery makers are researching new ratios of nickel-manganese-cobalt (NMC) to increase the cheaper nickel share and reduce the cobalt content.

35 Yiting Sun, "China's Massive Effort to Purify Seawater Is Drying Up," MIT Technology Review, July 11, 2016, https://www.technologyreview.com/s/601861/chinas-massive-effort-to-purify-seawater-is-drying-up/.

36 Across the Celebes Sea, the peoples of the southern Philippine Islands and the northern Moluku Islands of Indonesia are ethnically related.

37 Xi Jinping, "Secure a Decisive Victory in Building a Moderately Prosperous Society in All Respects and Strive for the Great Succss of Socialism with Chinese Characteristics for a New Era," speech delivered at the 19th National Congress of the Communist Party of China, Oct. 18, 2017, http://www.xinhuanet.com/english/download/Xi_Jinping's_report_at_19th_CPC_National_Congress.pdf.

38 The Nielsen Company, "The Sustainability Imperative: New Insights on Consumer Expectations," October 2015, http://www.nielsen.com/content/dam/nielsenglobal/co/docs/Reports/2015/global-sustainability-report.pdf.

39 Latin America and Africa have far poorer countries than even Yemen, such as Haiti and Congo, but neither region has nations as wealthy per capita as Qatar or Singapore.

40 Low-income countries are those with a per capita income between $1,000 and $4,000 (India, Pakistan, Indonesia, Vietnam, the Philippines) per year; and middle-income countries are those with a per capita income between $4,000 and $12,000 (Turkey, Iraq, Iran, China, Malaysia, Thailand); high-income countries are those with a per capita income of more than $12,000 (Singapore, Japan, South Korea).

41 "New 2025 Global Growth Projections Predict China's Further Slowdown and the Continued Rise of India," The Growth Lab, Center for International Development, Harvard University, June 28, 2017, https://growthlab.cid.harvard .edu/news/new-2025-global-growth-projections-predict-china%E2%80%99s -further-slowdown-and-continued.

42 Cristian Badarinza, Vimal Balasubramaniam, and Tarun Ramadorai, "The Indian Household Savings Landscape," paper presented at India Policy Forum 2016, July 12–13, 2016, http://www.ncaer.org/events/ipf-2016/IPF-2016-Paper -Badarinza-Balasubramaniam-Ramadorai.pdf.

43 Reliance Industries CEO Mukesh Ambani is Asia's richest man with a net worth estimated at $45 billion.

44 Alipay accounts for about 68 percent of third-party online payments, with Tencent far behind, although Tencent has 20 percent of the mobile payments market. WeChat has evolved from messaging to payments to personal finance with the launch of WeBank, an online-only bank, in 2014. Together, Alipay and WeBank account for an estimated 50 percent or more of bank deposits in China.

45 According to "EY FinTech Innovation Index, 2017," China and India rank ahead of the United Kingdom, Germany, and the United States in providing large-scale digital consumer banking and other financial products to the masses. https:// www.ey.com/Publication/vwLUAssets/ey-fintech-adoption-index-2017/$FILE/ ey-fintech-adoption-index-2017.pdf.

46 Mayuko Tani, "Asia's 'Tiger Cubs' Will Feast on FDI for the Next Decade," *Nikkei Asian Review*, August 2, 2017.

47 Geely's 800,000 car sales in Europe in 2016 were less than Volkswagen's 4 million, but for Geely, Europe is far less important than its core market of China itself. It considers overseas sales a bonus, not a necessity.

48 Jost Wübbeke, Mirjam Meissner, Max J. Zenglein, et al., "Made in China 2025: The Making of a High-Tech Superpower and Consequences for Industrial Countries," Mercator Institute for China Studies, December 2016, https://www .merics.org/sites/default/files/2017-09/MPOC_No.2_MadeinChina2025.pdf.

49 Commission on the Theft of American Intellectual Property, "Update to the IP Commission Report: The Theft of American Intellectual Property: Reassessments of the Challenge and United States Policy," National Bureau

of Asian Research, 2017, p. 4, http://ipcommission.org/report/IP_Commission
_Report_Update_2017.pdf.

50 Kyle A. Jaros, "Urban Champions or Rich Peripheries? China's Spatial
Development Dilemmas," Harvard Kennedy School Ash Center for Democratic
Governance and Innovation, April 2016, http://ash.harvard.edu/files/ash/files
/261226_ash_jaros_web.pdf?m=1461696669.

51 The largest share of GDP represented by the informal economy is found in
countries such as Russia, Thailand, the Philippines, Pakistan, and Bangladesh.

52 Emma Lee, "Nearly 90% Phones Sold in China in 2016 Came from Domestic
Makers," TechNode, Jan. 12, 2017, https://technode.com/2017/01/12/nearly-90-of
-560m-phones-sold-in-china-comes-from-domestic-makers-2016/.

53 Chris Cooper, "China to Surpass U.S. as World's Largest Aviation Market by
2024," Bloomberg, Oct. 20, 2016, https://www.bloomberg.com/news/articles
/2016-10-21/china-to-surpass-u-s-as-world-s-largest-aviation-market-by-2024.

5. Asians in the Americas and Americans in Asia

1 Pew Research Center, *Modern Immigration Wave Brings 59 Million to U.S.,
Driving Population Growth and Change Through 2065*, September 28, 2015, http://
www.pewhispanic.org/files/2015/09/2015-09-28_modern-immigration-wave
_REPORT.pdf.

2 United States Census Bureau, "Asian Alone or in Any Combination by Selected
Groups: 2015 American Community Survey 1-Year Estimates," https://www
.census.gov/history/pdf/acs15yr-korean62017.pdf.

3 United States Census Bureau, "Annual Estimates of the Resident Population by
Sex, Race Alone or in Combination, and Hispanic Origin for the United States,
States, and Counties: April 1, 2010 to July 1, 2016," https://factfinder.census.gov/
faces/tableservices/jsf/pages/productview.xhtml?src=bkmk.

4 Department of Homeland Security, "Persons Obtaining Lawful Permanent
Resident Status by Region and Country of Birth: Fiscal Years 2013 to
2015," table 3 in *Yearbook of Immigration Statistics 2015*, https://www.dhs.gov/
immigration-statistics/yearbook/2015/table3.

5 Ibid.

6 Gustavo López, Neil G. Ruiz, and Eileen Patten, "Key Facts About Asian
Americans, a Diverse and Growing Population," Pew Research Center. Sept. 8,
2017, http://www.pewresearch.org/fact-tank/2017/09/08/key-facts-about-asian
-americans/.

7 Pew Research Center, "Intermarriage across the U.S. by Metro Area," May 18,
2017, http://www.pewsocialtrends.org/interactives/intermarriage-across-the-u-s
-by-metro-area/.

8   Pew Research Center, *Modern Immigration Wave Brings 59 Million to U.S.*
9   Pew Research Center, "Chinese in the U.S. Fact Sheet," Sept. 8, 2017, http://www.pewsocialtrends.org/fact-sheet/asian-americans-chinese-in-the-u-s/; United States Census Bureau, "Los Angeles County a Microcosm of Nation's Diverse Collection of Business Owners, Census Bureau Reports," Dec. 15, 2015, https://www.census.gov/newsroom/press-releases/2015/cb15-209.html.
10   López, Ruiz, and Patten, "Key Facts About Asian Americans."
11   Shalene Gupta, "Big Fat Indian Weddings Get Bigger and Fatter," *Fortune*, Aug. 8, 2014, http://fortune.com/2014/08/08/indian-weddings/.
12   Sari Horwitz and Emma Brown, "Justice Department Plans New Project to Sue Universities over Affirmative Action Policies," *Washington Post*, Aug. 1, 2017, https://www.washingtonpost.com/world/national-security/justice-department-plans-new-project-to-sue-universities-over-affirmative-action-policies/2017/08/01/6295eba4-772b-11e7-8f39-eeb7d3a2d304_story.html?noredirect=on&utm_term=.808b27e06276.
13   Vivek Wadhwa, "The Face of Success, Part I: How the Indians Conquered Silicon Valley," *Inc.*, Jan. 13, 2012, https://www.inc.com/vivek-wadhwa/how-the-indians-succeeded-in-silicon-valley.html.
14   Ibid.
15   Jane Ciabattari, "Why Is Rumi the Best-Selling Poet in the US?," BBC, October 21, 2014, http://www.bbc.com/culture/story/20140414-americas-best-selling-poet.
16   Charles Lam, "The 115th Congress is History-Making for Asian Americans and Pacific Islanders," NBC News, Jan. 4, 2017, https://www.nbcnews.com/news/asian-america/115th-congress-history-making-asian-americans-pacific-islanders-n703261.
17   Statistics Canada, "Data Tables, 2016 Census: Citizenship, Place of Birth, Immigrant Status and Period of Immigration, Age and Sex for the Population in Private Households of Canada, Provinces and Territories, Census Metropolitan Areas and Census Agglomerations, 2016 Census—25% Sample Data," January 16, 2018, https://www12.statcan.gc.ca/census-recensement/2016/dp-pd/dt-td/Rp-eng.cfm?LANG=E&APATH=3&DETAIL=0&DIM=0&FL=A&FREE=0&GC=0&GID=0&GK=0&GRP=0&PID=110525&PRID=10&PTYPE=109445&S=0&SHOWALL=0&SUB=0&Temporal=2017&THEME=120&VID=0&VNAMEE=&VNAMEF=.
18   Wanyee Li, "More Mandarin than Cantonese Speakers in Metro Vancouver: Census," *Metro News*, Aug. 3, 2017.
19   Joshua Bateman, "China's Real Estate Investors on a $200B Global Spending Spree," CNBC, June 16, 2017, https://www.cnbc.com/2017/06/16/chinas-real-estate-investors-on-a-200b-global-spending-spree.html.

20 Ibid.

21 Institute of International Education, "Open Doors 2016 Executive Summary," https://www.iie.org/Why-IIE/Announcements/2016-11-14-Open-Doors-Executive -Summary.

22 Bethany Allen-Ebrahimian, "Chinese Students in America: 300,000 and Counting," *Foreign Policy*, Nov. 16, 2015, https://foreignpolicy.com/2015/11/16/ china-us-colleges-education-chinese-students-university/.

23 Ibid.

24 Pew Research Center, "Race and Social Connections—Friends, Family and Neighborhoods," June 11, 2015, http://www.pewsocialtrends.org/2015/06/11/ chapter-5-race-and-social-connections-friends-family-and-neighborhoods/.

25 Eva Li and Sarah Zheng, "Seeking Better Job Options, More Chinese Students Are Returning Home After Graduating," *South China Morning Post*, April 17, 2017, https://www.scmp.com/news/china/policies-politics/article/2088088/ seeking-better-job-options-more-chinese-students.

26 Cai Muyuan, "Hangzhou a Top Choice for Overseas Returnees," *China Daily*, Sept. 5, 2016, http://www.chinadaily.com.cn/business/2016hangzhoug20/2016-09 /05/content_26698859.htm.

27 Cheng Li and Lucy Xu, "Chinese Think Tanks: A New 'Revolving Door' for Elite Recruitment," Brookings Institution, Feb. 10, 2017, https://www.brookings .edu/opinions/chinese-think-tanks-a-new-revolving-door-for-elite-recruitment/.

28 Ka Ho Mok, "What Can We Learn from Returning Chinese Students?," *University World News*, July 7, 2017, http://www.universityworldnews.com/article .php?story=20170627134055924.

29 Liu, Cecilia, "Chinese Universities Ranked Among Global Elite," *China Daily*, May 31, 2018, http://www.chinadaily.com.cn/a/201805/31/ WS5b0ef93ea31001b82571d42b.html.

30 Jacob Passy, "Why Millennials Can't Buy Homes," MarketWatch, Oct. 30, 2017, https://www.marketwatch.com/story/student-debt-is-delaying-millennial -homeownership-by-seven-years-2017-09-18.

31 Tamara Hardingham-Gill, "The World's Most Liveable Cities in 2018," CNN Travel, Aug. 14, 2018, https://www.cnn.com/travel/article/worlds-most-liveable -cities-2018.

32 Van Jay Symons and Suzanne Wilson Barnett, eds., *Asia in the Undergraduate Curriculum: A Case for Asian Studies in Liberal Arts Education* (New York: Routledge, 2015).

33 NAFSA, "Trends in U.S Study Abroad: Study Abroad Participation and Demographics Data," https://www.nafsa.org/Policy_and_Advocacy/Policy _Resources/Policy_Trends_and_Data/Trends_in_U_S__Study_Abroad/.

34 Institute of International Education, "Open Doors 2016 Regional Fact Sheet: Asia," 2016.

35 Asian Development Bank Institute, "Labor Migration, Skills & Student Mobility in Asia," 2014, https://www.oecd.org/migration/Labour-migration-skills-student-mobility-in-Asia.pdf.

36 The US government is one of the few in the world that does not track its overseas citizens systematically, but estimates for the years 1999, 2013, and 2016, have been made by the State Department and are reported in the following sources, respectively: Jason P. Schachter, "Estimation of Emigration from the United States Using International Data Sources," United Nations Secretariat, November 2006, https://unstats.un.org/unsd/Demographic/meetings/egm/migrationegm06/DOC%2019%20ILO.pdf; US Department of State, Bureau of Consular Affairs, "Consular Affairs by the Numbers," January 2013, https://travel.state.gov/content/dam/ca_fact_sheet.pdf; US Department of State, Bureau of Consular Affairs, "Consular Affairs by the Numbers," March 2018.

37 HSBC, "Expat Explorer Report 2014," https://www.expatexplorer.hsbc.com/survey/files/pdfs/overall-reports/2014/HSBC_Expat_Explorer_2014_report.pdf.

38 Angus Whitley, "Chinese Airlines Wave Wads of Cash to Lure Foreign Pilots," Bloomberg, Aug. 17, 2016, https://www.bloomberg.com/news/articles/2016-08-17/chinese-airlines-lure-expat-pilots-with-lucrative-pay-perks.

6. Why Europe Loves Asia but Not (Yet) Asians

1 Wilhelm Hofmeister and Patrick Rueppel, eds., "The Future of Asia-Europe Cooperation," Konrad-Adenauer Stifung and European Union, 2015, http://www.kas.de/wf/doc/kas_40559-1522-2-30.pdf?160317100039, p. 6.

2 Max Bouchet and Joseph Parilla, "How Trump's Steel and Aluminum Tariffs Could Affect State Economies," Brookings Institution, March 6, 2018, https://www.brookings.edu/blog/the-avenue/2018/03/06/how-trumps-steel-and-aluminum-tariffs-could-affect-state-economies/.

3 "Countries and Regions: China," European Commission, April 16, 2018, http://ec.europa.eu/trade/policy/countries-and-regions/countries/china/.

4 European Central Bank, "ECB Completes Foreign Reserves Investment in Chinese Renminbi Equivalent to €500 million," June 13, 2017, https://www.ecb.europa.eu/press/pr/date/2017/html/ecb.pr170613.en.html.

5 German food companies are investing in deep-chill freezing techniques that would extend the shelf life of their goods by weeks, further expanding their offerings to far-off Asian markets.

6 Feng Xin, "China Railway Express: Freight Network Facilitates Trade Between

China and Europe," CGTN, April 28, 2017, https://news.cgtn.com/news /3d55444f31597a4d/share_p.html.

7   In 2018, Balkrishna Doshi became the first Indian to win the Pritzker Architecture Prize; his architectural projects have long promoted sustainable and affordable housing.

8   From 2015 to 2017, China invested 40 percent of its FDI in Europe, 24 percent in the United States, and 12 percent in East Asia.

9   Aoife White and David McLaughlin, "ChemChina Gets EU Nod for Syngenta Deal One Day After US," Bloomberg, April 5, 2017, https://www.bloomberg.com/ news/articles/2017-04-04/chemchina-wins-u-s-approval-for-43-billion-syngenta -takeover-j13z8ty8.

10 Jamie Robertson, "Qatar: Buying Britain by the Pound," BBC News, June 9, 2017, https://www.bbc.com/news/business-40192970.

11 "China Launches $11 Billion Fund for Central, Eastern Europe," Reuters, Nov. 6, 2016, https://www.reuters.com/article/us-china-eastern-europe-fund/china -launches-11-billion-fund-for-central-eastern-europe-idUSKBN13105N.

12 Mission of the European Union to ASEAN, "40 Years of EU-ASEAN Partnership & Prosperity: Trading and Investing Together," 2017, https://eeas.europa.eu/sites/ eeas/files/eu_asean_trade_investment_2017.pdf.

13 World Travel & Tourism Council, *Travel & Tourism Economic Impact 2017: Iran*, https://www.wttc.org/-/media/files/reports/economic-impact-research/ countries-2017/iran2017.pdf.

14 The European Union already gives 20 percent of its science and research grants to non-EU entities, especially in Asia, leading to growing numbers of academic exchanges and knowledge-based collaborations.

7. The Return of Afroeurasia

1   The Gulf nations, however, clearly don't coordinate their Africa policies. During the 2017 rift between the GCC countries and Qatar, countries such as Ethiopia, Sudan, and Somalia were caught in the diplomatic cross fire, forced to choose sides between Qatar, which has become a major political and aid donor across the region, and Saudi Arabia, which has been a major trade partner.

2   Irene Yuan Sun, "The World's Next Great Manufacturing Center," *Harvard Business Review*, May–June 2017, https://hbr.org/2017/05/the-worlds-next-great -manufacturing-center.

3   Yoon Jung Park, "One Million Chinese in Africa," *SAIS Perspectives*, May 12, 2016, http://www.saisperspectives.com/2016issue/2016/5/12/ n947s9csa0ik6kmkm0bzb0hy584sfo.

4   Jacqueline Musiitwa, "Despite Slowdown, China's Migrants Rooted in Africa,"

This is Africa, March 30, 2016, https://www.thisisafricaonline.com/News/Despite
-slowdown-China-s-migrants-rooted-in-Africa?ct=true.

5 Tom Hancock, "Chinese Return from Africa as Migrant Population Peaks,"
   Financial Times, Aug. 28, 2017, https://www.ft.com/content/7106ab42-80d1-11e7-
   a4ce-15b2513cb3ff.

6 Lily Kuo, "China Now Owns More Than Half of Kenya's External Debt,"
   Quartz Africa, June 15, 2016, https://qz.com/africa/707954/china-now-owns
   -more-than-half-of-all-of-kenyas-debt-2/.

7 Pavithra Rao and Franck Kuwonu, "India, Africa Rekindle Trade Ties,"
   AfricaRenewal, August–November 2016, https://www.un.org/africarenewal/
   magazine/august-2016/india-africa-rekindle-trade-ties; "China, Africa Trade,
   Investment 'Off to a Flying Start' in 2017," Reuters, May 11, 2017, https://
   af.reuters.com/article/africaTech/idAFKBN1870LJ-OZATP.

8 "Data: Chinese Workers in Africa," China Africa Research Initiative,
   January 2018, http://www.sais-cari.org/data-chinese-workers-in-africa/;
   Deborah Brautigam, Margaret McMillan, and Xiaoyang Tang, "The Role
   of Foreign Investment in Ethiopia's Leather Value Chain," PEDL Research
   Note, ERG Project 106, 2013, https://cms.qz.com/wp-content/uploads/2016/11
   /08072-researchnote_brautigam_mcmillan_tang.pdf, p. 1.

9 Rao and Kuwonu, "India, Africa Rekindle Trade Ties"; IOM Global Migration
   Data Analysis Centre, "Global Migration Trends Factsheet," International
   Organization for Migration, http://gmdac.iom.int/global-migration-trends-
   factsheet.

10 His granddaughter Ela Gandhi was elected a member of the first postapartheid
   South African parliament in 1994.

11 Yun Sun, "Rising Sino-Japanese Competition in Africa," Brookings Institution,
   Aug. 31, 2016, https://www.brookings.edu/blog/africa-in-focus/2016/08/31/rising
   -sino-japanese-competition-in-africa/.

12 Wade Shepard, "India and Japan Join Forces to Counter China and Build
   Their Own New Silk Road," *Forbes*, July 31, 2017, https://www.forbes.com/sites/
   wadeshepard/2017/07/31/india-and-japan-join-forces-to-counter-china-and-build
   -their-own-new-silk-road/#563e3aeb4982.

13 Amadou Sy, "What Do We Know About the Chinese Land Grab in Africa?,"
   Brookings Institution, Nov. 5, 2015, https://www.brookings.edu/blog/africa-in
   -focus/2015/11/05/what-do-we-know-about-the-chinese-land-grab-in-africa/.

14 Lily Kuo, "China's Xi Jinping Pledges $60 Billion to Help Africa Solve Its
   Problems Its Own Way," *Quartz,* December 4, 2015, https://qz.com/africa/565819/
   chinas-xi-jinping-pledges-60-billion-to-help-africa-solve-its-problems-its-own-way/.

8. The New Pacific Partnership

1 After the US withdrawal, the TPP was replaced by the Comprehensive and Progressive Agreement for Trans-Pacific Partnership (CPTPP).

2 Rosalind Mowatt, "Trade Policy Issues in Latin America and the Caribbean: Views from Country Authorities and Current State of Pay," International Monetary Fund, March 2017, https://www.imf.org/~/media/Files/Publications/CR/2017/cr1766-ap-1.ashx, p. 11.

3 A key ingredient of tofu and source of cooking oil, soy is also crushed into soya meal for chickens, pigs, and fish.

4 Daniel Bellefleur, "Spanning the Economic Gap Between Asia and Latin America," *The Diplomat*, March 16, 2017, https://thediplomat.com/2017/03/spanning-the-economic-gap-between-asia-and-latin-america/.

5 Peter A. Petri and Michael G. Plummer, "US Must Get Back into the Game in the Asia Pacific," Peterson Institute for International Economics, Oct. 23, 2017, https://piie.com/commentary/op-eds/us-must-get-back-game-asia-pacific.

6 David Dollar, "China's Investment in Latin America," Geoeconomics and Global Issues Paper no. 4, Brookings Institution, January 2017, https://www.brookings.edu/wp-content/uploads/2017/01/fp_201701_china_investment_lat_am.pdf.

7 Kevin P. Gallagher, "China Steps into the Latin American Void Trump Has Left Behind," *Foreign Policy*, March 6, 2017, https://foreignpolicy.com/2017/03/06/china-steps-into-the-latin-american-void-trump-has-left-behind/.

8 "China Makes a Power Play in Brazil and Argentina," Stratfor, June 2, 2017, https://worldview.stratfor.com/article/china-makes-power-play-brazil-and-argentina.

9 Philippe Le Corre, Yun Sun, Amadou Sy, and Harold Trinkunas, "Other Perceptions of China: Views from Africa, Latin America, and Europe," Brookings Institution, May 27, 2015, https://www.brookings.edu/blog/order-from-chaos/2015/05/27/other-perceptions-of-china-views-from-africa-latin-america-and-europe/.

10 Zhang Chun, "Latin America's Oil-Dependent States Struggling to Repay Chinese Debts," Chinadialogue, April 12, 2017, https://www.chinadialogue.net/article/show/single/en/9730-Latin-America-s-oil-dependent-states-struggling-to-repay-Chinese-debts.

11 R. Viswanathan, "Trump Triggers Greater Latin American Interest in India," The Wire, March 9, 2017, https://thewire.in/external-affairs/donald-trump-triggers-greater-latin-american-interest-in-india.

12 Akio Hosono, "Asia-Pacific and Latin America: Dynamics of Regional Integration and International Cooperation," UN ECLAC International Trade

Series no. 132, 2017, https://repositorio.cepal.org/bitstream/handle/11362/41813
/1/S1700439_en.pdf.

13 Antoni Estevadeordal, "How Trade, Investment, and Cooperation Between
Japan and Latin America and the Caribbean Can Inspire Our Future Trade
Relationship with Africa," Brookings Institution, Dec. 22, 2016, https://www
.brookings.edu/blog/up-front/2016/12/22/how-trade-investment-and-cooperation
-between-japan-and-latin-america-and-the-caribbean-can-inspire-our-future
-trade-relationship-with-asia/.

9. Asia's Technocratic Future

1 "Dangerous World 2017," IPSOS, June 14, 2017, https://www.ipsos.com/en/
dangerous-world-2017.

2 Justin McCarthy, "In U.S., 65% Dissatisfied with How Gov't System Works,"
Gallup, Jan. 22, 2014, https://news.gallup.com/poll/166985/dissatisfied-gov-
system-works.aspx.

3 Martin Gilens and Benjamin I. Page, "Testing Theories of American Politics:
Elites, Interest Groups, and Average Citizens," *Perspectives on Politics* 12, no. 3,
(2014): 564–81.

4 John Helliwell, Richard Layard, and Jeffrey Sachs, eds., *World Happiness Report
2017*, Sustainable Development Solutions Network, 2017, https://s3.amazonaws.com
/happiness-report/2017/HR17.pdf; Facundo Alvaredo, Lucas Chancel, Thomas
Piketty, et al., eds., *World Inequality Report* (Cambridge, MA: Belknap Press, 2018).

5 James Henry, a former chief economist at McKinsey & Co., has written that US
criminal justice for white-collar crimes is nothing but a "system of organized
impunity" in which the top twenty Western banks and the dozens of accounting
and consulting firms colluding with them have perpetrated hundreds of large-
scale financial crimes leading to $300 billion in fines between 1998 and 2017 but
without a single firm losing its license to operate or a single senior official being
imprisoned. On the contrary, perpetrators become regulators in the revolving door
of the United States' "bankster" system. See James S. Henry, "The Economics of
the Global 'Bankster' Crime Wave," *The American Interest*, Oct. 25, 2017, https://www
.the-american-interest.com/2017/10/25/economics-global-bankster-crime-wave/.

6 Roberto Stefan Foa and Yascha Mounk, "The Signs of Deconsolidation," *Journal
of Democracy* 28, no. 1 (2017): 5–16.

7 Woodrow Wilson, "The Study of Administration," *Political Science Quarterly* 2, no.
2 (1887).

8 I began making this argument well before moving to Singapore in 2012. For
example, one chapter of my book *The Second World* (2008) is titled "Singapore:
Asia's First-World Inspiration."

9   Peter Ho, "The Challenge of Governance in a Complex World," IPS-Nathan
    Lecture Series, Singapore, May 17, 2017.

10 Philip Tetlock, *Expert Political Judgment* (Princeton, NJ: Princeton University
    Press, 2017).

11 Chua Beng Huat, *Liberalism Disavowed: Communitarianism and State Capitalism in
    Singapore* (National University of Singapore Press, 2017).

12 Cheng Li and Lucy Xu, "The Rise of State-Owned Enterprise Executives in
    China's Provincial Leadership," Brookings Institution, Feb. 22, 2017, https://
    www.brookings.edu/opinions/the-rise-of-state-owned-enterprise-executives
    -in-chinas-provincial-leadership/; Cheng Li and Lucy Xu, "Chinese Think
    Tanks: A New 'Revolving Door' for Elite Recruitment," Brookings Institution,
    Feb. 10, 2017, https://www.brookings.edu/opinions/chinese-think-tanks-a
    -new-revolving-door-for-elite-recruitment/; David J. Bulman, "Governing
    for Growth and the Resilience of the Chinese Communist Party," Harvard
    Kennedy School Ash Center for Democratic Governance and Innovation,
    April 2016, http://ash.harvard.edu/files/ash/files/261226_ash_bulman_web.
    pdf?m=1461352909.

13 Jessica Teets, "Let Many Civil Societies Bloom: The Rise of Consultative
    Authoritarianism in China," *China Quarterly*, March 2013.

14 Sebastian Heilmann and Matthias Stepan, eds., *China's Core Executive: Leadership
    Styles, Structures and Processes Under Xi Jinping*, Mercator Institute for China
    Studies, June 2016, https://www.merics.org/sites/default/files/2018-01/MPOC
    _ChinasCoreExecutive.pdf.

15 Eric X. Li, "Why Xi's Lifting of Term Limits is a Good Thing," *Washington Post*,
    April 2, 2018, https://www.washingtonpost.com/news/theworldpost/wp/2018/04
    /02/xi-term-limits/?utm_term=.8b093d3d5c96.

16 Daniel Bell, *The China Model: Political Meritocracy and the Limits of Democracy*
    (Princeton University Press, 2015).

17 According to the World Bank's Worldwide Governance Indicators (WGI),
    most Asian countries made steady improvements in measures of state capacity
    between 2010 and 2016, with the most improvement reported in China,
    Indonesia, Thailand, Saudi Arabia, Vietnam, Iran, Kazakhstan, and the UAE.
    The worst backsliding was seen in Turkey and Malaysia.

18 Edmund Malesky, "Sincere Preference by Default: An Alternative Theory of
    Public Support for Party Labels in Single-Party Regimes," Presentation at Yale-
    NUS College, Singapore, November 22, 2017.

19 Tonia E. Ries, David M. Bersoff, et al., *2018 Edelman Trust Barometer*, Edelman,
    2018, p. 6.

20 Tatyana Stanovaya, "Rotating the Elite: The Kremlin's New Personnel Policy,"

Carnegie Moscow Center, Jan. 30, 2018, http://carnegie.ru/2018/01/30/rotating
-elite-kremlin-s-new-personnel-policy-pub-75379.

21 Neil Buckley, "Once-Repressive Uzbekistan Begins a Post-Karimov Opening,"
Financial Times, Feb. 12, 2018, https://www.ft.com/content/6c37419c-0cbf-11e8-
8eb7-42f857ea9f09.

22 US Department of State, *Trafficking in Persons Report, June 2017*, https://www.state
.gov/documents/organization/271339.pdf.

23 Danny Quah, "When Open Societies Fail," *Global Policy Journal*, Nov. 7, 2017,
https://www.globalpolicyjournal.com/blog/07/11/2017/when-open-societies-fail.

10. Asia Goes Global: The Fusion of Civilizations

1 Hyuk-Rae Kim and Ingyu Oh, "Migration and Multicultural Contention in East
Asia," *Journal of Ethnic and Migration Studies* 37, no. 10 (2011): 1563–81.

2 In 2017, the U.S.-China Economic and Security Review Commission
recommended that Chinese journalists be reclassified as foreign agents and
required to register as such.

3 Jonathan McClory, "The Soft Power 30: Global Ranking of Soft Power,"
Portland Communications and USC Center on Public Diplomacy, 2017, https://
softpower30.com/wp-content/uploads/2017/07/The-Soft-Power-30-Report-2017
-Web-1.pdf.

4 Kai-Ping Huang and Bridget Welsh, "Trends in Soft Power in East Asia:
Distance, Diversity and Drivers," *Global Asia* 12, no. 1 (2017): 112–17.

5 Indians also make up 22 percent of Kuwait's population, 20 percent of Oman's
and Bahrain's populations, and 16 percent of Qatar's population.

6 Jung-Mee Hwang, "Local Citizenship and Policy Agenda for 'Foreign Residents'
in East Asia," in *Multicultural Challenges and Sustainable Democracy in Europe and
East Asia*, ed. Nam-Kook Kim (New York: Palgrave Macmillan, 2014), 129–52.

7 Katharine H. S. Moon, "South Korea's Demographic Changes and Their
Potential Impact," East Asia Policy Paper no. 6, Brookings Institution, October
2015, https://www.brookings.edu/wp-content/uploads/2016/06/South-Koreas
-demographic-changes-and-their-political-impact.pdf.

8 It should be noted, however, that many Chinese women marrying Korean men
are ethnically Korean, known as the Chosonjok/Chaoxianzu (Korean tribe).
What began as a government-led strategy in 1992 to import Chosonjok women
from China has expanded rapidly into moneymaking "marriage tours" by
licensed matchmakers and unlicensed traveling marriage brokers.

9 Mark J. Hudson and Mami Aoyama, "Views of Japanese Ethnic Identity
Amongst Undergraduates in Hokkaido," *The Asia-Pacific Journal* 4, no. 5 (2006).

10 Heidi Østbø Haugen, "Destination China: The Country Adjusts to Its New

Migration Reality," Migration Policy Institute, March 4, 2015, https://www
.migrationpolicy.org/article/destination-china-country-adjusts-its-new-migration
-reality.

11 Arabs report the highest levels of racist sentiment in the world as expressed by
people's responses to questions such as whether they would accept as a neighbor
someone from another religious or ethnic group. See Roberto Foa, "Creating
an Inclusive Society: Evidence from Social Indicators and Trends," presention
at the UN Department of Economic and Social Affairs Expert Group Meeting,
2015.

12 UN World Tourism Organization, *UNWTO World Tourism Barometer*, vol. 15,
March 2017, http://cf.cdn.unwto.org/sites/all/files/pdf/unwto_barom17_02_mar
excerpt.pdf.

13 Hindi-language Bollywood films make up less than half of India's total output
of 2,000 films per year. India's highest-grossing film of all time comes from its
Telugu-language productions ("Tollywood"), *Baahubali* (parts I and II).

14 R. Viswanathan, "India and Latin America: A New Perception and a New
Partnership," Elcano Royal Institute, July 22, 2014, https://www.files.ethz.ch/isn
/182336/ARI37-2014-Viswanathan-India-Latin-America-new-perception-new
-partnership.pdf.

15 Notably, Western periodicals devoted to "Asia" have historically covered the
full geographic spectrum of the region, not just East Asia. Most prominently,
the British *Journal of the Royal Asiatic Society* has been publishing articles on the
literature and arts of cultures from Arabia to Southeast Asia since 1834. The
Royal Netherlands Institute of Southeast Asian and Caribbean Studies, part
of the University of Leiden, has since 1851 been assembling anthropological
materials on Indonesia especially and continues to be an important stop
for regional researchers. The first US publication covering the wider Asian
geography was titled *Asia*, the journal of the American Asiatic Association.
From the 1920s to the 1940s, it provided glossy reportage on and coverage of
European imperial machinations, as well as US entreaties to the region as the
United States' presence across the Pacific grew stronger after the defeat of Spain
in the Philippines in 1898.

Epilogue: Asia's Global Future

1 Henry Kissinger, *World Order* (New York: Penguin Press, 2014).

Bibliography

Abu-Lughod, Janet L. *Before European Hegemony: The World System, A.D. 1250–1350.* London: Oxford University Press, 1989.

Acharya, Amitav. "Asia Is Not One." *Journal of Asian Studies* 69, no. 4 (2010): 1001–13.

——. *The End of American World Order.* London: Polity Press, 2014.

——, and Barry Buzan. *Non-Western International Relations Theory: Perspectives on and Beyond Asia.* City: Routledge, 2010.

Alden, Edward. *Failure to Adjust: How Americans Got Left Behind in the Global Economy.* New York: Rowan and Littlefield, 2016.

Alexievich, Svetlana. *Secondhand Time: The Last of the Soviets.* New York: Random House, 2017.

Allen, Barry. *Vanishing into Things: Knowledge in Chinese Tradition.* Cambridge, MA: Harvard University Press, 2015.

Allison, Graham, Robert D. Blackwill, Henry Kissinger, and Ali Wyne. *Lee Kuan Yew: The Grand Master's Insights on China, the United States, and the World.* Cambridge, MA: MIT Press, 2012.

Amrith, Sunil. *Crossing the Bay of Bengal: The Furies of Nature and the Fortunes of Migrants.* Cambridge, MA: Harvard University Press, 2013.

——. *Migration and Diaspora in Modern Asia.* Cambridge, UK: Cambridge University Press, 2011.

Amyx, Jennifer, and Peter Drysdale, eds. *Japanese Governance: Beyond Japan Inc.* New York: Routledge, 2003.

Asian Development Bank. *Asian Development Outlook 2014: Fiscal Policy for Inclusive Growth.* Manila: Asian Development Bank, 2014.

——. *Asian Development Outlook 2016: Asia's Potential Growth.* Manila: Asian Development Bank, 2016.

——. *Asian Economic Integration Report 2016: What Drives Foreign Direct Investment in Asia and the Pacific?* Manila: Asian Development Bank, 2016.

—— and Asian Development Bank Institute. *Infrastructure for a Seamless Asia*. Manila: Asian Development Bank Institute, 2009.

Auslin, Michael. *The End of the Asian Century: War, Stagnation, and Risks to the World's Most Dynamic Region*. New Haven, CT: Yale University Press, 2017.

Ayoob, Mohammed. *Will the Middle East Implode?* London: Polity, 2014.

Ayres, Alyssa. *Our Time Has Come: How India Is Making its Place in the World*. New York: Oxford University Press, 2017.

Bagchi, Prabodh Chandra. *India and China: Interactions Through Buddhism and Diplomacy–A Collection of Essays by Professor Prabodh Chandra Bagchi*. Compiled by Bangwei Wang and Tansen Sen. Delhi: Anthem Press India, 2012.

Balazs, Étienne. *Chinese Civilization and Bureaucracy: Variations on a Theme*. Trans. H. M. Wright. New Haven, CT: Yale University Press, 1964.

Balwin, Richard E. *The Great Convergence: Information Technology and the New Globalization*. Cambridge, MA: Harvard University Press, 2016.

Banomyong, Ruth. "Supply Chain Dynamics in Asia," ADBI Working Paper no. 184, Asian Development Bank Institute, January 2010. https://www.adb.org/sites /default/files/publication/156039/adbi-wp184.pdf.

Basu, Prasenjit K. *Asia Reborn: A Continent Rises from the Ravages of Colonialism and War to a New Dynamism*. New Delhi: Aleph, 2017.

Bayly, Christopher. *The Birth of the Modern World, 1789–1914*. London: Blackwell, 2004.

Beckwith, Christopher I. *Empires of the Silk Road: A History of Central Eurasia from the Bronze Age to the Present*. Princeton, NJ: Princeton University Press, 2011.

Bell, Daniel. *The China Model: Political Meritocracy and the Limits of Democracy*. Princeton, NJ: Princeton University Press, 2015.

Benedict, Ruth. *The Chrysanthemum and the Sword*. New York: Houghton, Mifflin, 1946.

Bennett, Bruce W. "Preparing North Korean Elites for Unification." Santa Monica, CA: RAND Corporation, 2017.

Berger, Mark. *The Battle for Asia: From Decolonization to Globalization*. New York: Routledge, 2004.

Bestor, Theodore C. *Tsukiji: The Fish Market at the Center of the World*. Berkeley: University of California Press, 2004.

Bhabha, Homi K. *The Location of Culture*. New York: Routledge, 1994.

Biran, Michael, and Amitai Reuvan. *Nomads as Agents of Cultural Change: The Mongols and Their Eurasian Predecessors*. Manoa: University of Hawai'i Press, 2014.

Bose, Sugata. *A Hundred Horizons: The Indian Ocean in the Age of Global Empire*. Cambridge, MA: Harvard University Press, 2006.

Bourdaghs, Michael. *Sayonara Amerika, Sayonara Nippon: A Geopolitical Prehistory of J-Pop*. New York: Columbia University Press, 2012.

Brautigam, Deborah. *Will Africa Feed China?* New York: Oxford University Press, 2015.

Brierley, Saroo. *A Long Way Home: A Memoir.* New York: Penguin Books, 2014.

Bulman, David J. "Governing for Growth and the Resilience of the Chinese Communist Party." Harvard Kennedy School Ash Center for Democratic Governance and Innovation, April 2016. http://ash.harvard.edu/files/ash/files/261226_ash _bulman_web.pdf?m=1461352909.

Bunton, Martin, and William L. Cleveland. *A History of the Modern Middle East.* New York: Avalon Publishing, 2009.

Buzan, Barry. *Regions and Powers: The Structure of International Security.* Cambridge, UK: Cambridge University Press, 2003.

———, and Richard Little. *International Systems in World History: Remaking the Study of International Relations.* London: Oxford University Press, 2000.

Chakravorty, Sanjoy, Devesh Kapur, and Nirvikar Singh. *The Other One Percent: Indians in America.* New York: Oxford University Press, 2017.

Chaudhuri, Kirti N. *Asia Before Europe: Economy and Civilisation of the Indian Ocean from the Rise of Islam to 1750.* Cambridge, UK: Cambridge University Press, 1990.

Chellaney, Brahma. *Water, Peace, and War: Confronting the Global Water Crisis.* New York: Rowman & Littlefield, 2013.

Chong, Ja Ian. "Diverging Paths? Singapore-China Relations and the East Asian Maritime Domain." Maritime Awareness Project. April 26, 2017. http://maritime awarenessproject.org/wp-content/uploads/2017/04/analysis_chong_04262017-1 .pdf.

Chou, Rosalind, and Joe Feagin. *Myth of the Model Minority: Asian Americans Facing Racism.* New York: Paradigm Publishers, 2008.

Chua, Beng Huat. *Liberalism Disavowed: Communitarianism and State Capitalism in Singapore.* Singapore: National University of Singapore Press, 2017.

Clarke, Michael E. *Xinjiang and China's Rise in Central Asia—A History.* City: Routledge, 2011.

Coedès, George. Walter F. Vella, ed., Susan Brown Cowing, trans. *The Indianized States of Southeast Asia.* Manoa: University of Hawai'i Press, 1968.

Cohen, Warren I. *East Asia at the Center.* New York: Columbia University Press, 2000.

Cole, Bernard. *China's Quest for Great Power: Ships, Oil and Foreign Policy.* Annapolis: Naval Institute Press, 2016.

Coll, Steve. *Directorate S: The CIA and America's Secret Wars in Afghanistan and Pakistan.* New York: Penguin, 2018.

Conrad, Sebastian. *What Is Global History?* Princeton, NJ: Princeton University Press, 2016.

Cotterell, Arthur. *A History of Southeast Asia.* London: Marshall Cavendish, 2014.

Cunningham, Edward. "China's Most Generous: Understanding China's Philanthropic Landscape." Harvard Kennedy School Ash Center for Democratic Governance and Innovation, 2015. http://ash.harvard.edu/files/ash/files/china _philanthropy_report_final.pdf?m=1453851156.

Daly, Jonathan. *The Rise of Western Power: A Comparative History of Western Civilization.* London: Bloomsbury, 2013.

Desvaux, Georges, Jonathan Woetzel, Tasuku Kuwabara, Michael Chui, et al. "How a Private-Sector Transformation Could Revive Japan." McKinsey Global Institute, March 2015. https://www.mckinsey.com/featured-insights/employment -and-growth/how-a-private-sector-transformation-could-revive-japan.

Di Cosmo, Nicola. *Ancient China and Its Enemies: The Rise of Nomadic Power in East Asian History.* Cambridge, UK: Cambridge University Press, 2002.

Dikotter, Frank. *Mao's Great Famine: The History of China's Most Devastating Catastrophe, 1958–62.* London: Bloomsbury Publishing, 2010.

Dollar, David. "China as a Global Investor." Brookings Institution Asia Working Group Paper 4, May 2016.

Donald S. Lopez, Jr. *Living in the Chinese Cosmos: Understanding Religion in Late-Imperial China (1644–1911).* Princeton, NJ: Princeton University Press, 1996.

Dower, John. *Embracing Defeat: Japan in the Wake of World War II.* New York: W. W. Norton, 1999.

Duara, Prasenjit. *The Crisis of Global Modernity: Asian Traditions and a Sustainable Future.* Cambridge, UK: Cambridge University Press, 2015.

Dychtwald, Zak. *Young China: How the Restless Generation Will Change Their Country and the World.* New York: St. Martin's Press, 2018.

Ebinger, Charles K. "India's Energy and Climate Policy: Can India Meet the Challenge of Industrialization and Climate Change?" Brookings Institution Energy Security and Climate Initiative Policy Brief 16-01, June 2016. https://www.brook ings.edu/wp-content/uploads/2016/07/india_energy_climate_policy_ebinger.pdf.

Economy, Elizabeth, and Michael Levi. *By All Means Necessary: How China's Resource Quest Is Changing the World.* New York: Oxford University Press, 2014.

Ehteshami, Anoushiravan. *Dynamics of Change in the Persian Gulf: Political Economy, War and Revolution.* New York: Routledge, 2013.

Eichengreen, Barry, and Masahiro Kawai, eds. *Renminbi Internationalization: Achievements, Prospects, and Challenges.* Washington, DC: Brookings Institution Press, 2015.

Ellis, Peter, and Mark Roberts. *Leverage Urbanization in South Asia: Managing Spatial Transformation for Prosperity and Livability.* Washington, DC: World Bank, 2015.

Emmerson, Donald K. "ASEAN Between China and America: Is It Time to Try Horsing the Cow?" *TRaNS: Trans-Regional and National Studies of Southeast Asia 5,* no. 1 (2017): 1–23.

Ferchen, Matt. "China, Economic Development, and Global Security: Bridging the Gaps." Carnegie-Tsinghua Center for Global Policy, December 2016. https://carnegie endowment.org/files/CP_289_Ferchen_China_Final.pdf.

Fingar, Thomas. *The New Great Game: China and South and Central Asia in the Era of Reform*. Stanford, CA: Stanford University Press, 2016.

Flanagan, Owen. *The Geography of Morals: Varieties of Moral Possibility*. New York: Oxford University Press, 2017.

Frank, Andre Gunder, and Barry Hills, eds. *The World System: Five Hundred Years or Five Thousand?* New York Routledge, 1994.

Frankopan, Peter. *The Silk Roads: A New History of the World*. London: Bloomsbury, 2015.

Freier, Nathan P. "At Our Own Peril: DoD Risk Assessment in a Post-Primacy World." Strategic Studies Institute and Army War College Press, June 2017. https://ssi.armywarcollege.edu/pdffiles/PUB1358.pdf.

French, Howard. *Everything Under the Heavens: How the Past Helps Shape China's Push for Global Power*. New York: Victoria Scribe Publications, 2017.

Friedrich, Johannes, Mengpin Ge, and Thomas Damassa. "Infographic: What Do Your Country's Emissions Look Like?" World Resources Institute, June 23, 2015. http://www.wri.org/blog/2015/06/infographic-what-do-your-countrys-emissions -look.

Frost, Ellen L. *Asia's New Regionalism*. Boulder: Lynne Rienner Publishers, 2008.

Fujitani, Takashi. *Race for Empire: Koreans as Japanese and Japanese as Americans During World War II*. Berkeley: University of California Press, 2013.

Fukuyama, Francis. *Political Order and Political Decay: From the Industrial Revolution to the Globalization of Democracy*. New York: Farrar, Straus and Giroux, 2014.

Fuller, Graham. *World Without Islam*. San Francisco: Back Bay, 2012.

Gabuev, Alexander. "China and Russia: Friends with Strategic Benefits." The Lowy Institute, April 7, 2017. https://www.lowyinstitute.org/the-interpreter/china -and-russia-friends-strategic-benefits.

Gerges, Fawaz. *Journey of the Jihadist: Inside Muslim Militancy*. New York: Houghton Mifflin Harcourt, 2006.

Golden, Peter B. *Central Asia in World History*. London: Oxford University Press, 2011.

Goody, Jack. "Eurasia and East-West Boundaries," *Diogenes* 50, no. 4 (2003): 115–18.

——. *The Eurasian Miracle*. New York Wiley, 2013.

Gordon, Andrew. *A Modern History of Japan: From Tokugawa Times to the Present*. New York: Oxford University Press, 2003.

Graham, Allison. *Destined For War: Can America and China Escape Thucydides's Trap?* New York: Houghton Mifflin Harcourt, 2017.

Green, Michael. *By More than Providence: Grand Strategy and American Power in the Asia Pacific Since 1783*. New York: Columbia University Press, 2017.

Gupta, Anil K., Girija Pande, and Haiyan Wang. *The Silk Road Rediscovered: How Indian and Chinese Companies are Becoming Globally Stronger by Winning in Each Other's Markets.* London: Jossey-Bass, 2014.

Hamid, Shadi, and William McCants, eds. *Rethinking Political Islam.* New York: Oxford University Press, 2017.

Hansen, Valerie. *The Silk Road: A New History.* New York: Oxford University Press, 2012.

Hardy, Alfredo Toro. *Understanding Latin America: A Decoding Guide.* London: World Scientific, 2017.

He, Baogang. *Contested Ideas of Regionalism in Asia.* New York: Routledge, 2017.

Hellenthal, Garrett, George B. J. Busby, Gavin Band, James F. Wilson, et al. "A Genetic Atlas of Human Admixture History." *Science* 343, no. 6172 (2014): 747–51.

Herberg-Rothe, Andreas, and Key-young Son. *Order Wars and Floating Balance: How the Rising Powers Are Reshaping Our Worldviews in the Twenty-first Century.* New York: Routledge, 2017.

Hobsbawm, Eric J. *The Age of Empire, 1875–1914.* New York: Pantheon, 1987.

Hodgson, Marshall G. S. *Islam: Conscience and History in a World Civilization.* Chicago: University of Chicago Press, 1974.

——. *Rethinking World History: Essays on Europe, Islam and World History.* Cambridge, UK: Cambridge University Press, 1993.

Holcombe, Charles. *The Genesis of East Asia, 221 B.C.–A.D. 907.* Ann Arbor: Association for Asian Studies and University of Hawai'i Press, 2001.

——. *A History of East Asia: From the Origins of Civilization to the Twenty-first Century.* Cambridge, UK: Cambridge University Press, 2010.

Hong, Euny. *The Birth of Korean Cool: How One Nation Is Conquering the World Through Pop Culture.* London: Picador, 2014.

Hoodbhoy, Pervez. "Saudizing Pakistan: How Pakistan Is Changing and What This Means for South Asia and the World" In *Routledge Handbook of Contemporary Pakistan*, ed. Aparna Pande. Abingdon, UK: Routledge, 2018.

Hopkins, Antony G., ed. *Globalization in Word History.* London: Palgrave Macmillan, 2006.

Hopkirk, Peter. *The Great Game: The Struggle for Empire in Central Asia.* London: Kodansha International, 1992.

Horsley, Jamie P. "Will Engaging China Promise Good Governance?" Brookings Institution John L. Thornton China Center Strategy Paper no. 2, Jan. 2017. https://www.brookings.edu/wp-content/uploads/2017/01/fp_201701_will_engaging_china_promote_good_governance2.pdf.

Huang, Jing, and Alexander Korolev, eds. *International Cooperation in the Development of Russia's Far East and Siberia.* New York: Palgrave Macmillan, 2015.

——, eds. *The Political Economy of Pacific Russia: Regional Developments in East Asia.* New York: Palgrave Macmillan, 2017.

Hu-DeHart, Evelyn, and Kathleen López. "Asian Diasporas in Latin America and the Caribbean: An Historical Overview." *Afro-Hispanic Review* 27, no. 1 (2008): 9–21.

Huebner, Stefan. *Pan-Asian Sports and the Emergence of Modern Asia, 1913–74.* Singapore: National University of Singapore Press, 2016.

Huntington, Samuel P. *The Clash of Civilizations and the Remaking of World Order.* New York: Simon & Schuster, 1996.

Ikeda, Satoshi. "The History of the Capitalist World-System vs. the History of East-Southeast Asia." *Review* 19, no. 1 (1996): 49–77.

Ito, Takatoshi, Hugh Patrick, and David E. Weinstein, eds. *Reviving Japan's Economy: Problems and Prescriptions.* Cambridge, MA: MIT Press, 2005.

Jansen, Marius B. *The Making of Modern Japan.* Cambridge, MA: Harvard University Press, 2000.

Jaros, Kyle A. "Urban Champions or Rich Peripheries? China's Spatial Development Dilemmas." Harvard Kennedy School Ash Center for Democratic Governance and Innovation, April 2016. http://ash.harvard.edu/files/ash/files/261226_ash _jaros_web.pdf?m=1461696669.

Johnston, Alastair I. *Cultural Realism: Strategic Culture and Grand Strategy in Chinese History.* Princeton, NJ: Princeton University Press, 1995.

Joseph, Mathew C. "China-South Asia Strategic Engagements–2: Bhutan-China Relations." National University of Singapore Institute of South Asian Studies Working Paper no. 157, August 23, 2012. https://www.files.ethz.ch/isn/152366 /ISAS_Working_Paper_157_-_Bhutan_-_China_23082012174042.pdf.

Kang, David C. *East Asia Before the West: Five Centuries of Trade and Tribute.* New York: Columbia University Press, 2012.

——. "Hierarchy and Legitimacy and International Systems: The Tribute System in Early Modern Asia," *Security Studies* 4, no. 19 (2010): 591–622.

——. "Why Was There No Religious War in Premodern East Asia?" *European Journal of International Relations* 20, no. 4 (2014): 965–86.

Kaplan, Robert D. *Marco Polo's World: War, Strategy, and American Interests in the 21st Century.* New York: Random House, 2018.

——. *Monsoon: The Indian Ocean and the Future of American Power.* New York: Random House, 2010.

Katzenstein, Peter J., ed. *Sinicization and the Rise of China: Civilizational Processes Beyond East and West.* City: Routledge, 2013.

——, and Takashi Shiraishi, eds. *Beyond Japan: The Dynamics of East Asian Regionalism.* New York: Cornell University Press, 2006.

Kavalski, Emilian. *The Guanxi of Relational International Theory*. New York: Routledge, 2018.

Keen, Andrew. *How to Fix the Future*. New York: Atlantic Monthly Press, 2018.

Kikuchi, Tomoo, and Wang Zi. "The Missing Link: Financial Development and Technology in Southeast Asia." Brink Asia, Feb. 23, 2017. http://www.brinknews .com/asia/the-missing-link-financial-development-and-technology-in-south-east-asia/.

King, Stephen D. *Grave New World: The End of Globalization, the Return of History*. New Haven, CT: Yale University Press, 2017.

Kissinger, Henry. *On China*. New York: Penguin, 2011.

———. *World Order*. New York: Penguin, 2014.

Koo, Richard C. *The Other Half of Macroeconomics and the Fate of Globalization*. London: John Wiley & Sons, 2018.

Korolev, Alexander. "The Strategic Alignment Between Russia and China: Myths and Reality." Lee Kuan Yew School of Public Policy Research Paper no. 15–19, April 15, 2015.

———, and Jing Huang, eds. *International Cooperation in the Development of Russia's Far East and Siberia*. New York: Springer, 2015.

Kroeber, Arthur. *China's Economy: What Everyone Needs to Know*. New York: Oxford University Press, 2016.

Kulke, Hermann. "The Naval Expeditions of the Cholas in the Context of Asian History." In *Nagapattinam to Suvarnadwipa: Reflections on the Chola Naval Expeditions to Southeast Asia*, ed. Hermann Kulke, K. Kesavapany, and Vijay Sakhuja. Singapore: ISEAS-Yusof Ishak Institute, 2009.

Kumar, Niraj. *Asia in Post-Western Age*. New Delhi: KW Publishers, 2014.

Kushida, Kenji. "Japan's Startup Ecosystem: From Brave New World to Part of Syncretic 'New Japan.'" *Asian Research Policy* 7, no. 1 (2016): 66–77.

Kynge, James. *China Shakes the World: A Titan's Breakneck Rise and Troubled Future*. New York: Houghton Mifflin, 2006.

Lach, Donald F. *Asia in the Making of Europe*. Vol. 1: *The Century of Discovery*. Chicago: University of Chicago Press, 1965.

Lahoud, Nelly, and Anthony H. Johns, eds. *Islam in World Politics*. New York: Routledge, 2005.

Lai, Walton Look, and Tan Chee-Beng, eds. *The Chinese in Latin America and the Caribbean*. New York: Brill, 2010.

Lal, Vinay. *Empire and Knowledge: Culture and Plurality in the Global Economy*. London: Pluto Press, 2002.

Landes, David S. *The Wealth and Poverty of Nations: Why Some Are So Rich and Some So Poor*. New York W. W. Norton, 1998.

——. "Why Europe and the West? Why Not China?" *Journal of Economic Perspectives* 20, no. 2 (2006): 3–22.

Lankov, Andrei. *The Real North Korea: Life and Politics in the Failed Stalinist Utopia.* London: Oxford University Press, 2013.

Lapidus, Ira. *A History of Islamic Societies.* Cambridge, UK: Cambridge University Press, 1988.

Levitsky, Steven. *How Democracies Die.* New York: Crown, 2018.

Lewis, Martin M., and Karen Wigen. *The Myth of Continents: A Critique of Metageography.* Berkeley: University of California Press, 1997.

Li, Cheng. *Chinese Politics in the Xi Jinping Era: Reassessing Collective Leadership.* Washington, DC: Brookings Institution Press, 2016.

——, and Lucy Xu. "Chinese Think Tanks: A New 'Revolving Door' for Elite Recruitment." Brookings Institution, Feb. 10, 2017. https://www.brookings.edu /opinions/chinese-think-tanks-a-new-revolving-door-for-elite-recruitment/.

Lieberthal, Kenneth. *Governing China: From Revolution Through Reform.* New York: W. W. Norton, 1995.

Lipman, Jonathan. *Familiar Strangers: A History of Muslims in Northwest China.* Seattle: University of Washington Press, 1998.

Liu, John Chung-En. "Assembling China's Carbon Markets: The Carbons, the Business, and the Marginalised." Harvard Kennedy School Ash Center for Democratic Governance and Innovation, June 2016. http://ash.harvard.edu/files/ash /files/assembling_chinas_carbon_markets.pdf?m=1466106853.

Lockard, Craig. *Societies, Networks, and Transitions: A Global History.* New York: Houghton Mifflin , 2010.

Ma, Debin. "The Great Silk Exchange: How the World was Connected and Developed." In *Pacific Centuries: Pacific and Pacific Rim History Since the Sixteenth Century*, ed. Dennis O. Flynn, Lionel Frost, and A.J.H. Latham. London: Routledge, 1999, 38–69.

Ma, Laurence J. C., and Carolyn Cartier, eds. *The Chinese Diaspora: Space, Place, Mobility, and Identity.* New York: Rowman & Littlefield, 2003.

Macaes, Bruno. *The Dawn of Eurasia: On the Trail of the New World Order.* London: Allen Lane, 2018.

MacFaquhar, Roderick. *The Politics of China: Sixty Years of the People's Republic of China.* Cambridge, UK: Cambridge University Press, 2011.

Maddison, Angus. *Contours of the World Economy, 1–2030 AD: Essays in Macro-Economic History.* New York: Oxford University Press, 2007.

Mahbubani, Kishore. *The Great Convergence: Asia, the West, and the Logic of One World.* New York: Public Affairs, 2013.

——. *The New Asian Hemisphere: The Irresistible Shift of Global Power to the East.* New York: Public Affairs, 2008.

——, and Jeffery Sng. *The ASEAN Miracle: A Catalyst for Peace.* Singapore: National University of Singapore Press, 2017.

Manuel, Anja. *This Brave New World: India, China, and the United States.* New York: Simon & Schuster, 2017.

Mao, Joyce. *Asia First: China and the Making of Modern American Conservatism.* Chicago: University of Chicago Press, 2015.

Masterson, Daniel M., and Sayaka Funada-Classen. *The Japanese in Latin America.* Urbana: University of Illinois Press, 2004.

McGregor, Richard. *Asia's Reckoning: China, Japan, and the Fate of U.S. Power in the Pacific Century.* New York: Viking, 2017.

McNeill, William Hardy. *The Rise of the West: A History of the Human Community.* Chicago: University of Chicago Press, 1964.

Miller, James, ed. *Chinese Religions in Contemporary Societies.* Santa Barbara, CA: ABC-CLIO Press, 2006.

Miller, Tom. *China's Asian Dream: Empire Building Along the New Silk Road.* London: Zed Books, 2017.

Millward, James A. *Eurasian Crossroads: A History of Xinjiang.* New York: Columbia University Press, 2007.

Mishra, Pankaj. *From the Ruins of Empire: The Intellectuals Who Remade Asia.* New York: Farrar, Staus and Giroux, 2012.

Mittal, Sachin, and James Lloyd. "The Rise of FinTech in China: Redefining Financial Services." DBS and Ernst & Young, November 2016. https://www.ey.com /Publication/vwLUAssets/ey-the-rise-of-fintech-in-china/$FILE/ey-the-rise-of-fin tech-in-china.pdf.

Miyoshi, Masao, and H. D. Harootunian, eds. *Japan in the World.* Chapel Hill, NC: Duke University Press, 1993.

——, eds. *Learning Places: The Afterlives of Area Studies.* Chapel Hill, NC: Duke University Press, 2002.

——, eds. *Off Center: Power and Culture Relations Between Japan and the United States.* Chapel Hill, NC: Duke University Press, 1991.

——, eds. *Postmodernism and Japan.* Chapel Hill, NC: Duke University Press, 1989.

Morichi, Shigeru, and Surya Raj Acharya, eds. *Transport Development in Asian Megacities: A New Perspective.* New York: Springer, 2012.

Morris, Ian. *Why the West Rules—for Now: The Patterns of History, and What They Reveal About the Future.* New York: Profile, 2011.

Morris-Suzuki, Tessa. *Re-inventing Japan: Time, Space, Nation.* Armonk, NY: M. E. Sharpe, 1998.

Mounk, Yascha. *The People vs. Democracy: Why Our Freedom Is in Danger and How to Save It.* Cambridge, MA: Harvard University Press, 2018.

Nadella, Satya. *Hit Refresh: The Quest to Rediscover Microsoft's Soul and Imagine a Better Future for Everyone*. New York: HarperBusiness, 2017.

Nakane, Chie. *Japanese Society*. Berkeley: University of California Press, 1970.

National Geographic. "Asia: Human Geography." National Geographic, Jan. 4, 2012. https://www.nationalgeographic.org/encyclopedia/asia-human/.

National Geographic. "Asia: Physical Geography." National Geographic, Jan. 4, 2012. https://www.nationalgeographic.org/encyclopedia/asia/.

Needham, Joseph. *Science and Civilization in China*. Vol. 1. Cambridge, UK: Cambridge University Press, 1954.

Newland, Sara A. "Growing Apart? Challenges to High-Quality Local Governance and Public Service Provision on China's Ethnic Periphery." Harvard Kennedy School Ash Center for Democratic Governance and Innovation, July 2016. http://ash.harvard.edu/files/ash/files/growing_apart.pdf.

Nijman, Jan, Peter O. Muller, and Harm J. de Blij, eds. *Geography: Realms, Regions, and Concepts*. 17th ed. New York: Wiley, 2016.

Nisbett, Richard E. *The Geography of Thought: How Asians and Westerners Think Differently . . . And Why*. New York: Free Press, 2003.

Nussbaum, Felicity A., ed. *The Global Eighteenth Century*. Baltimore: Johns Hopkins University Press, 2003.

Ocampo, Anthony. *The Latinos of Asia: How Filipino Americans Break the Rules of Race*. Stanford, CA: Stanford University Press, 2016.

Orekhanov, Serafim. "Generation Youtube: How Millennials Are Shaping Russian Politics." Carnegie Moscow Centre, Apr. 2017.

Osnos, Evan. *Age of Ambition: Chasing Fortune, Truth, and Faith in the New China*. New York: Farrar, Straus and Giroux, 2014.

Pan, Zhongqi. "Guanxi, Weiqi and Chinese Strategic Thinking." *Chinese Political Science Review* 1, no. 2 (2016): 303–21.

Park, Cyn-Young Park. "Developing Local Currency Bond Markets in Asia," Asian Development Bank Economics Working Paper no. 495, August 2016. https://www.adb.org/sites/default/files/publication/190289/ewp-495.pdf.

Park, Jehoon, T. J. Pempel, and Gérard Roland, eds. *Political Economy of Northeast Asian Regionalism: Political Conflict and Economic Integration*. London: Edward Elgar, 2008.

Park, Yeonmi. *In Order to Live: A North Korean Girl's Journey to Freedom*. New York: Penguin, 2015.

Pei, Minxin. *China's Crony Capitalism: The Dynamics of Regime Decay*. Cambridge, MA: Harvard University Press, 2016.

——. *China's Trapped Transition: The Limits of Developmental Autocracy*. Cambridge, MA: Harvard University Press, 2006.

——. *From Reform to Revolution: The Demise of Communism in China and the Soviet Union.* Cambridge, MA: Harvard University Press, 1994.

Pempel, T. J. *The Economic-Security Nexus in Northeast Asia.* New York: Routledge, 2012.

——, ed. *Remapping East Asia: The Construction of a Region.* New York: Cornell University Press, 2004.

——, and Keiichi Tsunekawa, eds. *Two Crises, Different Outcomes: East Asia and Global Finance.* New York: Cornell University Press, 2015.

Plummer, Michael G., Peter J. Morgan, and Ganeshan Wignaraja, eds. *Connecting Asia: Infrastructure for Integrating South and Southeast Asia.* London: Edward Elgar Publishing, 2016.

Pollack, Jonathan D.. "Order at Risk: Japan, Korea and the Northeast Asian Paradox." Brookings Institution Asia Working Group Paper 5, September 2016. https://www.brookings.edu/wp-content/uploads/2016/09/fp_20160901_north east_asian_paradox_v2.pdf.

Pomeranz, Kenneth. *The Great Divergence: China, Europe, and the Making of the Modern World Economy.* Princeton, NJ: Princeton University Press, 2000.

Porter, Michael E., Jan W. Rivkin, Mihir A. Desai, and Manjari Raman. "Problems Unsolved and a Nation Divided: The State of U.S. Competitiveness 2016." Harvard Business School, September 2016. https://www.hbs.edu/competitiveness /Documents/problems-unsolved-and-a-nation-divided.pdf.

Rachman, Gideon. *Easternisation: War and Peace in the Asian Century.* London: Bodley Head, 2016.

Rein, Shaun. *The War for China's Wallet: Profiting from the New World Order.* Boston: Walter de Gruyter, 2017.

Roberts, Anthea. *Is International Law International?* New York: Oxford University Press, 2017.

Roberts, John Morris, and Odd Arne Westad. *The History of the World.* New York: Oxford University Press, 2013.

Robinson, Andrew. *India: A Short History.* London: Thames & Hudson, 2014.

Samuels, Richard J. *Securing Japan: Tokyo's Grand Strategy and the Future of East Asia.* New York: Cornell University Press, 2007.

Sanyal, Sanjeev. *The Ocean of Churn: How the Indian Ocean Shaped Human History.* New York: Penguin Random House, 2016.

Sato, Kazuo, ed. *The Transformation of the Japanese Economy.* Armonk, NY: M. E. Sharpe, 1999.

Schroder, Christopher. *Startup Rising: The Entrepreneurial Revolution Remaking the Middle East.* City: Palgrave Macmillan, 2013.

Schuman, Michael. *The Miracle: The Epic Story of Asia's Quest for Wealth.* New York: HarperBusiness, 2010.

Sen, Tansen. *India, China, and the World: A Connected History*. New York: Rowman & Littlefield, 2017.

——. "The Intricacies of Premodern Asian Connections." *The Journal of Asian Studies* 69, no. 4 (2010): 991–99.

Shambaugh, David. *China Goes Global: The Partial Power*. New York: Oxford University Press, 2013.

——. *China's Future*. Cambridge, UK: Polity Press, 2016.

——, and Michael Yahuda, eds. *International Relations of Asia*. New York: Rowman and Littlefield, 2008.

Sharma, Ashok. "Australia-India Relations: Trends and the Prospects for a Comprehensive Economic Relationship." ASARC Working Paper, February 2016. https://acde.crawford.anu.edu.au/sites/default/files/publication/acde_crawford_anu_edu_au/2016-09/asarc_wp_2016-02_sharma.pdf.

Shin, Gi-Wook, Michael H. Armacost, Takeo Hoshi, Karl Eikenberry, et al. "President Trump's Asia Inbox." Walter H. Shorenstein Asia-Pacific Research Center, Feb. 10, 2017. https://fsi-live.s3.us-west-1.amazonaws.com/s3fs-public/president_trumps_asia_inbox.pdf.

Simpfendorfer, Ben. *The New Silk Road: How a Rising Arab World Is Turning Away from the West and Rediscovering China*. New York: Palgrave Macmillan, 2011.

Singh, Daljit, Norshahril Saat, Malcolm Cook, and Tang Siew Mun. "Southeast Asia Outlook 2017." ISEAS Yusof Ishak Institute, January 2017. https://www.iseas.edu.sg/images/pdf/ISEAS_Perspective_2017_1.pdf.

Sioris, George A. "Buddhism in Asia: Tolerance and Syncretism." *The Tibet Journal* 13, no. 1 (1988): 20–29.

Smith, Patrick. *Somebody Else's Century: East and West in a Post-Western World*. London: Pantheon, 2010.

Sneider, Daniel C., Yul Sohn, and Yoshihide Soeya. "US-ROK-Japan Trilateralism: Building Bridges and Strengthening Cooperation." National Bureau of Asian Research Report no. 59, July 2016. http://www.nbr.org/publications/specialreport/pdf/sr59_trilateralism_july2016.pdf.

Spence, Jonathan. *The Chan's Great Continent: China in Western Minds*. New York: Penguin, 1999.

——. *The Search for Modern China*. New York: W. W. Norton, 1990.

Stanislaw, Joseph, and Daniel Yergin. *The Commanding Heights: The Battle for the World Economy*. New York: Free Press, 2008.

Steinfeld, Edward S. *Playing Our Game: Why China's Rise Doesn't Threaten the West*. Oxford: Oxford University Press, 2012.

Stockwin, Arthur, and Kweku Ampiah. *Rethinking Japan: The Politics of Contested Nationalism*. Lanham, MD: Lexington Books, 2017.

Studwell, Joe. *How Asia Works: Success and Failure in the World's Most Dynamic Region.* New York: Grove Press, 2014.

Su, Fei, and Lora Saalman. "China's Engagement of North Korea: Challenges and Opportunities for Europe." Stockholm International Peace Research Institute, February 2017. https://www.sipri.org/sites/default/files/Chinas-engagement-North-Korea.pdf.

Sun, Yun. "Rising Sino-Japanese Competition in Africa." Brookings Institution, August 31, 2016. https://www.brookings.edu/blog/africa-in-focus/2016/08/31/rising-sino-japanese-competition-in-africa/.

Sunstein, Cass R. *Can It Happen Here? Authoritarianism in America.* New York: HarperCollins, 2018.

Tan, Chee Beng, and Walton Look Lai, eds. *The Chinese in Latin America and the Caribbean.* Leiden, Netherlands: Brill, 2010.

Tanaka, Nobuo. "What Should China and India Do to Cooperate Globally in Energy Policies?" Lee Kuan Yew School of Public Policy Research Paper no. 14-02, March 31, 2014.

Teets, Jessica C. *Civil Society Under Authoritarianism: the China Model.* Cambridge, UK: Cambridge University Press, 2014.

Tellis, Ashely J., Alison Szalwinski, and Michael Wills, eds. *Strategic Asia 2016–17: Understanding Strategic Cultures in the Asia-Pacific.* Seattle: National Bureau of Asian Research, 2016.

Tharoor, Shashi. *Inglorious Empire: What the British Did to India.* London: Hurst, 2017.

Trenin, Dmitri. *What Is Russia Up to in the Middle East?* London: Polity Press, 2018.

Unschuld, Paul U. *The Fall and Rise of China: Healing the Trauma of History.* London: Reaktion Books, 2013.

Vaitheeswaran, Vijay. "What China Can Learn from the Pearl River Delta." *The Economist*, April 8, 2017.

Vlastos, Stephen. *Mirror of Modernity: Invented Traditions of Modern Japan.* Berkeley: University of California Press, 1998.

Vogel, Steven K. *Japan Remodeled: How Government and Industry Are Reforming Japanese Capitalism.* New York: Cornell University Press, 2006.

Wan, Ming. *The Political Economy of East Asia: Striving for Wealth and Power.* Washington, DC: CQ Press, 2008.

Weatherford, Jack. *Genghis Khan and the Making of the Modern World.* New York: Broadway Books, 2004.

Westad, Odd Arne. *The Global Cold War: Third World Interventions and the Making of Our Times.* Cambridge, UK: Cambridge University Press, 2007.

——. *Restless Empire: China and the World Since 1750.* New York: Basic Books, 2012.

Westerfield, H. Bradford. *Foreign Policy and Party Politics: Pearl Harbor to Korea.* New Haven, CT: Yale University Press, 1955.

White, Hugh. *The China Choice: Why We Should Share Power.* London: Oxford University Press, 2013.

Wood, Francis. *Great Books of China.* New York: BlueBridge, 2017.

World Atlas. "Asia." World Atlas, November 14, 2016. https://www.worldatlas.com /webimage/countrys/as.htm.

World Bank. "World Development Indicators." World Bank, 2017. http://databank .worldbank.org/data/reports.aspx?source=world-development-indicators.

World Economic Forum, "The Inclusive Development Index 2018: Summary and Data Highlights." World Economic Forum. http://www3.weforum.org/docs/WEF _Forum_IncGrwth_2018.pdf.

Wright, Robert. *Why Buddhism Is True: The Science and Philosophy of Meditation and Enlightenment.* New York: Simon & Schuster, 2017.

Wright, Tom. *All Measures Short of War: The Contest for the 21st Century and the Future of American Power.* New Haven, CT: Yale University Press, 2017.

Wu, Ellen. *The Color of Success.* Princeton, NJ: Princeton University Press, 2014.

Wu, Kang, and Jane Nakano. "The Changing Political Economy of Energy in China." Center for Strategic & International Studies, December 2016. https: //csis-prod.s3.amazonaws.com/s3fs-public/publication/161214_WuNakano _PoliticalEconomyEnergyChina_Web.pdf.

Xuetong, Yan, Daniel A. Bell, and Sun Zhe, eds. *Ancient Chinese Thought, Modern Chinese Power.* Trans. Edmund Ryden. Princeton, NJ: Princeton University Press, 2011.

Xuetong, Yan. "The Instability of China-US Relations." *The Chinese Journal of International Politics* 3, no. 3 (2010): 263–92.

Yamamura, Kozo, and Yasukichi Yasuba, eds. *The Political Economy of Japan 1: The Domestic Transformation.* Stanford, CA: Stanford University Press, 1987.

Young, Louise. *Japan's Total Empire: Manchuria and the Culture of Wartime Imperialism.* City: University of California Press, 1998.

Youngshik, Bong, and T. J. Pempel, eds. *Japan in Crisis: What Will It Take for Japan to Rise Again?* Seoul: Asan Institute, 2012.

Zahidi, Saadia. *Fifty Million Rising: The New Generation of Working Women Transforming the Muslim World.* New York: Nation Books, 2018.

Zhao, Tingyang. "Rethinking Empire from a Chinese Concept 'All-under-Heaven' (Tian-xia, 天下)." *Social Identities* 12, no. 1 (2006): 29–41.

Illustration Credits

Index

Page numbers in *italics* refer to maps and charts.

The Dunces of Doomsday